SECOND EDITION

Drawing the Human Form

methods, sources, concepts

WILLIAM A. BERRY
University of Missouri-Columbia

PRENTICE HALL, Englewood Cliffs, New Jersey 07632

Library of Congress Cataloging-in-Publication Data

BERRY, WILLIAM A.
   Drawing the human form : methods, sources, concepts / William A.
Berry. — 2nd ed.
      p.   cm.
   Includes bibliographical references and index.
   ISBN 0–13–219783–9
   1. Human figure in art.   2. Drawing—Study and teaching.
   I. Title.
   NC765.B39   1994 P AP
   743'.4—dc20   93-4354
                                                      CIP

Acquisitions editor: Bud Therien

Editorial production/supervision
   and interior design: F. Hubert

Production coordinator: Bob Anderson

Cover design: Maureen Eide

Cover art: George Segal, *Seated Nude*
   (detail). Allen Memorial Art Museum,
   Oberlin College; Charles F. Olney Fund
   1964 (64.10).

FOR ESTHER L. BERRY

 © 1977, 1994 by William A. Berry

Printed in the United States of America

10   9   8   7   6   5   4   3   2   1

ISBN 0-13-219783-9

PRENTICE-HALL INTERNATIONAL (UK) LIMITED, *London*
PRENTICE-HALL OF AUSTRALIA PTY. LIMITED, *Sydney*
PRENTICE-HALL CANADA INC., *Toronto*
PRENTICE-HALL HISPANOAMERICANA, S.A., *Mexico*
PRENTICE-HALL OF INDIA PRIVATE LIMITED, *New Delhi*
PRENTICE-HALL OF JAPAN, INC., *Tokyo*
SIMON & SCHUSTER PTE. LTD., *Singapore*
EDITORA PRENTICE-HALL DO BRASIL, LTDA., *Rio de Janeiro*

Contents

Preface   **vii**

Acknowledgments   *xi*
The Second Edition   *xi*

CHAPTER 1
Drawing a Simple Shape
prelude to the human form   **1**

Concepts of Form: The Basis for the Drawing Construct   *1*
Overlapping Shapes   *6*
Figure-Ground Relationships   *7*
Summary   *9*

CHAPTER 2
Seeing Large Forms
outline and silhouette   **11**

Objectives   *16*
Summary   *18*

CHAPTER 3
Drawing in Line
contour, constructs, visual measurement, movement, and memory   **19**

Vision and Eye Movement   *23*
Completing the Drawing   *26*
Body Forms and Line   *26*
Form and Visual Measurement   *34*
Variations and Combinations of Line   *44*
Classical Proportions   *48*
Proportional Canons and Studio Practice   *54*
Proportion and Symmetry   *56*
Line and Motion in Masterworks   *68*
Summary   *74*

CHAPTER 4
Modeling
relief, shadow, tone, and contour   **79**

Relief Modeling   *79*
Relief Modeling and the Perception of Form   *92*
Shadow Modeling   *97*
Transparency   *105*
Sculptured Relief and Shadow Modeling   *112*
Line and Modeling   *116*
Cross-Section Contours   *121*
Contour Hatching and Sculpture   *130*
Hatching and Form   *133*
Summary   *145*

CHAPTER 5
The Skeleton
the structural framework of body forms   **147**

Reference Sources   *147*
The Structure of the Vertebral Column   *152*
The Pelvis   *170*
The Rib Cage and the Shoulder Girdle   *174*
The Appendicular Skeleton   *176*
The Extremities: Comparable Structures   *180*
Summary   *189*

CHAPTER 6
The Muscles
the dynamics of the human form   **191**

Methods, Materials, and References *193*
Trunk Muscles: Front Side *202*
Trunk Muscles: Back Side *210*
The Neck Muscles *214*
The Arm Muscles *221*
The Lower Limb Muscles *227*
Muscles of the Lower Limb: Groups and Functions *229*
Summary *240*

CHAPTER 7
Advanced Studies
approaches to composition, color, and modeling   **245**

Composition *245*
Shape and Local Color in Composition *246*
Color Shapes in Black and White *247*
Shadow Modeling and Color *249*
Shadow Modeling and Subtle Tonal Values *250*
Shadow Modeling, Lighting, and Chiaroscuro *253*
Photography as an Aid to the Artist *264*
Drawing as Planning *268*
Summary *270*

CHAPTER 8
Drawing as Preparation
the development of visual concepts   **273**

Bibliography   **297**

Procedure for Photographing Drawings   **300**

Index   **301**

Preface

Many years ago when I was a student, a professor noticed I was carrying a book written in German, a language he knew I could not read. Chiding me, he asked what on earth I intended to do with it. I replied that I was going to look at the pictures. Undaunted, or perhaps simply stubborn, I have since continued to look at pictures in books I can't read. *Drawing the Human Form* offers information about drawing to those who, like myself, enjoy looking at pictures. It is organized around visual material so that you can learn directly from it—visually, technically, and creatively—without detailed reference to the text.

Illustrations include student drawings and masterworks, grouped to focus on one specific drawing principle at a time. The text follows a simple pattern, giving materials lists and procedures for each study as well as a short theoretical-historical explanation of the principle involved. Beginning with relatively simple studies, the sequence permits you to master individually the concepts that become components of the drawing methods, often more complex, that follow. The discussion is limited to drawing methods; stylistic preferences are avoided. The studies are designed to be repeated, with the understanding that only through practice can drawing concepts, however well described, become meaningful and useful to the artist. In this connection the illustrations can be helpful, especially for those who, like most artists, are visually oriented.

Many people have commented on the pleasure and satisfaction they derive from drawing. There is an undeniable sense of accomplishment in making something with your own hands, a feeling of particular value in the technological civilization of today. This is especially true if the object produced is a work of quality that has personal meaning for you. Satisfaction of this kind generally comes after the work has been completed.

I believe there is an even deeper satisfaction in drawing from life, which is felt before the drawing is completed. During the intense periods of concentration required by drawing, thoughts unrelated to the activity temporarily disappear. By transferring your total attention to another human being in an attempt to comprehend the uniqueness of the living form, you can experience a pleasurable release from self. This kind of satisfaction is a delightful side effect of the process of drawing.

Visual concentration while drawing can also produce a keen sense of discovery, though this may not be reflected in the completed drawing. Unfinished drawings can tell us more about the drawing process in many cases than those brought to completion by the artist. They also reveal the artist's method. For this reason I have used a camera to record drawings at various stages of development, paralleling projects described in the text.

The student drawings, with their freshness and flaws, indicate what you might reasonably expect to achieve in your first years of study in art school. I have also included some drawings by students who later became recognized masters, drawings that reveal how exceptional art students resolved problems similar to those described. Picasso's well-documented student work is of special interest in this connection. Mature graphic works of well-known artists are presented both as examples of the creative use of specific drawing concepts and as sources of inspiration.

Photographs are also employed to document something of the delicate relationship that exists between the drawing and the model, a relationship that vanishes as soon as the model ceases to pose. You can judge visually the successes and shortcomings of the students' draftsmanship. Since watching others draw is sometimes a strong inducement, I hope the photographs of art students at work will encourage you to explore drawing, whether independently or in the classroom environment.

Wherever you decide to draw, it is important to have suitable illumination, preferably with natural light (Figure 1). Drawing makes great demands on the eyes, so it is best to avoid drawing studios that have only artificial light, unless it is strong and even. "The illumination provided at eye level in artificially lighted rooms is commonly . . . less than 10 percent of the light normally available outdoors in the shade of a tree on a sunny day."[1] Traditionally artists have preferred studios with natural light from the north. No less an authority than Leonardo da Vinci advocated it ". . . in order that it may not vary. And if you have it from the South, keep the window screened with cloth, so that with the sun shining the whole day the light may not vary."[2] He also favored "a broad light high up and not too strong."[3] Before the advent of electric lamps Leonardo's instructions were closely followed in drawing studios (Figure 2). His insistence on a steady, unvarying light source remains valid today.

I should add here that, while I do not wish to discourage the independent study of drawing—many of the studies call for independent work—my experience as a teacher has convinced me that the subject is most easily mastered in a studio environment with other students. This view is shared by celebrated artists of the past, among them Rembrandt (Figure 3) and Leonardo da Vinci. Leonardo put it this way:

I say and insist that drawing in company is much better than alone, for many reasons. The first is that you would be ashamed to be seen lagging behind the other students, and such shame will lead you to careful study. Secondly, a wholesome emulation will stimulate you to be among those who are more praised than yourself, and this praise of others will spur you on. Another is that you can learn from the drawings of others who do better than yourself. . . .[4]

This book attempts to bring you, whether instructor, student, or interested layperson, into the drawing studio to share the problems and experiences of a group of serious young art students who are concerned with acquiring a basic mastery of drawing. Drawing from the model is one of the traditional ways of attaining such a mastery (Figures 1-1 and 1-2). Many art schools require it. In an age in which much studio art is nonfigurative, however, you might well question the relevance of drawing the human figure. Is the study of drawing from real life relevant only to figurative art? I think not. As Kenneth Clark has pointed out, ". . . our admiration of an abstract form, a pot or an architectural molding, has some analogy with satisfying human proportions."[5]

Human proportions are naturally best seen in the nude body. Your first experience in drawing from the nude model, however, may seem quite unnatural. Yet for centuries the social taboo against viewing another human being without clothes has been lifted in the artist's studio. Michelangelo once implored, ". . . who is so barbarous as not to understand that the foot of a man is nobler than his shoe, and his skin nobler than that of the sheep with which he is clothed. . . ."[6] Such reasoning holds true as long as the model appears noble. With many models, however, this is simply not the case, and yet they, too, are fascinating to draw. Noble or not, the nude figure has compelled the attention of artists through the ages.

Since the 1600s the nude model has been the standard subject in the study of drawing. Today as then the model poses on an elevated platform while students situated around the platform draw, usually with crayon and paper (Figure 3). Drawing instruction, however, has changed considerably. In Rembrandt's time, for example, students applied to the studio of a recognized master and often worked as apprentices. The apprentice system made possible a long period of continuous training with one teacher. Instruction was highly directed. "We know that Rembrandt used to teach his pupils by getting them to copy, stroke for stroke, his own drawings (Figure 4)."[7] Although drawing method remains as important now as it was then, you are encouraged to explore a variety of drawing methods as a way of discovering the approach that works best. Once discovered, you can pursue that approach in depth.

It is foolish to generalize about the relative merits of the various methods of drawing. Even the most traditional approaches to drawing can be a springboard to creativity. History reminds us that many of the most innovative artists of the past, including Picasso, studied drawing from the model with instruction that can only be termed academic. Even to the revolutionary artist the canons of form learned through the traditional study of life drawing are useful. In order to break the rules, it is helpful to know what they are.

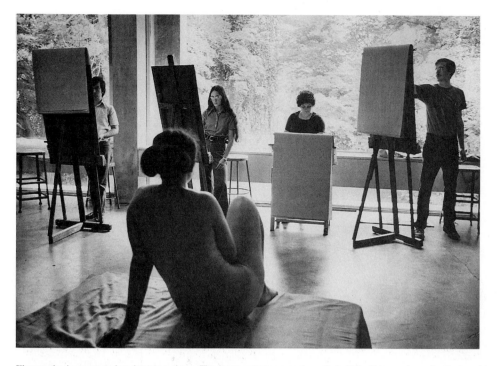

Figure 1. A present-day drawing class. The large windows and north light in this modern studio provide these students with natural, even illumination.

Figure 2. Mathieu Cochereau (1793–1817), *The Atelier of David*, 1814. Oil on canvas. Paris, the Louvre. Similar drawing sessions are still conducted in Paris. In the nineteenth century (and earlier) admittance to such an atelier required an arduous preliminary study of engravings and casts, a practice rarely seen in art schools today.

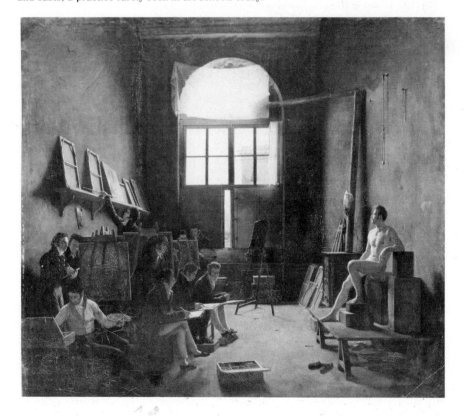

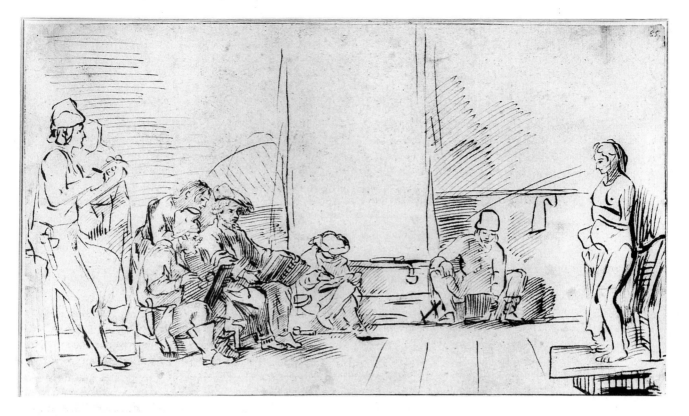

Figure 3. Rembrandt (school of), *Rembrandt with His Students in the Workshop Drawing from the Live Model.* Quill and ink. 180 × 317 mm. Weimar, Schlossmuseum. While some students appear to be drawing directly from the model, two students are shown looking over the shoulder of Rembrandt, in hopes of learning from the master's drawing.

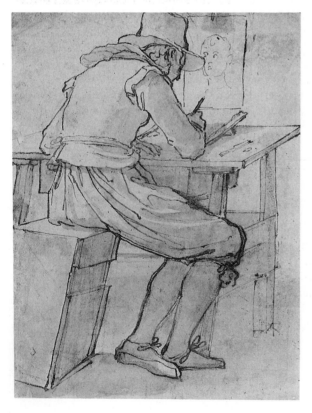

Figure 4. Iacopo Chimenti, called *da Empoli* (1551–1640), *Young Artist Copying a Master Drawing of the Head.* Brown over black chalk. 30 × 21.7 cm. Frankfurt, Städelsches Kunstinstitut and Städtische Galerie. Copying "model" drawings, or engravings, was standard practice in drawing instruction from the Renaissance well into the nineteenth century.

ACKNOWLEDGMENTS

Thanks must be given to my friend Sterling McIlhany, who originally proposed that I write a book on drawing and, more importantly, offered invaluable critical advice throughout the project. Under the spell of my drawing students' enthusiasm the book metamorphosed from a short work on drawing media to its present form. Like most teachers I learned much from my students. In the early stages of writing I also learned much from the sympathetic insights of Professor Harold Larrabee, who kindly consented to read the first draft. I also benefited enormously from the advice of Professor Janet Rollins Berry, my wife, whose wide-ranging knowledge of art history was a constant resource and whose objective criticism was a wonderful antidote to murky writing. Without her encouragement and assistance the book might have remained yet another unfinished project. I am grateful for the generosity of the studio models in allowing their images to be reproduced in these pages. It was a thrilling experience to receive the cooperation of great art museums and private collectors around the world who diligently filled my many orders for photographs. All photographs without credit lines are by the author.

Many people have contributed time, effort, and valuable advice. Special thanks to my colleagues, Professors Donald Weismann, Mort Baranoff of the University of Texas at Austin, Jack Kramer of Boston University, John Frazer of Wesleyan University, and Jerrold Simon of City College of New York. I am grateful to Robert Tyndall and Paul Russell for their assistance with computer graphics. Richard J. Wolfe, rare books librarian at the Francis A. Countway Library of Medicine, deserves thanks for personally introducing me to the treasured anatomical publications for which the library is justly famed. I am indebted to many people who assisted me in completing the second edition, especially to Janet Rollins Berry, who gave insightful advice on many aspects of the second edition, as she had on the first. I acknowledge the input received from the following instructors who reviewed the manuscript: Bob Jones, Northeast Missouri State University; James Mitchell Clark, Blackburn College; and Paul H. Davis, University of Utah. Brenda Warren also deserves credit for her skillful help with word processing.

THE SECOND EDITION

The assumption underlying the second edition remains the same as in the first: The student of drawing progresses more rapidly when there is a clear objective in mind. In accordance with that assumption the selection of illustrations and proposed studies focus on specific facets of drawing. In this way the student can explore a variety of concepts in drawing rather than simply repeat what has already been mastered. Sheer practice in drawing is important, but when it is backed by an idea or objective, it is possible to draw with a greater sense of purpose and to learn more.

The changes the reader will note in the second edition are not merely cosmetic, but represent an evolution of my ideas on drawing since the appearance of the first edition in 1977. Fortunately, the precepts underlying the original text have proven valid over the years, but my own experience teaching the subject has led to ways of developing some topics in directions that were only mentioned in the first edition.

There is also an expansion of the range of examples of master drawings as well as drawings by students. The examples of student work appearing in the first edition came exclusively from beginning drawing classes at the University of Texas at Austin. For the second edition I have selected some drawings executed by more advanced students at the University of Missouri-Columbia in hopes that these drawings will be of interest to art students at all levels of accomplishment.

The distinction commonly made between beginning and advanced drawing, though useful for purposes of instruction, is perhaps more academic than real. Student drawings by such masters as Degas blur even the convenient distinction separating master drawings and student drawings. In truth all drawings simply form part of the grand continuum we call art.

WILLIAM A. BERRY

Notes

1. Richard J. Wurtman, "The Effects of Light on the Human Body," *Scientific American*, vol. 233, no. 1 (July 1975), p. 70.

2. Leonardo da Vinci, *The Notebooks of Leonardo da Vinci*, vol. 1, ed. Jean Paul Richter (New York: Dover, 1970), p. 257.

3. Ibid., p. 257.

4. Ibid., p. 249.

5. Kenneth Clark, *The Nude: A Study in Ideal Form* (Garden City, N.Y.: Doubleday, 1959), p. 447.

6. Robert Goldwater and Marco Treves, *Artists on Art* (New York: Pantheon, 1945), p. 70.

7. Philip Rawson, *Drawing* (London: Oxford University Press, 1969), p. 292.

CHAPTER 1

Drawing a Simple Shape

prelude to the human form

Drawing is not form; it is your understanding of form.

—EDGAR DEGAS

S O CENTRAL IS the human form to the history of Western art that it inevitably became an accepted standard against which draftsmen tested and sharpened essential drawing skills. Some artists have maintained that a person who can draw the human figure can draw anything under the sun. There is some truth in this claim, for methods used to draw the human form can readily be applied to other subjects, yet it is likely that the reverse is also valid: A person who can draw any subject can also draw the human figure. Drawing the human figure raises many of the same problems that are encountered in drawing any observed form. It is useful, therefore, to begin by considering some of the principles that life drawing has in common with all drawing.

CONCEPTS OF FORM: THE BASIS FOR THE DRAWING CONSTRUCT

Seeing form is the first step in the drawing process, but perception alone is not sufficient to enable you to draw. In order to draw an observed form, think of form in terms that can be translated into marks on paper capable of representing the observed form. The formal concept of the artist provides a means of translating the raw data of visual observation into coherent constructs of marks on paper. In a master drawing

the resulting effect of forms described in this way can be so compelling that the formal concept employed by the artist may pass unnoticed by the casual observer. It is instructive to examine a relatively simple form in a drawing (Figure 1-1) by the German Renaissance artist Albrecht Dürer (1471–1528). For example, the artist may have conceived of the neck of his model Catherine in terms of a cylinder in space. Such a concept of form appears to underlie the curving-line constructs in that area of the drawing. Each curved mark of the pen conveys some information about the cylindrical form of the neck.

The richly complex construction of Dürer's drawing seems perfectly in keeping with the subtle perceptions it records. Such technical virtuosity, dazzling though it may be, is not the critical factor in determining the quality of a drawing. Artistic quality depends a great deal on the appropriateness of the drawing's constructs to the artist's perceptions. This partly explains the special charm of children's drawings, in which technical virtuosity plays no part. The boldly schematic constructs often seem admirably suited to the directness characteristic of a child's perceptions (Figure 1-2). The constructs in both drawings are effective in that they do not initially attract the viewer's attention: They seem to exist solely to communicate an essential image of the figure.

What are the origins of the constructs that enable a draw-

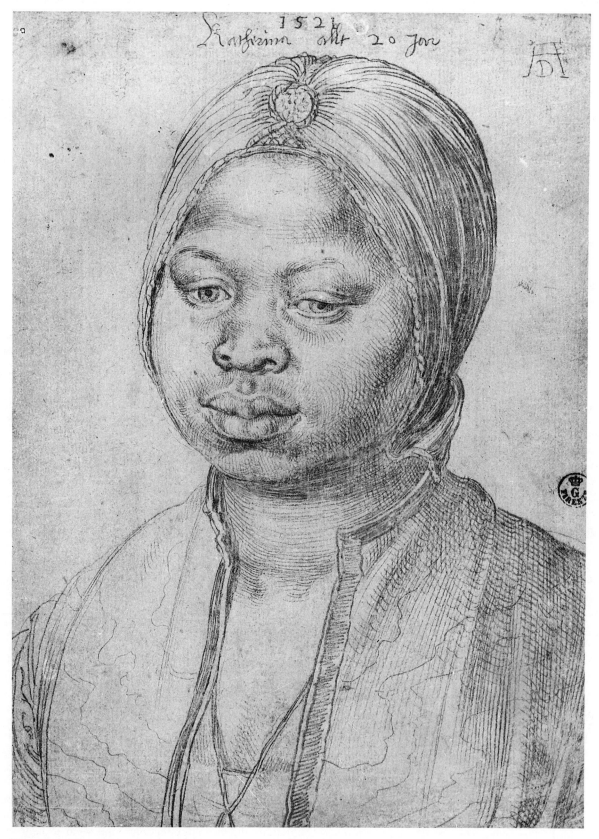

Figure 1-1. Albrecht Dürer (1471–1528), *Catherine*, 1521. Silverpoint on white ground. 200 × 140 mm. Florence, Galleria degli Uffizi. The complex structure of Dürer's drawings is often built with simple curving-line motifs that suggest rounded forms.

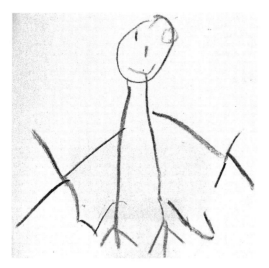

Figure 1-2. A five-year-old's drawing of the human body. Crayon. A simple schematic construction of a circle and lines represents the figure.

Figure 1-3. Villard de Honnecourt (c. 1225–c. 1250), *Gateway, Heads, Animals, and Heraldic Eagle,* c. 1240. Page from a notebook. Pen and ink over lead point on parchment. 9¹¹⁄₁₆ × 5¹⁵⁄₁₆″. Paris, Bibliothèque Nationale. Since early times artists have explored the use of geometric forms as the framework for drawing. Villard de Honnecourt, an artist in charge of building cathedrals, employed a compass and a ruler to construct his sketches. In the description at lower right he wrote that drawing is "easy to practice . . . as it is taught by the discipline of geometry."

ing to convey form so effectively? From early times artists have looked to geometry as one way of constructing form. This is not to say that artists necessarily employed rulers and compasses, as mentioned in the Bible,[1] though such instruments were used to rough out sculptured form, but simply that many artists have used geometry as a source of ideas for the formal concepts on which to build a drawing. In the Middle Ages the artist Villard de Honnecourt used triangles or circles as the framework for drawing a figure (Figure 1-3). His search for geometric construction is echoed centuries later in a figure by Dürer drawn with the aid of a compass (Figure 1-4). In the more complex portrait drawing by Dürer (Figure 1-1) geometry is less obvious, yet the parallel lines in the neck that seem to curve around the form are nothing more than freely drawn segments of circles—constructs based on a cylinder (see Figures 4-74 and 4-75).

Art history offers an early instance of the circle as a subject of drawing, as recorded by the sixteenth-century artist-chronicler Giorgio Vasari in a curious account from the life of the early Renaissance painter Giotto (c. 1266–1337). The story began in Rome, when Pope Benedict IX set about selecting an artist to decorate the basilica of Saint Peter. To help make

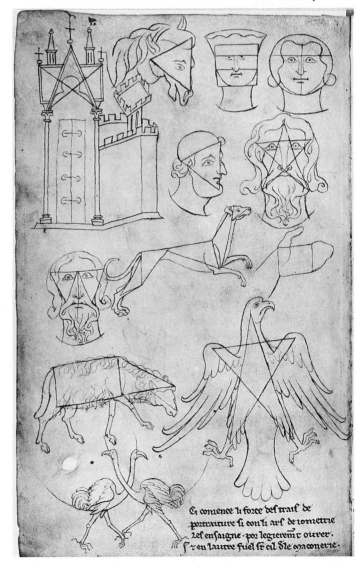

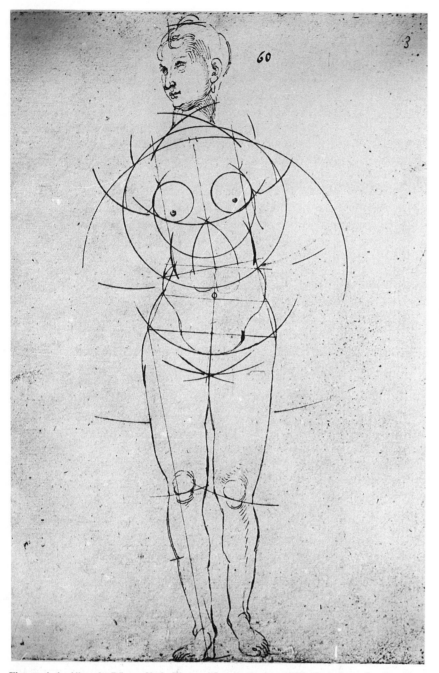

Figure 1-4. Albrecht Dürer, *Nude Woman, Constructed,* c. 1500. Page from the *Dresden Sketchbook.* Pen and ink with compass. 290 × 188 mm (11 ⅜ × 7⅜″). Dresden, Sächsische Landesbibliothek. Dürer used a compass in his search for a system of circular constructs in the figure. Even the parts of the figure drawn without the compass appear to have been constructed with arcs.

the selection, the pope wished to see examples of drawings by various artists of note, so he dispatched courtiers to the studios of noted artists to procure them. Upon being asked for a drawing,

> Giotto, who [Vasari assures us] was a very courteous man, took a sheet of paper and a brush dipped in red, closed his arm to his side, so as to make a sort of compass of it, and then with a twist of his hand drew such a perfect circle that it was a marvel to see. Then, with a smile, he said to the courtier: "There's your drawing."

As if he were being ridiculed, the courtier replied: "Is this the only drawing I'm to have?"

"It's more than enough," answered Giotto. "Send it along with the others and you'll see whether it's understood or not."[2]

Was this simply Giotto's way of saying that he felt no need to give proof of his ability as an artist? Or was he serious in submitting his drawing? The paradoxical nature of Giotto's response undoubtedly left the courtier puzzled, and no further explanation of its meaning has come to light. Although Giotto's purpose can only be guessed at, this anecdote suggests an awareness of the fundamental role that geometric shapes and forms play in drawing.[3]

It may come as a surprise to the beginner that formal concepts derived from geometry, unlike the rigid illustrations in geometry texts, are not constrictive in the drawing process. On the contrary, they can inspire the use of a wider range of options in the choice of drawing constructs because a single geometric shape can yield a variety of formal concepts. An example will make this clear. Although the circle is a single shape, it can be conceived in several ways, each of which invites the use of different drawing constructs: (1) You might conceive of the circle as a single line described by a point that changes its direction consistently and uniformly as it moves across a plane; (2) You can also regard a circle as the path of a moving point that maintains a constant distance from another point; (3) Or you can think of a circle as a shape composed entirely of points surrounding and equidistant from a central point on a plane. The three concepts are not merely superficially different: They differ to such an extent that each of them dictates a different way of making marks on the paper.

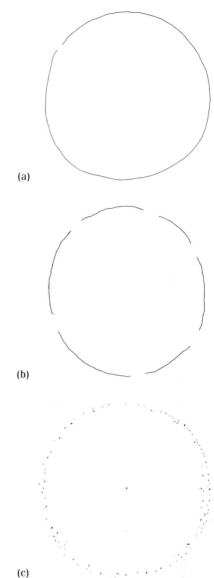

(a)

(b)

(c)

Figure 1-5. Three ways of drawing a circle: (a) as an evenly turning arc; (b) as a line drawn equidistant from a central point; (c) as a series of points equidistant from the center.

STUDY 1:   **The Circle**

materials: ❑ 36 × 24″ newsprint drawing pad
   ❑ 37 × 25″ piece of Masonite or ¼″ thick plywood (to back the drawing pad)
   ❑ drawing-board clamps (preferably the ball-bearing type) to hold drawing pad and drawing together
   ❑ easel (if none is available, rest the lower edge of the pad on the seat of a chair with the chair back supporting the back of the pad)
   ❑ dark brown or black drawing crayon (Nupastel or soft Conté brands)
time: ❑ 3–5 minutes

Keeping in mind the first concept of the circle, try moving the point of the crayon across the page in such a way that the direction of movement changes evenly and constantly, forming a uniform, even arc (Figure 1-5a). This arc, if it is uniform, will form a circle. Control of the hand and its swinging motion are very important in this exercise.

This first method is a natural way to draw a circle. Even scribbles by very young children often reveal rounded-contour patterns drawn with a swinging motion because

> The lever construction of the human body favors curved motion. The arm pivots around the shoulder joint, and subtler rotation is provided by the elbow, the wrist, the fingers. Thus, the first rotations indicate organization of motor behavior according to the principle of simplicity. The same principle also favors the priority of the circular shape visually.[4]

The resulting continuous contour is the drawing construct in this case.

The second concept of the circle provides a more measured way to draw it. If you first establish a center for the circle by making a dot in the center of the paper, you can draw around the point while concentrating on maintaining an equal distance between the crayon and the central dot (Figure 1-5b). It will seem natural to lift the crayon after a short arc is drawn, thereby breaking the line, and to replace the crayon after referring again to the central point. In this instance visual judgment is as important as muscular control. Errors caused by accidental movement of the arm are easily corrected by reevaluating the distance between the central point and the circumference (Figure 1-6) and redrawing the earlier stroke. The single stroke is the drawing construct suggested by this concept of the circle.

The third concept leaves no doubt about how to draw the circle: One dot must be drawn at a time, with each dot the same distance from the central dot. Obviously the dot is the drawing construct. A sufficient number of dots will appear to form a line describing a circle (Figure 1-5c). A perceptual phenomenon called *closure* explains the tendency of the mind's eye to fill the spaces between the outer dots with an illusory line, sometimes referred to as a *virtual line* or an *implied line*. This concept of the circle permits the artist to focus on the problem of visual distance and the principle of visual measurement. It is useful not only in estimating physical distance, as in the case of the circle, but also in drawing from life, since it is important to establish relative and apparent distance between points observed on the model and marks made by the artist on the paper in order to translate the solid form into a two-dimensional drawing.

The circle is also a convenient form to illustrate two important spatial principles of drawing: overlapping shapes and figure-ground relationships.

Figure 1-6. Drawing the circle. The student on the left has drawn a circle by the method illustrated in Figure 1-5a. On the right another student completes a circle as shown in Figure 1-5b. Note the Masonite panels supporting the drawing pads.

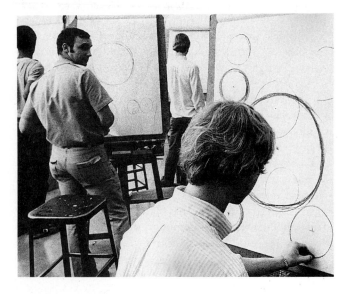

OVERLAPPING SHAPES

For purposes of clarity the word *shape* here refers only to a two-dimensional pattern, whether natural, as in the shape of a shadow, or human made, as in the geometric circle. *Form* refers to the three-dimensional structure of things. This distinction is useful in drawing, for flat shapes often are employed to represent the volume and structure of three-dimensional form.

If, for example, a drawing of a circle intersects another circle (Figure 1-7a), the result is an ambiguous spatial effect. Either of the circles may be seen as a transparent shape on top of the other: It is not clear which is on top. If the intersected arc of one circle is erased (Figure 1-7b), however, the apparent spatial relationship is clarified: The complete circle appears to be an opaque disk that covers part of another complete disk. Even though part of the latter circle has been erased, you continue to perceive it as a complete closed form rather than as a crescent shape next to a circle. The mind's eye tends to complete the regular shape of the incomplete circle. A slight separation of the two elements suffices to destroy the illusion of completeness (Figure 1-7c). The strong suggestion

Figure 1-7. The effect of overlapping forms: (a) an ambiguous, transparent effect results if two circles overlap; (b) if the overlapped portion of one circle is removed, the remaining circle appears to lie on top of and to hide part of the broken one; (c) the effect of overlapping form is destroyed if the two shapes are separated. The predominant visual interpretation of (b) is of overlapping circles, not of the independent shapes in (c).

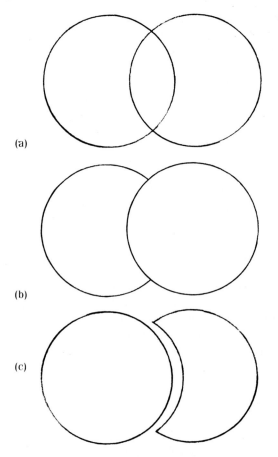

(a)

(b)

(c)

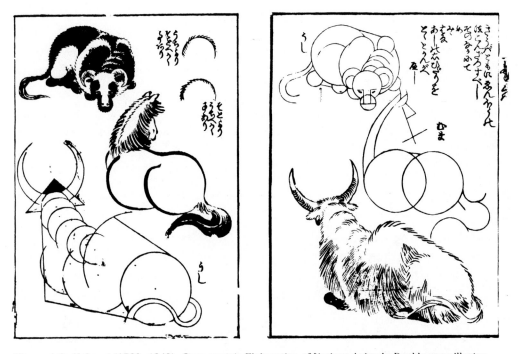

Figure 1-8. Hokusai (1760–1849), *Stereometric Elaboration of Various Animals.* Double-page illustration from *Rayakuga Haya Oshie,* vol. 3. Woodblock engraving from a brush drawing. 16 × 11.25 cm. London, British Museum. An important painter and graphic artist, Hokusai is also the author of a book explaining his drawing methods. Here he illustrates how to draw animal figures by means of overlapped circles that suggest hidden or "foreshortened" forms.

of spatial order brings with it a degree of three-dimensional effect. In short the two shapes now seem to represent form.

The manner in which the two elements are joined is essential to the integrity of the overlapped form. This is of special importance in contour-line drawing (see Chapter 3), which relies almost exclusively on the overlap principle to convey a sequence of forms in depth. Some artists in the past drew overlapping circles as constructs to represent the overlapping contours of forms observed in life (Figures 1-8 and 1-9), but the principle is not limited to rounded figures: Rectangles, triangles, and many other regular and irregular shapes can be repeated and overlapped to suggest spatial order.

FIGURE-GROUND RELATIONSHIPS

Research by psychologists has confirmed that a closed figure such as a circle establishes a special relationship between the figure and the background.[5] In particular, the closed figure appears more distinct in structure than the surrounding area or ground. Due to the assertive quality of the figure, artists often refer to it as the positive shape; the ground is called the negative space. Under certain conditions they are reversible: That is, the figure can be seen as the ground and vice versa (Figure 1-10).

The notion of "empty," or "negative" space applies not only to the ground surrounding a drawn enclosure, as in the case of the circle, but also to observations of the human form. An empty space, such as that between a model's arm and the rest of the body, can be perceived as a positive shape (Figures 1-11 and 2-6). Seeing a negative space as a positive shape involves the recognition of the empty space as an entity and therefore implies a figure-ground reversal similar to what you see in Figure 1-10. Once the "empty" space is perceived as a shape, the artist can readily compare it with the corresponding negative shape in a drawing of the model. Used in this way negative shapes are valuable as a means of checking the accuracy of positive form during the drawing process (see Study 9 in Chapter 3).

The relationship of negative and positive shapes is also the basis of pictorial composition, and therefore determines to a considerable extent the formal quality in visual art. The expressive power of negative and positive shapes in composition is most apparent in works with flat shapes of uniform tone (Plate II).

The figure-ground reversal itself can be used for expressive purposes. It is virtually the unstated subject of a collage entitled *Venus* by the French artist Henri Matisse (Figure 1-12). Seeing the figure of Venus requires a figure-ground reversal, for the goddess occupies the "empty" white space in the composition. In this way the artist enlists the active participation

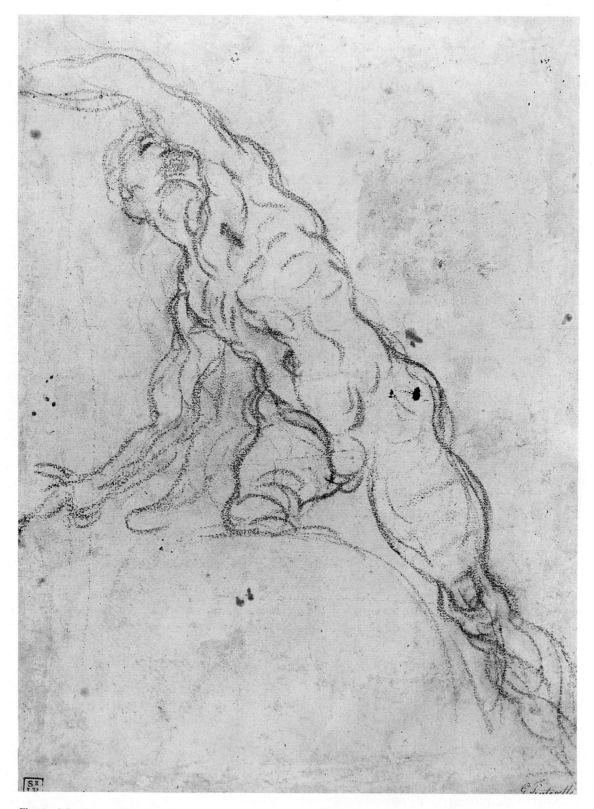

Figure 1-9. Jacopo Robusti, called *il Tintoretto* (1518–1594), *Nude Male Figure in Violent Action*, c. 1585. Black chalk on white paper. 348 × 251 mm. Oxford, Ashmolean Museum. Though less obvious than in Hokusai's didactic study of animals, the same principle of overlapping contours underlies the construction of this figure.

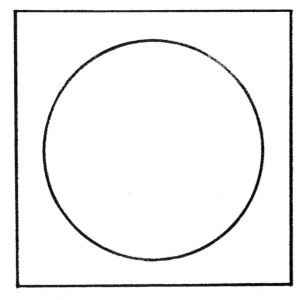

Figure 1-10. Both the circle and the square are usually seen as positive forms. If a circle is superimposed on a square, however, the former can be interpreted either as a positive shape surrounded by empty space or as a hole (i.e., negative space) in the square. This phenomenon, known as figure-ground reversal, has numerous applications in drawing.

Figure 1-11. The negative space between the model's arm and trunk can be viewed as a positive shape. A voluntary figure-ground reversal of this type provides the artist with a useful means of interpreting form in a drawing. A similar negative space, not completely enclosed, is apparent between the model's left leg and thigh.

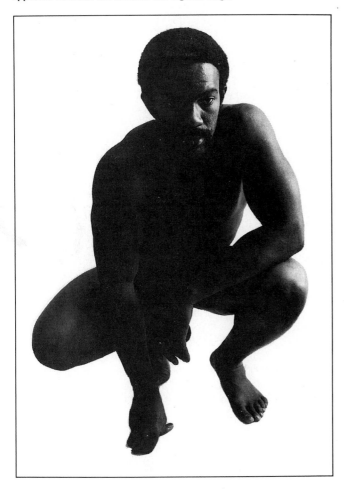

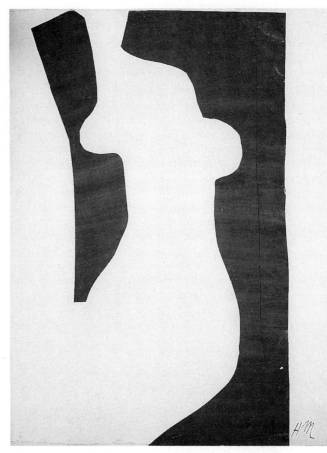

Figure 1-12. Henri Matisse (1869–1954), *Venus*, 1952. Paper pasted on canvas. 39⅞ × 30⅛″. Washington, D.C. National Gallery of Art, Ailsa Mellon Bruce Fund.

of the viewer in a figure-ground reversal, an experience usually reserved for the artist.

SUMMARY

The drawing exercises with the circle, simple though they may seem, can assist you in understanding several fundamental drawing principles, including positive and negative shape, overlapping form, and visual measurement. Only by actually drawing is it possible to comprehend the enormous range of application of such abstract principles in the drawing process. The circle, which requires a minimal degree of manual control to draw, demonstrates the principles without the complication of a figurative subject. In Chapter 2 we apply these and other principles to the process of drawing from life.

NOTES

1. Describing the procedure of an Assyrian sculptor, Isaiah recorded (44:13) that "... he marketh it out with a line; he fitteth it with planes and he marketh it out with the compass, and maketh it after the figure of a man according to the beauty of a man."

2. Giorgio Vasari, *Artists of the Renaissance, A Selection from Lives of the Artists*, trans. George Bull (New York: Viking, 1978), p. 35, p. 8. Vasari's stories have become professional myths and have a value unrelated to their historical accuracy. As Roger Shattuck commented in *The Banquet Years* (New York: Vintage, Random House, 1968), "As vividly as any museum, real or imaginary, these stories set the Renaissance still living before us. We need such mythologies in order to understand the past." Vasari's apocryphal account of Giotto accurately reflects a real concern of many Renaissance arts with geometry. Viewed as the intellectual aspect of art, geometry was a means of distinguishing fine art from craft. It also led to one of the most important discoveries of the Renaissance: linear perspective, the first systematic method for representing solid forms on a flat surface. Conceivably the anecdote of Giotto's circle was intended to illustrate the problem of drawing a circle in perspectival space, a problem familiar to Vasari as a practicing studio artist in the sixteenth century.

3. Works by such present-day artists as Ellsworth Kelly and Donald Judd have much in common with Giotto's drawing, in that their paintings and sculptures often feature single irreducible shapes such as circles or stripes. Called minimal art by critics, these works effectively eliminate any reference to a reality beyond that of the shapes themselves.

4. Rudolf Arnheim, *Art and Visual Perception* (Berkeley and Los Angeles: University of California Press, 1954), p. 167. An interesting discussion of how children create drawing constructs is found on pages 155–212.

5. The figure–ground relationship was first described by Kurt Koffka in 1922. M. D. Vernon, *The Psychology of Perception* (Harmondsworth, Middlesex, England: Penguin, 1962), pp. 52–53.

CHAPTER 2

Seeing Large Forms

outline and silhouette

*You must have the whole figure you want to draw
in your eye and mind*

JEAN-AUGUSTE-DOMINIQUE INGRES

O N A CLEAR DAY you can see a natural phenomenon that has much in common with the process of drawing (Figure 2-1). It is your shadow. The type of drawing most akin to the cast shadow is the silhouette. Like most drawings, a cast shadow is a two-dimensional transformation of three-dimensional form. In the silhouette, however, the transformation is far more severe than in most drawings, for it contains practically no visual information about the forms that may lie inside its dark, even tone (Figure 2-2). The silhouette provides a singular example of the large shape of the human form without most of the complex detail that sometimes lures the unwary art student into overworking a figure drawing. In fact, the only specific detail in a silhouette is in its sharply defined outer edge, or *outline* (Figure 2-3).

Drawing the human silhouette involves at least one important departure from the previous exercise: It requires a model. The circle, a simple unchanging shape, is easily remembered, whereas the human silhouette, a complex shape that changes with every movement of the body, is difficult to reconstruct from memory alone. Drawing from a model resolves some of the difficulty.

In drawing the circle you saw that the concept of form affects the way you draw. Before drawing the silhouette, consider these two concepts: (1) Viewed as an outline, the silhouette may be thought of as a pure line separating the figure from the ground; (2) The silhouette may also be regarded as a shape like a shadow, in which the edge is defined by tonal contrast rather than by an actual line. The first concept requires considerable concentration on a single aspect of the model, the apparent outside edge of the large shape of the body. Of course, you see much more than that. Your visual perception includes many patches of varied colors and tones in both the figure and the background. Only those patches that help define the boundary of the figure pertain to the outline: The rest can be temporarily ignored.

If this is your first experience in drawing from a model, you will appreciate the advantages of standard studio equipment, including a platform for the model and an easel for yourself. The platform elevates the model in order to eliminate unintentional visual distortion (Figure 2-4). As a further precaution against visual distortion you should adjust the easel so the center of the drawing paper is at eye level. This position has the added bonus of permitting easy movement of your arm to all parts of the drawing surface. In place of easels you may find adjustable drawing tables in the studio. If so, be sure to tilt the drawing table surface vertically in accordance with your line of sight before beginning to draw, for a horizontal drawing surface is a common source of unintended distortion. Lacking drawing tables or easels, it is possible to make do with an ordinary chair to support the drawing pad while you draw in a seated position (see Study 1), an arrangement that eliminates the need for a platform.

11

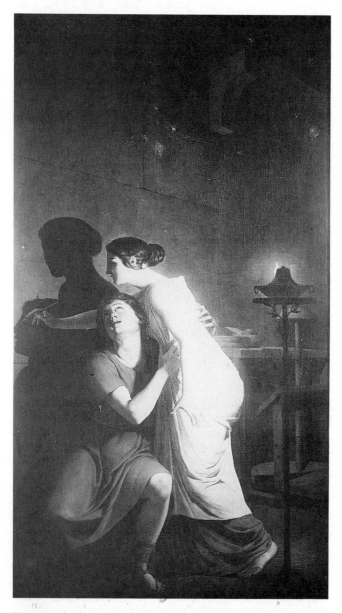

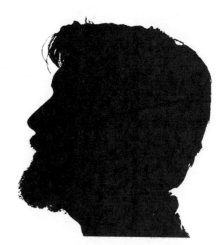

Figure 2-2. Profile. The outer limits of a three-dimensional form constitute the visual information conveyed by a silhouette.

Figure 2-3. Outline drawing in chalk by a police detective. The close relationship between the outline and objective reality makes this type of drawing useful in establishing the factual situation in an accident (photo by Lee Romero, courtesy of *The New York Times*).

Figure 2-1. Joseph Benoit Suvée (1743–1807), *The Daughter of Butades Drawing the Shadow of Her Lover*, 1799. Oil on canvas. Bruges, Groeningemuseum. The close relationship between the cast shadow and the representation of form in two-dimensional art is recognized in the folklore of art. "All agree," wrote the Roman author Pliny, "that it [painting] began with tracing an outline round a man's shadow. . . ." He recounts the tale of Butades's daughter, ". . . who was in love with a young man; and she, when he was going abroad, drew in outline on the wall the shadow of his face thrown by a lamp" (Pliny, *Natural History*, Book XXXV, 65–68, trans. H. Rackham [Cambridge, Mass.: Harvard University Press, 1968], pp. 271, 373).

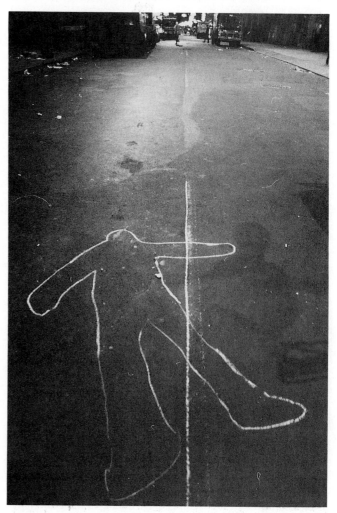

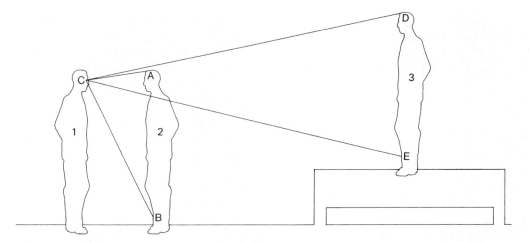

Figure 2-4. Unintended distortions in a drawing sometimes result from the relative location of the artist and the model in the studio. This is due to the nature of the visual field. Objects close at hand occupy a larger part of your field of vision than those at a greater distance. For this reason the closer forms may appear disproportionately large. This phenomenon would occur if figure (1) were observing figure (2). (CA) is a shorter distance than (CB), with the result that the head of figure (2) would appear disproportionately large compared with, say, the feet. Such distortion would not occur, however, if figure (1) were looking at figure (3). The greater distance separating (1) and (3) and the elevation provided by the model stand help to equalize the distances (CD) and (CE), eliminating the cause of the distortion. If, on the other hand, distortion effects are desirable in a particular drawing, you may wish to situate the model nearby.

STUDY 2:   The Outline

materials: ❑ 36 × 24″ newsprint drawing pad
  ❑ easel or straight-back chair
  ❑ Masonite or plywood board and clamps
  ❑ dark brown or black drawing crayon (Nupastel or soft Conté brands)
  ❑ felt-tip pen with broad point (optional)
reference: ❑ model
time: ❑ 10–15 minutes

Look at the entire shape of the model and select a point on the apparent edge of his or her form. If the point you choose is relatively high on the body, place the crayon at a relatively high point on the paper. Imagine the crayon point is resting on the model instead of on the page. Follow the edge of the model's form, moving your eye and the crayon in unison while looking *only* at the model (Figure 2-5). You will be able to register the slightest bumps in the outline by drawing slowly and carefully. The proverb that art, like nature, cannot be rushed is especially true of the outline drawing. It may require ten to fifteen minutes to complete.

It is possible to draw the outline in one continuous line except for negative spaces, such as between the arm and the trunk or between the legs of the model. These will appear as islands of closed (negative) shape within the larger shape. To draw them, you have to repeat the first step by selecting a new point of contact. Make sure to situate your crayon on the drawing at the same relative position as the point observed on the model; otherwise the drawn negative shape may not appear to be a part of the silhouette. Once you have replaced the crayon on the paper, avoid looking at the paper as you draw. Instead try to imagine the crayon is grazing the edge of the form you see in the model. You may be surprised at how easy it is to draw the outline in this way (Figure 2-6).

The primary aim of this exercise is to develop a sensitive, animated line based on observed form. Accuracy of proportion, while desirable in some drawings, is not a universal standard, nor is it the objective here. You should not feel discouraged with the results, however disproportionate, of your first outline drawing.

In drawing the outline concentrate on the edge of the silhouette, just as you did with the drawing of the circle. Continuing the analogy with the circle, try drawing the silhouette again, this time with the center of the form as the area of focus. In accordance with the second concept of form draw a dark inner shape, which, by its contrast with the white page, will generate an exterior linear effect.

STUDY 3:   The Silhouette

materials: ❑ 36 × 24″ newsprint drawing pad
  ❑ easel or straight-back chair
  ❑ Masonite or plywood board and clamps
  ❑ drawing crayon
reference: ❑ model
time: ❑ 10–15 minutes

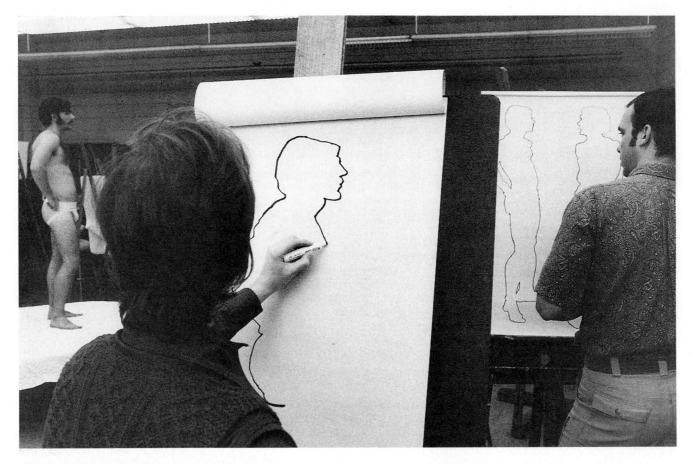

Figure 2-5. Drawing the outline with a felt marker on a newsprint pad. The student on the left is effectively transcribing the outline of the model. She is also committing the common error of drawing over her shoulder, making the drawing procedure unnecessarily tiring and at the same time somewhat restricting her view of the model. The problem is easily solved by shifting the easel to the left so the model appears to the right of the drawing pad.

In nature the silhouette is essentially a flat shape, determined by the three-dimensional form of the body. How can forms of the figure be analyzed for purposes of drawing the silhouette? One way is to imagine central cores that lie roughly midway between the outer edges of the model's body forms. Such imaginary cores can be estimated visually and drawn as median lines running through the longitudinal centers (*axes*) of body forms (Figure 2-8). The median lines bend in accordance with the general turn of the form rather than with the specific curves of the outer edge. For the artist this has the advantage of freeing the eye from the specific and detailed visual information of the outline. The median lines can also assist in controlling the scale and placement of the figure on the drawing page.

Once visualized in the model and drawn, median lines provide a framework for initiating the silhouette drawing, for the lines provide a useful reference for building up the silhouette figure with tone. Since a median line is only a rough estimate of the form's core, it can be rendered broadly with the flat side of the crayon. The dark tone of the silhouette

Figure 2-6. Student drawing. Two outline studies of the same model. Felt pen on newsprint pad. 36 × 24″. Negative spaces in an outline drawing tend to appear as isolated shapes.

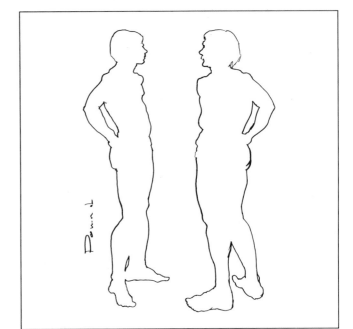

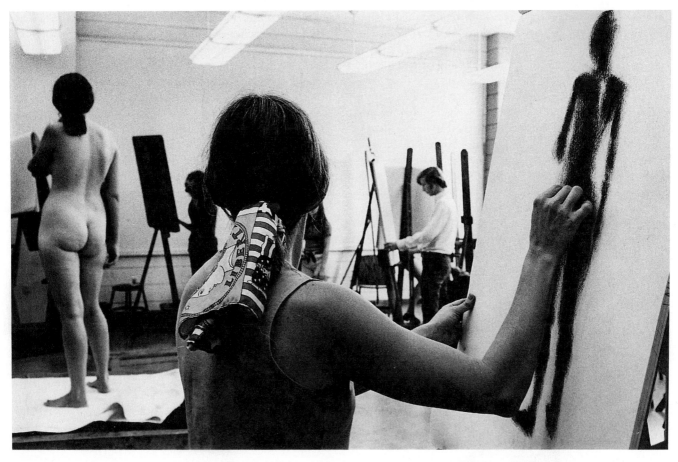

Figure 2-7. Student building up the form of the figure from the center out. Crayon on newsprint pad. 36 × 24″.

itself can be developed gradually by moving the crayon sideways right and left in zigzag fashion over the paper while pressing lightly against it. It is desirable to keep your eyes trained on the model rather than on the paper while drawing, for this permits a freer movement of the hand, and hence a greater breadth and spontaneity of drawing quality (Figure 2-7).

Free arm movement can also assist you in controlling the scale of the figure. It is not uncommon for beginning art students to draw the figure very small in relation to the format of the paper. This would be of no concern if it were done on purpose, but frequently it is not. The apparent lack of control over the scale of the drawing is sometimes due to the way the crayon is held. When it is grasped like a pencil, the hand tends to move it in small push-pull strokes similar to those of handwriting. Such restricted movements can produce unintentionally small figures. Fortunately this problem is easily resolved by grasping the crayon with the thumb and fingers so that the *broadside* of the crayon touches the paper (Figure 2-8). Moving the crayon constantly back and forth, continue the drawing by building outward from the median lines. The resulting tone will grow darker when the crayon is repeatedly dragged over an area, or when more pressure is applied. With

Figure 2-8. Student's drawing page with the silhouette figure at various stages of development. The darker central passages represent general median lines in the figure.

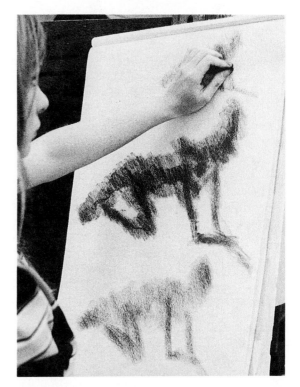

this method the figure will develop in somewhat the same manner as sculpture modeled in clay. Like a clay sculpture, the silhouette will appear to grow as more tone is added to the general fuzzy shape of the figure, until at last the full silhouette appears (Figure 2-9). After drawing the figure several times in this way, try holding the crayon parallel to the median line of the form being drawn while moving the crayon broadside back and forth over the median line. This version of the study will permit the advanced student to develop the figure more accurately while concentrating on the imaginary axes of the observed form.

It is essential in the silhouette study to see the bodily form in terms of the imaginary axes. Focusing on the axes draws your attention away from the visual edges of the figure toward the form as a whole so that contour edges are not isolated linear features but part of the boundary of the perceived form. If a form is drawn in this way, the linear edge per se becomes

Figure 2-9. Student drawing. Silhouette. Crayon on newsprint pad. 36 × 24″. The somewhat tentative quality of the silhouette edge results from a careful buildup of tone corresponding to the overall configuration of the model.

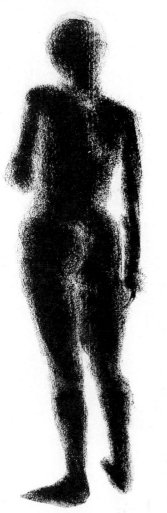

less important than the unit of perceived form it suggests. The problem of determining the linear edge of the drawn silhouette is thus postponed until the last.

The student might reasonably ask what is the advantage of a drawing method that begins with a generalized rendering of form—in this case the core of body forms—and describes specific visual information only as a last stage of the drawing process. In a word the answer is flexibility. The general-to-specific method offers the artist a greater opportunity to explore options before defining a contour edge. For example, it is much easier to change the position of a median line of the arm than a detailed outline that accurately describes both sides of the arm and their interrelationship. The method thus frees the draftsman from the visual tyranny of detail, making it possible to enlarge the scope of the artist's visual perception of form.

The beginner's experience in the perception of large shape or form may be quite limited. This is natural, for everyday life seldom requires it. Most people are conditioned through such activities as reading to see only very small units as complete shapes and to exclude larger visual forms from consciousness, even though they are within the visual field. All but a few words are usually excluded in the process of reading. To be sure, smaller formal units are important in figure drawing as in reading. Unless, however, they are perceived in context as parts of the larger bodily forms, the resulting drawing may appear as a series of unrelated, segmented forms, giving the figure an unintended puppetlike appearance.

OBJECTIVES

The main purpose of this study is to help overcome any difficulty you may have in relating the smaller, more easily perceived units of form to the totality of the figure. By intentionally looking for the largest units of form, you will gain a greater breadth of vision while drawing. Ingres may have had this in mind when he urged artists to "have the whole figure you want to draw in your eye and mind."[1]

To a certain extent drawing is a circular process. The experienced artist has a clear idea of form in mind and knows in advance what to look for in the model. As an aid to the less experienced artist, specific concepts of form are incorporated into the exercises in this chapter and in the chapters that follow. By practicing the exercises you will internalize the underlying concepts and thereby enlarge the circle of your drawing experience. Remember, however, that different drawing concepts are often combined in one drawing: They are rarely found in the "pure" state presented in the preceding two exercises.

Even though pure silhouettes and outlines are rare in art, they are appealing to the contemporary sensibility, as evidenced by certain drawings of modern masters (Figures 2-10 and 2-11). Paul Klee, the twentieth-century Swiss artist, once

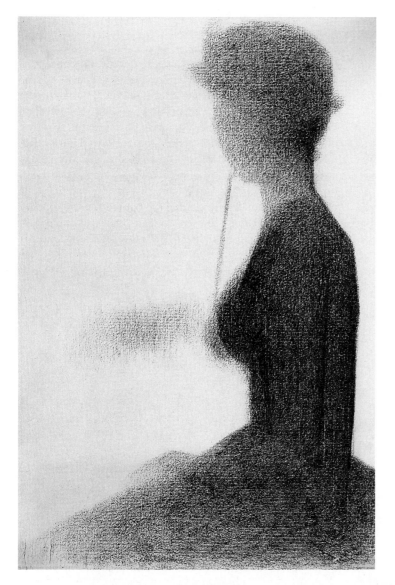

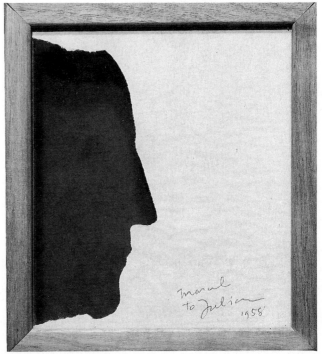

Figure 2-10. Georges-Pierre Seurat (1859–1891), *Seated Woman*, 1884–85. Conté crayon. 18⅞ × 12⅜″. The Museum of Modern Art, New York. Abby Aldrich Rockefeller Bequest. The subtle changes of value in this drawing convey far more visual information than is seen in a simple silhouette. Such subtleties are subordinate, however, to Seurat's overriding concern with the large form of the figure.

Figure 2-11. Marcel Duchamp (1887–1968), *Self-Portrait in Profile*, 1958. Torn paper. 5⅝ × 4⅞″. Julien Levy Collection (photo by Nathan Rabin). Duchamp simply tore away part of a piece of white paper to create the shape of the profile. A darker surface beneath the paper creates the silhouette effect. Although an empty space is normally seen as a negative shape, here it is perceived as the positive shape of the head. The figure-ground reversal, also common in nineteenth-century silhouettes, is enhanced by the unusual physical separation of the white paper from the dark surface.

wrote, "Graphic imagery being confined to outlines has a fairy-like quality and at the same time can achieve great precision."[2]

SUMMARY

Is art, as Max Lieberman maintained, "leaving out?" If so, the silhouette merits the attention of artists. The visual edge of the human form leaves out a great deal of visual information. It tells us little about the round three dimensionality of the body; it is a little more than a cross section of the figure. The deliberately incomplete description of form conveyed by the silhouette or outline drawing invokes the imagination of the viewer to complete it, thereby inducing a higher level of personal participation than that commonly experienced with more descriptive drawings.

Though derived from the same aspect of the figure, drawings based on the silhouette and the outline are conceptual opposites. In the case of the outline the artist draws the edge of the form first. The quality of the line used to define the edge tends to dominate the drawing, which is essentially a linear enclosure. With the silhouette, however, the artist can work from the inside core of the form outward. Linear edge, if it appears at all, appears last. Drawn in this way, the silhouette is associated with form in terms of mass and interior structure, while the outline is related to shape—the exterior edge of form, the boundary separating the figure from the ground. The two approaches represent fundamentally different ways of seeing form and underlie several other methods of interpreting it in drawing.

NOTES

1. Lorenz Eitner, *Neoclassicism and Romanticism*, vol. 2 (Englewood Cliffs, N.J.: Prentice-Hall, 1970), p. 137.

2. Paul Klee, *Inward Vision: Watercolors, Drawings and Writings* (New York: Abrams, 1959), pp. 5–10.

CHAPTER 3

Drawing in Line

contour, constructs, visual measurement, movement, and memory

*[T]he contour ought to round itself off and
so terminate as to suggest the presence of other parts behind it
also, and disclose even what it hides.*

—PLINY

ANY ARTISTS MAKE a distinction between *contour* and *outline*. The distinction is a subtle one often glossed over in dictionary definitions, but it is nevertheless implied in the derivations of the words. The word "contour" is derived from the Latin *con* ("with") and *tornare* ("to turn"), hence its meaning: a line that appears to turn with the form to which it pertains. A naturally occurring contour such as a fold or crease of the skin pertains to the form of the body and is therefore three dimensional in character. A curving line drawn on a flat surface can convey a powerful sense of the three-dimensional contour, and it is this type of line that artist commonly designate as contour (Figure 3-1). The drawn contour, as Pliny accurately observed, can also effectively suggest the continuity of volumetric form *beyond the visible edge of the object observed*. This is not the case with an outline, which is literally an outer line that limits the shape of the silhouette (Figure 3-2). Interesting for its graphic qualities, the outline tells us almost nothing of the volumes that lie within its edges: It is essentially flat.

The distinction between outline and contour is clarified by analogy with the familiar globe model of the earth. The outline of the globe is simply the edge of the circular outer shape, which is clearly visible when the globe is seen against a bright background. Contours of the globe are represented by the lines of latitude, which appear to curve and turn around the spherical surface before disappearing at the edge (or outline). By spinning the globe you can visualize many contours, for almost any point on the globe's surface describes a contour as the globe rotates. Two exceptions are the points of the poles. These, of course, define the globe's rotational axis.

Contours of the human body also appear to turn around the form, and, although body forms are more complex than the spherical form of the globe, body contours can usually be visualized around imaginary axes, or cores, as we discussed in Chapter 2. Just as a point on the spinning globe describes a contour in space, so can the point of a drawing instrument describe a contour of the body, although it is somewhat altered by the dictates of the flat surface.

The artist's contour drawings are generally less schematic than those of the globe but usually more interesting, for they are related to the sensuous experience of touch. To an even greater degree than the outline drawing, the contour drawing evokes the tactile sense. The contour line can mediate between vision and touch. This may be traced to the close coordination of the visual and the tactile experiences in childhood: "Since the child begins to learn how to identify objects by handling them and running his fingers round their edges,

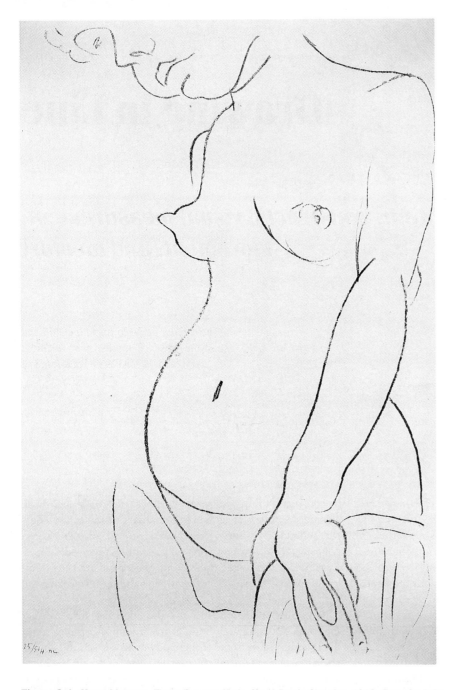

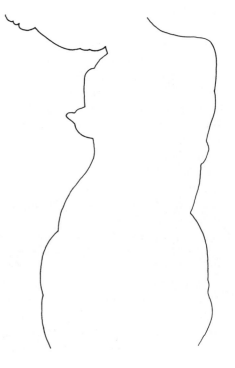

Figure 3-1. Henri Matisse, *Three-Quarter Nude, Head Partly Showing.* 1913. Transfer lithograph, printed in black. 19¹³⁄₁₆ × 12″. The Museum of Modern Art, New York. Frank Crowninshield Fund. Contour line endows this work with a suggestion of roundness and implies a complex sequence of forms with a remarkable economy of means.

Figure 3-2. Outline reduction of Figure 3-1. Outline, by eliminating overlapping contours, deprives the viewer of a means of interpreting the sequence of forms in space.

it is natural that this pattern of touch should become associated with the contour of the object perceived visually."[1] The child associates the contour with touch and vision in a natural, un-self-conscious way. The application of this principle to your first contour drawing must necessarily be more deliberate. With practice, however, the coordination of your vision with your sense of touch will become second nature. It is tempting to think that contour drawing reawakens a latent childlike spontaneity and responsiveness to the visual forms in nature. The lively spontaneity of contour drawings by many beginning students seems to affirm that possibility.

STUDY 4:   **Contour Drawing**

materials: ❑ 36 × 24″ newsprint drawing pad
             ❑ easel or straight-back chair
             ❑ Masonite or plywood board with clamps
             ❑ drawing crayon or felt-tip pen
reference: ❑ model
time: ❑ 30 minutes

You should observe the entire form of the model carefully before beginning a contour drawing. It helps to walk around the model to gain a more three-dimensional impression of the figure. After you return to your easel, select a point somewhere on the outer edge of the model's form. Then, as you touch your crayon to the drawing paper, imagine the point your crayon touches on the paper to be the point you observe on the model. Instead of actually touching the model, as a child might do, use your eye as an extension of your sense of touch. With this in mind, slowly draw the crayon across the paper while you simultaneously follow the model's contour, keeping your eye and hand in close coordination. When the contour on the model changes direction, your hand should also change direction. As you extend the contour line, you may notice that, although the contour originates from the edge (or outline) of the form, it does not necessarily continue along the edge. The contour line may turn inward on the form, at the same time curving around the volume of the figure. For best results try to focus solely on the model while you are drawing and avoid breaking your concentration by glancing back at the page (Figure 3-3).

When you have followed a contour as far as you can see it in the model, stop for a moment to regain your bearings on the page. Lift the crayon and go back to the point on the drawing at which the contour departs from the outline. With the crayon placed on that point, relocate the corresponding point on the form of the model before drawing the next contour. The second contour will probably also turn inward from

Figure 3-3. Student drawing. Crayon on newsprint pad. 36 × 24″. The sensitive and bold contour treatment of the figure is somewhat marred by the relatively fussy drawing of the head. It is evident the student looked at the paper while drawing that part of the model. Consistency of method ensures consistency of style.

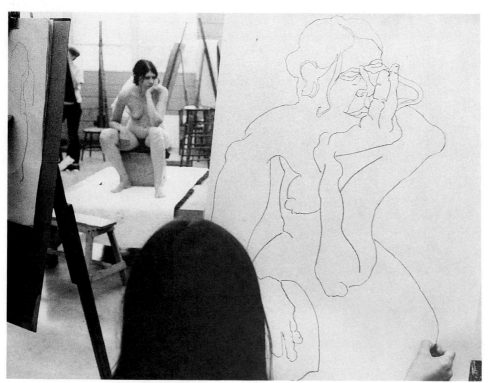

the outline. When you are unable to see this contour clearly enough to follow it further, stop again and repeat the process. With practice you will soon be able to follow a contour far inside the outline shape of the figure.

Wrinkles or creases in the skin may offer the clearest visible clues to the contours of the body. They are often noticeable in those portions of the body that bend, such as the waist or the joints of the limbs. If a crease line lies near the apparent outline of the figure, the contour may appear to turn sharply as it nears the outer limit of the silhouette. Contours of this type should be observed and drawn carefully, as they convey a great deal of visual information about the rounded volume of the form. Contour drawing need not be limited to representing such obvious linear features of the human form as wrinkles. Less clearly linear forms, such as muscle and bone patterns, can also be represented by means of the contour line.

The nature of contour drawing makes it advantageous to work from a standing position, for the slight shifts of viewpoint that occur quite naturally while standing enable you to see slightly beyond each side of the model and to follow contours further around the figure, both in life and in the drawing. The standing position also facilitates free arm movement, which is essential to a spontaneous line quality, since line itself is in a sense a trace of movement.

If the model is illuminated by a strongly directional light (i.e., a floodlamp), the boundaries between illuminated and shadowed surfaces on the model may appear as linear contours. For the purposes of this study such shadow contours, though useful in certain modeling techniques, are more related to the *effect of light* than to the *character of the form*, which is the primary concern in this exercise.

Concentration and patience are rewarded with this method of drawing; so it is wise to proceed slowly and carefully, drawing one contour at a time. Draw at a constant rate. The deliberately slow, unvarying speed will endow your drawing with a pleasing visual unity, no matter how erratic the lines may appear (Figure 3-4). What is more, a figure composed of contour lines can convey a sense of formal sequence, for the way in which each contour joins the next suggests overlapping (compare Figure 1-9 with Figure 3-1).

Figure 3-4. Student drawing. Contour study of the figure. Crayon on newsprint pad. 35 × 24″.

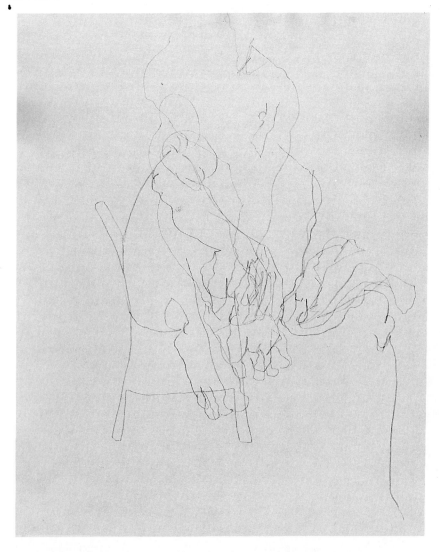

VISION AND EYE MOVEMENT

Despite the ease you experience in executing a contour drawing, one aspect of it may strike you as artificial: namely, the slowness it imposes on the hand and the eye. The eye prefers more movement. In fact under normal circumstances the eye moves constantly, even when you look at a single object. Its movement is not smooth, however: The eye scans in neat jumps from one point to another two or three times per second.[2] Each movement, called a *saccade* by physiologists, terminates with a *fixation*, during which the eye remains stationary for a short time while it records detailed visual information.[3]

The eye, as it moves and gathers information, seems at times to fix on points along the contours of forms (Figures 3-5 and 3-6). From this visual information the brain constructs a mental model of the object.[4] Exactly how the brain constructs this model and perceives it is one of the mysteries of science: to understand it fully would require an explanation of consciousness.[5] Yet it is believed that what is consciously perceived is the model, not the retinal image; that is, the continuously moving eye supplies the brain with visual information, but the eye itself does not see—the brain does. The striking similarity of the trails of eye movement to the

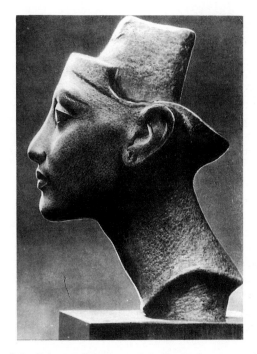

Figure 3-5. Unknown Egyptian artist, *Head of a Queen from El Amarna, Egypt,* c. 1370 B.C. Sandstone. 8⅝″ high. Berlin, Staatliche Museum.

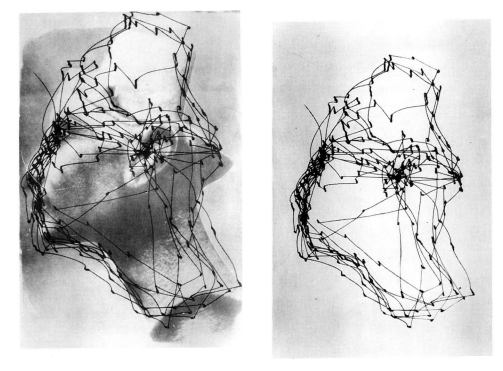

Figure 3-6. Alfred L. Yarbus, *Record of Eye Movements During Free Examination of a Photograph of the Sculptured Head of a Queen* [Figure 3-5] *for 2 Minutes.* The photographic recording was made by means of a small mirror attached to the eyeball. Darker spots on the trails indicate fixations, or short pauses, in the eye movement during which visual information is gathered. Although the trails of eye movement do not follow the contours of the head (Figure 3-5) precisely, nevertheless they suggest an as yet unexplained relationship between eye movement and drawing (photos courtesy of Alfred L. Yarbus, Institute for Problems of Information Transmission, Academy of Sciences of the USSR).

lines of a contour drawing may be coincidental, but it does suggest a contour-drawing exercise based on this modern concept of vision.

STUDY 5:   **Rapid Contour Drawing**

materials: ❏ 36 × 24″ newsprint drawing pad
  ❏ easel or straight-back chair
  ❏ Masonite or plywood board and clamps
  ❏ drawing crayon or felt marker
reference: ❏ model
time: ❏ 1–3 minutes

The brevity of this exercise makes it possible for the model to assume a pose of action, such as reaching or bending over. So it is helpful before putting crayon to paper to consider the type of action suggested by the pose. If, for example, the model is standing, let "the standing figure" be the subject of the drawing. This strategy will enable you to concentrate on the basic body forms that are possible to express within the time limit.

The starting position of the crayon on the drawing paper does not matter in this exercise, but it is vitally important to allow your eye to scan the entire length and breadth of the model freely as you draw and to avoid concentrating on small body features. The crayon should move continuously and, as much as possible, in unison with the eye as it scans the model. Remember to look for contours that do not lie on the edge of the form; they may appear to wrap around form in a way that strongly suggests sculptural volume. The resulting trails of line will develop into a wiry structure clearly related to the general contours and attitude of the model (Figures 3-7, 3-8, and 3-9).

Figure 3-7. Student drawing. Rapid contour study. Crayon on newsprint pad. 36 × 24″.

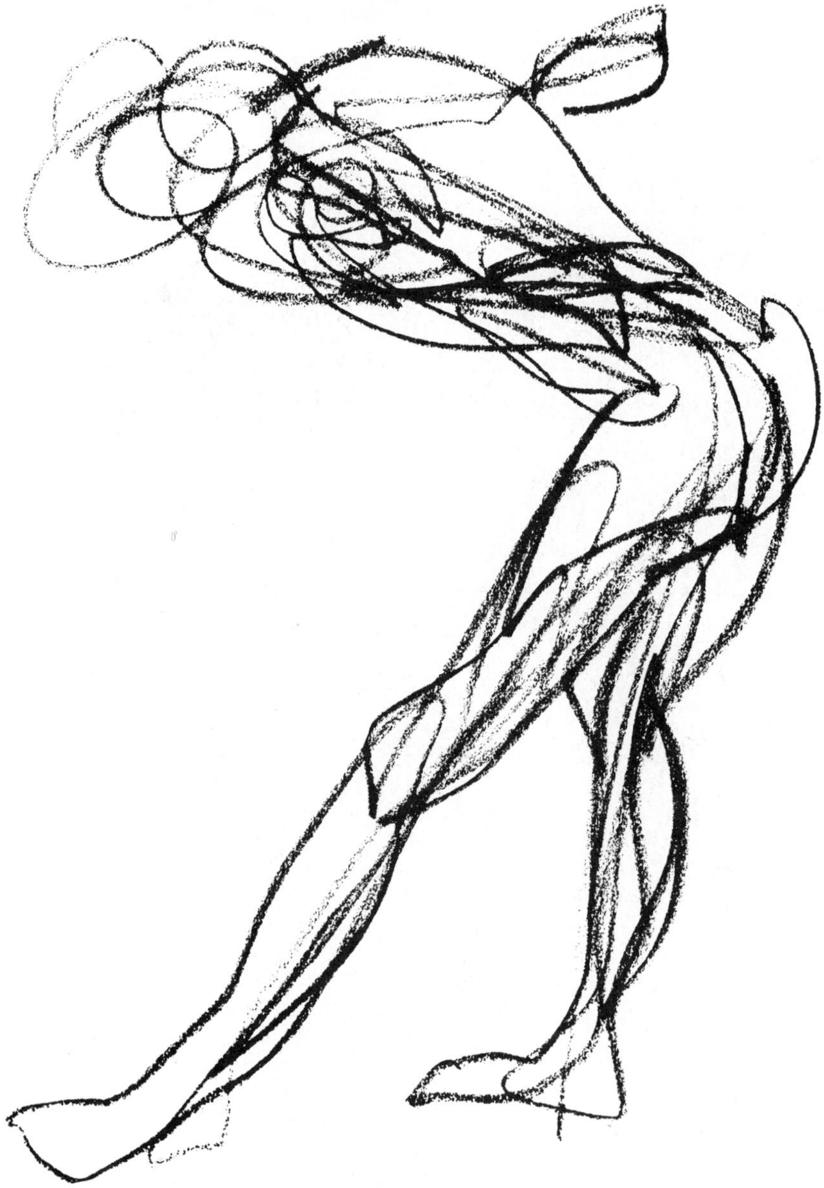

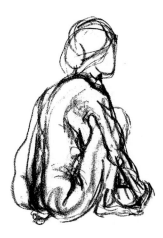

Figure 3-8. Student drawing. Rapid contour study. Crayon on newsprint pad. 36 × 24″. Holding the crayon on its side results in a greater tonal effect with contour line.

Figure 3-9. Jacopo da Pontormo (Jacopo Carrucci) (1494–1557), *Study for a* Madonna and Child, c.1524–1525. Black chalk heightened with white. 327 × 176 mm. Florence, Gallerie degli Uffizi.

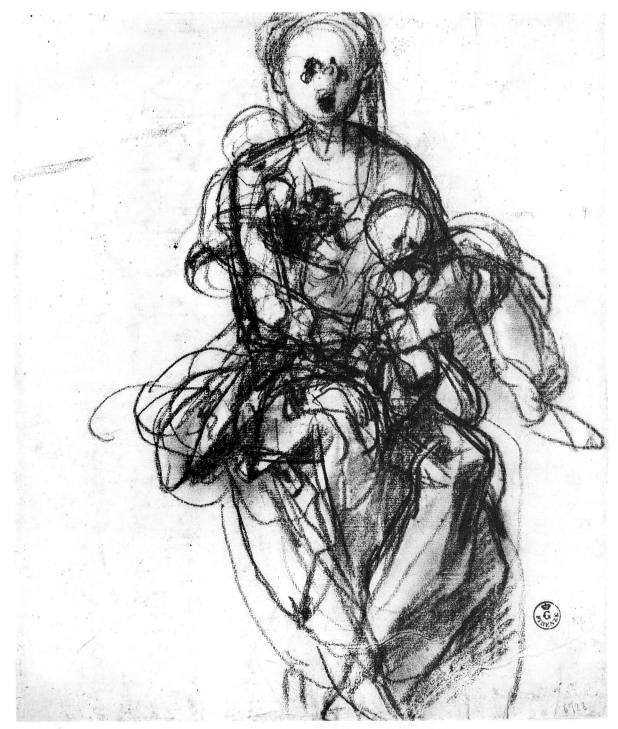

This procedure does not permit the eye to look back at the drawing pad, and it is just as well. To do so would interrupt your visual concentration and consequently the movement of your hand. The price will be a perceptible break in the unified development of the drawing.

The French sculptor Rodin—an artist also noted for his contour-line drawings—was convinced of the advantages of drawing the figure without looking at the paper. He gave eloquent testimony to the relation between visual observation and the sense of touch in the drawing process:

> I must become permeated with the secrets of all its [the body's] contours, all the masses that it presents to the eye. I must feel them at the end of my fingers. All this must flow naturally from my eye to my hand. . . . Not once in describing the shape of that mass did I shift my eyes from the model. Why? Because I wanted to be sure that nothing evaded my grasp of it. Not a thought about the technical problem of representing it on paper could be allowed to arrest the flow of my feelings about it, from my eye to my hand. The moment I drop my eyes that flow stops.[6]

These are words worth remembering. What Rodin has described may well be borne out by your own experiences in drawing with rapid contour.

COMPLETING THE DRAWING

Initially contour-line drawings may appear to be incomplete, lacking as they are in the nuances of tonal modeling. Such misgivings are understandable, but fail to take into account the special virtues of line as an artistic instrument. One of these is economy of means. Much can be expressed with few marks in line, leaving generous white areas of the paper intact. What matters in line drawing is the quality rather than the quantity of formal description. A complete line drawing is therefore one that meets the artist's objective, a condition the layperson may be less able to judge. Keenly aware of this problem, Matisse defended his line drawings, insisting that they

> . . . are more complete than they appear to some people who confuse them with a sketch. . . . Once I have put my emotion to line and modelled the light of my white paper, without destroying its endearing whiteness, I can add or take away nothing further.[7]

Due to time constraints of a drawing session, it is likely some of your drawings will not even be developed as completely as *you* would like. This is a common experience. Frustrating as this may seem, there is no need to feel discouraged. In fact these drawings are well worth saving as they are, without later reworking. The incomplete drawings may harbor a spontaneity that further development would have eliminated.

Save them. The incomplete work of art has long been appreciated for its own expressive quality. The Roman author Pliny informs us that certain "unfinished" paintings by Aristides and Apelles, important painters in ancient Greece, "are more admired than those which they finished, because in them are seen the preliminary drawings left visible and the artist's actual thoughts. . . ."[8]

BODY FORMS AND LINE

Outline and contour drawing demonstrate how line can serve as an instrument to describe the edge and the turning surface of form observed in the figure. Line can also be considered as a means of visualizing units of form in the figure. Extensive knowledge of anatomy is not necessary in order to visualize the parts of the body as structural units of form. Such units are already familiar as common words, such as *thigh*, *calf*, *head*, and *chest*. These and many other parts of the body can be seen to have in common a general roundness of form that can be seen and drawn as a unit. The turning, rotational nature of this formal unit invites the use of an analogous drawing construct—the oval—as a way of drawing the figure.

STUDY 6:   **The Figure as a Construction of Smaller Units**

materials: ❑ 36 × 24″ newsprint drawing pad
❑ easel or straight-back chair
❑ Masonite or plywood board and clamps
❑ drawing crayon
reference: ❑ model
time: ❑ 3–5 minutes

No more than five minutes are needed to complete this study, so you may choose to set the model in a pose of action or movement. Once the pose is set, observe body contours that appear as parts of the rounded form. The calf, for example, can be interpreted as a continuous ovoid (egg) form and drawn as an oval. The same is true of the other segments of the limbs, such as the thigh. The trunk, by virtue of its skeletal construction, is most readily conceived as two general ovoid masses, one corresponding to the egg shape of the rib cage and the other enclosing the pelvic mass of the lower abdomen. Both can be further broken down into smaller components, but it is helpful to keep the two essential masses in mind. Connecting the two masses are the spine and abdominal muscles, which appear to bend and change shape with the body's gesture.

Begin with a lightly drawn, rapid contour sketch of the entire figure to establish a frame of reference for placing the oval constructs. It is best to draw the oval constructs rapidly, exploiting the tendency to simplify complex form. Even the head, with all of its subtle complexities, can be reduced to bold oval constructs. As far as possible, however, you should strive for a correspondence between the oval constructs and the formal units observed in the figure. The oval discussed here is not the perfect and fixed form of geometry but a plastic form adaptable to the character of the formal unit observed. The character of the formal unit, rather than the quality of line or individual contour, is the aim of this study (Figure 3-10). The oval is merely a convenient construct, suggested by the rounded form of many shapes of the body.

Although it is relatively easy to interpret the body forms as ovals, it may require practice to relate those forms to the figure as a whole. The oval method may tend to produce

drawings of a somewhat doll-like, segmented character. You can control, if you wish, unwanted segmentation of form by adding contours that describe the formal transition observed between the oval constructs. However, you may find that the concept of the figure as a doll is of interest for your own artistic purposes, as indeed some artists have in the past.

Arcimboldo, an Italian painter of the Renaissance, conceived each construct as a separate object in itself, adding a second level of meaning—and humor—to his allegorical subjects (Figure 3-11). Artists such as Luca Cambiaso and Albrecht Dürer produced many drawings based on rectangle and box constructs. Likewise, some instructional anatomy

Figure 3-10. Student drawing. Crayon on newsprint paper. 36 × 24″. Familiar body forms can be drawn as overlapping oval constructs that suggest spatial sequence. A similar concept of form was expressed by Hokusai (Figure 1-8).

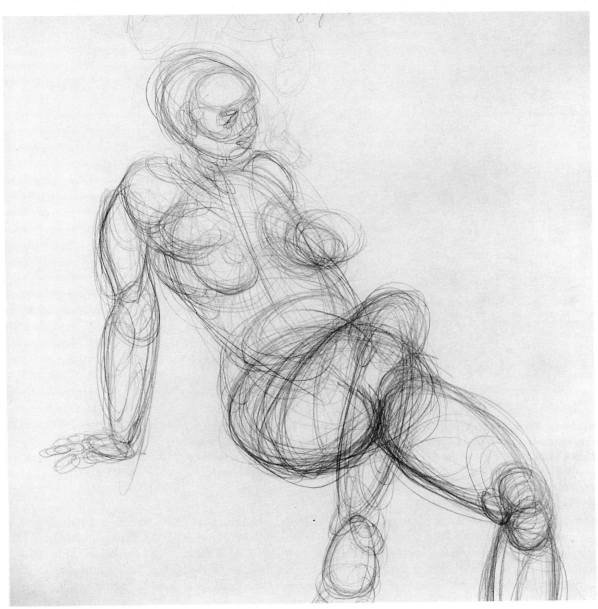

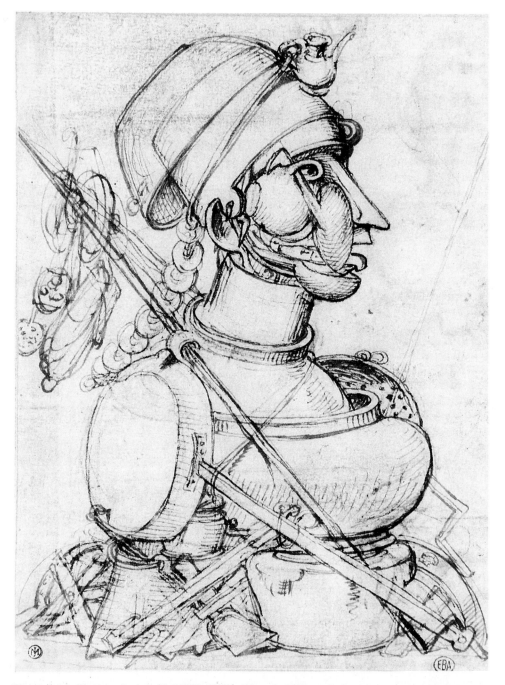

Figure 3-11. Giuseppe Arcimboldo (1527–1593), *Allegorical Figure of a Cook.* Pen and ink. Paris, L'Ecole Nationale Supérieure des Beaux Arts. Acknowledged as a precursor of surrealism, the Italian painter Arcimboldo developed figural constructs of larger forms to represent objects symbolic of the allegorical subject. Here the constructs represent the pots, pans, and other objects associated with the subject of the allegory—the cook.

books use the block as the basic construct of the figure.[9] For practical reasons dolls or manikins have long been used by artists as a substitute for the model, especially with a subject dressed in costume requiring very long drawing sessions. In the twentieth century the doll and manikin have been explored for their uniquely surreal qualities (Figure 3-12).

The oval constructs are far less obtrusive in Rico Lebrun's figure *Dusty Okie* (Figure 3-13), for they are subtly linked in an unbroken chain of formal units by means of the brush and ink wash. Because of the special, and perhaps less familiar qualities of the brush as a drawing instrument, it merits a separate study using the same approach just described.

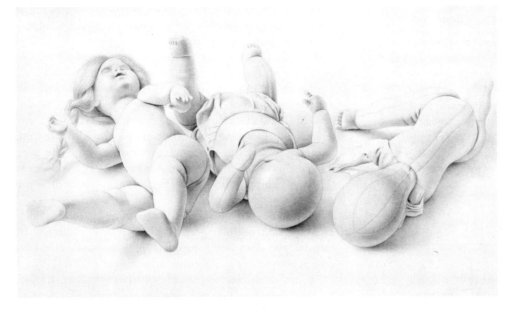

Figure 3-12. Rudolf Dischinger, *Dolls*, 1932. Watercolor. 18 × 24 cm. Stuttgart, Germany, Graphische Sammlung, Staatsgalerie.

Figure 3-13. Rico Lebrun (1900–1964). *Dusty Okie*. Sepia wash on white paper. 24½ × 19⅛″. The Nelson-Atkins Museum of Art, Kansas City, Missouri. Bequest of Katherine Harvey. (63-45)

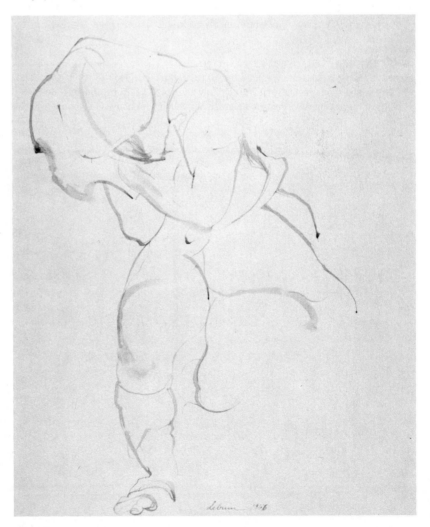

STUDY 7:   **Figure Construction with Brush and Ink**

materials: ❑ 36 × 24″ newsprint pad (or watercolor paper in
      a large size if expense is no problem)
    ❑ table or desk or drawing table (with top slightly
      tilted)
    ❑ Japanese bamboo-handled brush, no smaller
      than size 6 or flat bristle brush number
      9 or 10
    ❑ mason jar half filled with water
    ❑ small jar of India ink or tube of watercolor
      black
    ❑ saucer to hold washes
reference: ❑ model
time: ❑ 1–3 minutes

The need for a special arrangement of materials makes it advisable to devote an entire drawing session to brush drawing. Although brush drawings are possible with the paper set up on an easel, a more horizontal support such as a table allows the liquid brush strokes to dry without dripping down the page.

To begin, first squeeze out a small amount of black pigment into the saucer and dip the brush in the water. Use the wet brush to dilute some of the pigment to make a dark wash in the saucer. Load the brush moderately with the wash, and you are ready to draw. The drawing procedure is essentially the same as in the preceding rapid contour study. If this is your first attempt to draw with a brush, however, you may need some hints on how to hold it.

In order to experience the unique freedom of movement possible with the brush, try holding it in the traditional Oriental manner, near the top of the shaft between the thumb and the middle joint of the first finger (Figure 3-14). It should be held almost vertically, with the drawing pad flat on a table. This arrangement enables you to draw both with the large swinging motions of the arm and wrist and with the finer movements of the fingers. Oval constructs—and with them the large construction of the figure—may seem to come naturally.

Held high on the shaft, the brush registers even the slightest movements of the fingers. In fact, it seems to magnify such movements, often producing effects of great spontaneity. Liberty of movement is advantageous with the brush; so avoid the temptation to rest your hand or arm on the paper or table. By the same token, however, you may experience less control over the brush than you felt in drawing with the crayon because the sensation of touch and contact with the drawing surface is minimal. Practice is usually necessary to feel at ease drawing with the brush (Figure 3-15). But the special qualities of brush drawing make the effort worthwhile. These qualities are apparent in the calligraphy of the Far East, where brush drawing and writing are closely related expressions (Figures 3-16, 3-17, and 3-18), as well as in the more familiar master drawings by Western artists (Figure 3-19).

Figure 3-14. Hokusai, *How to Hold a Brush*, 1812. Double page illustration from Rajakuga Haya Oshie, vol. 2. Woodblock engraving from a brush drawing. 16 × 11.25 cm. Boston, Museum of Fine Arts. Gift of William Sturgis Bigelow. Holding the brush at midlength or above is helpful in creating free movement of line.

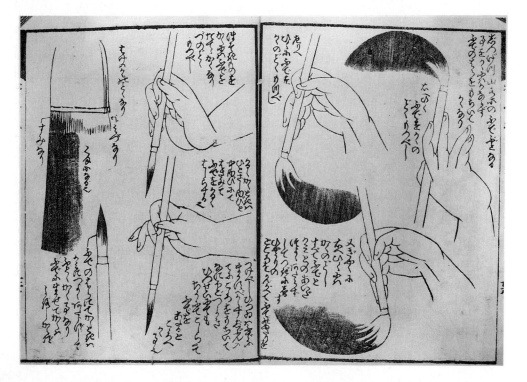

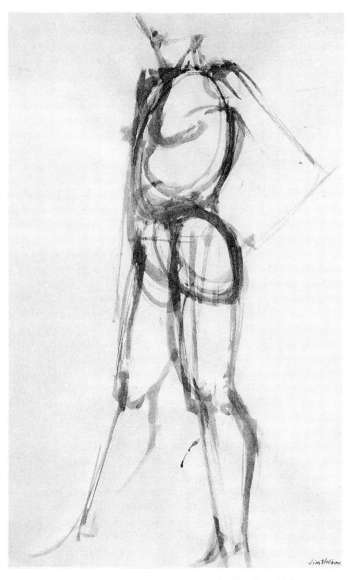

Figure 3-15. Student drawing. Contour study. Brush and ink on newsprint pad. 36 × 24″.

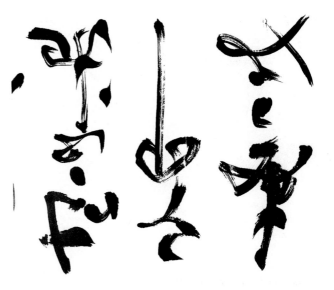

Figure 3-16. Calligraphy. Section of a poem by Chu Yun-ming (1460–1526), Ming Dynasty. Hand scroll, ink on paper. 18 × 624⅜″. Princeton University Art Museum.

Figure 3-17. Hokusai, *The Mirror Polisher.* Illustration from *Rajakuga Haya Oshie*, vol. 2. Woodblock engraving from a brush drawing. 16 × 11.25 cm. Boston, Museum of Fine Arts. The abstract cursive forms in the upper left are a calligraphic reduction of the figure of the mirror polisher, illustrating the affinity between writing and drawing in the Oriental tradition.

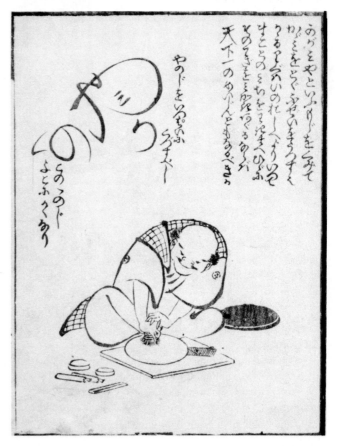

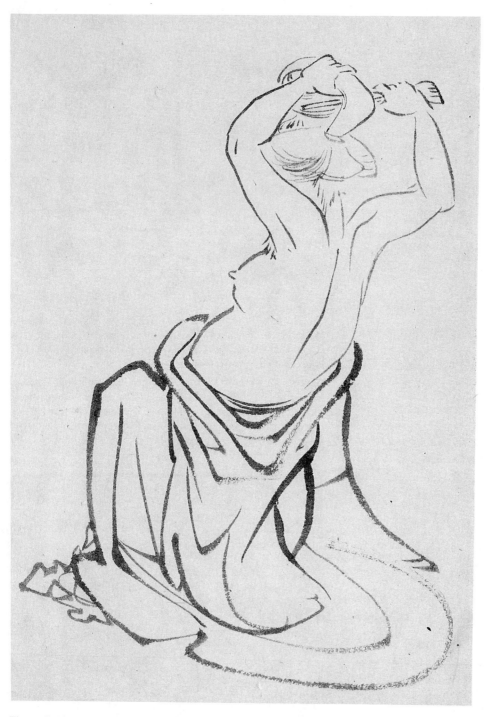

Figure 3-18. Hokusai, *Studies of a Woman Adjusting her Hair*. Brush and ink. 10⅛ × 6½″. New York, Metropolitan Museum of Art. Gift in memory of Charles Stewart Smith, 1914.

STUDY 8:	**Drawing the Figure from Memory**

materials: ❑ 36 × 24″ newsprint drawing pad
❑ easel or straight-back chair
❑ Masonite or plywood board and clamps
❑ drawing crayon
reference: ❑ model
time: ❑ 5 minutes for each drawing

Once you are familiar with the method described in Study 6, you can apply it to the problem of drawing the figure from memory. Drawing from memory is much easier than you may expect. In a sense you are already experienced at memory drawing, for every time you look at the paper while you draw, you are utilizing your short-term memory to recall forms you have just seen. This exercise makes use of the short-term memory in the same way but to a greater degree.

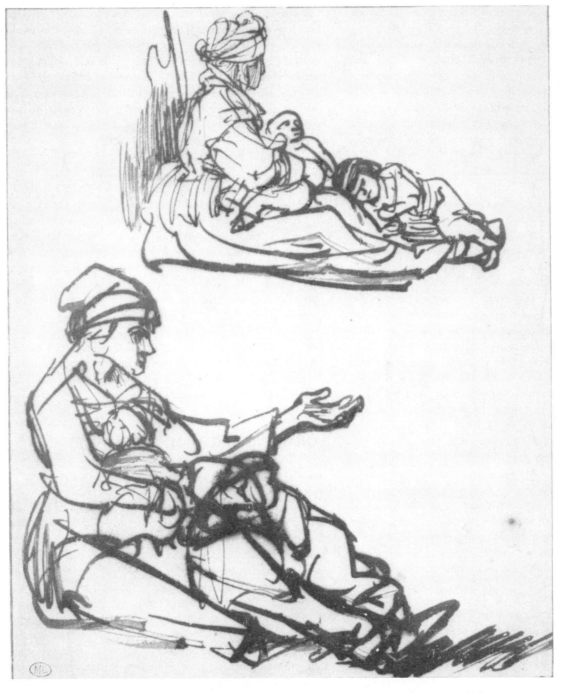

Figure 3-19. Rembrandt (1606–1669), *Two Studies of a Begging Woman with Two Children*, c. 1632–1633. Pen and gallnut ink. 6.9 × 5.5″. Paris, the Louvre.

The model should assume a simple pose, preferably with an ordinary gesture such as bending over to tie a shoe. When the pose has been decided on, be sure to mark the position of the feet with chalk or pieces of tape on the platform so the pose can be resumed later.

While the pose is set, observe the model for about three minutes without drawing at all. It may be helpful to walk around the model to gain a clearer sense of the disposition of body form as you did in the previous study. There are also two simple mental exercises that many students have found helpful: (1) Pretend you are drawing while you observe the model; (2) Imagine yourself performing the same gesture as the model. Both exercises rely on your natural ability to recall actions. By reinforcing your visual memory such exercises can assist you in recalling the gesture and forms of the figure.

As soon as the time is up, have the model step down from

the stand. That done, you are ready to commence drawing. But for the absence of the model, the drawing procedure is the same as that in Study 6. A light indication of the gesture with a rapid contour sketch can help set up the figure, but the oval constructs constitute the final drawing. Drawing time should be limited. For the best results allow a maximum time of five minutes. One advantage of the oval-construct method is that changes can be easily made while the drawing is in progress, particularly in the early stages when the constructs are still very general in nature.

When you have completed the memory study, it is instructive to make a second drawing of the same pose from life. Since the positions of the feet are marked on the model stand, the model can resume the same pose for another five-minute drawing session. It is vital that the second drawing be made immediately after the first in order to resolve any problems while they are still fresh in your mind. One memory study per drawing session is recommended.

Beyond its practical value as a diagnostic tool for improving your drawing, the memory drawing is an important genre in its own right, as demonstrated by the fact that countless master drawings, including many of the figure, were done from memory (or, if you prefer, from imagination). Constructs such as the oval serve as the basis for many of them, even though they may not be apparent in the finished drawings, be they cartoons of Mickey Mouse or classical figures on Greek vases.

Memory studies cannot be overstressed. Not only do they exercise your short-term memory, they also develop your long-term memory of body forms and their relative sizes—knowledge that can also be used in making studies from life.

Despite their value, memory drawing exercises are often omitted in art instruction courses. This may be partly due to the Western emphasis on empirical observation as the basis for objective reality. Whatever the reason, the omission reflects a misunderstanding of the interaction of visual perception and visual memory.

Visual memory differs from (visual) perception because it is based primarily on stored rather than on current information, but it involves the same kind of synthesis. Although the eyes have been called the windows of the soul, they are not so much peepholes as entry ports, supplying raw material for the constructive activity of the visual system.[10]

Visual perception is a creation of the brain. It is based on the input extracted from the retinal image, but what is seen in "the mind's eye" goes far beyond what is present in the input [of the retinal image]. The brain uses information it has extracted previously as the basis for educated guesses—perceptual inferences about the state of the outside world. Usually those guesses are correct and useful.[11]

If visual memory is useful in visual perception its role in drawing should not be underestimated.

Visual memory has proven useful to artists in the past. The French sculptor Auguste Rodin (1840–1917) credited his facility as a draftsman to the memory training he received as a young art student in the classes of Lecoq de Boisbaudran. He recalled that ". . . at home in the evening, before going to bed, it was his custom to practice what Lecoq de Boisbaudran had recommended, reproducing from memory what he had studied during the day."[12] Another major French artist, Edgar Degas (1834–1917), once remarked,

It is all very well to copy what you see; it is much better to draw what you see only in memory. There is a transformation during which the imagination works in conjunction with the memory. You put down only what made an impression on you, that is to say the essential. Then your memory and your invention are freed from the dominating influence of nature. That is why pictures made by a man with a trained memory who knows thoroughly both the masters and his own craft are almost always remarkable works. . . .[13]

The fact that both Rodin and Degas also produced superb drawings directly from life suggests that drawing from memory and directly from the model can be mutually enhancing approaches (Figures 3-36 and 6-51).

FORM AND VISUAL MEASUREMENT

Study 8 takes advantage of your ability to see and interpret body forms as rounded ovoid units in space. Essentially concerned with sculptural volumes, it is an approach to drawing that can be called *stereometric*. In order to learn how to make the fine adjustments of drawing associated with draftsmanship, however, a different approach is called for, one based on measuring the appearance of form seen as an optical image rather than as three-dimensional form. This method is known as *planimetric*, for it makes use of estimated visual measurement of form as it would appear on a plane of glass between you and the model. A visual measurement is the *apparent distance between features within the image*, not the actual distance separating those features in space. For example, the actual distance between a model's eyes is constant, but when the head is turned from a frontal view, the eyes may appear much closer. The apparent distance is thereby shortened. Visual measurement takes that into account in placing the eyes in the drawing of the head.

For purposes of visual measurement the simple straight line is a more effective tool in drawing than the curved (contour) line, with its infinite variations. The human body, however, presents few features with truly straight lines. Instead what confronts the artist is a complex array of contours—curves with varying degrees of shallowness or sharpness. The question then arises: How can the complexities of bodily form be described with straight lines on a flat surface? One answer lies

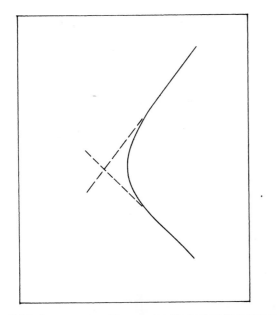

Figure 3-20. A curve reduced to an angle. The broken lines represent a visual reduction of a curve into straight lines that intersect to form an angle.

in the variety of the curves themselves. Put simply, the curves of the body bend more sharply in some places than they do in others. This gives many of them an angular character. By interpreting a contour as an angle the artist can estimate the angle of a contour and draw it as two straight lines that intersect at the sharpest point of the contour (Figure 3-20). Observing and drawing such intersections is the basis of the following exercise, which focuses on the problem of visual measurement in drawing.

STUDY 9:   Visual Measurement of Form in the Figure

materials: ❏ 36 × 24″ newsprint drawing pad
❏ easel or straight-back chair
❏ Masonite or plywood board and clamps
❏ drawing crayon
reference: ❏ model
time: ❏ 3 minutes for preliminary steps
❏ 20 to 30 minutes for visual measurements

Drawing 1

Formal Analysis with Angles. In this exercise two preliminary steps are advisable: (1) a rapid (two-minute) contour drawing of the figure to establish the placement and size of the intended drawing; and (2) a vertical and a horizontal line drawn through the center of the figure as a useful reference for your first visual measurements. The contour drawing should be rendered lightly, since dark tones might interfere with further development of form. Very light indications can

be achieved by holding the crayon on its side and moving it sideways across the paper. The two reference lines can be drawn by holding the crayon on its side and pulling it lengthwise across the pad. Use the edges of your drawing pad as a guide for proper vertical and horizontal alignment. Vertical alignment of the drawing paper is also important, so check the alignment of your drawing pad on the easel: Make sure it is not tilted or wobbly. A clamp may help hold the drawing pad in place.

With the preliminary steps completed you can begin the study by examining the form of the model for large contours that can also be interpreted as angles. Try focusing your attention on one angular feature only. Estimate the location of this feature in your preliminary drawing. Two straight lines will suffice to draw it, of course, but the key is to draw each line so it parallels the linear feature seen in the model (Figure 3-21).

A word of caution. Since your first angular measurement serves as a reference line for the rest of the drawing, take time and care with it. Consider carefully the angular direction of the line you observe in the model. Is it vertical or horizontal? If neither, how much does it depart from the vertical or horizontal of the reference lines?[14] If the line was drawn on the face of a clock, what time would it be? When you have answered these questions, use the vertical and horizontal reference lines in your preliminary drawing as a guide for drawing the line.

The crayon itself makes a useful instrument for angular measurement. You may find it helpful to hold the crayon at arm's length along your line of sight toward the model. Adjust the crayon's angular alignment so its length parallels the linear feature in the model you wish to draw.[15] Then, while retaining the alignment of the crayon, place it against the paper and move it lengthwise. This simple procedure will produce a line with the angular direction observed. The second line of the angle can be drawn in the same way.

After you have drawn the first angular intersection, you can shift your attention to another part of the figure in which an angular effect is apparent. The light preliminary drawing should prove useful in locating the second angle. Once you have placed it, repeat the process just described, taking equal care to make the lines parallel to those perceived in life. To place the second angle and all those that follow it, you can refer to the first to determine a more precise relationship among shapes of the body form. Observe their respective positions carefully in the model. Here, too, it may be helpful to imagine a clock face with the intersection of the first angle as its center. The angle of the clock's hand can help you estimate the position of the second angle. By repeating the steps described here to construct additional angular intersections, you can build up linear structures that accurately reflect body forms.

When you have completed the broad angular construction of the figure, you may wish to develop the form further by searching out the smaller angular indentations within the large

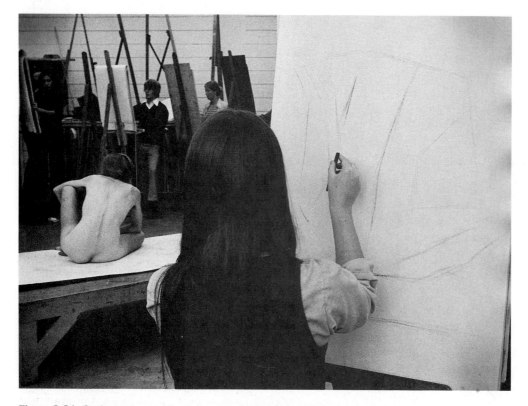

Figure 3-21. Student using angular measurement. The student holds the crayon on its side and examines the model for contours that can be interpreted as straight lines. Parallel alignment of the crayon with the observed line facilitates visual correspondence between the model and the drawing. Note the relationship of the crayon to the line drawn just above it. The first line indicates the spinal column. It was used as the reference line for determining the general placement of all additional lines. Vertical and horizontal guidelines, not shown in this drawing, can be helpful in gauging the alignment of the initial reference line.

Figure 3-22. Developing the drawing. The student blocks in the shape, holding the crayon parallel to the contour observed on the lower left side of the model. At this point in the drawing the head should have been developed to the same degree as the rest of the figure.

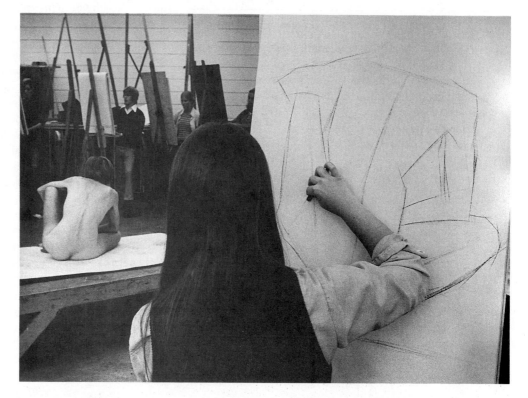

shapes (Figure 3-22). You can use the same method to place these smaller shapes within the framework of the larger ones. The task is somewhat simplified by the presence of the larger framework: It requires visual measurement only within the local area, since the problem of the larger relationship has already been solved by the more generalized shapes. This kind of visual measure can often be seen in terms of fractions—for example, one-half the length of the larger shape. The smaller measurements can be critical in areas with more complex features, such as those of the head; but fortunately the angular constructs of the large contours tend to favor both economy of detail and accuracy. It follows that the better the large framework in the early stage, the better your drawing will sustain the burden of detailed rendering. When an erroneous measurement is detected in the large framework, as sometimes happens while drawing the smaller type of form, it can be corrected at any time in the drawing process.

Figure 3-23. Completed student drawing, 30-minute session. Crayon on newsprint pad. 36 × 24″. Mistakes left unerased do not impair the quality of the drawing. An important correction was made in the angular intersection on the right-hand side of the figure's trunk at waist level. Drawing the shape of the head after that of the body contributed to the visual inconsistency in the two portions of the drawing. Certain other parts, such as the lower lines of the right leg, also need the reassessment of placement seen in the trunk.

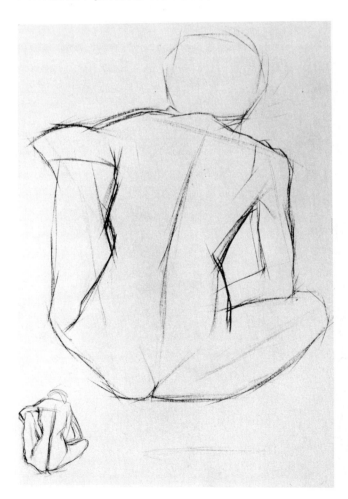

Although there is no fixed time period for this exercise, you will find that fifteen minutes should be allowed to complete the most general forms of the figure. The amount of additional time depends on the extent to which you wish to develop the drawing. For your first experiment with this technique an additional fifteen minutes is suggested.

A chief virtue of this method of drawing is its flexibility: It permits constant reevaluation of visual measurement, since you can simply draw another angular intersection to conform to your new estimate of the original's location.[16] In many cases the original angular intersection need not be erased, as it will not affect the quality of the drawing. Several instances of such reevaluation are visible in Figure 3-23, a drawing in which no erasures were made. The "extra" lines do not mar the quality of the drawing. On the contrary, they seem to add a kind of graphic excitement, implying the artist's search for shape and form. Remember that graphic effects of this sort are a by-product rather than the goal of the method.

Reevaluation of your drawing can also be accomplished by means of negative spaces. If, for example, parts of the figure seem to enclose a negative (or empty) space, you can compare the shape seen in the pose and the shape you have drawn by visualizing the negative space as an abstract positive shape (Figure 1-11). Simple as it is, the figure-ground reversal offers a fresh point of view, which can help you to be more self-critical of your draftsmanship.

The examples of student work in Figures 3-23 through 3-25 demonstrate the use of angular construction to describe and enclose form. Figure 3-26, however, illustrates a more economical use of this drawing method: By restricting the angular construction to areas of intersection the artist leaves "open" the spaces between those angles. Yet the forms of the figure seem completed, or closed (in accordance with the closure principle described in Chapter 1).

Limiting the drawing to angular intersections clearly observed in the model has several advantages. It tends to facilitate focusing attention on the abstract relationships of the angular measurements, which carries with it the bonus of keener draftsmanship. Aesthetically, the greater selectivity in the drawing process may enhance the personal quality in the resulting drawing. On the practical side, the "open" forms in the drawing are relatively easy to erase and modify. Whether the shapes drawn are "open" or "closed," all three examples of student drawings demonstrate that the angular method tends to favor a heightened clarity of structure. The angular analysis can also be applied to the earliest stages of drawing, as seen in the following study.

Drawing 2

Directional Lines and Framework of the Figure. Effective as it is in drawing apparent features of the figure, angular measurement is also useful in establishing the general frame-

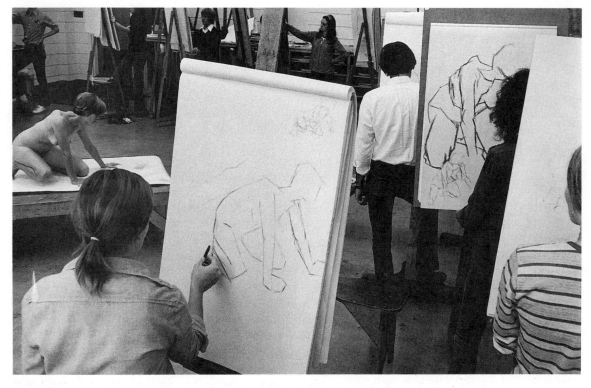

Figure 3-24. Observing and drawing angular intersections of the figure. Careful visual measurement is necessary in drawing the model's form in terms of angular intersections.

Figure 3-25. The flat brush, held so that the tip parallels a linear feature observed in the figure, makes a convenient instrument for gauging angular orientation.

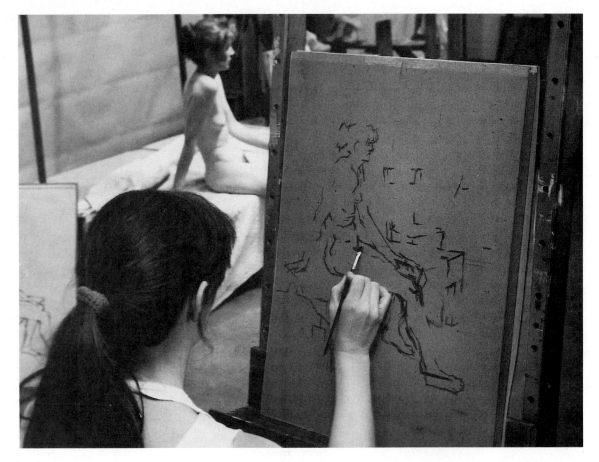

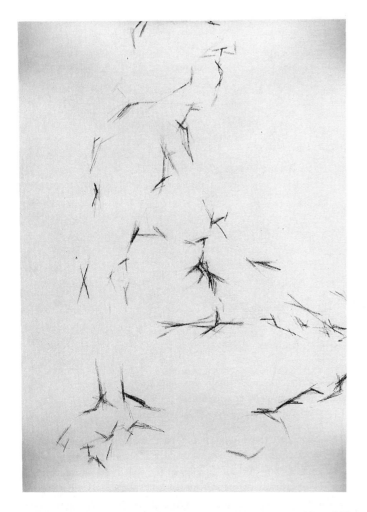

Figure 3-26. Student drawing. Crayon on newsprint pad. 36 × 24″. Angular intersections are registered only in areas where visual information is concentrated, allowing the forms to appear complete even though unenclosed by line.

work of the figure before proceeding to its visible contours. The body forms that are displayed most clearly in the pose will make a good starting place to apply this approach the first time. After examining the form of the arm, for example, try estimating the angular orientation of the model's arm with one or more straight line segments that reach from the shoulder to the wrist of the figure (Figure 3-27). The first directional line is likely to suggest a second one, connecting and relating the position of the two shoulders, enabling you to apply the same procedure to the other arm. Although the directional lines are imaginary, they can be visualized as running midway between the outer contours of body forms, as seen in the case of the arm. An exception is seen in the groove of the back, a *visible* feature that can provide a valuable directional sense of the trunk (Figure 5-47). As we noted in the case of the shoulders, directional lines are also an effective way to relate features common to both sides of the body. In particular the bony features of the trunk, notably the collar-

bones and the tips of the hipbone (pelvis) are helpful cross references (see Figure 3-33). Directional lines can also be used as a tool for relating *different* features of the figure. Such a line was drawn diagonally in Figure 3-27 to check the position of the figure's left hand in relation to the right shoulder.

In its early stages the drawing may resemble a stick figure; however, you should feel free to use as many directional lines as you need to indicate an adequate framework for drawing the visible exterior contours—the second phase of this study—using the angular measurements described in Drawing 1. In practice the second phase will become a logical, unbroken continuation of the first, capable of producing a crystalline clarity of construction unique to line drawing (Figure 3-33).

Drawing 3

Foreshortening. The foreshortening in the figure is often explained as a visual effect of perspective. Indeed it is. But in studio practice foreshortening commonly refers to any view

Figure 3-27. Student drawing. 15-minute study of the kneeling female figure. Dark blue crayon on grey paper. 12 × 8½″. Completed in fifteen minutes, the drawing shows initial development of the figure with lightly drawn interior directional lines followed by external contours, all based on angular measurement.

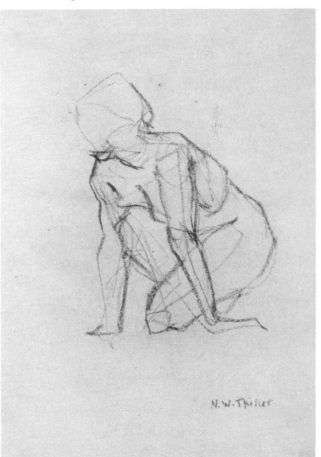

of the figure in which features of the body appear disproportionate due to an unfamiliar longitudinal view of the model or to the close proximity of the model. The foreshortened figure challenges the artist to represent the figure as it appears, and at the same time to convey a sense of wholeness.

The reclining figure offers a typical effect of foreshortening. If, for example, the prone model is situated with the feet toward the observer, the feet may appear disproportionately large (Figure 3-28). Likewise, the head, when seen from below, may appear relatively small, even though in both cases there is no sense of distortion (Figure 3-29). Indeed the viewer will perceive normal proportions in the figure.

Since the effects of foreshortening are more pronounced when the viewpoint is nearest the model, place your drawing board close by the model. If the model assumes a sitting pose on a raised platform, a "worm's eye view" may result. A reclining pose, as noted, can present a view with even more exaggerated effects of foreshortening.

The visual measurement of angles (described in Drawing 1) is especially helpful as a way of discovering the structure of the foreshortened figure, for it enables the artist to analyze

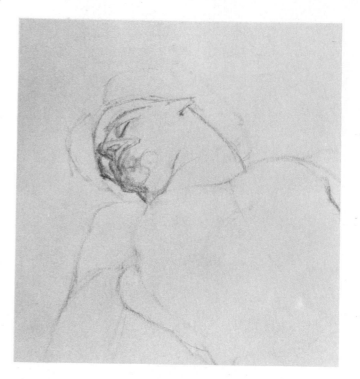

Figure 3-29. Student drawing. 20-minute study of the head with foreshortening. Crayon on newsprint pad. 24 × 18″.

Figure 3-28. Charles Cajori (b.1921), Study, 1963. Graphite pencil. 14 × 10½″. Courtesy Ingber Gallery Ltd., New York.

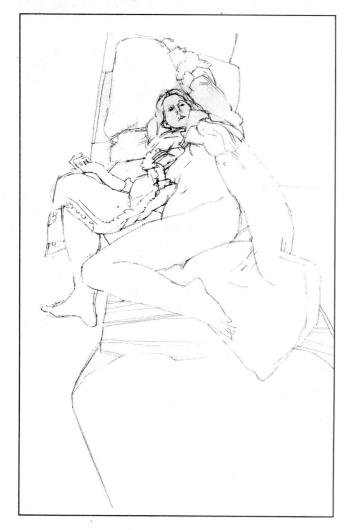

the image of the body—in this case an unfamiliar image—strictly in terms of abstract formal relationships. Despite its unfamiliarity (or perhaps *because* of it), the foreshortened figure is surprisingly easy to draw using the visual measurement method. The very novelty of the foreshortened view can make it a source of discovery for fresh and expressive interpretation of the figure.

Approach and Concept

Visual measurement in drawing is conceptually related to Cézanne's view that "art is a harmony parallel to that of Nature."[17] For Cézanne, parallel harmony did not merely refer to a method, such as that described here, of drawing lines parallel to those observed in nature. Rather, it encompassed all components of art, including color, value, composition, and form. Yet Cézanne's drawings reveal a similar method (Figure 3-30). This is less surprising in view of the fact that parallelism and angular measurement were a standard part of drawing instruction in the late nineteenth century. Among the earliest examples of drawings by the young Picasso are studies based on angular measurement, offering proof that he, like most of the art students at that time, learned to draw using this general method (Figures 3-31 and 3-32). Angular measurement is not limited to the nineteenth-century practice, however. The same general approach can be found in the work of contemporary artists. The Swiss artist Alberto

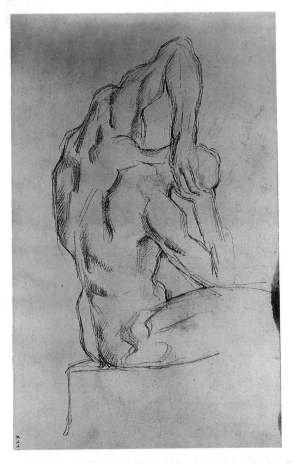

Figure 3-30. Paul Cézanne (1839–1906), *Sketchbook Study of the Ecorché*. Pencil on white paper. 12.4 × 21.7″. Courtesy of The Art Institute of Chicago. The method used by Cézanne to construct form with line is similar to that described in Study 8, but with the added feature of parallel hatch marks, which reinforce the angular constructs and add an effect of sculptural relief. Especially noteworthy are the three open spaces conceived and drawn as negative shapes.

Figure 3-31. Pablo Picasso (1881–1973), *Study of a Profile*, 1892–1893. Conté crayon. 9.3 × 12.2″. Barcelona, Museo Picasso (courtesy of SPADEM). An early study by the precocious Picasso reveals the drawing method he was taught. Initial vertical and horizontal reference lines (intersecting at the eye) were a guide for constructing the other lines. Note the lightly drawn lines that indicate the general angle of the profile: They serve as the reference for smaller angular intersections of the lines composing the features.

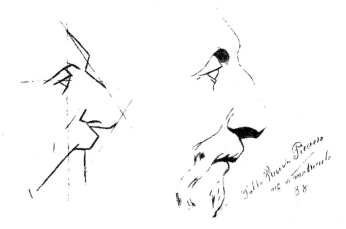

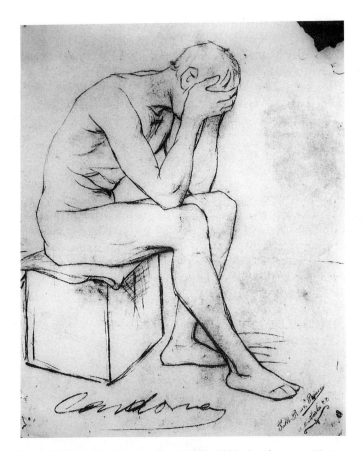

Figure 3-32. Pablo Picasso, *Study*, 1892–1893. Conté crayon. 20.4 × 14.4″. Barcelona, Museo Picasso (courtesy of SPADEM). Picasso's astonishingly early grasp of drawing principles is apparent in this study, created when he was approximately eleven years old.

Giacometti, for example, used an angular method to build up an almost abstract linear framework of the figure (Figure 3-33). His linear analysis of the interior as well as the exterior aspect of form led him to explore the "transparency" of line constructs, endowing his drawings with the monumental quality seen more commonly in architecture.

A self-portrait drawing by the young Josef Albers, a German-American artist, demonstrates how angular measurements can be applied in a pencil drawing of the head (Figure 3-34). The uncompromising search for form seen in the drawing yields a paradoxical effect, for the painstaking visual measurements yield an image that is highly personal. Better known today for his abstract painting, in 1917—when he produced this self-portrait—Albers was deeply immersed in his study of the art of Cézanne. It was then that, in his words, "Cézanne got into my bones." Inspired as he was by the French artist, the result was a remarkable series of portrait drawings that would not be confused with the drawings of Cézanne. Though angular measurement can be used to further a style, it is of a more fundamental nature than a style. Angular measurement is a method.

Angles and Perception

Students drawing with the angular method for the first time often experience a dramatic enhancement of the visual correspondence between the drawing and the model. The method was the technical advantage of "objectifying" the image of the model, that is, making the image itself an object whose formal qualities can be observed and analyzed with a degree of detachment. This can be refreshing. It enables the artist to set aside preconceived notions of the figure and concentrate on a single aspect of observed form. Surprisingly the effectiveness of the angular method may have its basis in the perceptual system of the brain. Scientists now believe the brain has a special capacity for detecting and distinguishing the visual angles seen in contours.[18] In addition, it now appears the awareness of one's own body gestures is also due in

Figure 3-33. Alberto Giacometti (1901–1966), *Trois Femmes Nues*, 1923–1924. Drawing. 44.5 × 28 cm. Kunsthaus Zürich. The three versions of the same figure can be seen as a progression from the more generalized forms of the figure on the right to the richly complex construction in the two other figures. The artist's drawing method, though highly personal, includes careful angular measurement in line.

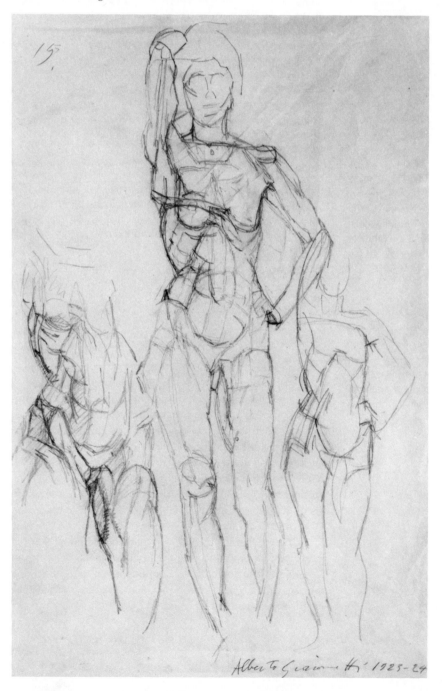

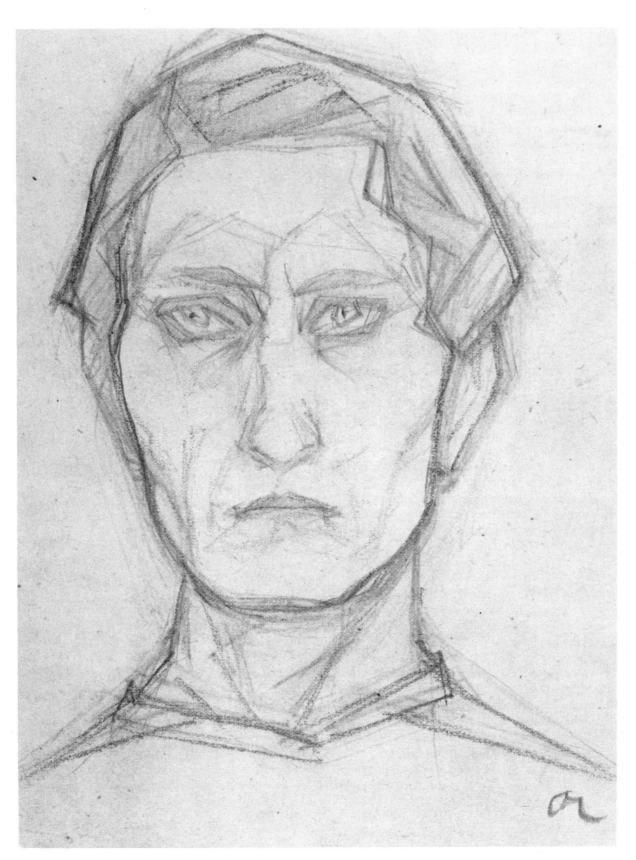

Figure 3-34. Josef Albers (1888–1976), *Self-Portrait IV*, c. 1917. Soft pencil on gray woven paper. 13 × 10″. Orange, Connecticut, Josef Albers Foundation (photo by Joseph Szaszfai).

part to a sense of the angles formed by the skeletal bones at the joints.[19] The visual perception of your own body gestures as well as those observed in other people thus appear to involve sensory information about angles.

A computer model of visual perception developed by the scientist David Marr has produced drawing constructs remarkably like those of the angular method of drawing. In attempting to represent the low-level feature description of a solid object, the computer drew line segments of a specific angular orientation. Some of the segments link together, implying continuous contours and other features.[20] The result is a drawing construction not unlike that seen in Figure 3-34. This is a tantalizing similarity, for the computer drawing represents an unconscious level of visual perception.

VARIATIONS AND COMBINATIONS OF LINE

Concentrating on one concept at a time, as we suggest in the studies outlined in this chapter, offers advantages to the beginner as well as to the more advanced student of drawing. Before a drawing concept can become a useful tool for the artist, however, you must repeat each study many times. Practice is a key ingredient in the study of drawing. Repetition of the exercises, however, need not follow the order of presentation shown in this book. Feel free to invent variations or combinations of the different exercises. You may wish, for example, to execute a more controlled contour drawing than is possible by concentrating exclusively on the model (as recommended in Study 1). This can be accomplished by glancing back at your drawing page while you work in order to check the relative location of the crayon. Even though paying greater attention to the placement of the crayon on the paper may run the risk of a less spontaneous drawing, you are likely to gain in control of formal rendering (Figure 3-35). Seeing and analyzing form remains the primary objective.

There are also ways of combining the concept of silhouette (Chapter 2) with the rapid contour method. The drawings of Rodin illustrate a way of combining contour line drawn in pencil with silhouette painted in watercolor wash (Figure 3-36). It is noteworthy that Rodin assigned a slightly different role to each component. The silhouette therefore does not merely reinforce the contour drawing, as it would if it neatly filled in the space between the lines. Instead it flows freely in and around the contours, representing a fresh reevaluation of the general form. The resulting interaction of the two simple drawing modes creates a surprisingly rich visual effect, strongly suggestive of motion.

Technically Rodin's drawings are disarmingly simple. He drew rapidly in pencil on small sheets of paper, generally about 10 by 12 inches, looking all the while at the model. Later he added a watercolor wash. The wash silhouette, though it follows the general shape defined by the pencil

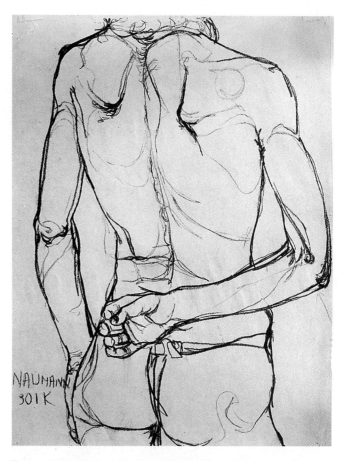

Figure 3-35. Student drawing. Contour line. Compressed charcoal pencil on newsprint paper. 36 × 24″. Unlike the technique of Study 4, here the student looked at both the model and the paper, which resulted in a more controlled drawing.

contours, is often a reevaluation of the form, adding a unifying sense of the body as a whole and at the same time creating a visual counterpoint between the two media. For the wash Rodin often used a diluted earth color. The resulting effect is not unlike that seen in reflected lights on bronze (Figure 3-37).

Rodin himself supplies a rare insight into his method of drawing:

> . . . I try to see the figure as a mass, as volume. It is this voluminousness that I try to understand. This is why . . . I sometimes wash a tint over my drawings. This completes the impression of massiveness, and helps me to ascertain how far I have succeeded in grasping the movement as a mass. . . . My object is to test to what extent my hands already feel what my eyes see.[21]

Rodin's drawings have their three-dimensional counterparts in his clay "sketches," which were created for much the same purpose as the drawings: namely, as preparations for

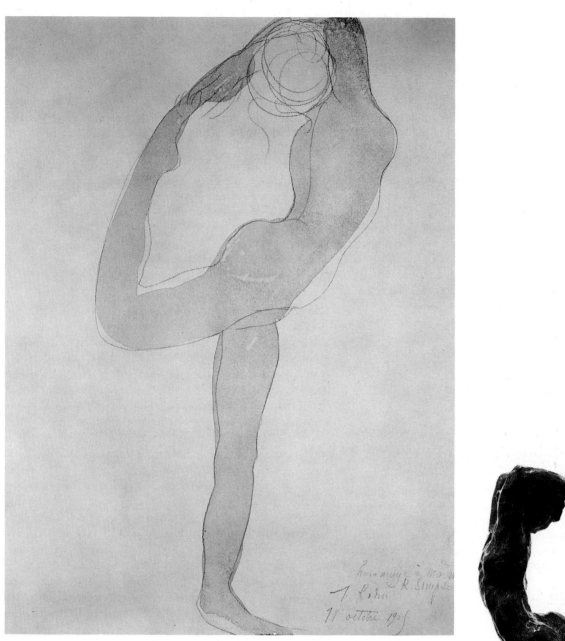

Figure 3-36. Auguste Rodin (1840–1917), *Dancing Figure*, pre-1908. Graphite pencil and water-color wash. 12³⁄₁₆ × 9³⁄₄″. Washington, D.C., National Gallery of Art.

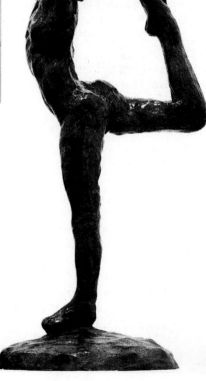

Figure 3-37. Auguste Rodin, *Dance Movement A*, 1911. Bronze. 12¹⁄₄″ high. Philadelphia, Rodin Museum.

larger works of sculpture. It is likely that his predilection for sculptural form influenced his drawing procedure: Only *after* making the contour drawing from life did he add the silhouette wash.

In studio practice it can be advantageous to begin with the silhouette wash, thereby establishing the large form of the figure directly from life. The wash, when it has dried, can then function as an armature around which to construct the figure in contour line. While the first wash is drying there is time to lay in additional silhouettes on other sheets, before returning to the first with pencil.

As Rodin's drawings demonstrate, the combined outline and contour methods allow the artist to be more selective in describing form. In places where the shape is sufficiently interesting, for example, you can use the more economical outline method. The interplay of the two methods can extend the expressive range of a line drawing. Intuition is the best guide in deciding which passages of the figure to draw in contour and which in outline. This simple variation of line can create a surprisingly personal drawing idiom.

Wire as Line

The analogy of line drawing with sculpture implied in Rodin's contour studies is carried one step further in the wire figures of Alexander Calder (Figure 3-38). Here the line is

Figure 3-38. Alexander Calder (1898–1976), *Two Acrobats,* 1928. Brass wire. 34″ high. Honolulu Academy of Arts. Gift of Mrs. Theodore A. Cooke, Mrs. Philip E. Spalding, and Mrs. Walter F. Dillingham, 1937. (HAA 4595). Line is not the exclusive property of the flat surface. Whether it is viewed as a sculpture or as a three-dimensional line drawing. Calder's work suggests a creative and amusing use of an unconventional medium.

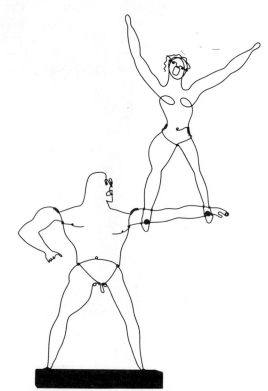

actually three dimensional. Such an unconventional use of line calls for unconventional drawing tools. If you wish to experiment with this medium, you may find pipe cleaner wire suitable for figures. It is easily bent and manipulated without tools. Contour drawings from the model will assist you in shaping the contours in wire. The line produced in wire is not likely to be as spontaneous as that resulting from a crayon on paper. As a medium it requires considerable manipulation. Nevertheless it offers a fascinating means of exploring the role of line in space and a unique approach to the structure of the skeleton, as we discuss in Chapter 5.

The Classic Drawing Method: Contour and Oval Construct

Combining outline and contour in a line drawing is not difficult, and after a few experiments with it, you may be ready to combine contour line with yet another factor: the oval constructs described in Study 6. In that study, you will recall, form was drawn in terms of body shapes that were interpreted as ovoid units. Instead of actually drawing the complete oval constructs of the figure, as you did in Study 6, try drawing only those portions that are part of a contour of the form you wish to represent (Figure 3-39). As you draw, it is helpful to visualize the complete construct, even though your drawing will show only portions of that construct. This technique is simply a more economical version of the procedure followed in Study 6; much that was drawn in that study can be left out. Nevertheless, a certain amount of practice is usually necessary in order to bring the oval and contour constructs together in a free, spontaneous drawing. Unlike the freewheeling scribbling seen in the drawings of Study 6, here few of the ovoid constructs are complete. Instead they are drawn as "open" forms so as to suggest overlapping in space. Concentration is necessary in order to see body structure in terms of ovoid units and at the same time to draw only

Figure 3-39. Oval drawing constructs. (a) Intersection of two oval constructs. (b) Two oval constructs, similar to (a) but with most of the intersecting portions eliminated. The spatial order of the two constructs is suggested by overlapping on the left side; the right side shows only outline.

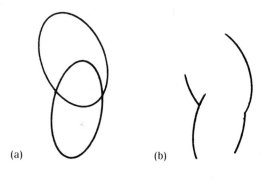

(a)   (b)

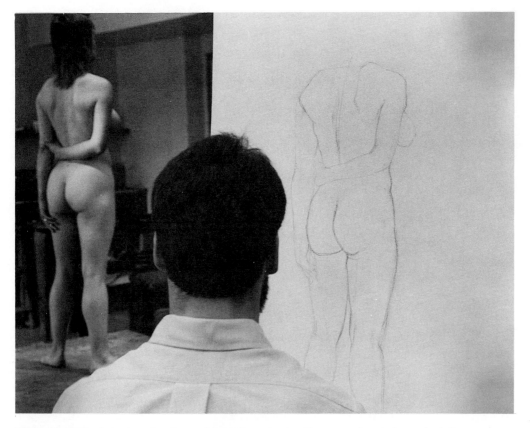

Figure 3-40. Contours based on incomplete oval constructs offer a way of analyzing and relating many formal units of the body.

enough of them to communicate the forms they encompass. Economy of means is of the essence, for it is the capacity to suggest rather than to completely describe form that gives this method its characteristic elegance of line (Figure 3-40).

Antecedents in Art History

The contour drawing method just described is similar to the method employed by Greek artists in the fifth to fourth century B.C., the classical period (Figures 3-41, 3-42, and 3-43), and for this reason we refer to it as *classic*. The conventions of classic drawing, however, were not limited to the art of ancient Greece: They are part of the visual arts of cultures as diverse as those of Japan, Mexico, Egypt, and India (Figure 3-44). Western ideas of classic methods, however, are derived largely from the art of ancient Greece.

The contour-line method of classical art was revived in Renaissance Italy when artists began to reject the relatively flat, schematic constructs of medieval art (Figure 1-3) in favor of the rounded constructs of ancient art.[22] An especially clear instance of the classic contour method is seen in Antonio Pollaiuolo's fresco, *Dancing Nudes* (Figure 3-45). Not only are

the rounded constructs and the sharp separation of figure and ground classical in quality, but the gestures of the figures themselves—including an example of classical *contrapposto*—recall those of Greek vase painting. Despite their obvious derivation the frescoes are unmistakably Renaissance in feeling, partly because of the description of anatomical structure and detail, which goes beyond the more general rhythmic forms of classical art, resulting in a slight awkwardness of the figures.

The vitality of the classic drawing method has been demonstrated in periodic revivals not only in Renaissance Italy but also in nineteenth-century France. Leading artists such as Ingres found inspiration in the linear mode of ancient art (Figures 3-79 and 3-80). In the twentieth century, which has been largely dominated by abstract art, classic methods have enjoyed a more limited revival, yet paradoxically the modern movement has sometimes produced art that is closer in spirit and technique to ancient Greece than was realized in the preceding century when classical art was more in vogue. Picasso, for example, returning to the severe outline-contour method seen in ancient mirror drawings (Figure 3-43) and vases, created line drawings that closely parallel classical art (Figure 3-53).[23]

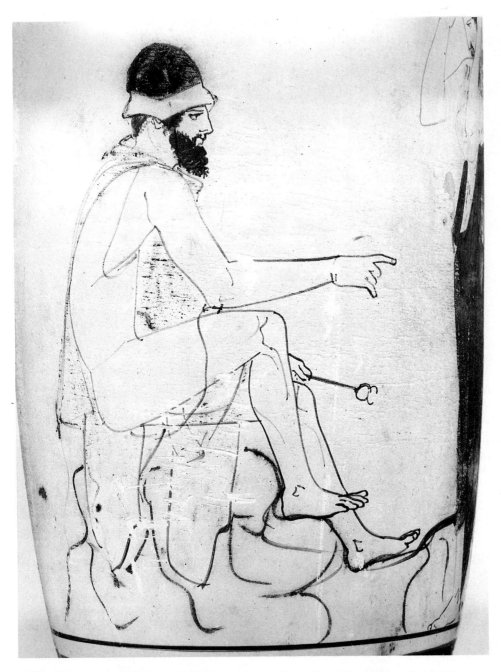

Figure 3-41. Greek, Phiale painter, *Hermes Waiting for a Woman* [partially visible on the right] *Departing for the Underworld*, c. 440–430 B.C. White-ground lekythos (pottery oil flask). Munich, Glyptothek.

CLASSICAL PROPORTIONS

The figure, when drawn with the classic contour method, is conceived and constructed in terms of ovoid forms, as we noted in Study 6. Drawing the figure in this way thus becomes a question of how big or how small to draw the ovoid forms, in other words, a question of proportions. In the broadest sense proportion in drawing simply refers to the relative size (*ratio*) of one part to another. In classical antiquity artists made use of a system of *ideal proportions* expressed in sets of ratios called a *canon*. Though based on the natural forms of the human body, ratios of ideal proportions presuppose the existence of "ideal" human form. This concept is not inconsistent with Greek idealism, a school of philosophy that interpreted material things as imperfect reflections of transcendent "perfect" ideas.

The canons themselves remain a subject of speculation, for none has been preserved in a complete written form. Ac-

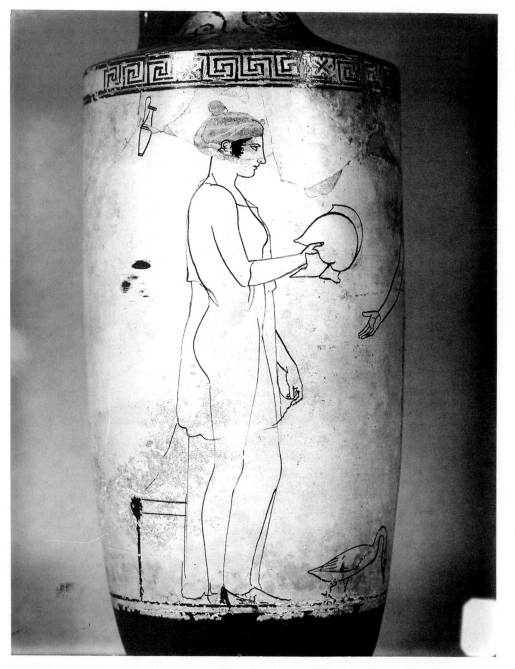

Figure 3-42. Achilles painter (active c. 460–430 B.C.), *A Woman Holding a Warrior's Helmet*. Attic brush drawing on a pottery oil flask (lekythos). London, British Museum.

cording to the Roman architect Vitruvius, the Greeks preferred the word *analogia* (analogy) to describe the proportional relationships of ideal form.[24] Indeed visual analogy of one part of the body to another part—in a word, proportion—is central to the Greek idea of ideal form in the figure. As the Roman writer Galen put it,

> Ideal form consists . . . in the harmonious proportion of the parts, the proportion of one finger to the other, of all the fingers to the rest of the hand, of the rest of the hand to the wrist, of these to the forearm, of the forearm to the whole arm, *in fine* of all parts to all others as it is written in the canon of Polyclitus.[25]

Prior to the classical period, Greek sculpture evidences some of the formal conventions of Egyptian sculpture. It was not until the fifth century B.C. that Greek figural representations reflected a closer correspondence to human proportions

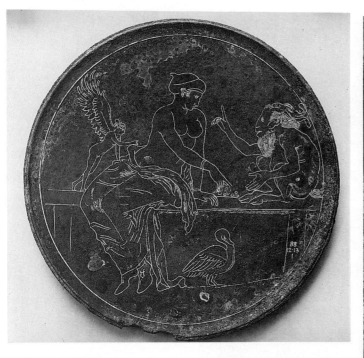

Figure 3-43. Anonymous Greek artist, *Aphrodite and Pan Playing at Dice,* fourth century B.C. Engraved underside of a mirror cover. London, British Museum.

Figure 3-44. Anonymous Indian artist, *Woman and Parrot,* Bengal, Kalighat school, c. 1875. Black line on paper. 45 × 29 cm. New Delhi, The National Museum.

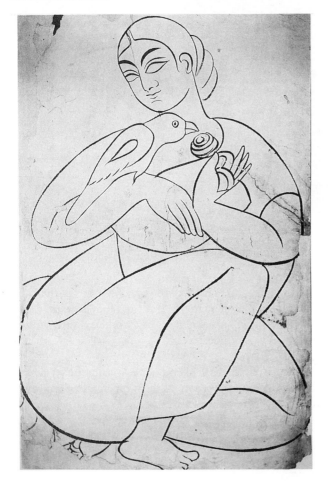

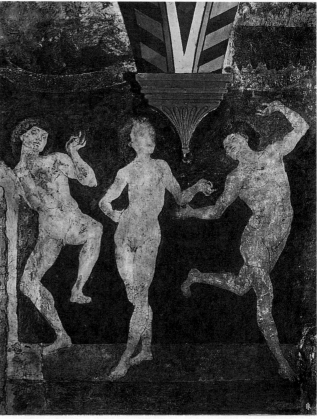

Figure 3-45. Antonio Pollaiuolo (1431–1498), *Dancing Nudes.* Fresco. Florence, Torre del Gallo (courtesy of Alinari).

and anatomy, a development which appears to coincide with the appearance of proportional canons, including the canon codified by Polyclitus. The origins and practical use of the canons are unclear. Were the canons the result of measured translations of the body forms of live models by artists such as Polyclitus (as in the case of the proportional drawings of Dürer and Leonardo centuries later)? Or were they a system of proportional norms of an ideal human figure, gradually modified and refined and passed on by generations of artists as artistic techniques evolved?[26]

Polyclitus himself is believed to have said, ". . . the beautiful comes about, little by little through many numbers."[27] The Greek idea of a canon based on numerical fractions was later adopted by Roman artists and architects, as recorded by Vitruvius. Writing in the first century B.C., he explained how proportional relationships of the ideal figure were incorporated in the design of buildings, such as temples. In addition to numerical fractions, he found "perfect" geometrical forms (i.e., the circle and the square) in the body.

Although the writings of Vitruvius were not unknown in the Middle Ages, medieval artists largely ignored the classical canons and resorted to schematic representations of the human figure (Figure 1-3). The geometrical system of proportions was revived in the fifteenth century when Italian artists began to rediscover the monuments and writings of the classical past. Some of the most important artists of the day, including Leonardo and Dürer, drew studies of the figure according to the instructions of Vitruvius (Figures 3-46 and 3-47), not only to learn how to draw the figure in classical proportions but also as a form of speculative research aimed, it seems, at establishing a correlation between visual art and philosophy.[28] In the eyes of the Renaissance artist, Vitruvius's writings conferred a new intellectual status on Renaissance art by linking the perfect forms of geometry with the forms of the body. Such status was one way of justifying the Renaissance artist's claim to superiority over the "craftsmen" of the Middle Ages.

Despite many careful proportional studies by Renaissance artists, no conclusive mathematical relationships among "harmonious" forms of the body were established, as with musical harmony.[29] Yet studies of proportions were an influential factor that contributed to the harmonious appearance of the figures and compositions of many works by Renaissance artists. In some instances Renaissance proportional studies are autonomous works of art in themselves. Leonardo's proportional study based on Vitruvius (Figure 3-47), for example, presents an unsurpassed image of man as the measure of all things, a creative expression of the rational humanism of the Renaissance. His abiding interest in proportions is also found in his writings, which give practical advice on animal as well

Figure 3-46. Albrecht Dürer, *Nude Woman with Staff, Constructed*, c. 1500. Pen and ink with ruler. 290 × 194 mm (11⅜ × 7⅝″). Dresden, Sächsische Landesbibliothek. Based on a proportional canon of the Roman author Vitruvius, the figure shows cross axes that relate the forms of the shoulders with those of the lower abdomen. These axes are helpful in constructing a figure from life.

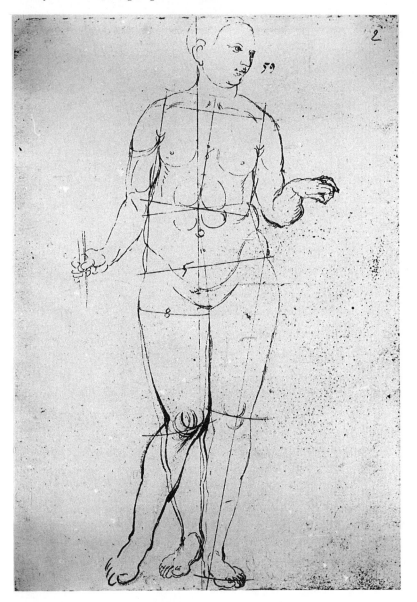

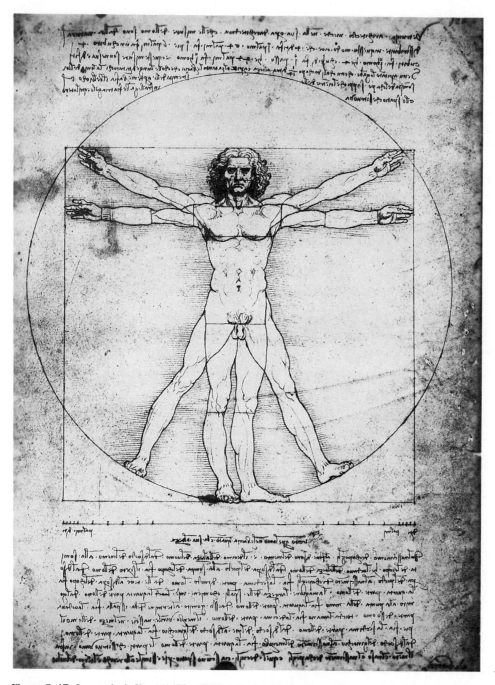

Figure 3-47. Leonardo da Vinci (1452–1519), *A Study of Proportions after Vitruvius*, 1485–90. Pen and ink. 34.3 × 24.5 cm. Venice, Accademia. In this drawing Leonardo interpreted a statement on proportions by Vitruvius: ". . . the navel is naturally the exact centre of the body. For if a man lies on his back with hands and feet outspread, and the centre of a circle is placed on his navel, his figure and toes will be touched by the circumference. Also a square will be found described within the figure, in the same way as a round figure is produced." (*On Architecture*, Book III, C. 1)

as human proportions: "All parts of any animal exist in relationship to the whole; that is, those short and stocky ought to have each part short and stocky, and those long and thin should have parts that are long and thin, and the medium-sized should also have medium-sized parts."[30] Essentially a rephrasing of Polyclitus, Leonardo's statement reveals that the enduring idea from classical art is the concept of proportion

as formal relationships of parts to the whole, rather than a set of numerical ratios.

Following the Renaissance period artists continued to be haunted by the concept of ideal human proportions and the symmetry that such proportions imply. Bernini, the seventeenth-century sculptor and architect, drew an allegorical male figure embracing Saint Peter's Square in order to

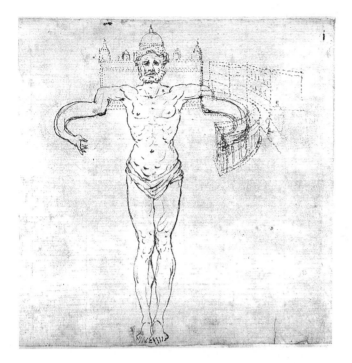

Figure 3-48. Gian Lorenzo Bernini (1598–1680), *Allegorical Drawing of the Plan of Saint Peter's Basilica and Square*, c. 1656. Rome, Library of the Vatican.

explain his design for the loggia of the Vatican, even though it was necessary to bend the figure's arms out of shape to fit the design (Figure 3-48).

It is natural that human proportions should be relevant to the architectural structures designed for human habitation, and it is for this reason that the concept of ideal proportions has survived to a greater extent in the field of architecture than in the pictorial arts. The architectural studies of the twentieth-century architect Le Corbusier provide an outstanding example. In a manner not unlike that of Vitruvius, Le Corbusier derived geometric shapes and ratios from a schematic drawing of the figure—the Modulor—representing proportional norms (Figure 3-49). Instead of deriving the Vitruvian circle and square from the figure, however, Le Corbusier derived the *golden section,*[31] a rectangular proportion of ancient Greek origin.

The study of ideal proportion was inherent in the curriculum of most European art academies. In the French Academy, for example, a drawing instructor would not hesitate to "correct" a student by imposing classical proportions on a figure that by academic standards was drawn too naturalistically. Although such academic instruction produced draftsmen of great expressive power in the seventeenth and eighteenth centuries, by the late nineteenth century classical proportion was no longer a vital art concept. It had come to be the hallmark of many lifeless paintings and sculptures produced by members of the academic art establishment, a

circumstance to which is owed the modern pejorative term *academic.*

Yet ancient sculpture, usually in the form of plaster casts, continued to be a standard subject for the study of drawing in most art schools even into the early twentieth century. By drawing from classical sculpture (as did the young Picasso) it was believed possible to gain a sense of ideal human proportions embodied in classical art (Figure 4-60). Although there is today a revival of interest in drawing from casts of ancient sculpture, it is done less out of concern for ideal proportions than for the practical advantage of a truly stationary model without color changes to complicate the study of form.

The study of human proportions is a vital discipline in medical morphology, however, where it is used as a diagnostic tool (Figure 3-50). Although the medical study of human proportions is not concerned with idealized form, it does represent a continuation of the investigation of actual body forms begun by Renaissance artists as the basis for theories of ideal form.[32]

The concept of ideal human proportions has not recently aroused interest as a vehicle of expression in the visual arts. Yet two ideal-figure representations were recently sent into outer space by the National Aeronautics and Space Administration as a means of communicating with intelligent beings of other worlds (Figure 3-51). The figures are rendered in a mediocre linear style vaguely resembling that of classical art.

Figure 3-49. Le Corbusier (1887–1965), *Proportional System Based on a Schematic Figure, Le Modulor,* 1949. Illustration from the book *Le Modulor* by Le Corbusier.

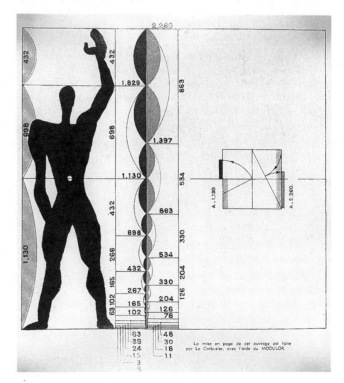

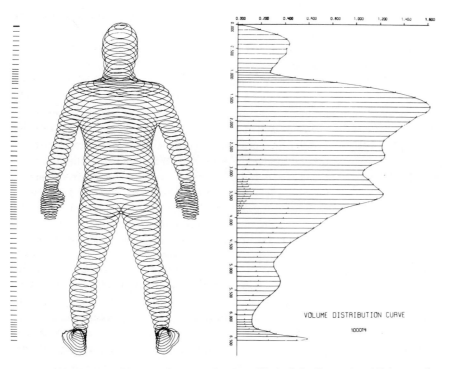

Figure 3-50. Dr. R. E. Herron, *Computer Drawing (Plot) of the Proportional Volumes of a Human Subject* (courtesy of Biostereometrics Laboratory, Baylor College of Medicine, Houston). The cross-sectional figure (above left) is translated into a bar graph that illustrates relative and absolute volumes of the body.

Figure 3-51. National Aeronautics and Space Administration, *Pioneer F Plaque*, 1972. Etched gold-anodized aluminum plate. 152 × 229 mm (photo courtesy of NASA). "'The Pioneer F spacecraft, destined to be the first man-made object to escape from the solar system into interstellar space," NASA states, "carries this pictorial plaque. It is designed to show scientifically educated inhabitants of some other star system—who might intercept it millions of years from now—when Pioneer was launched, from where, and by what kind of beings."

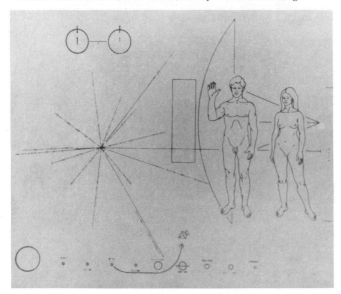

Perhaps the intelligent beings in outer space will recognize this work for what it is—the product of a scientific rather than an artistic effort.

PROPORTIONAL CANONS AND STUDIO PRACTICE

One of the most enduring ideas to come to us from the artists of ancient Greece is not a canon of proportion, but the underlying idea that the human form is best understood in terms of relationships of parts to the whole. That remains a valuable idea in drawing the figure today. What, then, is the most effective way to create figure drawings that embody this concept? In studio practice the analogous relationships of parts to the whole develop largely as a side effect of the artist's drawing method and purpose rather than from a conscious effort to use proportional rules and measures. A systematic drawing method is therefore the most reliable way of creating convincing proportions in a figure. For this reason the actual method of constructing drawn forms and the concept implicit in the method are stressed in this book: Visual measurement of angles, rather than proportional norms, is presented as a specific method of achieving correspondence with objective reality.

A number of popular texts optimistically present proportional guides as the answer to "how-to-do-it." Unfortunately the application of such memorized rules can impede and restrict rather than help you in drawing from life because of the preconceptions they impose between you and objective observation. Although the proportions given in such books are usually derived from an ideal figure, their origin is often left unexplained, implying that the rules are in some way absolute. This has the effect not only of masking the unintended cultural bias present in the rules but also of ignoring the existence of other canons of proportion, which though not classical, are nevertheless equally valid, such as those admired and studied by Modigliani in African art (Figures 3-81 and 3-82).

Although strict rules of proportion have little application in life drawing today, some basic proportional guides can be useful as a means of checking the figure you have drawn. If you tend to draw the top of the figure too large in proportion to the lower portion or vice versa, for example, it can be helpful to know that the midpoint of the body generally lies just above the genitals (the top of the genital triangle), as seen in Leonardo's *Vitruvian Man* (Figure 3-47) and in Raymond Duchamp-Villon's *Study of Proportions* (Figure 3-52). By

Figure 3-52. Raymond Duchamp-Villon (1876–1918), *Homme Nu— Debout, Etude de Proportions*, c. 1910. Crayon. 480 × 315 mm. Paris, Musée National d'Art Moderne (photo courtesy of Musées Nationaux, Paris).

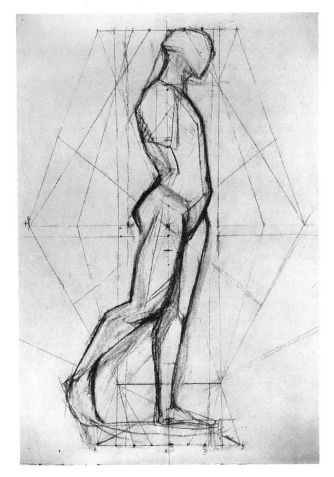

marking light lines at this point and under the heel of the figure you can estimate the proper measure from the top of the genital triangle to the top of the head in the standing figure, which should be the same as the lower interval. Note, however, that this measurement is valid only for the standing figure—and the average (ideal) standing figure at that. In drawing from life the rule is useful primarily as a way of checking or reevaluating what you have done.

A second type of guide, more anatomical than proportional, is seen in a Vitruvian study by Dürer (Figure 3-46). In this study the cross axes of the body are shown as straight lines that traverse the figure at the hip (pelvic) level and at the shoulder level. Their respective tilt reflects a natural shift of forms that is due to the underlying skeletal structure. Known as the shoulder and pelvic axes, these lines can be very helpful in constructing convincing and consistent connections (articulations) of the arm with the shoulder and the leg with the abdomen, problems that often baffle the beginning draftsman. These and other basic proportional features of the body are best appreciated by analyzing your own drawings of the figure.

STUDY 10:   Study of Basic Proportions

materials: ❑ 36 × 24″ newsprint drawing pad
❑ easel or straight-back chair
❑ Masonite or plywood board and clamps
❑ drawing crayon and graphite pencil
❑ straight edge or yardstick
❑ tape measure

alternative ❑ 14 × 11″ bound sketchbook of smooth bond
materials: paper
❑ HB pencil and kneaded eraser
❑ tracing paper and tape for an overlay
❑ straight edge

reference: ❑ model or cast of figure sculpture
time: ❑ 30 minutes

If you wish to rediscover for yourself the basic proportions discussed here, the angular measurement method offers a practical approach, for it focuses on the visual relationships of form that determine proportions in a drawing. The *Study of Proportions* by Duchamp-Villon (Figure 3-52) is an example of a modern proportional study constructed in this way. As with all studies it helps to plan the purpose of your proportional study. You might prefer to direct your study toward a speculative investigation of the figure and perfect geometrical forms in the Renaissance tradition. From a practical point of view, however, you may find it more beneficial to your drawing skills to focus on proportions that will assist you in drawing the figure.

Since proportions are best seen in the standing figure, the following objectives can be studied when you have completed a drawing of the model in simple standing pose. You may already have in mind the type of proportions to investigate. What follows is a list that may suggest additional objectives:

1. Framing the figure. Using a straight edge and pencil, determine and draw a rectangle that encompasses the height and the widest horizontal dimension of the standing figure. If the model is seen directly from the front or back, estimate and draw a vertical line that divides the rectangle down the middle. Does the line divide the figure into two equal halves? Holding the tape measure beside the model, record the height and the breadth.

2. The middle of the figure. Divide the rectangle of the figure in half to locate the horizontal middle of the figure, again making use of the pencil and straight edge. Where on the drawn figure does the midline fall? Where does it fall with respect to the life model? This can be checked with the tape measure by determining half of the model's height.

3. Quarter dimensions. Subdivide the rectangle of the figure into quarters. With the figure drawn and quartered, so to speak, you will be able to discover whether the subdivisions correspond with visible features, such as joints of the knees or horizontal axes of the shoulders.

4. Segmentation of the figure. What are the simplest irreducible units of form in the figure as determined by angular measurement? If you were designing a suit of armor, how would you divide the form of the body with the fewest parts of armor?

5. Tapering of body forms. Determine with pencil and straight edge the general degree of tapering in the thigh and the leg. Is there a more general tapering that would include both the thigh and the leg?

6. Checking the head's height. After drafting a line connecting the two shoulders, use that as a base for a triangle whose apex touches the top of the head. Do the resulting angles correspond with what is seen in the model?

These are proportion studies that can be executed either with crayon and the format of the newsprint pad or with pencil and the smaller format sketchbook. The sketchbook offers the advantage of drawing the proportional lines on an overlay sheet of tracing paper, thereby leaving the original pencil drawing intact.

PROPORTION AND SYMMETRY

Today the artist exercises practically unlimited freedom in drawing proportions of the human form, which has its disadvantages as well as advantages. In ancient times the same proportional canons were accepted within the classical world, since artists shared a common standard and training.[33] Modifications were slight and came gradually. Today's more pluralistic society lacks the cultural consensus necessary to codify rules of this kind, which leaves the artist with what can be an exciting but sometimes bewildering variety of choices. The choices, however, are narrowed greatly by the artist's purpose. In drawing from life your purpose may be to create a two-dimensional analogy of the proportions perceived in the live model rather than an analogy with a preconceived canon of classical proportion. Such a decision on your part need not be final, of course, but it will strongly influence the character of your drawing. By drawing from classical sculpture, as did the young Picasso, it is possible to gain a sense of the formal relationships that presumably made up ideal proportions.

The expressive qualities of classical canons of proportion are immediately apparent when you consider two drawings that are technically similar but differ greatly in figure proportions. Such a contrast is apparent in Picasso's ink drawing *Little Girl Playing Ball* (Figure 3-53) and the lithograph *Bourgeois Society* by the modern German artist George Grosz (Figure 3-54). In the ink drawing Picasso maintains the consistent and harmonious relationship of "all parts to the others" that is traditionally associated with classical proportions. In the lithograph by Grosz, however, the relative size of figural components (i.e., head, arm, and hand) is altered with the unbridled freedom of a child. The oval construct of the head, for example, is proportionally a different size in almost every figure. Such proportional variation enables the artist to include an astonishing amount of narrative detail, much of which is anything but childish. The deliberate violation of ideal proportions is emphasized all the more by Grosz's use of the classic outline-contour method, adding to the sense of outrage and social criticism that the drawing communicates. The word *deliberate* bears repeating in connection with this drawing, as Grosz was an accomplished draftsman, well known for his masterly studies from the live model (Figure 6-21).

What accounts for the immediacy with which we comprehend the figures of the Grosz drawing despite their lack of correspondence with objective or ideal proportions? And why do so many works of so-called primitive art exhibit figures with a similar set of proportions? At present there is no satisfactory answer to such questions, but the answer must include cultural, psychological, and physiological factors.

Reactions to such figures may spring from an intuitive inner sense of individual body form. If you close your eyes for a few moments and try to imagine the form of your body, you may find it difficult to retain an objective sense of your body proportions. Your head and particularly your face may seem very large in relation to the rest of your body. Yet you will probably retain a sense of equal proportion between the right and left sides of your body—in other words, a sense of your body's *symmetry*. For example, no matter how small your arms may seem, your right and left arms will seem to be the same size. The Grosz drawing shows a similar phenomenon:

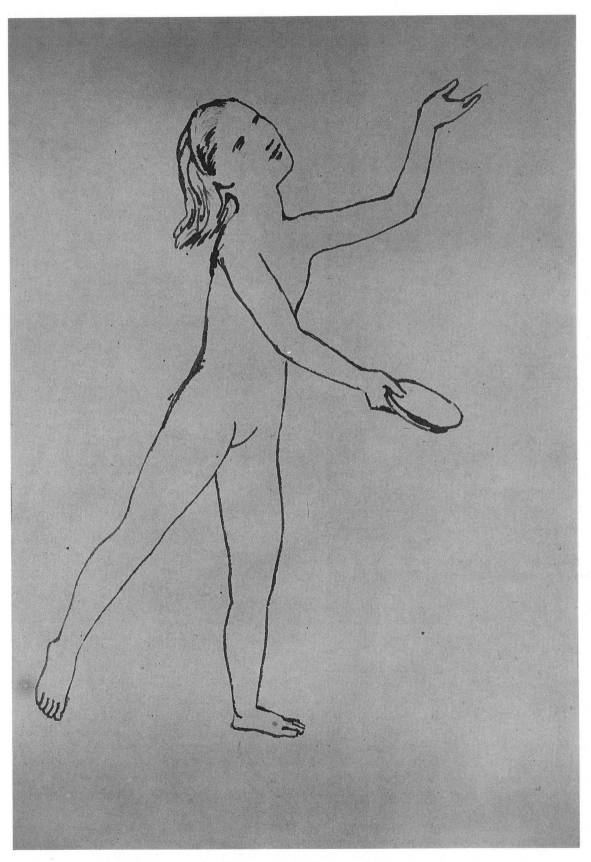

Figure 3-53. Pablo Picasso, *Little Girl Playing Ball*, 1902. India ink. 28.8 × 19 cm. Baltimore Museum of Art. Cone Collection.

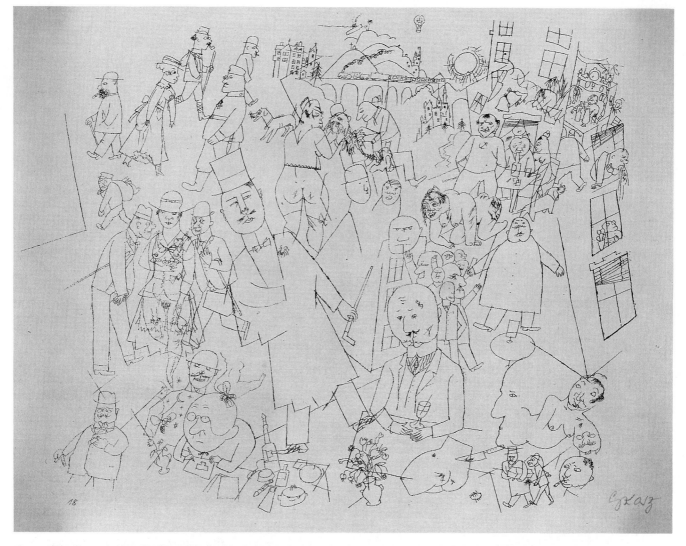

Figure 3-54. George Grosz (1853–1959), *World of the Bourgeoisie*, plate 18 from *Ecce Homo*, 1918. Lithograph, printed in black. 8¼ × 10⅜″. The Museum of Modern Art, New York. Abby Aldrich Rockefeller Fund.

The head is drawn disproportionately large in some of the figures, but the symmetry of the forms is maintained.

Symmetry, though traditionally associated with ideal proportions and classical art (Figure 3-55), can be developed as an independent concept, as in primitive or anticlassical figure representation. This suggests that symmetry is a more fundamental feature in art than ideal proportion. Psychologists have discovered a general human tendency to perceive any shape with the maximum degree of simplicity, regularity, and symmetry.[34] This may account in part for the frequently strong and disturbing emotional impact of seeing a markedly asymmetrical representation of the human face, a form whose features are basically symmetrical (Figure 3-56).

Symmetry in art parallels the bilateral symmetry of the body, which is seen not only in its exterior forms but also in its structural makeup, notably in the skeleton, the muscles, and the nervous system.[35] The eyes themselves partake of the body's bilateral structure. It seems reasonable that our sense of symmetrical structure in visual form has its basis in the symmetrical structure of the body. Attempts to represent proportionate areas of the brain as devoted to parts of the body have resulted in figures that appear to correspond more with primitive proportions than with those of classical art (Figure 3-57). Such figures suggest a possible physiological parallel to the proportions intuitively created by primitive artists. Conversely, a sense of ideal proportions as an artistic phenomenon may be as much a product of observation and study as of intuition or instinct.

Motion and Changing Points of View

The studies by Leonardo and Dürer explore human proportions with the figure assuming multiple gestures, as if seen in motion (Figures 3-46 and 3-47). Studies focused on the figure in motion can be a key to a better understanding of the human

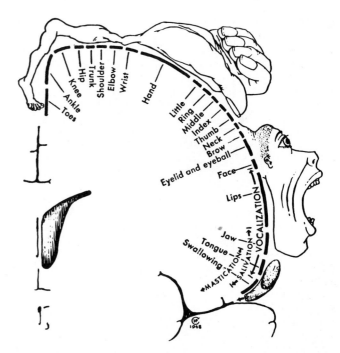

Figure 3-57. *Homunculus* (Wilder Penfield and H. Rasmussen, *The Cerebral Cortex of Man* [New York: Macmillan, 1950], Figure 22). The homunculus, a disjointed human figure, illustrates how much of the human cortex (represented in cross section) is devoted to motor control of various regions of the body; compare Figure 1-2.

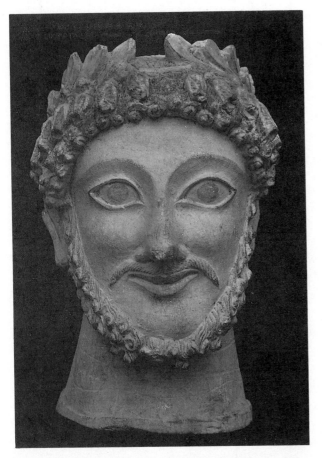

Figure 3-55. Unknown Greek Cypriote artist, *Stone Carving,* fifth century B.C. Rome, Museo Barracco. Formal elements of the head appear to have been conceived along a vertical line of bilateral symmetry, which is analogous to the natural symmetry of the human body.

Figure 3-56. Pablo Picasso, *Man's Head.* Study for *Guernica.* June 4, 1937. Pencil and wash on paper. 9¼ × 11½″ (© 1993 ARS, New York/SPADEM, Paris).

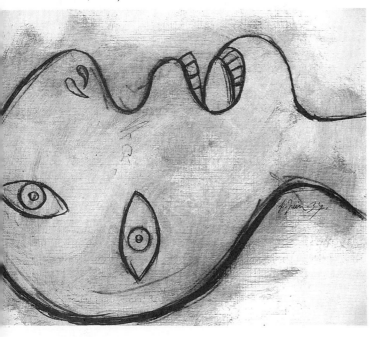

form. Even today, however, some artists tend to think of the figure as if seen from a specific point of view in time and space. This is a traditional concept of visual representation that is apparent in many works of art, particularly those based on linear perspective. It is an idea, moreover, that has been reinforced by much (though not all) still photography. Yet when you observe a person in life, it is usually not in the context of a stationary situation. Even when drawing from the life model it is likely that the model will move slightly during the drawing session. This involuntary shifting of position can be a source of frustration for the beginner. There is no real cause for alarm, however, because the changes in the model's pose can enhance the artist's understanding of the gesture and result in a more animated figure drawing (Figure 3-58). So closely is motion associated with visual perception that it warrants special attention in drawing.

STUDY 11:   The Rotating Pose

materials: ❑ 36 × 24″ newsprint drawing pad
              ❑ easel or straight-back chair
              ❑ clamps
              ❑ felt-tip pen or drawing crayon
reference: ❑ model
time: ❑ 10 minutes

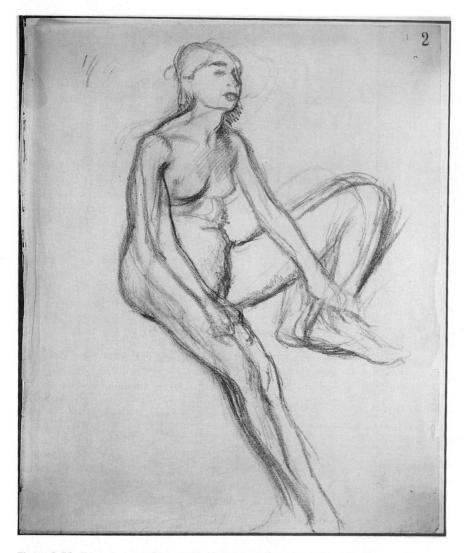

Figure 3-58. Edgar Degas (1834–1917), Plate 2 from sketchbook. Black chalk on tracing paper. 10⁹⁄₁₆ × 8⅝″ (26.8 × 21.9 cm). New York, Metropolitan Museum of Art. Fletcher Fund, 1973. When the model shifts position during a drawing session the displaced parts of the figure can be redrawn without erasing the earlier versions. Instead of harming the quality of the drawing, the changes add a sense of animation.

The "transparency" of contour line, coupled with its special capacity to suggest form beyond the visible edge, makes it especially effective in representing a figure in motion—the objective of this study. The suggestion of motion will be accomplished by means of multiple drawings of the figure drawn one on top of the other with each representing a different point of view. This can be easily arranged: The different points of view will be the result of the model turning while holding the same pose (see Figures 3-59 and 3-60).

The drawing procedure recommended for this study is essentially the same as the rapid contour method (Study 5). It is helpful to observe the model continuously, checking the location of your crayon only when necessary. The model should hold a simple standing pose that can be turned 45

degrees approximately every two minutes (Figure 3-59). This can be accomplished by either rotating the model stand or by requesting the model simply to redirect the same pose in quarter turns at two-minute intervals. After ten minutes the model will have returned to the original position. The drawing executed during this interval should consist of a partial or complete contour description of the five different views of the model. As a consequence, the drawing may exhibit a considerable amount of superimposed form as well as dislocated shapes (Figure 3-60). Seen as a whole the drawing may present a symmetrical appearance, making it possible to cross check the figures for the height of common features.

Rotation implies an *axis*, a stationary line around which a given form turns. The word *axis* commonly refers to the lon-

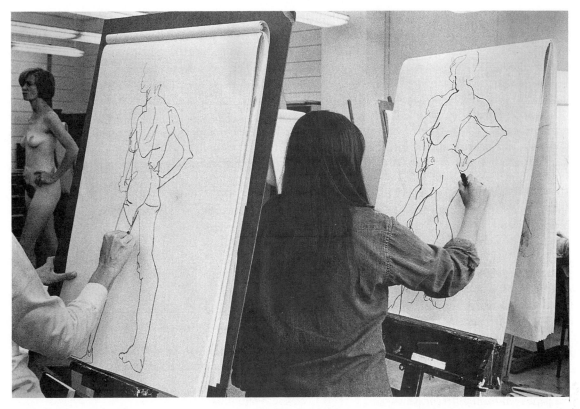

Figure 3-59. Drawing the rotating model, early stages. With the model facing a different direction every two minutes the artist's attention tends to focus more on the model than on the drawing page.

Figure 3-60. Drawing the rotating model, final stage. The model has turned 180 degrees after ten minutes. The resulting drawings reflect not only that movement but also a multiplicity of views of the figure.

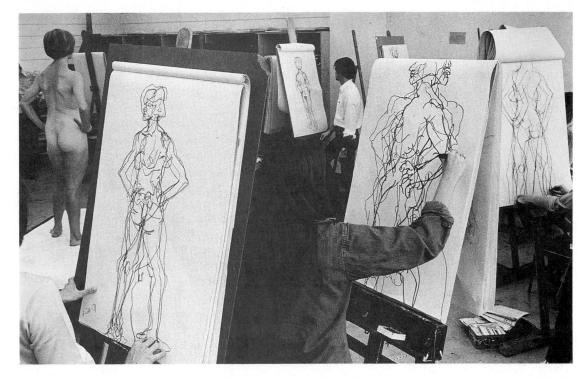

gitudinal centers of three-dimensional forms, including the forms of the body. Since the contour line often appears to turn around a drawn form, the idea of rotation around an axis is closely associated with contour drawing.

In a sense, drawing a rotating model is comparable with the way you see things in daily life. With each change of the model's position your vantage point as an observer changes, too. You may have noticed a similar thing happen when you look from the side window of a moving automobile, for, as you travel past them, people and objects appear to turn. The same apparent rotation occurs when you walk, though it is less obvious. Motion of this kind is an important aid in comprehending three-dimensional form. Scientific studies in perception have found that movement, "far from obscuring the shapes and spatial relations of things . . . generally clarifies them."[36]

Another visual phenomenon frequently occurs in drawings of the rotating model: *simultaneity*. Instead of suggesting motion the drawing may seem to present a figure composed of forms that, while belonging to the same body, are seen from different points of view *at the same time* (Figure 3-61). If you wish to aim for this effect, it is advisable to request the model to rotate slowly and continuously without sudden shifts of position. Then try erasing parts of some of the figures, leaving a figure composed of parts seen from different views.

Like a map of the globe, a simultaneous drawing manifests

Figure 3-61. Pablo Picasso, *Seated Nude,* 1956. Page from a sketchbook, pen and ink. 42 × 33 cm (courtesy of SPADEM).

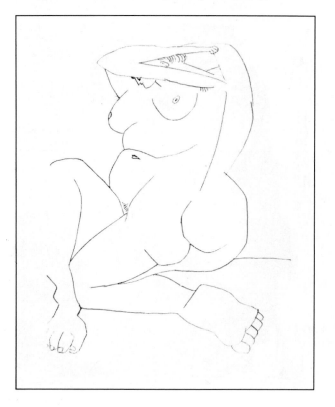

unavoidable dislocations and distortions of the rounded form. Shapes may seem to join or extend in ways that do not correspond to the conventional representation of the figure. Such a concept of form violates the canons of Western art as they were conceived from the fifteenth through the nineteenth centuries. Yet it is an idea that flourished in the art of India and of ancient Egypt, where different views of form appear even in the description of the face. Simultaneity was also important in the development of cubism in the early part of this century. A key member of this movement was Pablo Picasso, who created many drawings based on the principle of simultaneity (Figure 3-61). Cubism—and with it simultaneity—challenged the prevailing artistic conception of time and space in much the same way that topology in mathematics challenged certain ideas of Euclidean geometry. As a way of clarifying the form of the figure, however, a simpler study of movement, though less revolutionary, may be more rewarding.

STUDY 12: Simple Movement: The Double Pose

materials: ❏ 36 × 24″ newsprint drawing pad
❏ easel or straight-back chair
❏ clamps
❏ drawing crayon
reference: ❏ model
time: ❏ 20 minutes

A simple shift of weight from one foot to the other while standing in the same place can cause a remarkable change in body posture and position: It is a movement of *gesture*. The standing model can perform the movement with relative ease if you explain clearly that the feet are to remain in place. To move the feet would change the focus of the study and make it difficult to see the specific movement of the gesture. It is recommended that the model shift weight at regular one- to two-minute intervals for a period of twenty minutes (Figure 3-62). If an additional gesture, such as lifting the arm, is included in the movement, the one-minute interval is preferable for the model's sake. If you prefer, the arm gesture alone can be made the subject of a less strenuous double pose for the seated model (Figure 3-63).

The double pose has special advantages for the drawing student. Knowing the pose will change momentarily, you are encouraged to observe keenly and to draw rapidly, even in a relatively long session. Since the pose is continually alternating, it is best to work only on the figure drawing that corresponds to the pose then being held. In this way when the pose changes you may return to the first drawing fortified by what you learned from the other figure.

The aim of the study is to suggest movement by representing the figure at two stages of the gesture. The rapid-contour-line method is well suited to this aim. It is especially important even in the early stages of the drawing to indicate shifted so it falls mostly on one foot, the lower abdomen (pelvic region) tends to tilt upward on the weight-bearing side and downward on the other side, as in the classical contrapposto position (Figure 3-46). The weight-bearing leg is almost always straight (completely extended), while the other leg may be partially flexed as a consequence of the downward pelvic tilt. At the same time you may observe the reverse in the shoulder region. On the weight-bearing side of the body the shoulder may be lowered while the other shoulder is raised. If the model is relaxed, the body displacements are more pronounced. In nature a state of equilibrium exists when the center of gravity divides the masses of the body equally (Figure 3-64). When the body's weight rests mostly on one foot, the center of gravity can be traced from the middle of the weight-bearing foot to the base of the skull (or just behind the ears). If the weight falls equally on both feet, the center of gravity lies somewhere between them.

After you have completed Study 12, test the equilibrium of the figures by drawing a vertical line from the center of the weight-bearing foot. The edge of the drawing paper makes a convenient guide for such a line. If the drawn figure is balanced, the plumb line should pass through the middle of the head.[37] If it does not do so, the line itself will suggest a more convincing placement of the head, which can then be

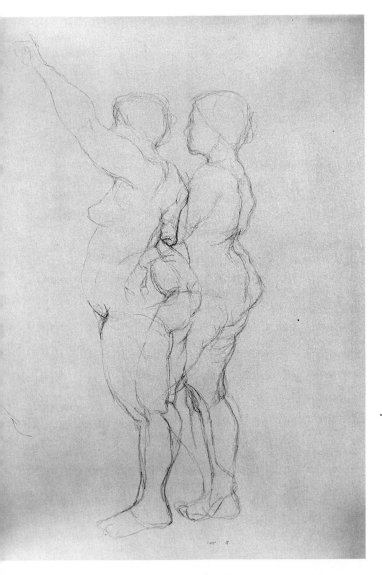

Figure 3-62. Student drawing. Double pose standing. Crayon on newsprint paper. 36 × 24″.

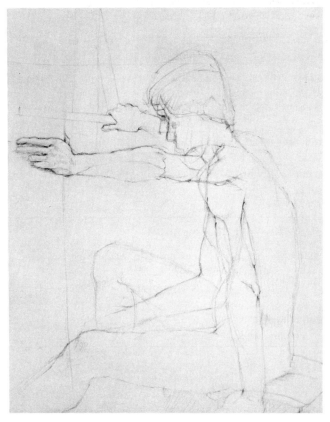

Figure 3-63. Student drawing. An optional version of the double pose. Crayon on newsprint paper. 36 × 24″.

the general forms of the lower portion of the figure. In all likelihood the model will move to the second position before your drawing of the first position is complete. This is no cause for concern, however, because the model will later resume the first position, and you can continue the original drawing. The motion is one of shifting weight, not of walking, so it is helpful to draw the figure's feet in the same location in both positions. For this reason you may wish to begin the second figure drawing by indicating the forms of the lower limbs, which will necessarily overlap those in the first drawing.

The difficulties that some beginners experience in drawing the standing figure may be avoided by a better understanding of the way equilibrium is achieved by the body. As you will notice in this study, a shift of weight in the standing figure is usually accompanied by a set of gestural changes if the body is to maintain equilibrium. For example, if the weight is

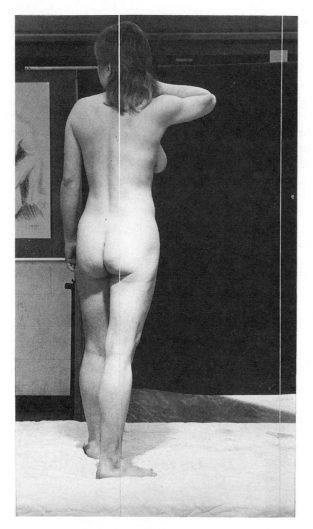

Figure 3-64. A simple plumb line made with string and suspended with drawing clamps can demonstrate the relationship of true vertical and equilibrium in the standing figure.

redrawn in accordance with the whole figure. The bodily shifts required for equilibrium are equally important in more complex actions, such as walking—the subject of the next study.

STUDY 13:   The Walking Model

materials: ❏ 36 × 24″ newsprint drawing pad
               ❏ easel or straight-back chair
               ❏ Masonite or plywood board and clamps
               ❏ drawing crayon
reference: ❏ model
time: ❏ 20 minutes

As a drawing subject the walking model is similar to the previous study, but carried several steps further, figuratively and literally. Instead of a simple shift in weight the model takes

two carefully planned steps on the model stand. The model should first walk across the stand a few times to decide on the most natural way in which the movement can be performed in the limited space. The steps can be marked with crayon so as to easily be repeatable.

The action of walking involves moving in equilibrium while shifting the body weight from one foot to the other. For the convenience of drawing, the action can be frozen midway when the weight is distributed evenly on both feet as well as when the weight rests on one foot alone. The two steps, broken down into component parts, amount to five different poses. No more than one minute should be allowed for each position, and each position should be repeated during the drawing session, allowing you to develop the figures continuously as a single drawing (Figure 3-65). As in the previous study, the feet act as pivots for the figure, so their positions can serve as reference points for the placement of the individual figures of the drawing. That being the case, the lower limbs can serve as a primary focus of your study (Figure 3-66). Observation of the model, as always, remains a vital factor in determining the quality of your drawing, making it imperative that you work only on the part of the drawing representing the position then held by the model.

Motion and Rhythm

The premise of Study 13 is *cinematic motion*: motion interpreted as a sequence of images of the same subject seen at different points in time. Historical precedents can be found in some ancient works of art, notably in certain Greek vase

Figure 3-65. Drawing the walking model. The walking motion can be "frozen" at convenient intervals for purposes of study.

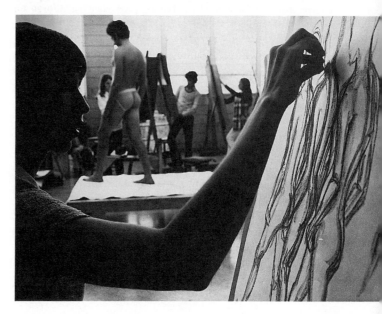

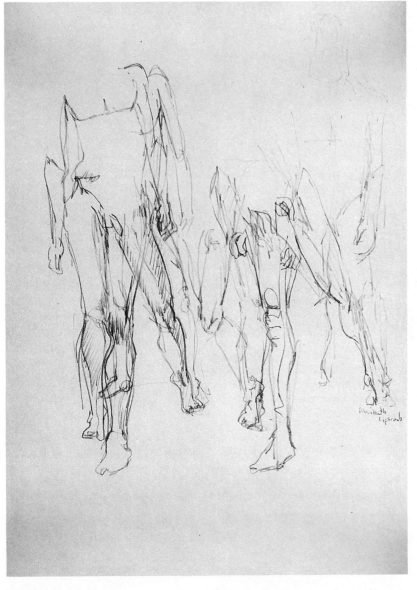

Figure 3-66. Student drawing. Study of a walking figure. Compressed charcoal pencil on newsprint paper. 36 × 24".

paintings (Figure 3-67), as well as in representations of the Hindu deity Shiva in Indian art, in which a multiplicity of similar figural elements suggests the motion of one form. In the nineteenth century Eadweard Muybridge and E. J. Marey recorded the figure in motion photographically for the first time. Although their sequential photographs eventually led to the invention of motion pictures, the unexpected patterns and visual rhythms revealed in their studies were of interest to artists and scientists alike. As early as 1884 the American realist painter Thomas Eakins made photographic studies of the nude figure in motion (Figure 3-68).[38] Since that time sequential images of the figure have been employed by a number of artists, notably by the twentieth-century French painter

Marcel Duchamp. Inspired by the multiple images of photography, Duchamp adapted them creatively as a source of visual rhythm in his well-known painting *Nude Descending a Staircase*.

The idea of *rhythm* is inherent in many forms of motion and is a visible aspect of cinematic images. In Thomas Eakins's photograph visual rhythm is apparent in the regular repetition of a similar but changing pattern, a repetition in which the space between each figure corresponds to a precise interval of time. Seen as a whole the figures form a large undulating pattern. A secondary rhythm is apparent in the arching pattern created by the movement of the legs (Figure 3-68).

In most works of art visual rhythm is not as mechanically

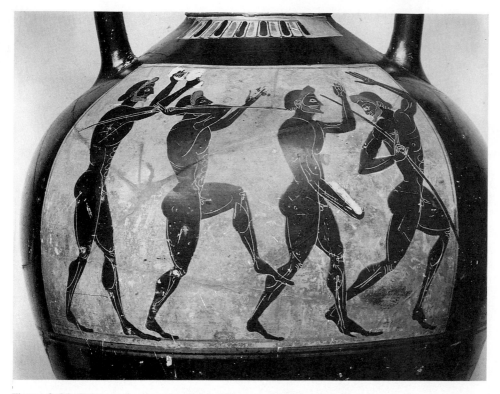

Figure 3-67. Unknown Greek artist, *Painted Figures of Athletes*. Panathenaic vase, late sixth century B.C. London, British Museum. The repetition of similar figural elements sets a visual rhythm that can also be interpreted as motion. *Rhythmos*, the word from which "rhythm" derives, was a term used in ancient Greece to designate "compositional patterns, especially of figures in movement" [J. J. Pollitt, *The Art of Ancient Greece 1400–31* B.C. *Sources and Documents* (Englewood Cliffs, N.J.: Prentice-Hall, 1965), p. 57].

Figure 3-68. Thomas Eakins (1844–1916), *Marey Wheel Photographs of Jesse Godley Running*, 1884. New York, Metropolitan Museum of Art. Gift of Charles Bregler, 1941. A noted exponent of realism in painting, Eakins was also an accomplished photographer. For this study of motion he used the newly invented Marey wheel, a revolving-disk shutter that permitted multiple exposures on a single plate.

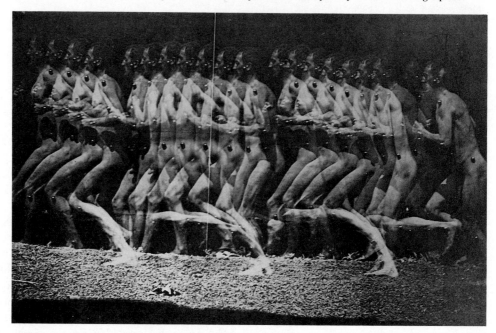

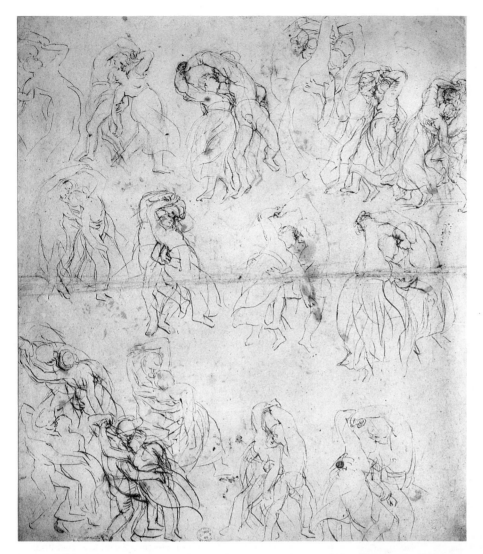

Figure 3-69. Peter Paul Rubens (1577–1640), *Peasant Dance*, 1629–1632. Black chalk with traces of red, reworked in pen and ink. 502 × 582 cm. London, British Museum.

Figure 3-70. Peter Paul Rubens, *Peasant Dance*, 1636–1640. Oil on wood. 28¾ × 39¾″. Madrid, the Prado.

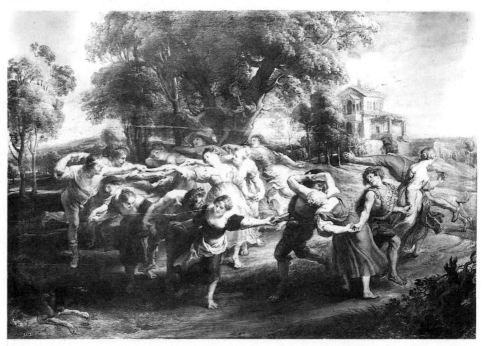

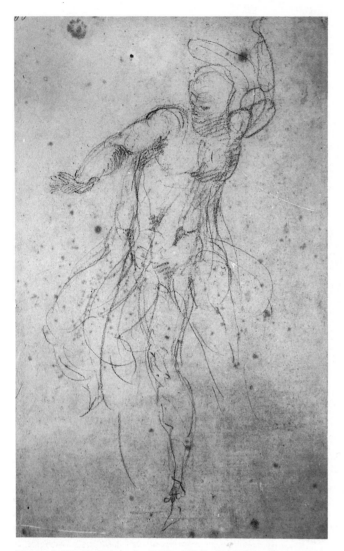

Figure 3-71. Michelangelo (1475–1564), *Study for a Resurrection*, 1523–1533. Black chalk. 16.2 × 12 cm. Florence, Casa Buonarroti (courtesy of GFSG).

motion both in individual figural elements and in compositional arrangements of figures in which the figures join in an unbroken rhythmic pattern, such as a circle or an ellipse. The principle is perhaps clearest, however, in works that present subjects involved in physical movement, such as dance (Figures 3-70 and 3-72).[39]

Rubens's drawing (Figure 3-69) reveals how he resolved problems of movement and gesture by means of numerous versions of two figures, perhaps drawn from life, before using them as part of the composition of his painting *Peasant Dance* (Figure 3-70). In the painting the couples are linked together as part of a larger pattern, like a visual chain forming an ellipse. The effect of swirling dance movement is enhanced by the similarity of types, giving rise to a visual rhythm and an implied cinematic movement that, in combination with the rollicking flow of line around the ellipse, makes the painting a centrifugal tour de force.

Like Rubens, Matisse also employed contour line as an instrument for expressing the movement of a ring of dancing figures (Figure 3-72). Drawing without the use of models, Matisse gave free reign to his visual memory, emphasizing movement more by means of the visual properties of the contour line itself.

STUDY 14:   **Using a Masterwork as a Resource: Movement**

materials: ❏ 14 × 11″ bound sketchbook of smooth bond paper
      ❏ India-ink drawing pen (2.5 Castell TG, 0.5 mm Mars Staedtler, or Rapidograph)
      ❏ optional medium: HB pencil and kneaded eraser
      ❏ single-edge blade for sharpening the pencil
reference: ❏ art museum or art books
time: ❏ 10–30 minutes (depending on the complexity of the work)

---

regular as in Eakins's photograph, but repetitive figures can suggest movement when integrated within a larger compositional pattern. Certain art works on the subject of the dance seem as if made to illustrate this aspect of rhythm. The recurring but varied figural elements seen in Figures 3-69, 3-70, and 3-72, for example, produce visual rhythms that evoke the unheard rhythmic beat of dance they represent.

LINE AND MOTION IN MASTERWORKS

Just as rhythm and motion are inseparable in dance, so motion and contour line are closely related in the visual arts. While the line seen in outline often serves primarily to isolate and clarify figural elements, contour line is capable of suggesting

There is a practical advantage to using a sketchbook for studying masterworks: It is portable. You can carry it with you into the art museum or library, and generally you are allowed to use the sketchbook on the spot. As a matter of form, however, it is proper to request permission from the museum attendant or librarian. In many European museums a written permit is required for this purpose. If an art museum is not accessible, you can simply turn to the nearest library. Many art books today have reproductions of sufficient quality to serve in place of original artworks for study purposes. What is more, art books can offer a greater range of masterworks than is possible in most museums.

In selecting a drawing instrument, bear in mind the purpose of your study. A study is not necessarily a copy, and for that reason a mechanical pen is recommended. Incapable of subtle tonal nuance, the pen eliminates the temptation to copy and encourages concentration on the particular aspect

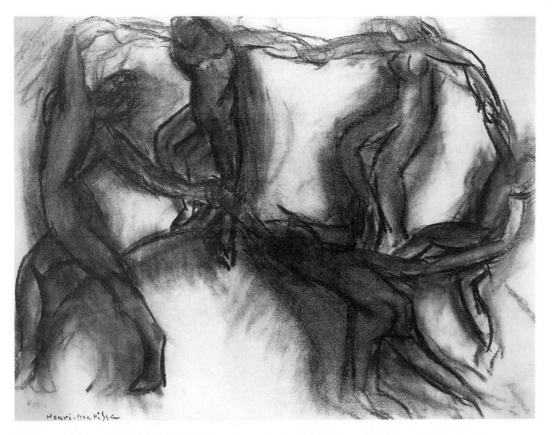

Figure 3-72. Henri Matisse, *Study for* The Dance, 1909. Charocal, on white paper 18⅞ × 25⅝″. Grenoble, Musée de Peinture et de Sculpture. Agutte-Sembat Bequest (photo by André Morin).

of the work under consideration. This is a real virtue, for the aim of studying—as opposed to copying—a masterwork is to uncover the concepts that produce the effect which interests you, in this case the effect of movement. This means you need draw only those features that appear associated with movement. If you decide to study Rubens's *Peasant Dance* (Figure 3-70), for example, the undulating ellipse formed by the dancing figures and the smaller, interlocking units of form (i.e., the arms of the figures) will be of special interest. In a student study (Figure 3-73), based on a drawing by the sixteenth-century Italian artist Luca Cambiaso, a different means was used to express motion—an explosive pattern of diagonal figure gestures. In place of the flowing contours of Rubens's dancers a curious block construction of form was favored by Cambiaso, yet the suggestion of movement is apparent. A drawing by Michelangelo (Figure 3-71) offers another approach to drawing the figure in motion: superimposing contours of the body in different positions as a way of resolving the gesture of the moving body. In Matisse's *Study for* The Dance (Figure 3-72), boldly simplified contours establish rhythms echoed in faint contours left by smudged erasures of preliminary lines. Like Michelangelo, Matisse expressed movement through the drawing process, allowing the earliest stages of the drawing to remain at least partially visible.

Figure 3-73. Student drawing. Study from Cambiaso's *The Return of Ulysses* (drawing in line and wash). Mechanical pen and ink on sketchbook page. 9 × 11″. The sixteenth-century artist Cambiaso is of special interest for his use of the geometric block as a construct in drawing.

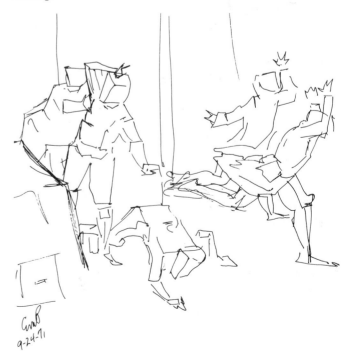

Further Study with the Sketchbook

Movement is but one topic to study in masterworks. You may wish, for instance, to record in your sketchbook the composition of masterworks in terms of abstract design. The sketchbook is also a practical means for the study of anatomy (see Chapters 6 and 7). Whatever the focus of your study, the sketchbook enables you to discover approaches and concepts that are best revealed through drawing, for drawing provides a uniquely visual way of learning from other works of art.

Artworks of the past are a self-renewing resource for study. "The past," wrote Italo Svevo, "is always new; it changes continuously as life goes on. Parts of it, seemingly forgotten, emerge again. . . ."[40] Perhaps it is the paradoxical newness of the past that has stimulated many artists—painters and sculptors alike—to draw from works of the past throughout their careers.

A drawing by the adolescent Michelangelo offers an interesting example of the study of earlier artworks (Figure 3-74). Like many other young art students in late fifteenth-

Figure 3-74. Michelangelo, *Copy After Two Figures from* The Ascension of St. John the Evangelist *by Giotto,* c. 1488. Pen and ink. 31.7 × 20.4 cm. Paris, the Louvre.

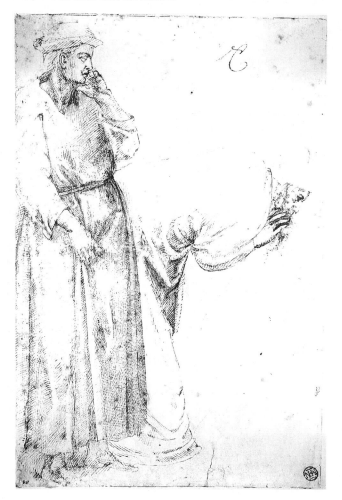

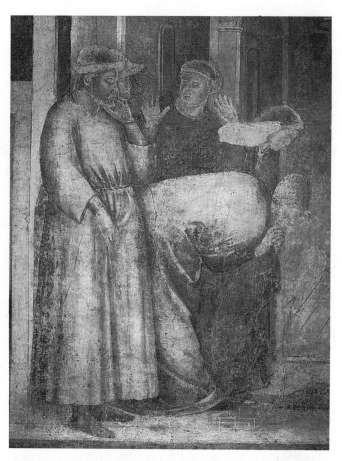

Figure 3-75. Giotto (1266?–1337), detail from *The Ascension of St. John the Evangelist,* c. 1318. Fresco. Florence, Santa Croce, Cappella Peruzzi (courtesy of GFSG).

century Florence, Michelangelo drew from figures he saw in a fresco wall painting by Giotto, a work already two hundred years old (Figure 3-75). His drawing, which has survived in somewhat better shape than the fresco, shows his interest in the compositional relationship of two of the five figures depicted in the fresco. Leaving out the stylistic details peculiar to Giotto's work, as well as two figures in the background, Michelangelo invested his version of the figures with his own sculptural sense of form and roundness while preserving the gestures and compositional relationships of the originals. The result is a creative study, not simply a copy reproducing the original.

Another example of an artist learning from earlier masterworks comes from seventeenth-century Holland. A quick study by Rembrandt of Raphael's *Portrait of Baldassare Castiglione,* made while the painting was on the auction block in Amsterdam, led to a subsequent self-portrait incorporating some of the compositional features of the Raphael (Figures 3-76, 3-77, and 3-78). Together the works cited represent a model of how drawing can be used to reinterpret earlier art for the purpose of furthering new creative efforts.

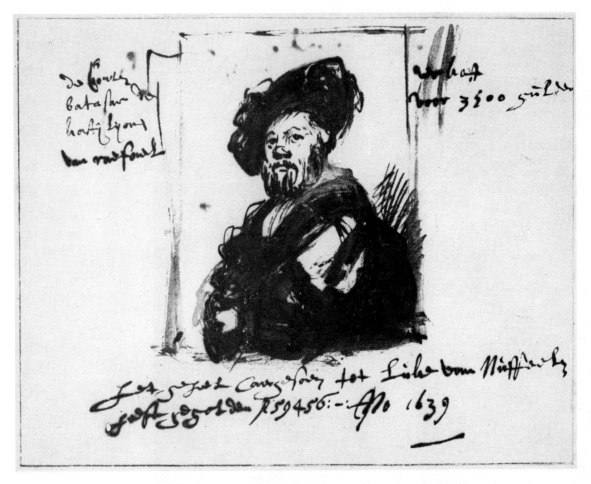

Figure 3-76. Rembrandt, *Sketch After Raphael's* Baldassare Castiglione, 1639. Pen and bister with some white body color. 163 × 207 mm. Vienna, Albertina. Art museums did not exist in Rembrandt's time, but public auctions, such as the one at which Rembrandt made his sketch of Raphael's painting, afforded an opportunity to see and possibly purchase artworks from other countries and periods. Rembrandt's writing at upper right records the price that the Raphael painting brought (3,400 guilders) and the date.

Figure 3-77. Raphael (1483–1520), *Baldassare Castiglione*, c. 1510. Oil on canvas. 32⅜ × 26½". Paris, the Louvre.

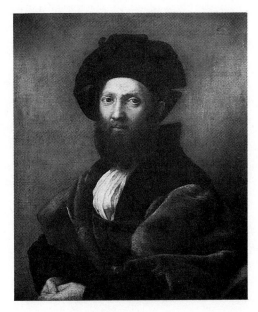

The history of art provides numerous instances of nineteenth- and twentieth-century artists using sources remote from their own time and culture. Ingres, a French painter of the nineteenth century and an excellent draftsman, continued throughout his lifetime to study the art of ancient Rome and Greece. Inspired both by ancient and Renaissance art, Ingres developed a way of constructing form with line that owes much to these sources, even though it is unmistakably his own. In some cases it is possible to trace the origin of a gesture in his drawing to an ancient prototype he studied (Figures 3-79 and 3-80).

The art of other cultures was not neglected by artists of the twentieth century. The Italian artist Modigliani, for example, drew studies of African sculptures in order to learn the rhythmic constructs and proportional relationships that he recognized as a source of expressive power. Similar constructs became the basis for some of his most original paintings and sculptures (Figures 3-81 and 3-82).

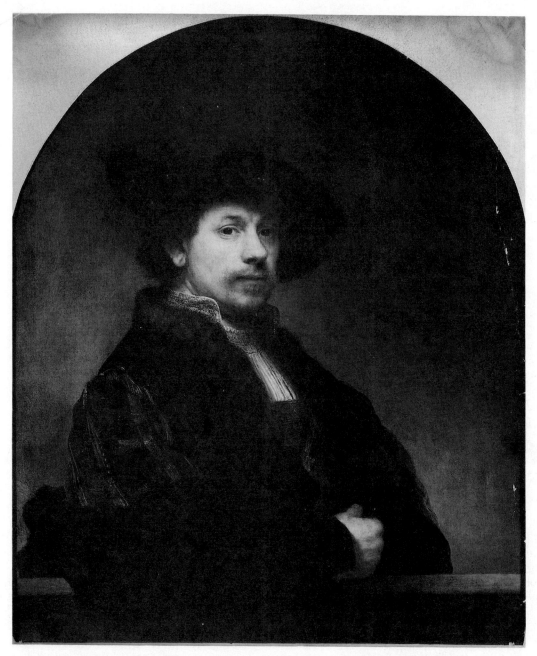

Figure 3-78. Rembrandt, *Self-Portrait*, 1640. Oil on canvas. 40⅛ × 31½″. London, National Gallery.

Figure 3-79. Jean-Auguste-Dominique Ingres (1780–1867), *Study for the Portrait of Madame Moitessier*, c. 1851. Charcoal over graphite on thin white woven paper squared with graphite. 7⅜ × 7⅞″. Cambridge, Massachusetts, Fogg Art Museum, Harvard University. Bequest of Charles A. Loeser.

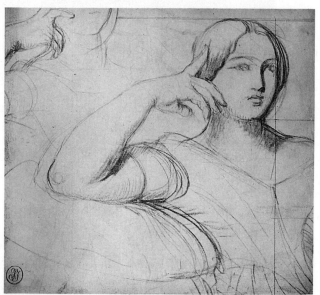

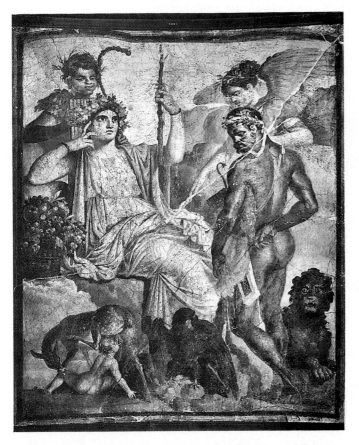

Figure 3-80. Unknown Herculanean artist, *Hercules and Telephus*, c. A.D. 70. Wall painting. Naples, National Museum.

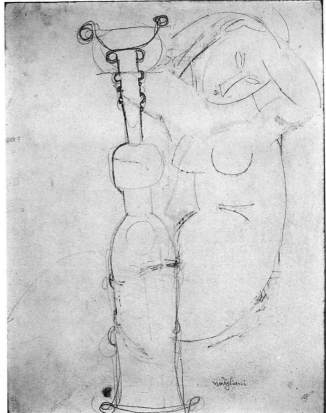

Figure 3-81. Amedeo Modigliani (1884–1920), *Caryatid with African Sculpture*, c. 1913. Pencil. 10⅜ × 8⅛". Mr. and Mrs. James W. Alsdorf collection.

Figure 3-82. Unknown Baoule (Ivory Coast) artist, *Horned Dance Mask*. 15" high. Private collection.

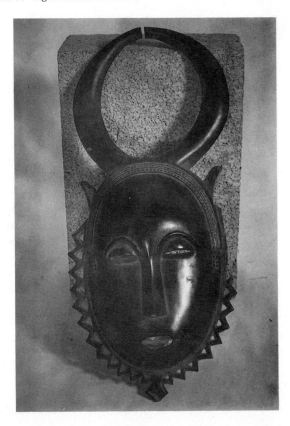

The Sketchbook and Sketching

It is misleading, however, to discuss the sketchbook only as a means of analyzing artworks of the past, for it is also a repository of the most informal type of art: the sketch. The sketchbook fulfills an important need of the artist and student—it helps to maintain a continuing sense of pleasure in drawing. This need is sometimes overlooked in the quest of "serious" artistic expression. In this regard it is refreshing to see pages from the sketchbooks of Picasso (Figure 3-83). Many of their pages may appear inconsequential, but what fun they are! The intermingling sketches and smears, like a visual stream of consciousness, evidence an enthusiasm for drawing rarely seen outside the sketchbook.

If you have never kept a sketchbook, you may profit from a suggestion from Leonardo, who had definite ideas on its use: "When you are out for a walk, see to it that you watch and consider men's postures and actions as they talk, argue, laugh, or scuffle together; their own actions, and those of their supporters and onlookers; and make a note of these with a few strokes in your little book which you must always carry

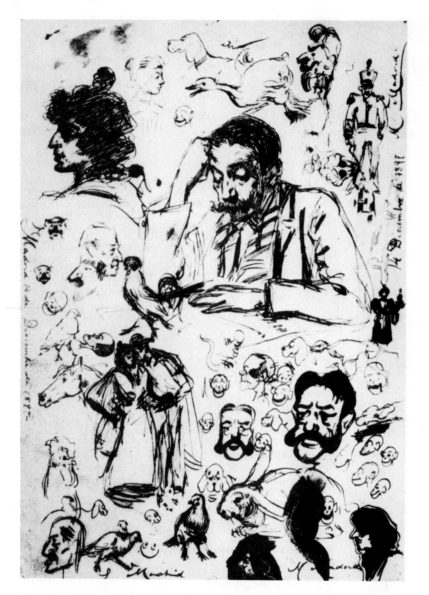

Figure 3-83. Pablo Picasso, *Page from a Sketchbook,* 1897. Pen and ink. 30.8 × 21 cm. Barcelona, Museo Picasso (courtesy of SPADEM).

with you."[41] To this sage advice may be added the suggestion that a sketchbook is handy for jotting down an idea while it is still fresh in your mind.

SUMMARY

You can gain an understanding and mastery of line by the practice of exercises with the objective of clarifying a single aspect of line at a time. The most distinctive aspect of line is its capacity to separate the figure from the ground, as in the outline of the silhouette. The contour line, on the other hand, is capable of suggesting a degree of sculptural depth by describing linear features within the silhouette. This is espe-

cially noticeable with features near to the silhouette edge, where turning and overlapping contours tend to be most apparent. Both the beginner and the more advanced student can appreciate the way in which contour drawing frees the eye and the hand from preconceived notions of proportion and scale. The deliberately slow movement of the eye and hand in the first contour exercise (Study 4) can result in an exquisitely sensitive line that, like a seismograph, records the small changes of form, albeit often at the expense of the figure as a whole. The basic formal unity of the figure is more readily expressed through the rapid contour drawing method (Study 5).

Like the slow contour drawing, rapid contour studies are recommended for both beginners and advanced students. The unbridled freedom of arm movement encouraged by rapid contour drawing makes it an effective warm-up exercise for beginning a drawing session. The heightened sense of breadth and movement in the rapid contour drawing more than compensates for the lack of delicacy or detail.

The effective use of line in drawing goes hand in hand with the artist's concept of formal construction. Since a common denominator of bodily forms is the egg, or ovoid form, a drawing construct based on that form can be helpful. Ovoid construction facilitates drawing the figure by providing a drawing construct that both corresponds with the basic forms of the body and produces a harmonious, sculptural drawing. The ovoid construct challenges the artist to discover the wholeness of form in the body and thereby to see relationships between one side of the figural form and the other side. The overlapping oval constructs often create angular intersections, which in turn suggest an approach to line emphasizing visual measurement.

Visual measurement as an approach to drawing works best with straight lines. While it is true that there are few, if any, features in the body that form straight lines, some contours of the body are sharp enough to be interpreted as two intersecting straight lines. The angle formed can easily be measured visually. Our natural ability to see subtle differences of angular intersections—as when reading the hands of a clock—provides a practical way to analyze the appearance of the figure with a surprising degree of accuracy. Unlike the previous exercises the visual measurement deals with the figure primarily as an image composed of shapes. Thus effects of apparent distortions of form, as seen in the foreshortened view, can be analyzed more effectively with visual measurement than with the ovoid construction.

It is possible to arrive at a more sophisticated mode of line drawing by carrying the ovoid construction one step further—eliminating the invisible lines. This approach, because of its affinity to ancient Greek drawing, is called classic. Classic line drawings have the appearance of combining outline and contour, but the oval underlies the construction of the figure and produces the characteristic harmonious relationship of parts of the figure. The relationship of parts in ancient and Renaissance art was itself the subject of study and conjecture, although today these canons are little used by artists except as a means of checking basic proportions and symmetry of the standing figure.

In addition to understanding the importance of line in establishing the relationships between the different parts of the body, both classical and Renaissance authors and artists appreciated line for its ability to convey a sense of motion. By drawing the figure in multiple poses inspired by specific types of movement, it is possible to explore a variety of gesture and form in a single study. The study of masterworks can also be a source of ideas for representing motion as well as other subjects. Museum restrictions favor the sketchbook for studies of this type. For reasons of clarity as well as economy of time, line is often the preferred drawing mode for sketchbook studies.

In general, line is a uniquely graphic tool, most commonly associated with drawing, though it is sometimes apparent in painting and sculpture. Line is also uniquely abstract, yet, as we have seen, capable of communicating realistic imagery with great economy. Picasso, himself a master of line, summed up the exceptional nature of this drawing mode when he stated, "Only line drawing escapes imitation."[42]

NOTES

1. M. D. Vernon, *The Psychology of Perception* (Harmondsworth, Middlesex, England: Penguin, 1962), p. 40.

2. David Noton and Lawrence Stark, "Eye Movements and Visual Perception," *Scientific American*, vol. 224, no. 6 (June 1971), p. 35.

3. Much of the visual information is gathered by the *fovea*, "the small central area of the retina that has the highest concentration of photoreceptors" (ibid.).

4. It is clear the eye does not normally function like a still camera, a common misconception that has "dominated philosophy and psychology for many years." Ulric Neisser, "The Processes of Vision," *Scientific American*, vol. 219, no. 3 (Sept. 1968), p. 206.

5. For an interesting discussion of current knowledge of human visual perception, see *The Mind's Eye, Readings from Scientific American* (New York: Freeman, 1986).

6. Quoted originally in Charles H. Caffin, *Camera Work*, no. 2, 1903, pp. 22–23; reprinted in Albert E. Elsen, *Rodin* (New York: Museum of Modern Art, 1963), p. 163.

7. Henri Matisse, "Notes of a Painter on his Drawing," quoted by Victor I. Carlson in *Matisse as a Draughtsman* (Greenwich, Conn.: Baltimore Museum of Art, 1971), p. 18.

8. Pliny, *Natural History*, Book XXXV, 65–68, trans. H. Rackham (Cambridge, Mass.: Harvard University Press, 1968), p. 367. Though not an artist himself, the Roman author Pliny recorded much of what is known about ancient Greek and Roman art. His brilliant insight into the nature of contour line is contained in a paragraph praising the Greek artist Parrhasius, whose works were prized for their linear quality, a quality Pliny considers to be "the high-water mark of refinement." Pliny clearly favored the line techniques of classical art over the use of modeling for effects of mass and volume: ". . . to paint bulk and the surface within the outlines, though no doubt a great achievement, is one in which many have won distinction, but to give the contour of the figures, and make a satisfactory boundary where the painting within finishes, is rarely attained in successful artistry. . . . This is the distinction conceded to Parrhasius. . . ." It is one of the ironies of history that Pliny's writings on ancient painting have survived the centuries, but the paintings themselves have not.

9. An outstanding example of the box construction of the figure is found in George B. Bridgman's *Constructive Anatomy* (New York: Dover, 1960).

10. Ulric Neisser, "Processes of Vision," p. 214.

11. *The Mind's Eye, Readings from Scientific American* (New York: Freeman, 1986), p. 80.

12. "At the Petite Ecole—now known as the Ecole Nationale Supérieure des Arts Decoratifs (Paris)—the painter Horace Lecoq de Boisbaudran was teaching a revolutionary method of drawing from memory, and a whole generation of artists was influenced by him, among them Dalou, Fantin-Latour, and Legros. . . . Rodin wrote in 1913: 'Most of what he taught me then, still remains with me.' " Robert Descharnes and Jean-François Chabrun, *Rodin* (New York: Viking, 1967), p. 15.

13. Elizabeth Gilmore Holt, *From the Classicists to the Impressionists* (Garden City, N.Y.: Anchor Books, Doubleday, 1966), p. 401.

14. In the French Art Academy of the nineteenth century the art student "centered his sketch with horizontal and vertical guide lines formed with a plumb line." Albert Boime, *The Academy and French Painting in the Nineteenth Century* (London: Phaidon, 1971), p. 32.

15. Artists in the past sometimes used the thumb instead of the crayon to estimate parallelism, hence the stereotyped gesture of the artist with arm extended.

16. An inexperienced draftsman might reason that it would be simpler and more accurate to take measurements not by eye but by a measuring instrument, such as the carpenter's calipers. This type of method ignores the discrepancy between appearance and objective reality, a discrepancy that visual measurement takes into account. Nevertheless, some artists have utilized actual measuring instruments. The naïveté of this approach is suggested by Apollinaire's account of the "primitive" artist Henri Rousseau, who began a portrait by measuring his model and inscribing on the canvas reduced measurements in proper proportion. Charming though they are, Rousseau's portraits offer mute testimony to the accuracy of draftsmanship derived from physical measurements of the model.

17. Amédée Ozenfant, *The Foundations of Modern Art* (New York: Dover, 1952), p. 323.

18. Studies in perception show that the human brain may be especially equipped to detect angles and sharp curves in edges of visual patterns. David H. Hubel and Torsten N. Wiesel of the Harvard Medical School have found angle-detecting cells in the visual cortex of cats and monkeys, "and recordings obtained from the human visual cortex by Elwin Marg of the University of California at Berkeley give preliminary indications that these results can be extended to man." As Professor Jeremy Wolfe of M.I.T. explains, "a set of channels (in the cerebral cortex) to identify the precise orientation of a contour, for example, might include a channel for horizontal contours, one for contours tilted 30 degrees from the vertical, and so on." David Noton and Lawrence Stark, "Eye Movements," p. 37, and Jeremy M. Wolfe, *The Mind's Eye* (New York: Freeman, 1986), p. 38.

19. Until recently scientists believed our "sense of position and movement of the joints" depended on a "mysterious muscle sense" deriving in some way from the relative length of the muscles. Research by J. E. Rose and V. B. Mountcastle, however, disclosed that

nerve receptors in the joints of the limbs serve as pickups informing the brain of the angular attitude of the limbs. James J. Gibson, *The Senses Considered as Perceptual Systems* (Boston: Houghton Mifflin, 1966), pp. 110–111.

20. For an example of this type of feature description see Figure 10 in John P. Frisby, *Seeing* (Oxford, England: Oxford University Press, 1980).

21. Quoted originally in Charles H. Caffin, *Camera Work*; reprinted in Elsen's *Rodin*, p. 163.

22. A much earlier classical revival occurred in ancient times. *Neo-atticism*, as it is now called, was "an artistic movement which evolved in Athens and was popular at Rome from the middle of the first century B.C. until the early part of the first century A.D. The artists who flourished during this period imitated or copied works of the fifth and fourth centuries, but also drew inspiration from the archaic period." Ranuccio Bianchi Bandinelli, *Rome: The Center of Power* (New York: George Braziller, 1970), p. 430.

23. Classical drawings and mirror engravings share a technical as well as a conceptual similarity with Picasso's drawings of the Rose Period: They utilize a line that has a constant width. This form of line, called *monoline*, is also characteristic of ancient Greek writing styles, which lack the swells and thins of later Roman letters.

24. Vitruvius, *On Architecture*, book III, trans. Frank Granger (Cambridge, Mass.: Harvard University Press, 1970), c. 1, p. 159.

25. Galen, *Placita Hippocratis et Platonis*, V, 3, as quoted in Erwin Panofsky, *Meaning in the Visual Arts* (New York: Doubleday, 1955), p. 64.

26. The system of classical proportions permitted the artist to compensate for effects of foreshortening by means of deliberate distortion. In this respect it was a freer concept of form than that exhibited in earlier art.

27. Vitruvius, *On Architecture*, p. 68. For a thorough study of the proportional canons of Polyclitus see the exhibition catalog *Polyklet der Bildhauer der griechischen Klassik* (Frankfurt am Main: Verlag Philipp von Zabern, 1990).

28. Such a link was established with music in ancient Greece when the philosopher Pythagoras divided a vibrating string into fractional parts, thereby demonstrating the mathematical basis of harmony.

29. In 1525 Venetian writer Francesco Giorgi attempted to demonstrate a relationship between the intervals of bodily forms and musical intervals of tones (*Francisci Giorgii Veneti de harmonia mundi totius cantica tria*, cited in Erwin Panofsky, *Meaning in the Visual Arts* [New York: Doubleday, 1955], p. 91).

30. Leonardo da Vinci, *The Treatise on Painting*, vol. 1, trans. A. Philip McMahon (Princeton, N.J.: Princeton University Press, 1956), p. 119.

31. The golden section is the division of a line or the proportion of a rectangle in which the smaller dimension is to the greater as the greater is to the whole: "The golden section has for centuries been regarded as . . . a key to the mysteries of art" (Herbert Read, as quoted in Webster's *Third New International Dictionary* [Springfield, Mass.: Merriam, 1971]).

32. For a fascinating example of a Renaissance study of body proportions, see *The Human Figure by Albrecht Dürer, The Complete Dresden Sketchbook* (New York: Dover, 1972).

33. The consensus of opinion on proportional norms (and on art in general) in ancient times may have been achieved partly at the expense of restrictive practices limiting drawing instruction to persons of a certain class: "Drawing . . . has always consistently had the honour of being practiced by people of free birth, and later on by persons of station, it having always been forbidden that slaves should be instructed in it. Hence it is that neither in painting nor in the art of statuary are there any famous works that were executed by any person who was a slave" (Pliny, *Natural History*, books XXXV and XXXVI [Cambridge, Mass.: Harvard University Press, 1967]), 77–80).

34. M. D. Vernon, *Psychology of Perception*, p. 51.

35. In some respects the bilateral symmetry of the brain is not matched by a symmetry of function. Doreen Kimura reports ("The Asymmetry of the Human Brain," *Scientific American*, vol. 228, no. 3 [March 1973], pp. 72–76): ". . . evidence that the right hemisphere is . . . primary for some very fundamental visual processes. . . . In the simplest kind of spatial task—the location of a single point in a two-dimensional area—the right hemisphere is dominant. . . . It has been known for some time that injury to the right posterior part of the brain (the parieto-occipital region) results in the impairment of complex abilities such as drawing, finding one's way from place to place, and building models from a plan or picture." Both spheres of the brain, however, seem to be equally capable of perceiving shape, a function that, according to Kimura, apparently involves neural systems "relatively independent" of those that analyze information about the location of objects in space.

36. Ulric Neisser, "Processes of Vision," p. 206. In an article on visual perception of motion, Gunnar Johansson writes, "The eye has evolved to function essentially as a motion-detecting system. The concept of a motionless animal in a totally static environment has hardly any biological significance; the perception of physical motion is of decisive importance. In many lower animals the efficient perception of moving objects seems to be the most essential visual function. A frog or a chameleon, for example, can perceive and catch its prey only if the prey is moving." Gunnar Johansson, "Visual Motion Perception," *Scientific American*, vol. 232, no. 6 (June 1975), p. 76.

37. Leonardo preferred to drop the vertical line from the hollow of the model's throat. Leonardo da Vinci, *Treatise on Painting*, p. 131.

38. The British photographer Eadweard Muybridge, who learned the technique from its inventor E. J. Marey, taught Eakins how to use the "Marey Wheel" camera. For a detailed history of Marey's photographic work, see *E. J. Marey, 1830/1904, La Photographie du Mouvement* (Paris: Centre Georges Pompidou), 1977.

39. Julius Held, in *Rubens' Selected Drawings* (London: Phaidon, 1959), mentions the London drawing as a work sheet for the same painter's *Kermesse* in the Louvre. He omits reference to *Peasant Dance*, though the two paintings are listed by Reginald H. Wilenski in *Flemish Painters* (London: Faber & Faber, 1960) as probably dating from the same period and including similar dancing figures.

40. Italo Svevo, quoted in Udo Kultermann, *New Realism* (Greenwich, Conn.: New York Graphic Society, 1972), p. 24.

41. Leonardo da Vinci, *Trattato della Pittura* 169, quoted in Kenneth Clark, *Leonardo da Vinci* (Harmondsworth, Middlesex, England: Penguin, 1959), p. 79.

42. Picasso, quoted in Pierre Daix and George Boudaille, *Picasso: The Blue and Rose Periods, A Catalogue Raisonné of the Paintings, 1900–1906* (Greenwich, Conn.: New York Graphic Society, 1966), p. 67.

CHAPTER 4

Modeling

relief, shadow, tone, and contour

There are no lines in nature, only lighted forms and forms which are in shadow, planes which project and planes which recede.

—FRANCISCO GOYA

T HE VIEW OF NATURE espoused by the Spanish artist Francisco Goya is not merely a rationale concocted to explain why so few contour lines appear in his work: It expresses an attitude that has been held by many artists of many different persuasions and is shared by contemporary psychologists concerned with visual perception. Studies in this field draw attention to the fact that ". . . the world we ordinarily look at consists mostly of surfaces, at various angles and in various relations to one another."[1]

What you may interpret as the lines of an object often prove on closer inspection to be sharply turning areas on its surface, like the corners of a cube (Figure 4-1). Such surface discontinuities are commonly reinforced by the effects of light, resulting in comparable discontinuities of tone on the surface. A line drawing of a cube, for example, defines the form strictly in terms of discontinuities, suppressing the essential surface continuity of the object (Figure 4-2). It is understandable, therefore, that some artists prefer a mode of drawing which takes into account the physical surface continuity of forms in nature—its "planes which project and planes which recede" and their attendant effects of tonality. This alternative approach to drawing is generally called *modeling*.

Modeling is more, however, than a mere graphic representation of the surface of an object. A lithograph by the American artist Jasper Johns (Figure 4-3) helps to clarify this point. It is an impression made in the manner of a fingerprint from the actual surface of the human head. The resulting image of human topology, though derived from a solid form, lacks any suggestion of the surface's orientation in three-dimensional space. Moreover, the limitations of human vision are ignored in the lithograph, which shows more of the surface of the head than is normally possible at one time from any single point of view. (A comparable representation of a box would show it unfolded as a flat piece of cardboard.) Johns has documented an actual continuous surface divorced from its spatial context; modeling techniques, by contrast, enable the artist to describe surfaces of forms within the context of three-dimensional space. A drawing by the French sculptor Aristide Maillol for example (Figure 4-4) uses tone to model the body surfaces turning around volumetric form as seen from a specific point of view.

RELIEF MODELING

Maillol's drawing employs a beautifully simple modeling principle. Dark tones are used to signify surfaces that are turned away from the viewer; light tones, surfaces that front (face) the viewer. The dark tones in the Maillol drawing are

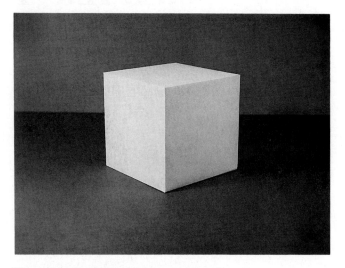

Figure 4-1. The effect of light on a white cube.

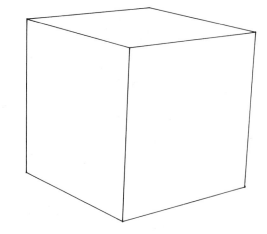

Figure 4-2. Line representation suppresses the surface continuity of a cube.

imposed systematically without reference to natural lighting effects in order to give a sense of sculptural relief to the form. For this reason the method is called *relief modeling.*

Relief modeling has much in common with the modeling of clay: The term itself is borrowed from sculpture (Figure 4–5). In making a clay relief the sculptor works and shapes the clay, pushing back forms that are meant to recede in space. The fingers often serve directly as modeling instruments. By an extension of the sculptor's technique you also can use your hand as an instrument for modeling the figure in a drawing.

Figure 4-3. Jasper Johns (b. 1930), *Study for* Skin 1, 1962. Lithograph. 22 × 34″. Artist's collection. Adopting a technique borrowed from police fingerprinting, the artist recorded the surfaces of his face, palms, and fingers, producing an image of the head's surfaces without a sense of its volumes.

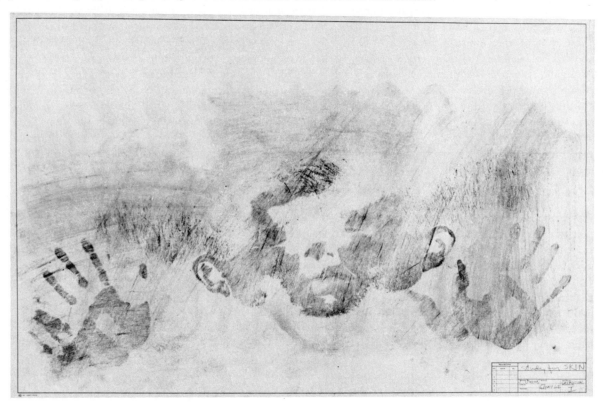

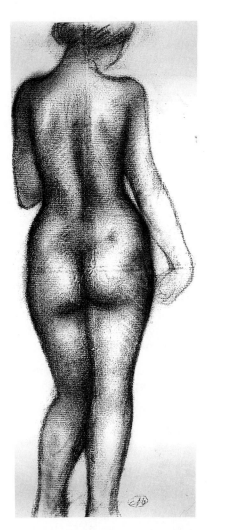

Figure 4-4. Aristide Maillol (1861–1944), *Female Nude Seen from the Back*. Red chalk. 12½ × 4½″. Philadelphia Museum of Art. McIlhenny Fund.

STUDY 15:   Relief Modeling with Printing Ink

materials: ❑ 36 × 24″ newsprint drawing pad
 ❑ easel or straight-back chair
 ❑ Masonite or plywood board and clamps
 ❑ stand or small table
 ❑ black or brown oil-base woodblock
 ❑ printing ink
 ❑ 5″ ink roller
 ❑ pane of glass (minimum size 10 × 12 × ⅛″)
 ❑ small roll of masking tape (to cover the sharp
  edges of the glass)
 ❑ turpentine or mineral spirits and rag (to clean
  the plate and your hands)

reference: ❑ model
time: ❑ 15 minutes

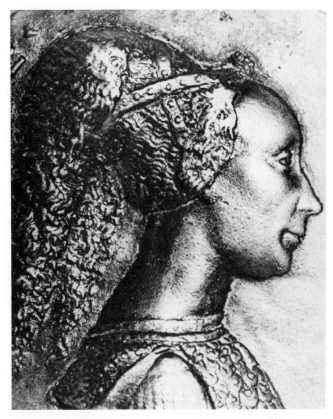

Figure 4-5. Matteo d'Pasti, *Isotta da Rimini* (1446–1467). Bronze medal (enlarged). Florence, Museo Nazionale. (Ludwig Goldscheider, *Unknown Renaissance Portraits* [New York: Phaidon, Praeger, 1952]. Photo courtesy of Phaidon Photo Archive.)

For your first experience in modeling the figure, it is helpful to arrange your easel and drawing pad so you can draw while you observe the model from the same side and direction as the source of light. With this setup the visual effect of relief modeling appears ready-made on the model so that, in the words of Leonardo, "the greater density of shadows are created on the sides where the parts of the body are most curved (turned from you), and the least dark shades will be found on the flattest sides (facing you)"[2] (Figure 4-5). In a studio with window illumination this may require a drawing position between the window and the model stand. If this arrangement is not possible, you can simply disregard the appearance of light and dark values on the model and following Maillol's example apply tone to the drawing in accordance with what you perceive as its sculptural form, using dark tones to signify surfaces that turn away. The highest value, the white of the paper, can be reserved for areas of the figure representing the surfaces that are flat with respect to your field of vision.

 You may find it practical to arrange your drawings materials on a stand beside your easel so the pane of glass may be laid flat and is within easy reach when you begin to draw. To prepare, squeeze a small amount of printing ink on the glass pane and spread it with the roller until it has the con-that you are reaching for and touching the model. Above all keep in mind the objective: the effect of sculptural relief. Search out the ways in which forms recede and turn. Within a period of fifteen minutes the figure should take shape in your drawing. The illusion of volume and relief may be quite strong even on your first try (Figures 4-6, 4-7, and 4-8).

Using your fingerprints to draw may seem so natural that it scarcely needs explanation, but a few hints can make it easier. With your fingers lightly inked you can lay in the general shape of the figure with light tones, saving the deeper values until you are more certain of their position. Portions of the figure only slightly turned from you may need no additional tone.

As in virtually all drawing, the quality of your work tends to improve when you work with a plan or procedure in mind. In this study it is advantageous to aim at modeling the larger, more general forms first. In modeling the head, for example, first establish the general large, ovoid form of the head as a whole before attempting the finer modulations of the facial features. The larger forms of the figure when modeled adequately serve as a formal setting within which you can place

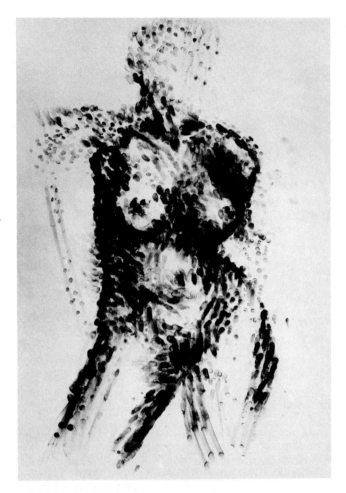

Figure 4-6. Student drawing. Figure seen from the front. Woodblock printing ink applied with the fingertips on newsprint paper. 36 × 24″.

sistency of a thin film. Before you start to draw, however, take time to study the model as form.

From a single viewpoint the three dimensionality of the model's form may not be apparent. By walking slowly around the model and observing the disposition of the form in space, it becomes somewhat easier to interpret the specific view of the figure seen from your position at the easel. When you are ready to begin to draw, press the fingertips of your drawing hand into the film of ink on the glass pane. The ink your hands pick up will mark the paper wherever you touch it.

Observe the model carefully, asking yourself which surfaces of the figure are most turned from your line of sight and which face you. Your recollections of form gained by walking around the model will help you determine the answers to such questions. With a general notion of the form in mind press your inked fingers against the drawing paper, imagining as you do so that you are pushing back the surfaces which are most recessive, as you might if you were modeling a clay relief. Work rapidly, concentrating on the larger, simpler forms of the figure. Throughout the drawing process it can be helpful to exploit your tactile sense of form pretending

Figure 4-7. Student drawing. Figure seen from the back. Woodblock printing ink applied with the fingertips on newsprint paper.

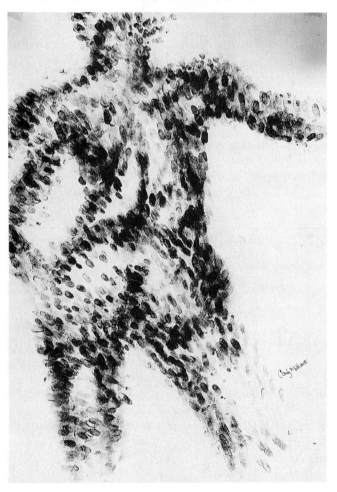

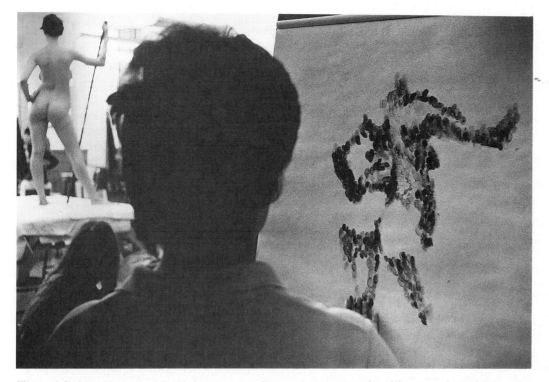

Figure 4-8. Drawing the model with fingerprinting. The tactile sensation of modeling is made vivid by using the fingers as drawing instruments.

and model the subtler changes of form. This procedure also helps avoid fragmentation of the drawing into isolated dark patterns. Although such disconnected tonal passages are sometimes necessary, they tend to break up the sculptural unity of the drawing and to produce an unintended flatness of effect, a common problem in beginners' work. Generally the most sharply turned surfaces of the figure are also the farthest. In some instances, however, turned surfaces may be relatively near to you and therefore pose a special problem in modeling. In relief modeling it is the orientation of form rather than the distance that governs the tone. You are likely, therefore, to discover passages in the figure that despite their proximity require modeling with darker tones than the more distant surfaces (Figure 4-9).

STUDY 16:   Relief Modeling with Stippling

materials: ❑ 36 × 24″ newsprint drawing pad
 ❑ easel or straight-back chair
 ❑ Masonite or plywood board and clamps
 ❑ warm black[3] or dark brown blunt-point felt-tip pen
 ❑ optional colors: medium yellow, process blue, and magenta
reference: ❑ model
time: ❑ 15 minutes

The principles of modeling discussed in Study 15 apply equally to this study. Surfaces that appear to turn away from your line of sight are translated into deeper tones than surfaces that face you; deepest tones are reserved for surfaces that turn the most. Instead of making fingerprints to create tone you can create tonal effects with dots of black. The necessary variation of tone is achieved by varying the number (density) of dots in different areas of the drawing: If you wish to deepen the tonal values in one area, simply add more dots until the desired effect is achieved (Figures 4-10 and 4-11). A readily available instrument for this purpose is the blunt felt-tip pen. By simply tapping the pen against the paper you can produce many dots with little effort. Tapping rapidly and at random within a given area of the figure will help you think of the dots as tonal areas of a modeled surface rather than as individual points. Since the eye tends to perceive areas of dots as tone and texture rather than as independent dark units, it is doubly important to use the pen in this way.

If this is your first experience in modeling with dots, a few suggestions may be helpful. Before initiating a study of the model try making simple areas of tone with dots to get an idea of the tonal range possible with this technique. Starting with a wide area of sparsely placed dots, add more to create a middle tone, and still more so that the dots cluster to form a deeper value.

A similar order of tones can be used for modeling the figure following the procedure of modeling the large forms

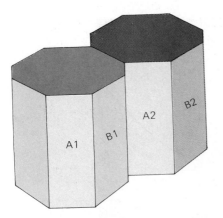

Figure 4-9. Two prisms with modeled surfaces. Though facet (B1) appears nearer to the viewer than facet (A2), the latter is represented as lighter because of its spatial orientation. At first glance this use of lighter value may seem to be a contradiction in terms of modeling but is actually a common occurrence in complex passages of the human form.

Figure 4-10. Student drawing. Modeling by stippling. Felt-tip marker on newsprint paper. 36 × 24″. Dots are concentrated in areas where the form appears to turn and/or recede. The changing density of dots corresponds to changing distances and orientations of the body surface.

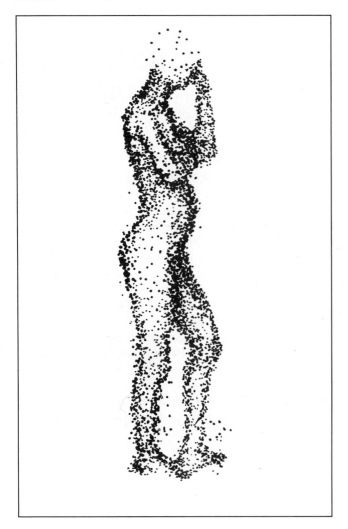

of the body first. Begin by placing dots randomly on the page at a considerable distance from one another in order to establish the general breadth and height of the figure. As the drawing evolves, a more unified effect of form can be created by developing the figure as an integral whole rather than modeling one small area at a time. You can lay in a nebulous general form by tapping continuously with the pen. With further modeling the figure will seem to emerge as if through a fog. A gradual development of form in the drawing permits you to exploit the special advantage of dots in making visual estimates of form.

It is important to avoid stringing dots together into virtual lines in this exercise. Modeling describes form primarily in terms of surfaces and volumes, not contours or edges. Although effects resembling edges and contour may appear in a highly modeled drawing, they are a by-product, not the aim, of the technique. As with the silhouette study, any crisp modeling of detail is generally more convincing if it appears last in the modeling process and integrated with the larger forms. An advantage of the dot technique is that the variation in tonal value is automatically accompanied by a corresponding variation in texture, with the recessive areas richest in both elements. Such textural effects greatly enhance the power of tone to suggest form.

The role of the dot in visual art is greater than might be expected for so modest a mark. Interest in the dot as a studio technique began with the development of the graphic process called *aquatint* in the eighteenth century: a process that Goya exploited to create grainy tonal areas in many of his prints (Figure 4-109). In the nineteenth century dot stippling became part of the standard repertoire of drawing techniques, and ultimately the basis for a controversial new painting technique, called *pointillism*, which is associated most closely with the French artist Georges Seurat (1859–1891). In his paintings dots of pigment produce effects of color and tonal modulation while creating a unifying texture (Figure 4-12). Through Seurat's careful juxtaposition of dots of different colors the figure appears as if viewed through a screen. Since the "screen" seems to lie on the painting surface, the viewer is constantly made aware of the two-dimensional nature of painting despite the opposing three-dimensional relief effects of the modeling.

Seurat was condemned by critics and fellow artists alike for his new technique. Gauguin, a contemporary painter, derided pointillists as "young chemists who accumulate some small points."[4] Few, however, would agree with such a negative assessment today. The initial unfavorable reception to Seurat's work may have been due to the sheer novelty of the dot technique and a prevailing skepticism within the artistic community toward industrial technology. A radical innovator, Seurat was one of the first artists to see the creative possibilities inherent in commercial mass media printing processes.

The deliberate breaking up of imagery into small dots of pigment, characteristic of Seurat's painting, echoed devel-

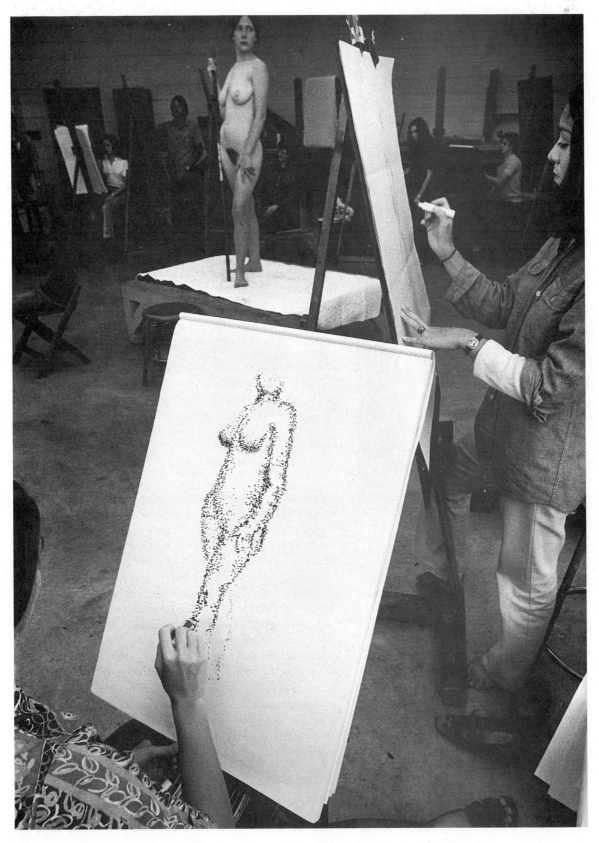

Figure 4-11. Modeling the figure by stippling. A rapid random tapping motion with the marker frees the modeling of unintended linear effects.

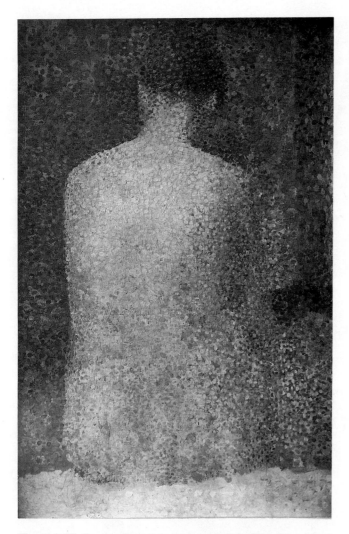

Figure 4-12. Georges Seurat, *La poseuse de Dos*, 1887. Oil on board. 9⅝ × 6¼″. Paris, the Louvre. This is a preparatory sketch for a figure in the painting *Les Poseuses*, "the first of Seurat's pictures to be conceived and executed from the start in small separately applied dots" (Normal Brouse, "New Light on Seurat's 'Dot'; Its Relation to Photo-Mechanical Color Printing in France in the 1880's," *The Art Bulletin,* LVI [Dec. 1974], p. 58.)

opments then occurring in science and technology. The newly invented photographic plate, for example, recorded images composed of dotlike particles of light sensitive silver bromide (i.e., grain). The nineteenth century also witnessed renewed interest in atomic theory, which postulated a world composed of irreducible particles of matter so small that they were comparable to points in space. Language itself was reduced to dots and dashes by means of the new telegraphic code. The most direct link to Seurat's art, however, remains the color printing process,[5] specifically the nineteenth-century *chromotypogravure*,[6] which utilized colored dots to sug-

gest imagery. The way dots are used in printing today is different, however, for at present the standard printed image is composed of evenly spaced dots with varying thicknesses, produced by means of a screen. Because of their even spacing these dots tend to have a smooth, even texture quite different in effect from chromotypogravure. The varying density of dots of chromotypogravure creates a singular richness of texture and tone also found in the paintings of Seurat and in some stipple drawings.

The affinity of stippling with early color printing suggests another application of the technique to drawing. The variety of colors seen in "full-color" reproductions are produced with small dots of only four colors of ink. By using a medium-yellow marker, a process-blue marker, and a magenta marker along with your original black marker, you can create full-color stippling effects. A more practical application of stippling is found in scientific illustration, where the technique is often employed because of its clarity of description and ease of reproduction.

STUDY 17:   Relief Modeling with Continuous Tone

materials: ❑ 36 × 24″ newsprint pad
 ❑ easel or straight-back chair
 ❑ Masonite or plywood board and clamps
 ❑ black or brown medium-soft or soft drawing crayon
reference: ❑ model
time: ❑ 15–30 minutes

The traditional drawing crayon is an effective instrument for modeling. If it is held with the broad side against the paper and moved sideways back and forth, it produces a grainy but unbroken (i.e., continuous) dark tone. The tone can be deepened by either moving the crayon over the paper for a longer time, while maintaining an even pressure against it, or by pressing harder—the stronger pressure producing a correspondingly darker tone. The relationship between the tone and the pressure makes crayon especially useful in pushing back the receding forms in a drawing. Too much pressure, however, can break the crayon, so it is more practical to make several strokes with moderate pressure to obtain the darkest tones. While drawing with the broad side of the crayon you may experience beneficial feedback, for the limitations imposed by the wide tonal mark may encourage you to see and draw primarily the larger masses and volumes of the figure—a most worthy objective in relief modeling.

A drawing period of fifteen minutes is suitable for your first attempt at modeling with the crayon. Holding the crayon on its broad side, establish the general shape of the figure first with a light tone without attempting to model forms within. Keep the figure shape vague and fuzzy. With this shape es-

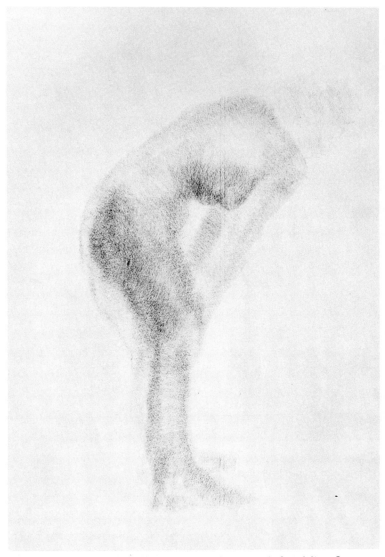

Figure 4-13. Student drawing (early stage). Study in relief modeling. Crayon on newsprint paper. 36 × 24″. Even in the beginning stages the drawing should encompass the general forms to be modeled. Holding the crayon with the flat side against the paper permits the artist to model general form without linear effects.

tablished on the drawing paper you then can begin to search out the receding surfaces of the massive forms of the body—trunk, head, and limbs—as distinct from smaller parts or details of the forms (Figure 4-13). At this stage it is advisable to work continuously over the whole figure as much as possible.

An analogy with sculptural relief offers a key to the technique of relief modeling. While drawing a receding form of the figure try imagining that you are pushing back the clay in a relief when you apply pressure to the crayon on the drawing page (Figure 4-14). In principle relief modeling is simple enough to produce satisfactory results on the first try, yet it challenges the most experienced draftsman. After a few fifteen-minute studies you may wish to increase the drawing period to thirty minutes or more to develop a modeled figure

more completely (Figure 4-15). In an extended drawing period you may prefer to establish the size and placement of the figure with contour line as a reference for modeling with tone (Figure 4-14). Lightly drawn contour line will best serve the purpose because it will permit changes as the drawing develops.

Modeling in Tone and in Clay

The close relationship between relief modeling in drawing and in sculpture is especially clear in the work of certain artists. The work of the French artist Honoré Daumier (1808–1879) offers a case in point. As a political caricaturist Daumier

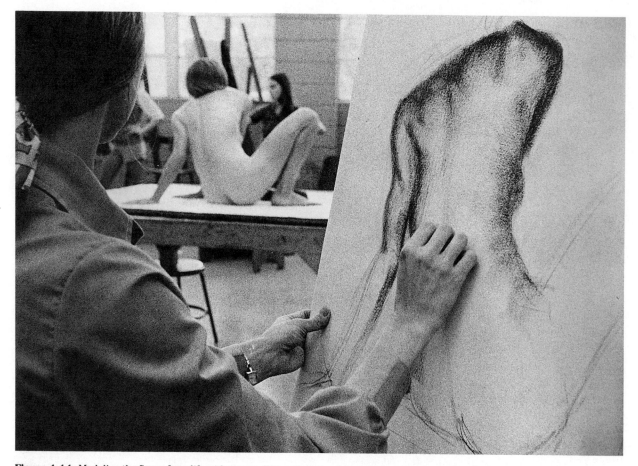

Figure 4-14. Modeling the figure from life with crayon. Forms that recede or turn in space can be "pushed back" in the drawing by putting more pressure on the crayon to produce correspondingly darker tone.

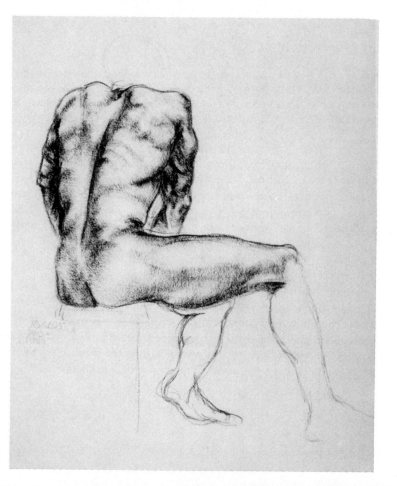

Figure 4-15. Student drawing. Figure viewed from the back. Crayon on newsprint paper. 36 × 24″. Relief modeling creates a sense of volumes only suggested by the preliminary contour-line drawing, still visible in the lower portion of this study.

often modeled his subjects in clay before drawing them with lithographic crayon. This method enabled the artist to experiment with different viewpoints of the clay portrait and to select the angle from which the subject's salient features are visible. Daumier heightened the realistic effect by painting the clay bust before drawing it.

In creating the sculpture and lithograph of the French deputy Ganneron (Figures 4-16 and 4-17), Daumier

> concentrated on warping the structure of the head itself. Ganneron, with his huge lumpy brow hiding his tiny eyes, his crooked potato nose, and his big broad chin, is . . . one of Daumier's most extraordinary conceptions. . . . The translation of the [sculptured] bust with its large, smooth, irregular areas into broad areas of lights and darks is especially successful in this lithograph. The bronze, one of the first cast, also reproduces these largely modeled areas particularly well.[7]

Beyond their satirical intent, Daumier's caricatures attest to an underlying humanism and a high artistic quality that continues to set a standard for the serious artist who wishes to employ relief modeling in drawing the human form.

Figure 4-16. Honoré Daumier (1808–1879), *Ganneron.* Bronze cast from the artist's unfired painted clay sculpture. 179 mm high. Washington, D.C., National Gallery of Art. Lessing J. Rosenwald Collection.

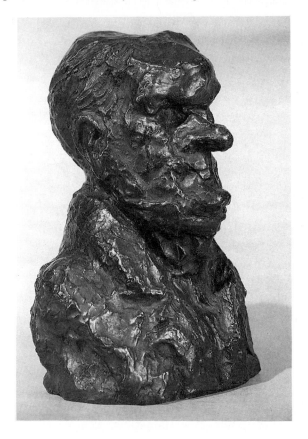

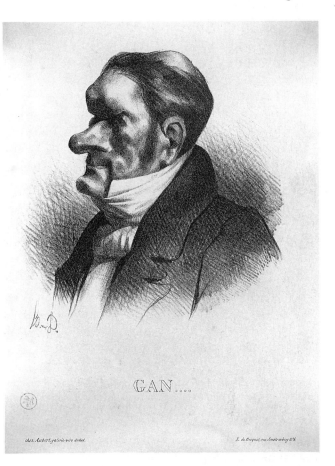

Figure 4-17. Honoré Daumier, *Gan. . . . L.D.* Illustration from *Charivari,* September 6, 1833. Lithograph on white paper. 142 × 132 mm. Boston Public Library. A wealthy manufacturer of candles and president of the French Chamber of Commerce, Ganneron became a subject of political caricature as a result of his strong support of the July Monarchy. During his long career as a journalist-illustrator Daumier produced over four thousand lithographs, many of which satirized the restored French monarchy. The artist himself was a Republican.

STUDY 18: **Modeling Actual Size**

materials: ❑ 36 × 24″ newsprint pad
❑ easel or straight-back chair
❑ Masonite or plywood board and clamps
❑ drawing crayon
reference: ❑ model
time: ❑ 30 minutes

If you wish to explore bolder effects of relief modeling, drawing on a larger scale can be rewarding. The broad area of tone produced by the side of the crayon is well suited to drawing on a large scale. Drawing life size affords an additional advantage: You can use your own body as a rough measure to check the accuracy of the drawing (Figure 4-18). An actual size

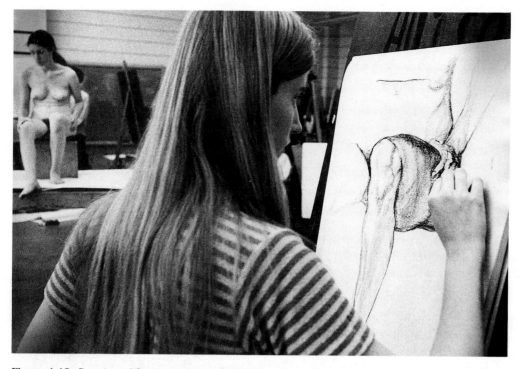

Figure 4-18. Drawing a life-size study in relief modeling of one portion of the figure. Darkly modeled surfaces correspond to the volumes seen in the model, not to the effect of observed light and shadow.

drawing of the whole figure cannot fit on a newsprint pad, of course, so this study focuses on a more limited objective: a selected portion of the figure.

Even when drawing only a portion of the figure it helps to understand how that portion relates to the whole. For this reason it is useful to begin with a small contour study of the entire figure on the margin of the page (Figure 4-19). No more than one minute is needed for this thumbnail sketch. As you work on the preliminary sketch, you are likely to notice one region of the figure that has particular visual interest, either in terms of form or as a challenge to your drawing skills. Let it be the subject of your actual size study.

Begin the actual size study by developing it lightly in contour, taking care to draw the selected portion as large as it appears. If you decide to draw an arm, for example, try using your own arm to estimate roughly the size. Your drawing may include more than the area selected. If so, simply model the portion you wish to study, and leave the rest of the drawing in line. The modeling procedure is the same as for Study 16, but the larger scale will enable you to model more boldly, taking advantage of broader tonal effects of the crayon. Thirty minutes is sufficient for a study of this kind, not counting the time for the preliminary sketch.

For your first experiments with actual size modeling two suggestions may prove helpful: (1) Avoid drawing the head at first. Later, when you have acquired a mastery of the relief modeling technique, you will be able to model the head as sculptural form integrated with the rest of the figure, without

Figure 4-19. Student drawing. Life-size study of the arm. Crayon on newsprint paper. 36 × 24″. Above the life-size study is a small preliminary sketch of the entire figure.

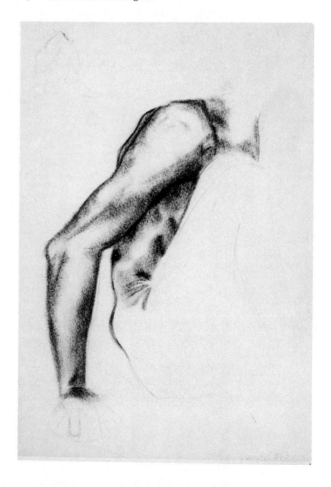

succumbing to the temptation of cliché facial features. (2) Use your design sense. Drawing and design are often closely linked, especially in a drawing of this type.[8] You may find it helpful to select the area for your study by sketching a rectangle around that part of the figure in the preliminary sketch. In the following study compositional design is a primary consideration.

STUDY 19:   Modeling Nonsequential Forms

materials: ❏ 36 × 24″ newsprint pad
          ❏ easel or straight-back chair
          ❏ Masonite or plywood board and clamps
          ❏ drawing crayon
reference: ❏ model
   time: ❏ 20–30 minutes

Within a single gesture certain passages of bodily form appear more interesting than others as subjects for modeling, as you can see in Study 18. Although such passages are usually drawn in the context of a unified, figural structure, they can be divorced from it and modeled as abstract form, which is the focus of this study. A preliminary study of the whole figure is therefore not needed. Instead, you can start by looking for regions of the figure with special visual qualities, paying particular attention to transitions of intersecting planes, recessive turns of form, or forms around a negative space—in short, forms that are well suited to modeling.

Draw first the passage of form that interests you most. After modeling that portion to your satisfaction, you may begin another part or region without regard to its location in the context of the figure. You may, for example, complete a drawing of an upper region of the body and then model a lower portion above or beside the first (Figure 4-20). The

Figure 4-20. Modeling body forms as separate elements out of the context of figure structure.

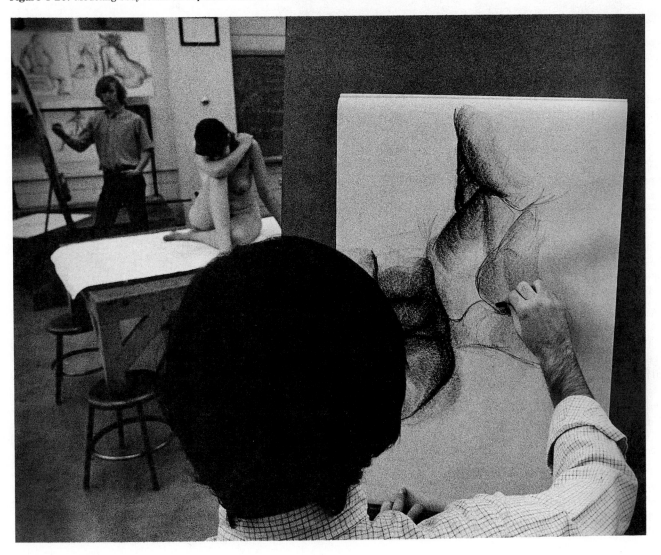

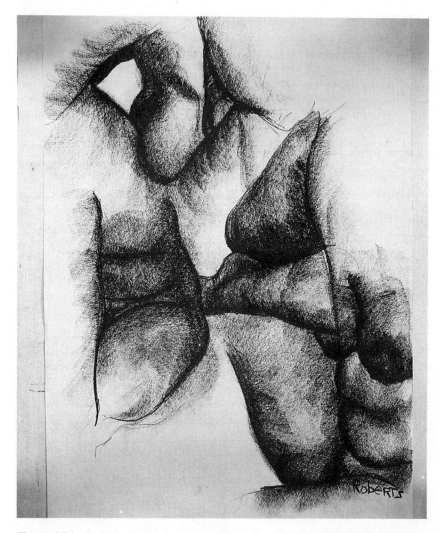

Figure 4-21. Student drawing. Nonsequential forms of the human body. Crayon on newsprint paper. 36 × 24″.

two portions may overlap and fuse together as you move from one part of the drawing to another. Feel free to change your view of the model. When you have exhausted the possibilities of the figure as seen from one viewpoint, move to another location in the studio and continue the same procedure from the new point of view.

Nonsequential drawing may enable you to compose more freely because it permits you to select parts of the figure for study without the constraints imposed by the natural structure that normally governs relationships between parts of the figure and the whole (Figure 4-21). This is an enjoyable study. With the complexities of body structure set aside temporarily, you can indulge in the more sensuous aspect of modeling—searching out surfaces that lend themselves to tonal description as abstract volumes. Relief modeling offers an effective way of seeing the figure in abstract terms, for, like line, it interprets form without recourse to naturalistic effects of light and shadow.

RELIEF MODELING AND THE PERCEPTION OF FORM

Although natural lighting on the model can simulate the tonal effects used by the artist in relief modeling, as for example when the viewer and the light source trained on the model come from the same point (imagine you are wearing a miner's hat with the light turned on the model), such circumstances seldom occur in nature.

Relief modeling is not based on observed effects of natural light; it is rather an artificial artistic convention with a long history.[9] The antiquity of relief modeling in representational art attests to its illusionistic power and causes us to wonder how this modeling convention communicates the roundness of form so vividly. At present there is no definitive answer; however, recent studies in the field of visual perception point to texture as an important factor. It appears that relief modeling is related to our perception of form through surface texture.

In its broadest aspect relief modeling is an approach to drawing that utilizes textural and tonal values to describe form. Texture and tone play key roles in the visual perception of form in nature as well as in art. Although people often perceive tone (shadow) and texture of an object simultaneously, each has distinguishing qualities. Shadows are determined by such variable factors as the type of illumination (i.e., directional or diffused) on the object and the position of the viewer with respect to the light source and the object. Consequently, shadows in nature tend to be ephemeral, changing with the time of day. Under harsh direct lighting conditions the side of an object that faces the sun shields the back side from the light, casting a shadow over it. Unlit parts of the object may appear to vanish into a uniformly dark pattern of cast shadow. Photographs often record this type of image simplification. Such cast shadows do not necessarily clarify the form of the object: They sometimes have quite the opposite effect by creating misleading visual patterns, though these can also be of interest to the artist.

Unlike shadow, textural elements are often a permanent feature of the object's surface. Not entirely dependent on lighting conditions, texture can be perceived not only visually but also through the sense of touch, the sense that is associated with the perception of solid form. Studies by the psychologist James J. Gibson confirm that uniform surface-texture patterns provide important visual cues that assist human perception of three-dimensional forms and their orientation in space.[10]

The key roles that texture and tone play in the perception of form can be demonstrated by examining their appearance on a simple object, the faceted column (Figure 4-22). If the viewer is situated in the same location as the source of light (S), facet (A) appears lighter in value than the other facets (B and C) of the column (Figure 4-23). In this arrangement facet (A) reflects more light to the viewer for two reasons. (1) As the plane nearest the light source, A is illuminated before the light weakens as a result of diffusion by distance; thus it reflects more light than the more distant planes B and C. (2) Facing both the light source and the viewer, facet (A) tends to reflect more light in that direction than in other directions—in other words, it acts somewhat like a dull mirror.[11] Facets (B) and (C), on the other hand, are turned away from the light source and the viewer. For this reason they not only present less reflective surface to the light source but also reflect less light in the direction of the viewer, who as a result perceives them as darker in tone than facet (A).

When a column with more facets is illuminated in a similar way (Figure 4-24), the gradation from light to dark is more gradual. In a fully rounded column the gradation of tone may be imperceptibly smooth, but the principle seen in the faceted column prevails; that is, surfaces of an object appear darker if they are turned away or more distant from the viewer.

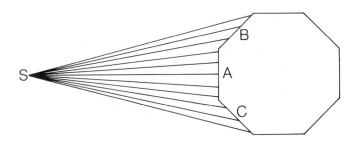

Figure 4-22. Leonardo da Vinci, diagram from his *Treatise on Painting*. (S) represents the source of light and the position of the viewer observing facets (A,B,C) of an octagonal column from above.

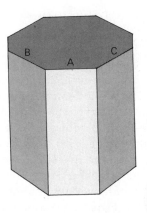

Figure 4-23. Octagonal column. Seen from (S), the position of the viewer, the surfaces of the column appear to have different values. Facet (A), a plane that faces the viewer and the source of light, reflects a greater amount of light toward (S) than the planes (A,B), which are turned at an angle from the viewer.

Figure 4-24. Sixteen-sided column. A greater differentiation of tonal values occurs if the octagonal column becomes a 16-sided column. The tone of each facet is an expression of its orientation with respect to the viewer.

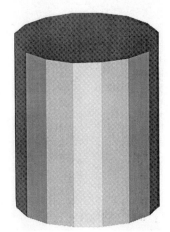

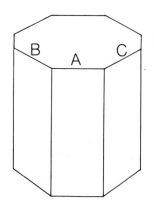

Figure 4-25. The octagonal column represented without tonal values.

A surprisingly similar result occurs if a column is drawn merely as a faceted surface without regard to the effects of light (Figure 4-25). This is demonstrated by subdividing the facets of the column so it becomes successively a 16-sided polygon (Figure 4-26), a 32-sided polygon (Figure 4-27), and a 64-sided polygon (Figure 4-28). As with the illuminated column, surfaces that turn away from the viewer appear darker, and the column looks as if it were modeled in relief. A comparable effect of roundness can be observed in a photograph of a cylinder (Figure 4-81) with a surface pattern of equally spaced vertical lines. The principal difference between the drawing and the photograph is the apparent progressive thinning of line width near the edge of the cylinder. In both figures the apparent roundness of surface is suggested primarily by the changing intervals of the vertical lines, which the eye interprets as a regular surface texture. In order to account for this let us consider how the eye gathers visual information.

When viewing an object the eye focuses an image (or *array*) on the retina, the inner back surface of the eyeball. Like the image inside a camera viewfinder, the size of the object's

Figure 4-26. The 16-faceted column shown without tonal values.

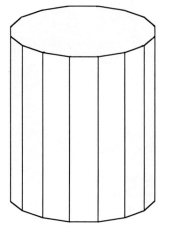

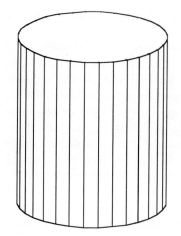

Figure 4-27. A 32-sided column.

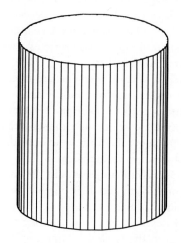

Figure 4-28. A 64-sided column. The apparent contraction of facet width near the sides of the column produces a gradual change of texture and tone that suggests recession and roundness of form. Compare with the tonal and textural changes in Picasso's *Self-Portrait* (Figure 4-33).

retinal image varies with distance (Figure 4-29): The more distant the object, the smaller the absolute size of its retinal image.[12] Another factor that affects the size of the retinal image is the orientation of the object in space with respect to the eye (Figure 4-30). When an object is turned with respect to the viewer, as in Figure 4-30, the corresponding retinal image contracts.

The retinal image of a surface composed of equal elements of a texture likewise exhibits size variations in accordance with the orientation and distance of each element (Figure 4-31). When the elements being viewed form a plane, there results a retinal image in which the elements appear graduated from large to small, with the most distant represented by the smallest component. The optical contraction of the elements in the retinal image (visible in diagrammatic form in Figure 4-31) produces a ratio that the visual system recognizes as

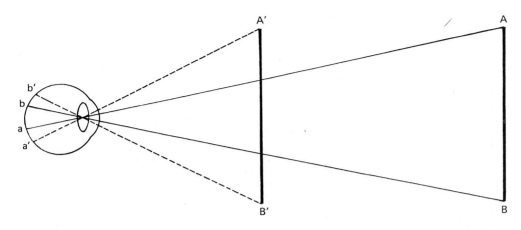

Figure 4-29. The retinal image. An object's image on the retina of the eye varies according to the object's distance from the eye. Bars (AB) and (A'B') are identical in size, but (A'B'), which is nearer to the eye, produces a larger retinal image (a'b') than image (ab) projected by (AB).

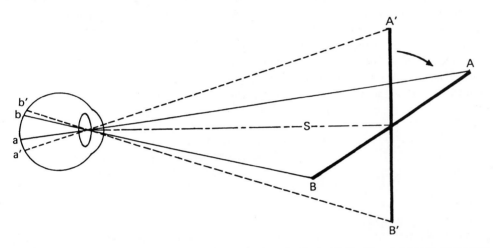

Figure 4-30. The retinal image. The orientation of a plane (or line) with the line of sight affects the size of the retinal image. If bar (A'B') turns from a position of 90-degree alignment with the line of sight (S) to a new position (AB), the retinal image contracts from (a'b') to (ab).

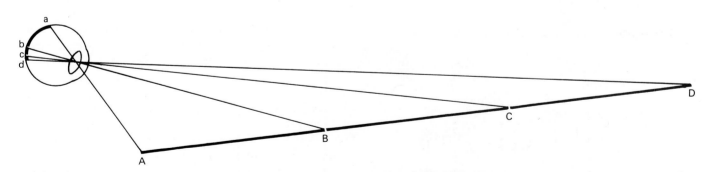

Figure 4-31. The retinal image. (Illustration after Ulric Neisser, "The Processes of Vision," *Scientific American*, vol. 219, no. 3 [Sept. 1968], pp. 206–207.) Elements of equal length result in a retinal image in which their projected lengths diminish in a specific proportion. This proportional reduction in image size, the gradient of texture density, informs the observer of the orientation and character of the surface. A common instance is observed in railroad track ties, which gradually appear to become more closely spaced with distance but are perceived as evenly spaced. The same phenomenon occurs on a smaller scale with such textures as cloth, hair, and skin.

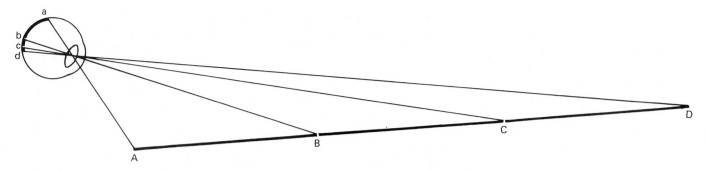

Figure 4-32. The retinal image. If equal elements are turned, as on the surface of a column, the proportional contraction of the retinal image is greater than that seen if the elements form a flat surface (as in Figure 4-31). The contraction of retinal image caused by distance is enhanced by the changing orientation of the elements. Compare with Figure 4-28.

specific to a flat surface. When, however, the equal-size elements are arranged so as to turn at equal angles with one another (Figure 4-32), a sharper gradient of texture density results, which is particularly noticeable in the projected retinal images of element (CD). It occurs primarily because of the different orientation of the elements. Although (CD) is the same size in both diagrams, the retinal image (cd) is much smaller in Figure 4-32 than in Figure 4-31. As the actual elements turn away from the viewer, they appear closer together on the retina than they would if they were extended on a flat plane. The resulting difference of gradient thus provides the brain with enough visual information to detect the roundness of surface. Although the physiological process by which the perception of form is accomplished is only partially understood at present, the *gradient of texture density* is believed to play a major role.[13]

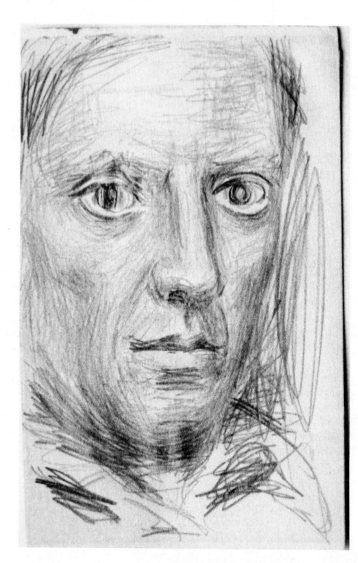

Figure 4-33. Pablo Picasso, *Self-Portrait*, August 11, 1940. Pencil. 6.3 × 4.3″. Geneva, Walters (photo courtesy of Galerie Jan Kruglier). Differences of texture and tone within this work correspond to observed differences of orientation of the surfaces of the head and provide the basis for the effect of relief modeling.

Given the role of texture in the visual perception of form, it makes just as much sense to model form with texture as it does with tone. In fact they often go hand in hand. Stippling, for example, is based on such a union of texture and tone (Figure 4-10). The change of texture seen in a stippled drawing of the figure plays as much a part in describing the form of the figure as the darkened tone where the dots are dense. The "artificial" textures are made to correspond with micro-density gradients of the surfaces of the body. Artificial textures of a similar kind are apparent in Picasso's *Self-Portrait* (Figure 4-33). In this drawing accumulated line strokes serve to model the facial features in relief rather than describe the actual texture of the skin. The lines are freely, almost sketchily drawn; yet they succeed in modeling a complex and irregular form accurately and spontaneously. Receding planes of the head are drawn with closely packed lines; flatter planes are represented with more widely spaced lines. The resulting "artificial" texture is comparable to a gradient of texture density that varies in accordance with the orientation of the surface. The accumulation of lines in the denser areas of the drawing also produces a darker tone, which heightens the relief effect.

By drawing on paper with a textured surface it is possible to model with a texture in a different way. The surface of a woven or laid paper, for example, tends to produce a specific texture when marked with a crayon. A "laid" paper such as that used by Maillol and Seurat, for example, features regularly spaced ridges (tooth) that tend to darken first when a crayon is dragged over the surface (Figures 4-34 and 4-4). The result is a combination of texture and tone well suited to relief modeling, but subtly different from the texture effect in Picasso's *Self-Portrait* (Figure 4-33).

Since the tooth of the paper becomes visible only where it is touched with crayon, texture is virtually absent in the lightest areas of both figures, but fairly evenly spaced in all medium to dark tones. Only in the very darkest areas does the texture once again disappear. Thus, while Seurat and Maillol employ both texture and tone to achieve relief modeling, it is tonal contrast that plays the major role. The insistent, regular linear pattern of the paper texture contributes to the drawings in another way; it adds an overall unifying effect that suppresses detail in favor of larger, more monumental construction. Picasso shared this concern with an earlier artist, Ingres, who, although not a sculptor, warned that "one must not dwell too much on the details of the human body; the members must be, so to speak, like shafts of columns; such they are in the greatest masters."[14]

The drawings by both artists are superb examples of the creative interplay of the drawing surface and the drawing instrument. If you wish to follow the example of Maillol and Seurat by modeling the figure on a laid paper, you will find several brands suitable for this purpose, including Strathmore charcoal paper, Ingres paper (made by Fabriano), and Canson.

The Maillol drawing (Figure 4-4) is a fairly straightforward application of relief modeling. The artist has methodically modeled the figure in terms of large generalized forms. This does not mean he perceived simple forms only, but rather that he exercised creative selectivity, omitting what he felt to be trivial visual information and focusing instead on the more massive forms of the body. Like sculpture in the round, the Maillol figure is an isolated positive form standing alone in the surrounding negative space.

Seurat, however, puts relief modeling to a far more complex and subtle use in his *Study for* Les Poseuses (Figure 4-34). Here the figure is not represented as an isolated form as in the Maillol drawing, but is carefully integrated pictorially in an interior space. Does the artist employ more than relief modeling in this drawing? Perhaps so. On the wall behind the model we see a new element: a diffused cast shadow of the model. Seurat has thus created an enigmatic image that has the formal qualities of relief modeling but seems to cross over into another model of drawing: shadow modeling.

SHADOW MODELING

The natural effects of light and shadow on the model, while not essential to relief modeling, are of considerable visual interest and provide the basis for a fundamentally different approach to tonal modeling.

STUDY 20:   **Shadow Modeling**

materials: ❑ 36 × 24″ newsprint pad
     ❑ soft or medium-soft black or brown drawing crayon (Conté or Nupastel recommended)
     ❑ optional: India ink or acrylic black and water-color brush
reference: ❑ model or cast of sculpture illuminated by 200-watt flood lamp (bell type with clamp)
time: ❑ 20 minutes

The location of the light source with respect to the positions of the artist and model are important in shadow modeling. For this study you should be situated so you can see part of both the illuminated and the shaded sides of the model. If the illuminated side only is visible, the visual effect is the same as in the previous exercise; if the dark side only is visible, a silhouette results. The quality of the light is also important in shadow modeling. An ordinary window can provide sufficiently directional illumination, but you may prefer to use an artificial light source such as a flood lamp for a clearer division between light and shadow. A flood lamp with a bell-type reflector can be raised or lowered with respect to the model

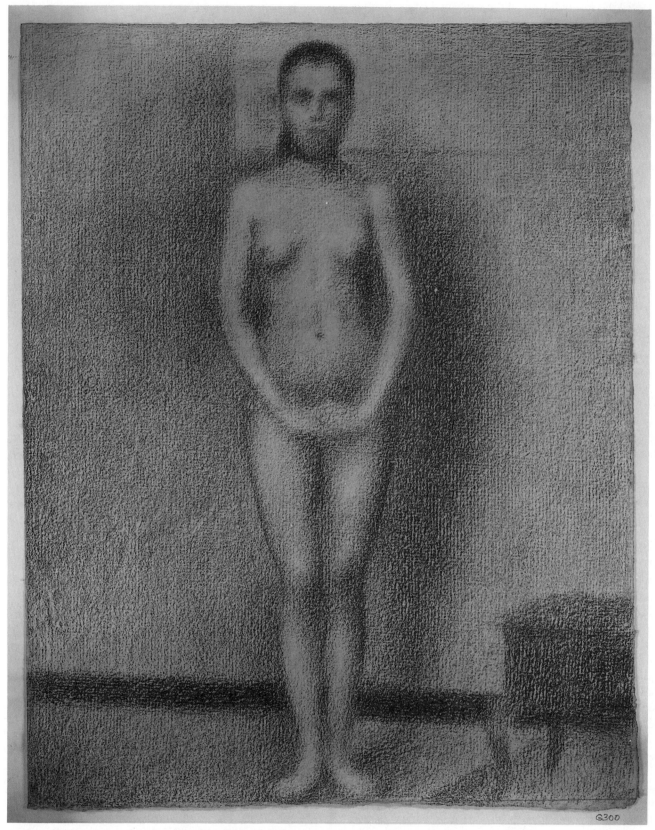

Figure 4-34. Georges Seurat, *Study for* Les Poseuses, c. 1887. Conté crayon on Ingres paper. 29.7 ×
22.5 cm. New York, Metropolitan Museum of Art. Robert Lehman Collection, 1975.

in order to discover the most interesting play of light and shadow on the figure. The flood lamp can then be clamped to an easel for support. The advantages of such an arrangement will become apparent as you work.

Shadow modeling is essentially a way of drawing form purely in terms of the patterns of light and shadow observed in the subject. Although this objective is simple in principle, the tonal values that comprise such patterns are often complex: Gradations of value in nature are in fact infinite. It is useful, therefore, to limit the number of tones in your first studies to four, including the white of the paper (Figure 4-35). These four tones, though arbitrary in number, are analogous to four fairly distinct tonal steps that are usually discernible on the model: (1) the areas of the form that reflect the most light; (2) the intermediate tone of surfaces that reflect less light but are not themselves in shadow; (3) the areas in darkest shadow; and (4) the portions of form in shadow that receive some reflected light or the shadow cast by the object onto the ground plane (Figure 4-36).

For your first experiment in shadow modeling, begin by making a carefully constructed line drawing of the figure, and then examine the model for tonal patterns. Look first for the division between intermediate tones (2) and darkest tones (3), a division that is usually a distinct shadow contour. Draw this contour lightly in line; then look for similar divisions between the other tones. If a separation between light (1) and intermediate (2) values is not distinct, simply estimate it. You may

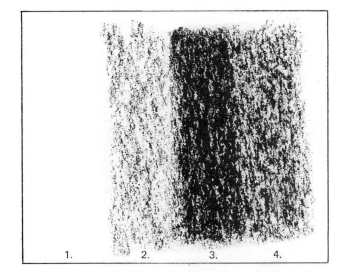

Figure 4-36. Four tones produced by crayon and white paper.

also have to estimate the shadow contour separating the lighter dark (4) within the cast shadow (Figures 4-37 and 4-38). For greater precision the angular method (Study 9 in Chapter 3) can be employed to construct the figure's contours and shadow patterns (Figure 4-40).

When the shadow contours are complete, you can use the broad side of the crayon to apply even tones within them in accordance with the four shades shown in Figure 4-36. In your first studies resist the temptation to rub and blend the tonal gradations of the drawing. The unblended tones show the grain of the paper and contribute a unifying texture that rubbing tends to destroy. The crisp contours also permit easy corrections.

By limiting the tones in number you may find it easier to develop and control the value relationships within the drawing, which is especially important in a complex compositional study (Figures 4-41 and 4-44). Some shadow contours may enclose a tonal area extending the entire length of the figure; others may form separate islands of tone. The larger patterns generally lend visual cohesion and unity to the drawing.

Shadow Modeling with the Brush

Restricting the number of tones in a crayon drawing may seem arbitrary, given the ease with which the tones blend into smooth gradations. In a liquid medium such as watercolor, however, there is a practical advantage to limiting the tones. A watercolor tone is usually applied with a brush loaded with wash (pigment highly diluted in water). In order to model with some degree of control, wait for the first wash to dry before applying another wash. This process takes time, and it is best to keep the number of washes to a minimum if you wish to complete the drawing in one sitting (Figure 4-39). You can see a superb example of shadow modeling

Figure 4-35. Light and shadow effects on a white hexagonal prism. A light source on the right side produces four distinct tones ranging from white to dark gray, with two middle tones for the prism's center and top.

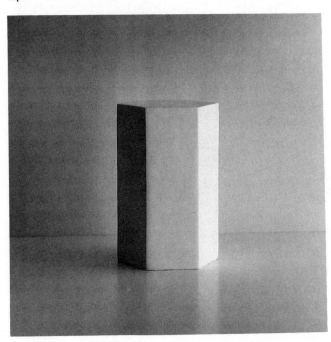

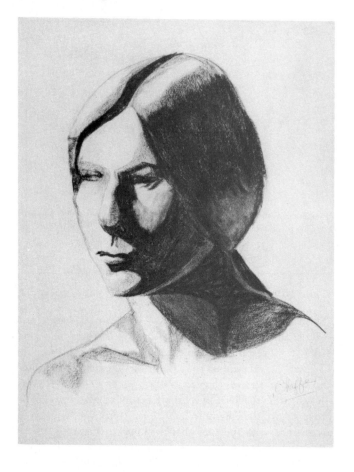

Figure 4-37. Student drawing. Life-size portrait. Crayon on newsprint pad. 36 × 24″. It is useful to limit the number of tones in shadow modeling. Here there are four tonal values, counting the white of the paper.

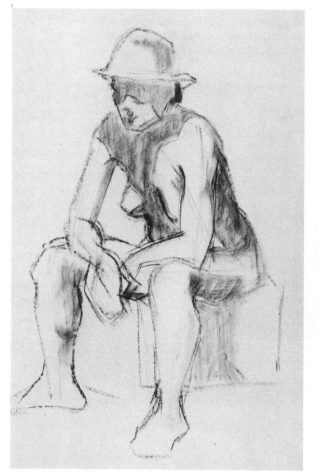

Figure 4-38. Student drawing. Crayon on newsprint pad. 36 × 24″. Study of the figure with shadow modeling. Angular measurement was employed to describe shadow patterns. The cast shadow patterns of the hat describe the head and chest of the figure.

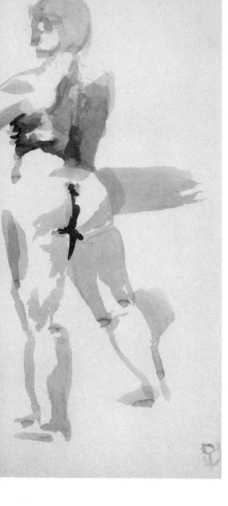

Figure 4-39. Student drawing. Ink wash on bond pad. 24× 18″.

Figure 4-40. Henri de Toulouse-Lautrec (1864–1901), *The Model Nizzavona.* Charcoal. Courtesy of The Art Institute of Chicago. In modeling the figure the artist made a careful estimate of the shadow contours, blocking them with the same precise angular measurements seen in the rest of the drawing. The flexibility of the charcoal medium is seen in the redrawing of the head and neck.

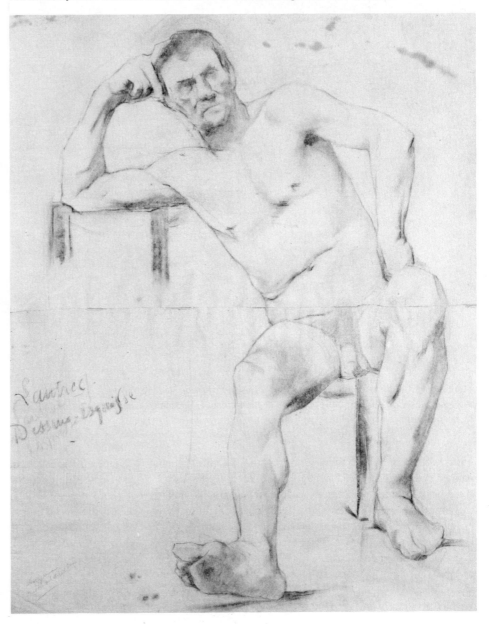

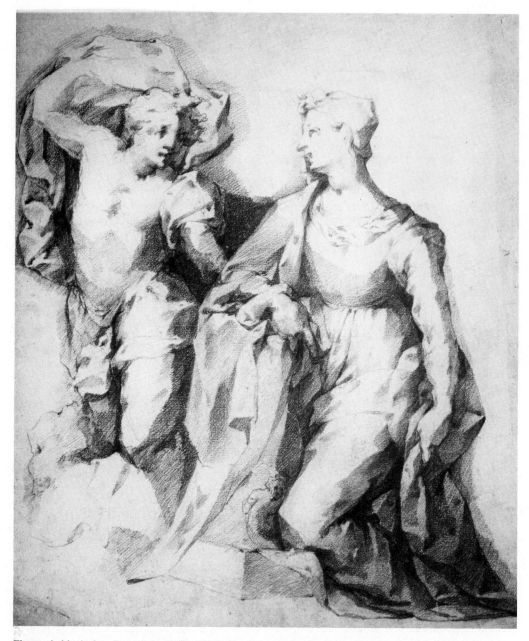

Figure 4-41. Andrea Boscoli (c. 1560–1607), *The Annunciation*. Red crayon. 14¼ × 11⅜″. Cambridge, Fogg Art Museum, Harvard University. The shadow modeling in this drawing remains clearly visible as an orderly progression of value steps from light to dark.

with watercolor in a drawing (Figure 4-42) by the French painter Théodore Géricault (1794–1824). The layered washes are especially evident in the head area, where, incidentally, the tones appear to correspond in number with those recommended in the preceding crayon study (Figure 4-43). Dense cast shadows dramatically define the figure and separate it spatially from the shallow depth of the tonal background, implying a single light source illuminating the model from above.

The peculiar qualities of an artificial light source are evi-

dent in a brush and wash drawing of the figure by the American artist Philip Pearlstein (Figure 4-44). The multiple layers of sharp-edged shadows cast by the right leg on the left as well as those seen under the right foot are characteristic effects of the incandescent lamp, and are used expressively by the artist to dramatize the figure. They find echo in the banded pattern of the bed cover. A less obvious, but instructive feature of the artist's method can be seen in the faint dotted lines drawn to map shadow contours of the figure before laying in the wash.

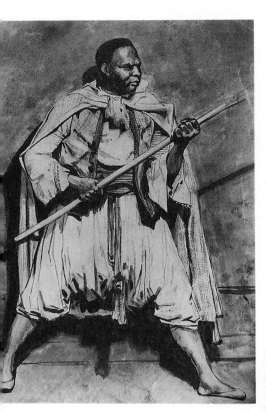

Figure 4-42. Théodore Géricault (1791–1824), *Soldier Holding a Lance*, 1820–1824. Brush with brown and gray wash. 13³⁄₁₆ × 9¹³⁄₁₆″. Cambridge, Fogg Art Museum, Harvard University. Bequest of Meta and Paul J. Sachs.

Figure 4-43. Théodore Géricault, *Soldier Holding a Lance* (detail), 1820–1824. The figure's head reveals a series of discrete tonal steps from light to dark, applied as watercolor washes.

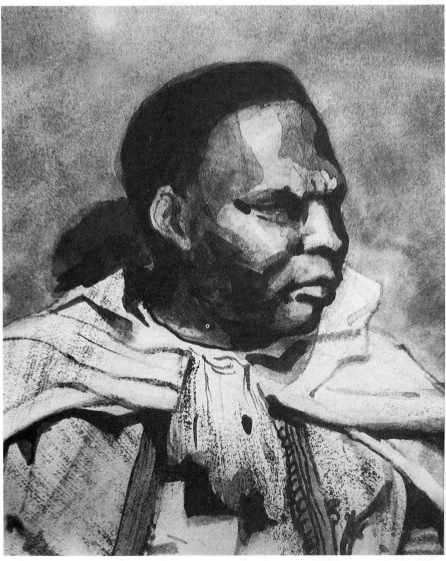

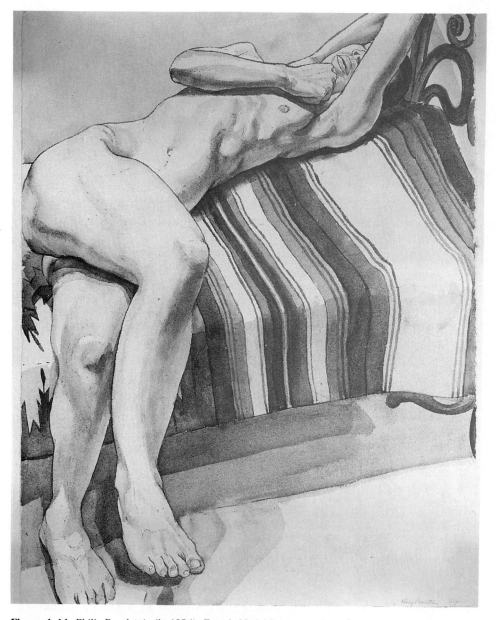

Figure 4-44. Philip Pearlstein (b. 1924), *Female Model Lying on a Bed, Feet on Floor.* Brush and brown wash on heavy paper. 29¾ × 22⁷⁄₁₆″. Baltimore Museum of Art.

Cast Shadows

When a strong directional light is trained on the model, some parts of the body are likely to throw shadows on other parts, resulting in an effect peculiar to shadow modeling. Cast shadows of this sort are found in student drawings (see Figures 4–37 and 4–38). In both drawings the head casts a shadow on the shoulder of the figure. By interpreting the cast shadows as abstract shapes—again applying the method of visual measurement—you will be able to draw them without difficulty. They are of interest for the way they can relate one form with another without their being perceived as forms themselves. Leonardo recognized the special nature of such shadows, and advised artists to "Take care that the shadows cast upon the surface of [a] body by different objects undulate according to the various curves of the limbs which cast the shadows and of the objects on which they are cast."[15] In some master drawings the cast shadow effect plays a major role in dramatizing form. In the *Self-Portrait* (Figure 4-45) by the Swiss artist Henry Füseli (1741–1825), for example, the cast shadow patterns create contours that describe not only the volumes of the arm and the head but also those of the much smaller forms,

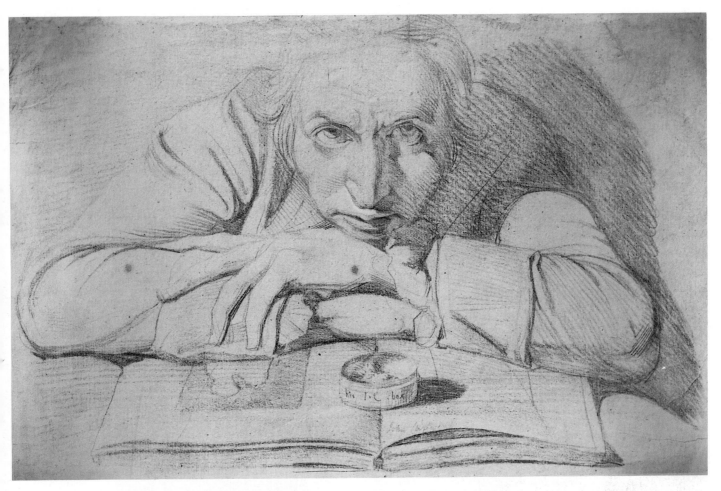

Figure 4-45. Henry Füseli (1741–1825), *Self-Portrait.* Black chalk with white. London, National Portrait Gallery.

including the eyeball. The calculated consistency of Füseli's shadow modeling is responsible for the luminous, transparent quality of the work.

A similar transparency of shadow is achieved in a charcoal drawing entitled *Dark Background* by the contemporary American artist Wayne Thiebaud (Figure 4-46). True to Leonardo's dictum, the cast shadows in this drawing "undulate according to the various curves" of the figure, an effect underscored in places by emphatic shadow contours. The crisply defined shadow patterns become expressive elements themselves, adding unexpected visual drama and fusing the dark background with the figure in a symmetrical composition of stark monumentality.

TRANSPARENCY

The effect of *transparency* of shadows represented in drawings touches on a curious principle of everyday human perception known in psychology as *value constancy*.[16] Value constancy is best explained by a visual example of a folded piece of paper (Figure 4-47). If the folded paper is illuminated from one side, it seems lighter in value on that side than on the other, yet we tend to perceive the whole paper as uniform (constant) in value. Although the principle of value constancy is simple, how it works is less so. It appears that memory of past visual experiences is an important factor. The observer is conditioned by experience to recognize that a strong light source causes an object of uniform color to appear darker on the shadow side. Since a shadow cast by the object often extends to neighboring surfaces or nearby objects, the continuity of the shadow can act as a visual cue to favor perception of the uniform tone of the object. This can be demonstrated by covering the cast shadow at the base of the folded paper in Figure 4-47. With the cast shadow covered, the folded paper appears to consist of two pieces, a gray and a white, instead of a single sheet of folded white paper.

In shadow modeling the transparency effect of shadow patterns likewise depends on the consistency and continuity of those patterns in relation to the forms drawn. It is therefore

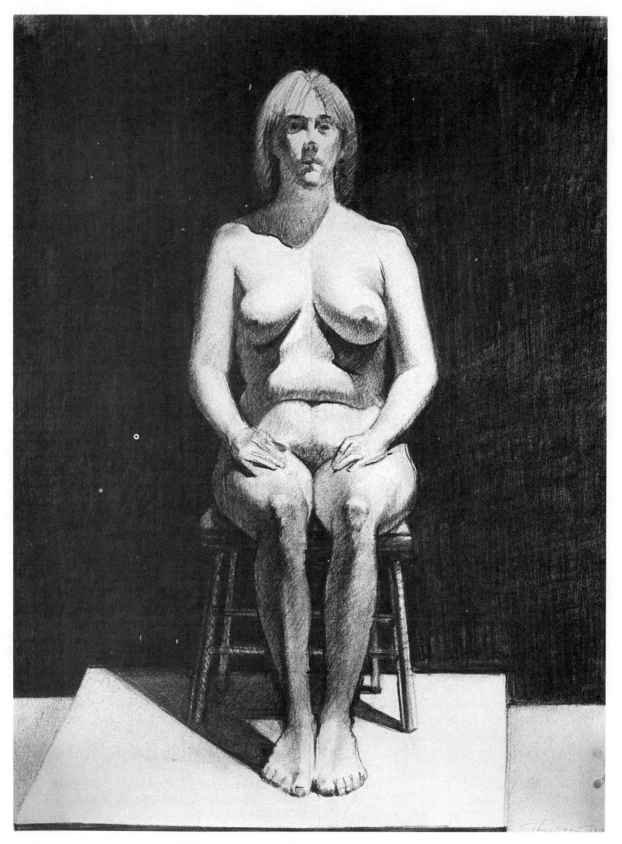

Figure 4-46. Wayne Thiebaud (b. 1920), *Dark Background*, 1976. Charcoal. 30 × 22″ (photo courtesy Thiebaud-Campbell Gallery, San Francisco).

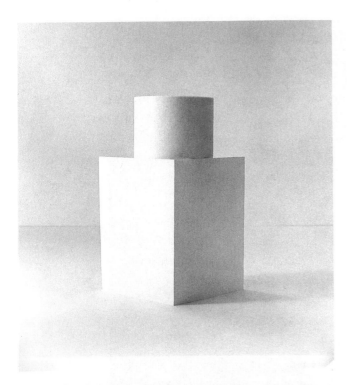

Figure 4-47. Value constancy: folded paper and a cylinder. Despite the apparent differences of tone caused by light and shadow, both the folded paper and the cylinder are perceived as uniform (constant) in value—white. The cylinder displays a more graduated value change, which enhances the effect of value constancy. The cast shadow at the base of the folded paper reinforces the effect of value constancy.

important to draw shadows as continuous patterns so they are perceived as natural effects of light on integral form rather than simply as separate darker areas or objects. In shadow modeling the effect of light on the subject thus assumes an importance on a par with the form of the subject represented. In some drawings, as we will see, light and shadow truly become part of the subject.

Your studio experience with shadow modeling and relief modeling will demonstrate how they differ technically. They also differ conceptually. Shadow modeling encourages the artist to observe and attempt to capture natural tonal relationships as they appear under specific lighting conditions. The temporary and ephemeral aspect of light is of paramount importance. In relief modeling, on the other hand, the values of light and dark are based on an imaginary, timeless light source. Such a close association with an imaginary, unchanging source of light suggests profound philosophical differences between the two drawing methods.

The artist who adopts the shadow modeling technique shares some of the same concerns as the photographer who takes pictures in available natural light, yet few people would mistake a photograph for a drawing! The physical difference between the surface of a drawing and the chemical bromide surface of the photograph is usually self-evident. Unless the

drawing is itself based on a photograph, another factor distinguishes the photographic process from the drawing process—human binocular vision. The human visual system, unlike most cameras, normally gathers visual information from at least two points in space. Also, the slight shifts of position that usually accompany the drawing process permit many more points of view. Drawings made by direct observation of a subject are thus the result of a process that encompasses more *spatial* information about form than is seen in most photographs, a fact which both enriches and distinguishes drawings even when shadow modeling is restricted to only a few tonal steps.

Shadow Modeling
and Directional Lighting

In a lithograph (Figure 4-48) by the German artist Käthe Kollwitz (1867–1945), shadow modeling yields an almost sculptural sense of form, emphasizing the general structure of the head illuminated by a low source of light, suggestive of a hearth. Intended as a poster for a homecraft exhibition, the shadow modeling in the lithograph becomes part of the expressive content of the work. A related charcoal drawing—one of several preparatory studies for the poster—reveals how the artist used discrete steps of tone to define form by shadow modeling (Figure 4-49). The tonal steps are especially clear in the lower hand. Beginning, it seems, with a general contour-line construction the artist delineated the boundaries of shadow contours within the outer contours before proceeding to lay in tone. In the study of the head, planes that are commonly modeled with tone, such as the plane under the lower lip and at the base of the nose, are instead left white, in accordance with the directional light from below. It appears that shadow modeling of the structure of the head was her primary objective, more important than the description of facial features, which came last, or, as in the case with the right eye, was simply left out. The unorthodox shadow modeling combined with the artist's masterful draftsmanship confer a poignant grandeur to the poster's humble subject.

It is instructive to compare Kollwitz's use of light and shadow with that of Leonardo, whose ideas on the subject are known through his writings.

> Above all, [he advised,] see that the figures you paint are broadly lighted and from above, that is to say all living persons that you paint; for you will see that all the people you meet out in the street are lighted from above, and you must know that if you saw your most intimate friend with a light (on his face) from below you would find it difficult to recognize him.[17]

Recent studies in the field of visual perception seem to confirm Leonardo's intuition. The human "visual system not

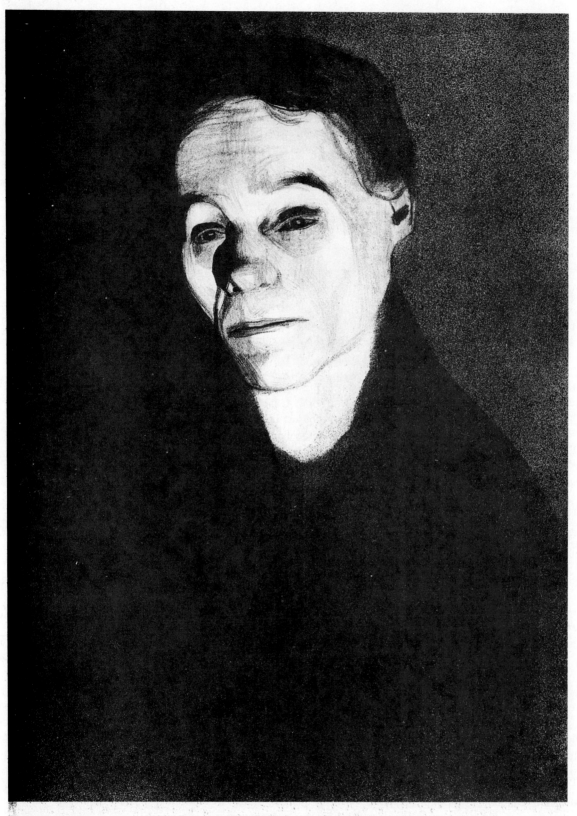

Figure 4-48. Käthe Kollwitz (1867–1945), *The German Homecrafts Exhibition Poster*, 1906. Lithograph. Berlin Kupferstichkabinett and Sammlung der Zeichnungen. The artist selectively stressed the opposing formal values of shape and modeled this haunting figure by reducing the form of the dress and hair to flat shapes while modeling the sculptural form of the face.

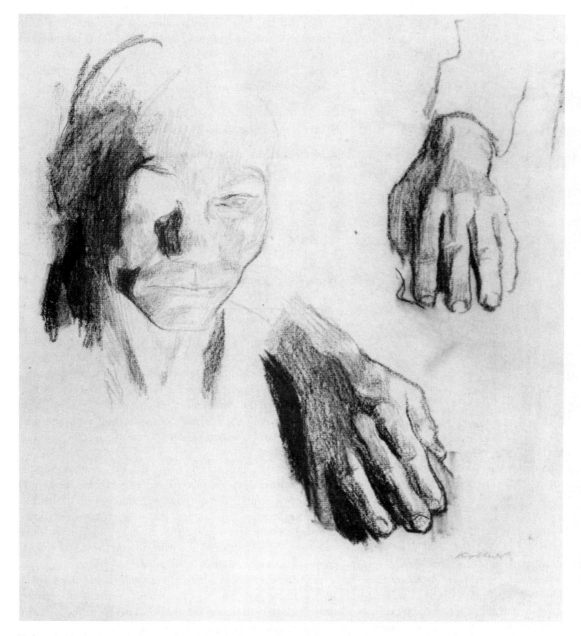

Figure 4-49. Käthe Kollwitz *Studies of the Head and Hands,* 1906. Detail studies for the German Home-crafts Exhibition poster. Charcoal on Ingres paper. 42.5 × 38 cm. Private collection.

only assumes a single light source but also tends to assume, naturally enough, that the light comes from above."[18] The unexpectedly low light source indicated in Kollwitz's shadow modeling thus appears to go against a natural bias in our visual system, a fact which may account in part for the drama of the otherwise conventionally, albeit masterfully drawn head.

Kollwitz's choice of shadow modeling reflects her aims, which were quite different from those of Leonardo. Her work reflects a deep concern with the social conditions of the working class. For this reason it was not important that her subjects be seen as if under an ideal light, nor was it necessary

that the individual be easily recognized as a unique person. Of greater concern was the general humanity of an entire class of people. Her philosophical and political views are thus inseparably connected with the formal means she adopted in her work, just as Renaissance attitudes about individualism and rationalism are related to the works of Leonardo.[19] That the uses of shadow modeling changed and evolved in the four hundred years separating Leonardo and Kollwitz is not surprising, but it is remarkable that this mode of drawing has continued to be a rich expressive vein from the Renaissance into this century.

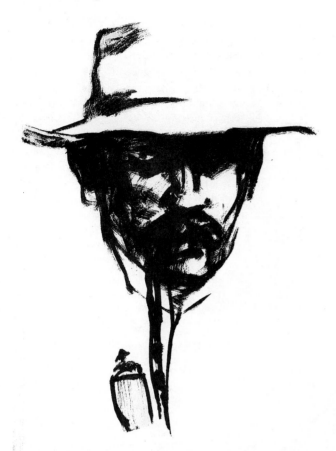

Figure 4-50. Emil Nolde (1867–1956), *Self-Portrait*, 1907. Lithograph. Cambridge, Fogg Art Museum, Harvard University.

The tonal simplification apparent in the works of Kollwitz is carried further still in a *Self-Portrait* (Figure 4-50) by Emil Nolde (1867–1956), who was a compatriot and contemporary of Kollwitz. A master of the woodcut, a medium that dictates a bold black-and-white effect, Nolde imparted a graphic severity to his lithographic *Self-Portrait*. He apparently used a flat-tipped brush dipped in undiluted tusche (lithographic drawing ink), thus ensuring the intensely high contrast apparent in this work. His choice of instrument and medium necessarily reduced the amount of visual information contained in the drawn image, yet, as in the Kollwitz lithograph, a remarkable sense of form and structure remain. For example, although one side of the hat represented in the *Self-Portrait* is not delineated, the portion drawn suggests the entire form. The *Self-Portrait* is not a mere simplified image of the head but rather a reduction that retains a sense of the complexity of form observed in life. Crisp areas of black boldly

model the form in shadow, leaving illuminated parts uniformly white. Here and there Nolde relieves the harshness of pure black and white with the textured marks of the "dry brush." The economy of means inherent in this method makes it well worth exploring.

STUDY 21: **Black-and-White Shadow Modeling**

materials: ❏ 36 × 24″ newsprint pad
❏ easel or straight-back chair
❏ Masonite or plywood panel and clamps
❏ stand or small table
❏ India ink
❏ Japanese brush or flat-tipped long bristle brush (number 6 or 7)
❏ 200-watt flood lamp (optional)
reference: ❏ model
time: ❏ 10 minutes

Several drawing media can be used for this study, including crayon, but liquid media offer advantages. Like the liquid tusche used in lithographs, India ink can be brushed on undiluted. A flat-tipped bristle brush or a Japanese brush is a good carrier of the ink. Both types of brush will last longer if you dip them in clear water before loading with the ink. Excess ink can be wiped off on a scrap of paper before you begin to draw.

The drawing procedure is basically the same as for the previous study: Draw for shadow pattern and form. The black ink makes it possible to compress your description of shadow into a single tone, a reduction that may require several attempts before you are satisfied with the results. This study requires only ten minutes, however, so you should be able to complete several drawings in an hour.

A strong directional light, such as that provided by a single large window or a 200-watt flood lamp, is useful in creating clear shadow patterns on the model. These shadow patterns should be drawn as directly as possible, translating observed dark values into black in the drawing.

If you are not familiar with the brush as a drawing instrument, you may wish to begin your drawing with what is called a *dry brush* technique because it permits light sketching before laying in solid black tones. A brush fully loaded with ink can be prepared for dry brush by blotting it on a piece of scrap paper until the bristles are slightly moist with ink, but incapable of making a solid black stroke. The stroke produced by the dry brush tends to be broken and often registers the texture of the paper in the manner of a crayon. The result can be spontaneous half-tone effects identical to those produced by lithographic tusche in Nolde's *Self-Portrait*.

STUDY 22:   Shadow Modeling and Sketching

materials: ❑ 14 × 11″ bound sketchbook of bond paper
❑ HB drawing pencil and kneaded eraser
❑ single-edge blade for sharpening the pencil
❑ 200-watt flood lamp (optional)
reference: ❑ model
time: ❑ 15 minutes

Shadow modeling, as shown in the previous study, is not limited to drawing sessions of long duration. It adapts surprisingly well to the needs of sketching, not only with the brush, but also with pointed drawing tools, such as the graphite pencil. Modeling with pencil involves no new drawing procedure; the visual measurement of angles will serve to establish the figure on the page, as outlined in Study 9. Once the general contours of the figure are established, you may begin searching out the shapes of the largest shadow patterns, taking special care to define the *terminator lines* (the lines separating shadow areas from lighted areas of the figure) (see Figure 4-51). The visual measurement method is also recommended for establishing the terminator lines. When the terminator lines have been determined, the shadow patterns can simply be filled in with tone. This can be done expediently with closely spaced marks drawn in the same direction.

Figure 4-51. Student drawing. 15-minute study with shadow modeling. Graphite pencil. 14 × 11″ sketchbook page.

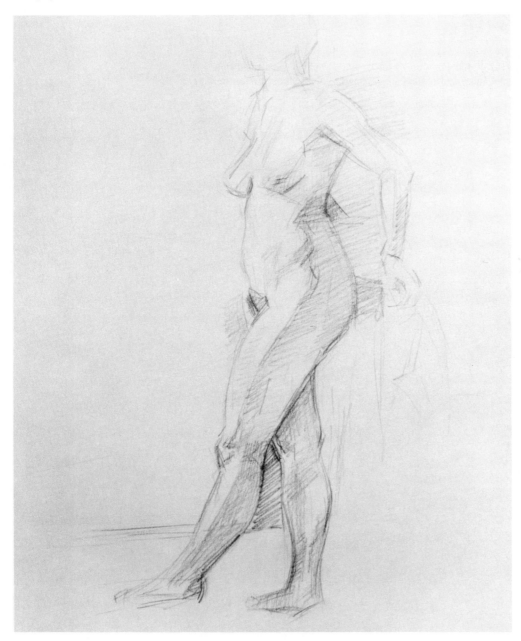

If you prefer a smoother tone, it can be laid in with the pencil held like a crayon, at a low angle. (The low angle has the virtue of sharpening the pencil as you draw the tone.) By linking shadow patterns throughout the figure, whenever possible, a greater sense of formal coherence will result.

A pencil drawing by the German painter Lovis Corinth (1858–1925) demonstrates how a figure can be modeled rapidly with undisguised buildup of marks describing shadow patterns over a preliminary line construction (Figure 4-52). In this case, the shadow patterns, which cover much of the figure, define dramatically the illuminated planes left white within the line drawing. The pencil marks themselves are applied freely in different directions, but in some shadow areas, notably the right arm and hand, they follow the direction of the form. Corinth evidently filled in the shadow patterns throughout the figure as a way of defining borders without drawing terminator lines beforehand. In the same way he established the cast shadow of the figure on the floor plane,

creating a literal figure-ground relationship. In this small drawing—intended as a study for the figure of Abel in a painting—the artist succeeds in combining the spontaneity of the sketch with the solidity of form unique to shadow modeling.

SCULPTURED RELIEF AND SHADOW MODELING

Regardless of the means used to represent it, form remains the element most commonly identified with drawing. Form in nature, however, is often disguised by effects of color. One solution to this problem is offered by sculptures or casts, in which the effects of color are virtually absent. Relief sculptures or, if they are not available, casts of relief sculptures are of special interest to the artist who is also concerned with pictorial form, for sculptured reliefs share many of the qualities of painting. Both painting and relief sculpture usually

Figure 4-52. Lovis Corinth (1858–1925), *Abel Prostrate on the Ground.* Graphite pencil on offwhite laid paper. 12 × 18⅜". Allen Memorial Art Museum, Oberlin College, Oberlin, Ohio. Gift of Thomas Corinth, 61.90.

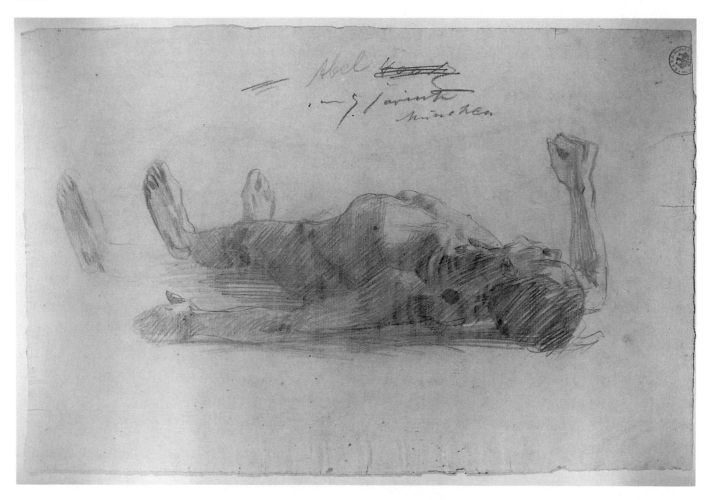

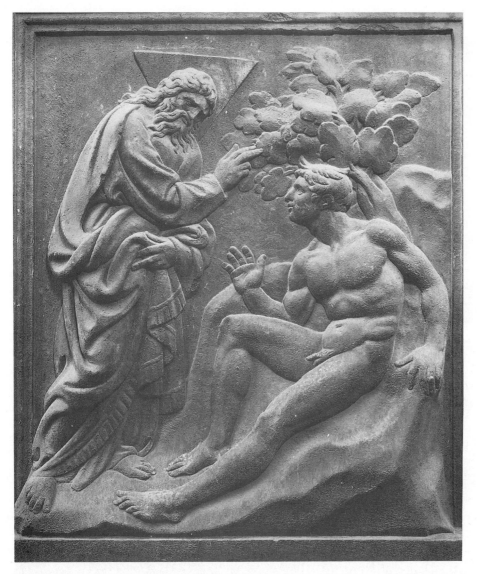

Figure 4-53. Jacopo della Quercia (c. 1374–1438), *The Creation of Adam*, c. 1430. Marble relief. 34½ × 27½″. Bologna, main portal, San Petronio.

function within a rectangular planar format. Although relief sculpture physically modulates the pictorial surface, the surface modulations, like those represented in painting, are in part illusionistic, for the relief represents volumes in a relative rather than an absolute way. In a relief by the Italian sculptor Jacopo della Quercia (1374–1438) entitled *The Creation of Adam* (Figure 4-53), the figure of Adam does not physically rise from the surface to form fully rounded features of the body, as in a free-standing sculpture, but rather protrudes only to the degree necessary to give the *effect* of rounded forms.

Another illusionistic spatial device common to both relief sculpture and painting is that of overlapping form (see Chapter 1). A clear example of overlapping form is seen in the della Quercia panel, in which the head of the figure of God, by interrupting the triangular form of a halo, appears to be in front of it. Such spatial relationships as overlapping form and the relative representation of volumes are most apparent

if the reliefs are illuminated, as they often are, by a directional light source. Under such lighting conditions the tonal values observed on the relief are a remarkably clear function of form (Figures 4-53 and 4-54). The highest values occur on the leading edges of planes that face the direction of the light source. Here a clear separation of values occurs between the darker tones of the adjoining plane. Like a line, the separation corresponds to a discontinuity of surface in the sculpture. The darkest values occur in shadow areas in which the surface turns sharply away from the light, resulting in a value contrast of dark and middle tones. Tonal steps of this kind help to establish a pictorial figure-ground relationship and lend themselves to straightforward translation into shadow modeling.

The French artist Nicolas Poussin (1593–1665) accomplished such a translation in his drawing of an ancient Roman relief found on the Arch of Titus (Figures 4-54 and 4-55). Using line to establish the contours of the relief, he laid in

113

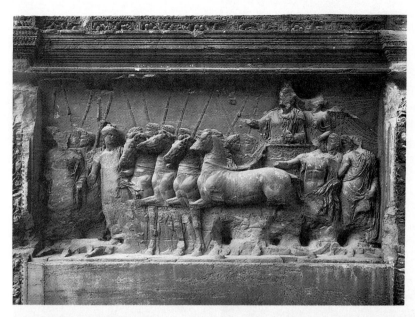

Figure 4-54. Unknown Roman artist, *The Triumph of Titus*, A.D. 81. Stone relief. Arch of Titus, Roman Forum.

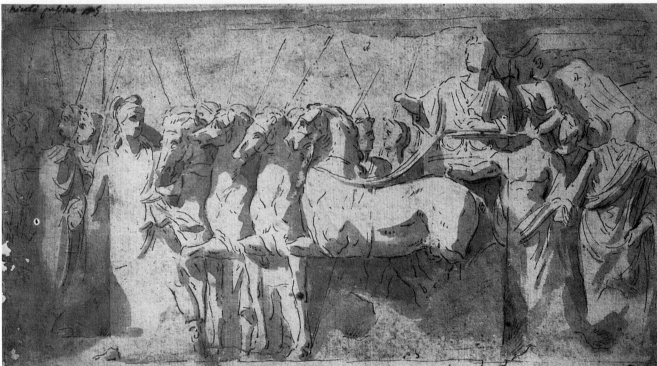

Figure 4-55. Nicolas Poussin (1594–1665), *Study after* The Triumph of Titus, 1640–1645. Pen, brown ink, and wash. 15.1 × 27.7 cm. Stockholm, Nationalmuseum.

transparent washes to model shadow tones. In some later drawings, such as *The Triumph of Galatea* (Figure 4-56), he reduced the number of tones to obtain a bolder effect. Many leading edges represented in this drawing are not separated from the background by tones but rather by faint contour lines drawn with chalk. Despite this tonal abbreviation the drawing retains the qualities of values and form that are peculiar to relief sculpture.

The order and effect of shadows on sculpture can easily be altered by changing the location of the light source. Rubens's two drawings of the same relief sculpture—a youthful work by Michelangelo—demonstrate how dramatically the effects of shadow modeling can change when the light source is transferred from one side to the other (Figures 4-57 and 4-58).

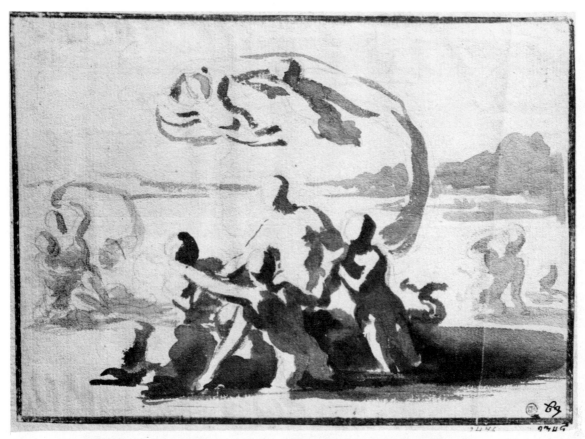

Figure 4-56. Nicolas Poussin, *The Triumph of Galatea*, c. 1635. Black chalk and brown wash. 14.2 ×
20.2 cm. Stockholm, Nationalmuseum.

Figure 4-57. Peter Paul Rubens, *After Michelangelo's Carved Relief: "The Battle of Lapiths and Centaurs,"* 1600–1603. Black and white chalk. 240 × 237 mm. Rotterdam, Museum Boymans-van Beuningen.

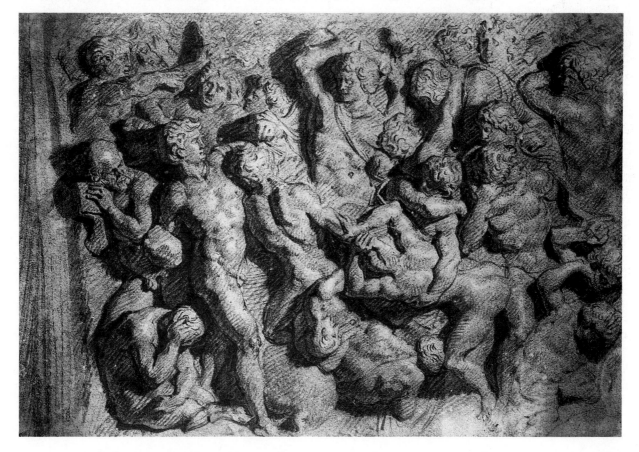

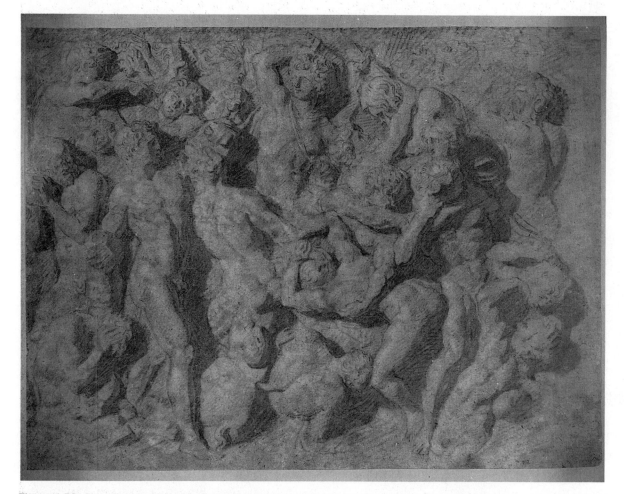

Figure 4-58. Peter Paul Rubens, *After Michelangelo's Carved Relief: "The Battle of Lapiths and Centaurs,"* 1600–1603. Black and white chalk. Fondation Custodia (coll. F. Lugt) Institut Néerlandais, Paris. Inv. no. 5422.

Relief sculpture as well as sculpture in the round were commonly available in art schools of the past in the form of plaster casts, which, like the original sculptures, enabled students to study the human form without the sometimes confusing elements of color and movement (Figure 4-59). Casts also provided a means of acquainting young art students with the classical sculpture tradition of Rome and Greece. For both reasons drawing from the cast was an important feature of art instruction in Western Europe from the seventeenth through the nineteenth century, especially in France. Only after considerable practice drawing casts, often of different parts of the body (such as the casts of heads in Figure 4-59), was the student admitted to life classes in the art academy.[20] The unbroken tradition of such instruction is seen in the student work of Picasso (Figure 4-60). Today, however, casts have fallen into disuse as a means of study, though many can still be found in art schools. This is perhaps regrettable, for the cast can ease the transition for the beginning student from basic drawing problems to the complexities of the human form.

LINE AND MODELING

A plaster cast can be used to demonstrate yet another instrument of modeling—*line.* Although line is perhaps better known for its capacity to represent form in terms of edges and discontinuities, it is also capable of defining the continuous aspect of form and can therefore be used for modeling. By projecting a thin beam of light on the model or on a cast (Figure 4-61), it is possible to see contour lines over the entire surface of the form instead of the more familiar contours normally perceived along edges and other surface discontinuities.[21] Seen bending and turning in accordance with the sur-

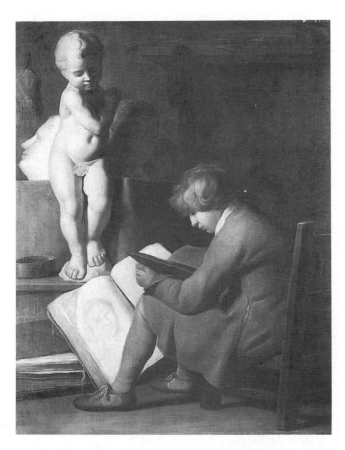

Figure 4-59. Wallerant Vaillant (1623–1677), *Young Artist Drawing from a Cast.* Oil on canvas. London, National Gallery.

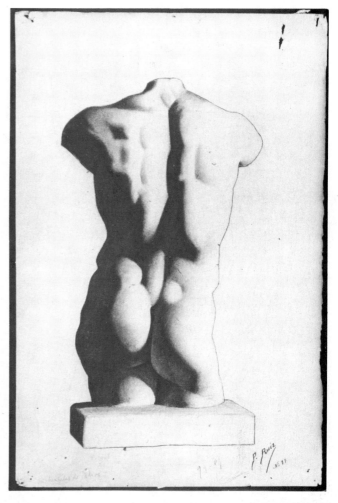

Figure 4-60. Pablo Picasso, *Study of a Torso After a Plaster Cast,* 1894–1895. Conté crayon. 19⅜ × 12½″. La Coruña (courtesy of Museo Picasso, Barcelona). While still in his early teens Picasso drew this study from a cast from an ancient Roman sculpture of a satyr. The knowledge of classical form acquired as a student emerged later in his mature work.

Figure 4-61. Cross-section contours. A time exposure of a cast of the head of the Aphrodite of Melos, recording many cross-section contours projected by means of a specially prepared slide (see Note 21, Chapter 4).

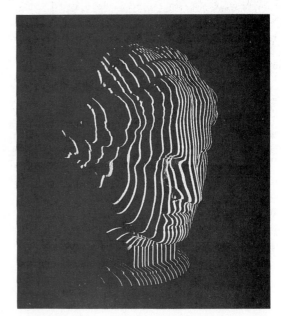

face of the head, these lines can be likened to a form of modeling. Ordinarily, of course, surface contours are not visible on the human form, and it would be difficult to draw them with such a projected light on the model. A similar effect can be achieved, however, with the draped model.

STUDY 23:   Drawing Contours of Fabric Patterns

materials: ❏ 3½ × 12″ or larger bound sketchbook of smooth bond paper
❏ India ink drawing pen (2.5 Castell TG or 0.5 mm Mars Staedler or Rapidograph)
reference: ❏ model draped in striped material
time: ❏ 20–30 minutes

A striped pair of overalls or a bathrobe or simply a striped cloth draped over the model will provide the necessary visual pattern for this study (Figure 4-62). Because the pattern is in the cloth and changes when the cloth shifts, the study is best completed in one session, with the model holding a sitting pose. The drawing session need not exceed twenty or thirty minutes.

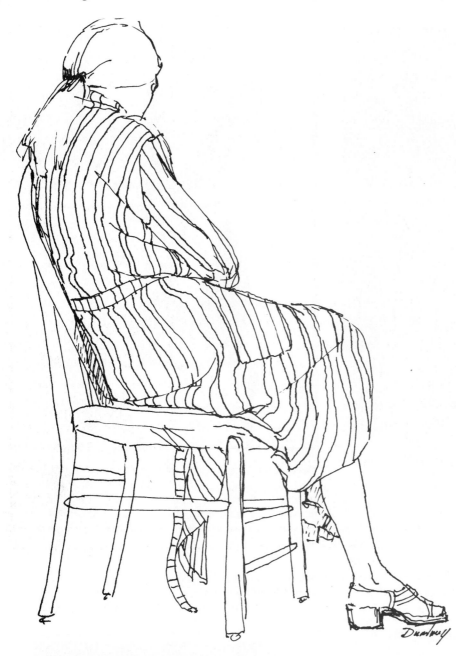

Figure 4-62. Student drawing. Seated model in a striped robe. Pen and ink on bond sketchbook paper. 11 × 14″. Textile patterns often reveal contours analogous to cross sections and provide an elegantly simple means of describing complex form in contour line.

With the model posing in the striped clothing, you may begin by making a preliminary contour drawing in pen and ink. When the contour drawing is established to your satisfaction, draw one by one the undulating contours that appear on the cloth. Many such contours reflect the form of the body beneath; others result from folds in the cloth. Together they can communicate a sense of surface relief similar to modeling.

The peculiar ability of the striped pattern to suggest volume and the undulations of folds apparently intrigued the French artist Jean-Antoine Watteau (1684–1721), who exploited the pattern's special qualities in a brilliant series of drawings of women in striped gowns (Figure 4-63).

Drawing forms covered by striped material is a helpful introduction to the construction of surface relief with line.

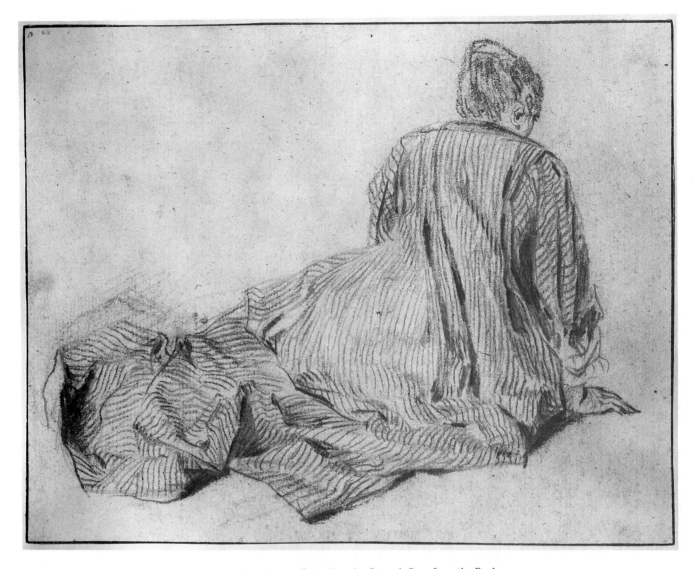

Figure 4-63. Jean-Antoine Watteau (1684–1721), *Woman Seated on the Ground, Seen from the Back.* Crayon. 181 × 146 mm. London, British Museum. The pattern of the material worn by the model informs the artist not only of the nature of cloth folds but also of the form of the body. Both functions can be observed in this drawing, in which the richly undulating contours suggested by the model's dress are echoed in the linear patterns of the model's hair.

The lines of the stripes are said to *follow* the form; that is, they suggest volume of the figure by means of their direction. This principle also can be applied in drawing cloth folds without stripes. Instead of the continuous contours of actual stripes, short line segments can follow the form where no actual lines exist—a true form of modeling. An instance of this line is observed in Netherlandish drawing (Figure 4-64), in which short strokes describe planes and crevices of folds reminiscent of Gothic woodcarving. The artist modeled receding form by increasing the density of the line strokes, causing correspondingly deeper values and richer textures in the valleys of folds and along the sides of the upper figure. The artist employed the same type of line segment to model the heads as well, thereby maintaining the formal unity of drawing. Modeling technique aside, the drawing represents a superb achievement in linking two figures together in a single composition by means of rhythmic patterns of the folds.

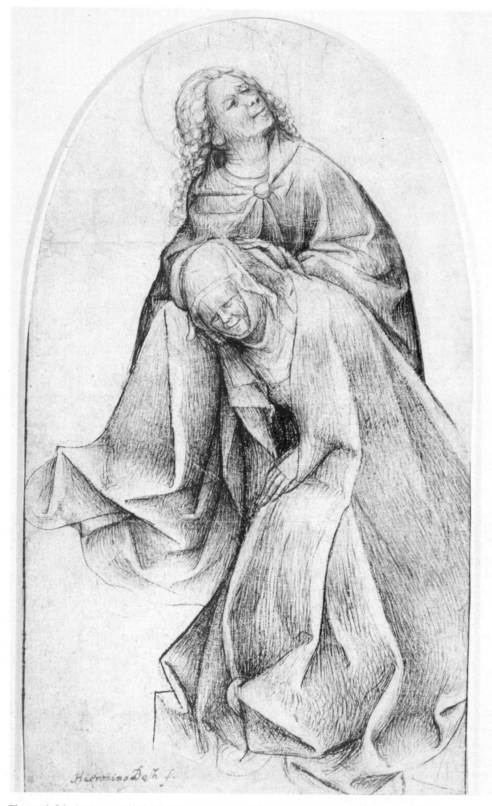

Figure 4-64. Anonymous Netherlandish master, *Mary and Saint John*, 1425. Pen, brush, and brown ink. 302 × 772 mm. Dresden, Staatliche Kunstsammlungen.

CROSS-SECTION CONTOURS

The surface contours projected on the plaster cast shown in Figure 4-61, though similar in some ways to those in the Watteau and the Netherlandish drawings (Figures 4-63 and 4-64), are simpler and more readily understood. The projected contours represent *cross sections* (slices) resulting from the intersection of the solid form of the cast by parallel vertical planes of light. The cross sections in the photograph are seen at an angle from one side, conveying a strong sense of the cast's form. If the cast had been photographed from the same angle as the direction of the light, however, the projected lines would appear straight and vertical without any suggestion of the relief form of the head. The capacity of the cross-section contour to suggest relief and volume thus depends on the angular orientation of the cross-section plane with respect to the viewer's line of sight.

An early application of this principle is seen in an anatomical study of the legs by Leonardo (Figure 4-65). The horizontal lines on the leg on the right side of the drawing represent the same cross sections that are shown in two "exploded" views as separate segments on the left side. In order to show the volume of the segments, however, it was necessary either to tilt the segment, as seen in the small leg in the center, or to shift the angle of intersection with respect to the viewer (Figures 4-66 and 4-67). Leonardo's study suggests an amusing way to explore the cross section in the figure.

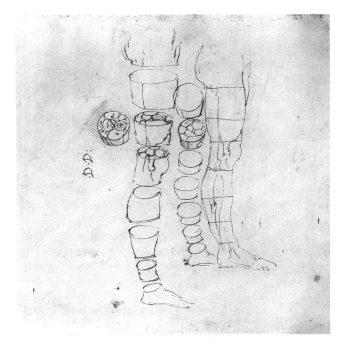

Figure 4-65. Leonardo da Vinci, *Anatomical Study: Cross-Sectional Rendering of a Man's Right Leg.* Windsor Castle, Royal Library. The horizontal lines on the right represent planes that visually cut through the form, producing the separate sections seen from a different angle on the left. Compare with Magritte's *Studies for Sculpture: Delusions of Grandeur* (Figures 8-30, 8-31, 8-32, and 8-34).

Figure 4-66. Model of a cylinder intersected by a plane.

Figure 4-67. A cylinder marked to show intersections by parallel planes.

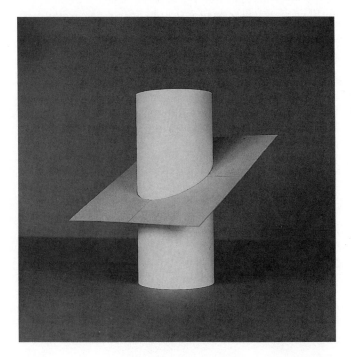

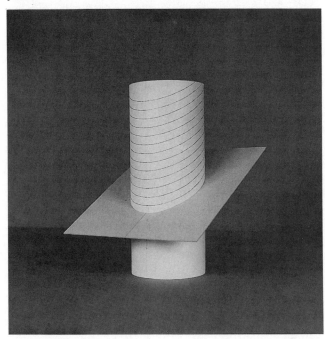

STUDY 24: **Cross Sections—**
An Imaginary Segment of the Figure

materials: ❑ 36 × 24″ newsprint drawing pad
❑ easel or straight-back chair
❑ Masonite or plywood panel and clamps
❑ drawing crayon
reference: ❑ model
time: ❑ 20 minutes

This exercise is a playful introduction to the cross section and its application to figure drawing. After developing a contour drawing of the figure, draw two imaginary cross sections. For best results draw them slowly, taking care that they describe the perceived surface of the figure. The portion of the figure between the two cross sections can then be erased and redrawn to show parts of the cross section hidden from view in the original drawing (Figure 4-68). For a clearer idea of the hidden contours, try observing the model from different points of view. Beyond the immediate objective of visualizing the cross section, this exercise brings into play your under-

Figure 4-68. Student drawing. After erasing a section of a figure study, the artist visualized and drew an open cross section.

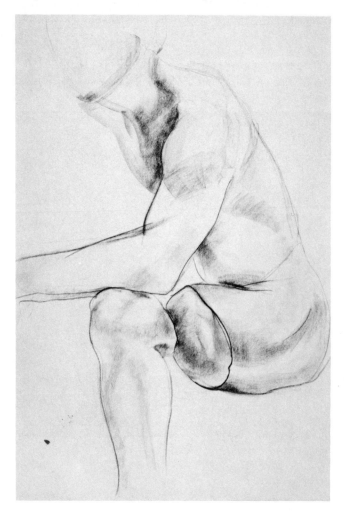

standing of the figure as volume—also an objective in the following study.

STUDY 25: **Drawing Cross-Section Contours**
of the Human Form

materials: ❑ 36 × 24″ newsprint drawing pad
❑ easel or straight-back chair
❑ Masonite or plywood panel and clamps
❑ drawing crayon
reference: ❑ model
time: ❑ 20 minutes

To begin this study, lightly indicate the figure in contour, paying special attention to the general gesture of the body. Try to draw a contour that would appear if the body were intersected (sliced) by an imaginary plane. Any region of the figure can be used for this purpose, but you may find it easier to use the more cylindrical forms of the leg or arm. Draw slowly, allowing the crayon to follow the apparent contour of the imagined intersection (Figure 4-69). Observe the model carefully as you draw: The contour, though generally rounded like an oval, must follow the undulations of the body's irregular volumes if it is to be accurate. (Only in the Michelin rubber-tire figure are contours truly regular!) If you find it difficult to construct a cross-section contour in a particular passage of the body, try drawing a rectangle representing the plane that intersects the form, as shown in Figure 4-67. The plane of the rectangle makes it easier to visualize the contour produced by the plane. Special care is necessary as the contours approach the apparent edge of body forms, for they may appear to turn sharply. If the cross sections are

Figure 4-69. Drawing cross sections. The preliminary contour drawing provides a visual armature for a study of cross-section contours.

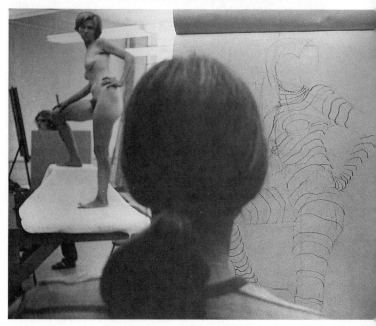

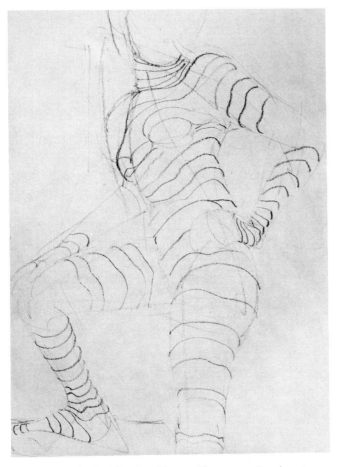

Figure 4-70. Student drawing. Figure with cross-sectional contours. Crayon on newsprint paper. 36 × 24″. Apparent irregularities of contour result from careful observation of external form. A relatively slow drawing speed is suggested for such studies.

drawn sensitively, curving in accordance with observed form, they seem to have a light, transparent quality (Figure 4-70); if they are drawn inconsistently and do not correspond with the turning of form, they tend to appear as opaque stripes painted on the figure.

The Cross Section and Art

The volumetric nature of the cross-section contour may account for the fascination it held for some artists of the Renaissance. For the Venetian artist Carpaccio the principle of the cross-section contour offered a way of drawing folds of cloth so they described the form they cover (Figure 4-71). Other Renaissance artists in addition to Leonardo used the cross-section contour as a tool for investigating the human form directly. For Piero della Francesca it became an instrument for investigating the effect of perspective on the proportions of the head (Figures 4-72 and 4-73). Dürer, the Ger-

man contemporary of Leonardo, employed the cross-section contour as a measuring device in his search for ideal human proportions (Figure 4-74). Continuing this tradition the cross-section contour now appears in medical studies of body volume (Figure 4-75). In these medical studies, however, Piero della Francesca's painstaking measurements are replaced with modern mapmaking and computer techniques, resulting in unique cross-sectional "portraits" of human subjects.[22]

The cross-section contour lends itself to scientific studies because it is capable of describing form with unequaled completeness and accuracy. Paradoxically, these very qualities may explain why it is seldom employed in realist art: The cross-section contour records more information about forms than the human eye normally takes in. The superrealistic, or more precisely, surrealistic, aspect of the cross-section contour is apparent in some computer studies of the human body and has been exploited by several twentieth-century artists associated with the surrealist movement (Figures 4-76 and 4-79).[23]

Figure 4-71. Vittore Carpaccio (c. 1465–1525), *Three Studies with Drapery, Leg and Foot* (Verso). 199 × 142 mm. Fondation Custodia (coll. F. Lugt), Institut Néerlandais, Paris. Inv. no. 5070 (Verso).

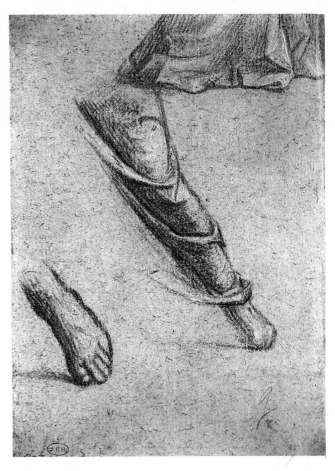

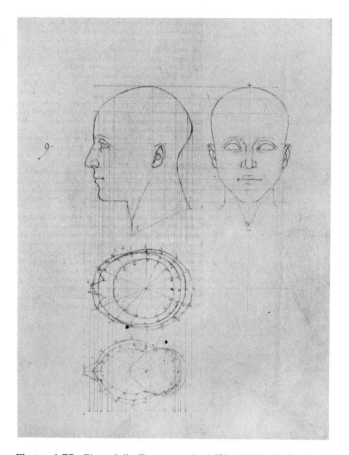

Figure 4-72. Piero della Francesca (c. 1420–1492), *Study of Proportions of the Head.* Milan, Biblioteca Ambrosiana. An artistic innovator with linear (geometric) perspective, Piero also experimented with cross-section constructions of the head. The horizontal lines cross the profile and frontal views of the head in the upper portion of the drawing at specific points. From those points the artist dropped vertical lines, which measure the corresponding points on the cross-sectional representation below.

Figure 4-73. Piero della Francesca, *Study of the Proportions of the Head.* Milan, Biblioteca Ambrosiana. By showing the cross-sectional contours inclined with respect to the drawing surface of the artist illustrates a systematic way of representing the volumes of the head.

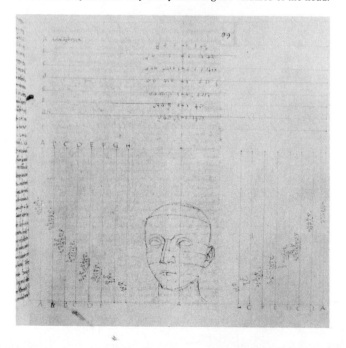

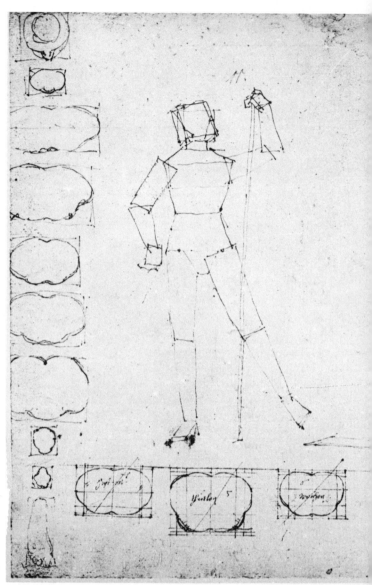

Figure 4-74. Albrecht Dürer, *Stereometric Man: Thirteen Cross Sections of the Body*, c. 1527. Page from *The Dresden Sketchbook.* Pen and ink. 11⅜ × 8″. Dresden, Sächsische Landesbibliothek. This is one of a large number of studies that Dürer made in preparation for the last of his *Four Books on Human Proportion.*

The cross-section contour also appears in some works by artists concerned primarily with formal analysis. The French painter Jacques Villon (1875–1963), for example, made use of such contours to interpret the volumes of a bust of Baudelaire by the artist's brother, Raymond Duchamp-Villon (Figure 4-77). Here cross-section contours are not drawn as they might appear around the sculptured form but are rather laid out like a deck of cards. Treated as objects complete with cast shadows the cross sections become a statement about the paradox of three-dimensional form in a two-dimensional drawing.

A deceptively similar mode of drawing utilizes the spiral: Closely spaced spiral contours tend to be perceived as a series of cross sections. This phenomenon is seen in the fanciful calligraphic coils of certain seventeenth-century decorative figures (Figure 4-78) as well as in the more monumental white spiral drawings (Figure 4-79) of Pavel Tchelitchew (1898-1959). Tchelitchew deliberately exceeds the limits of human visual perception, causing us to perceive what is not

there, cross-section contours. The apparent cross-section contours of the head in Tchelitchew's drawing appear to be formed on planes that lie parallel to the drawing surface. It is remarkable that this mode of figural representation, commonly used in mapmaking, has so rarely been adopted by artists. Contour relief maps of the body, though made for scientific purposes, reveal graphic possibilities of the map contour that merit the attention of artists concerned with rep-

Figure 4-75. Dr. R. E. Herron, *Cross-Sectional Representation of an Individual, Drawn (Plotted) by Computer.* Pen and ink. Houston, Biostereometrics Laboratory, Texas Institute for Rehabilitation and Research, Baylor College of Medicine. This is essentially the same construction as that improvised by Piero della Francesca (Figure 4-73) but drawn with the accuracy possible only with computer and mapmaking techniques. The drawing process of the computer is suggested by the slightly jerky line quality, produced as the pen moves in a straight line from one calculated point to another. Upon command the computer can generate a different view of the same figure. The angle of cross-section inclination can be gauged by the apparent angle of the figure's feet.

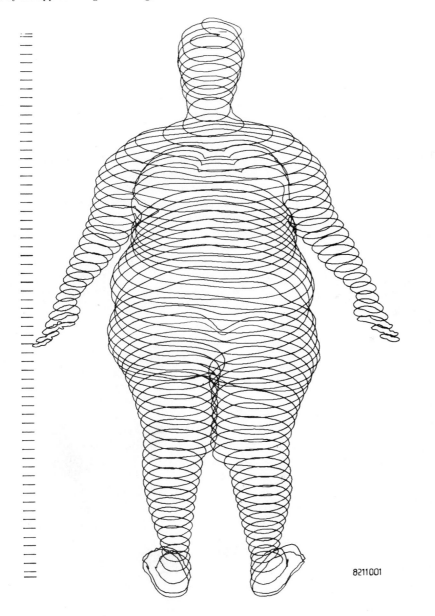

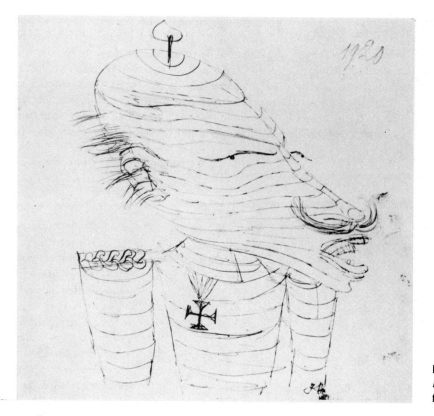

Figure 4-76. Paul Klee (1879–1940), *The Angry Kaiser Wilhelm,* 1920. Pen and ink. 7½ × 8″. Bern, from Felix Klee collection.

Figure 4-77. Jacques Villon (Gaston Duchamps) (1875–1963), *Abstract Construction,* 1920. Pen and ink on paper. 21.2 × 14 cm. New Haven, Yale University Art Gallery.

Figure 4-78. Geobattista Pisani, *Figure from a Calligraphic Scroll,* 1640. Pen and ink. Genoa. The pen produces calligraphic effects that often carry over into pen drawings, though seldom in so decorative a manner. The systematic thicks and thins of cursive writing apparent throughout the drawing are characteristic effects of the broad-point pen, which produces a line that varies in width according to the direction in which it is pulled (and not according to the pressure of the tip against the surface, as is the case with the Oriental brush). As in Figure 4-79, the form of the figure is perceived as though it were constructed with cross-section contours.

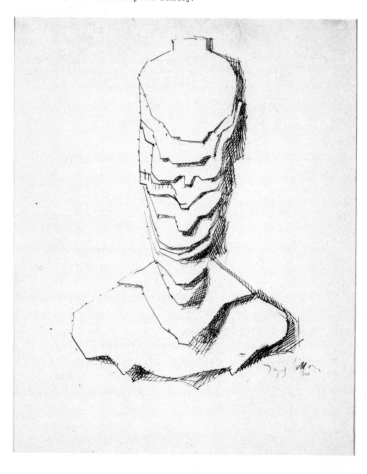

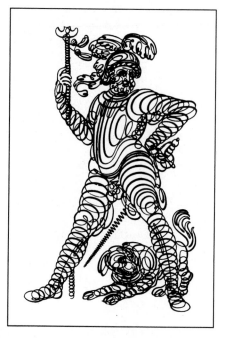

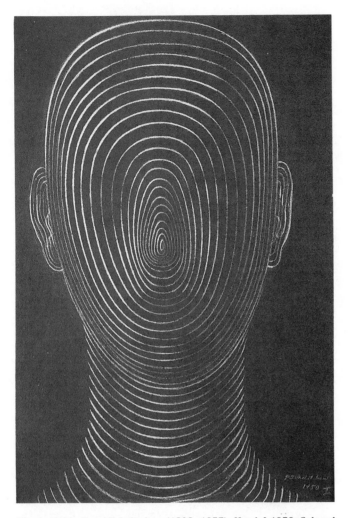

Figure 4-79. Pavel Tchelitchew (1898–1957), *Head, I.* 1950. Colored pencil on black paper. 18⅞ × 12½". The Museum of Modern Art, New York. Purchase. Only the form of the neck is modeled in regular cross-section contours, for Tchelitchew conceived the head as a virtuoso conceit of unbroken spiral line, originating at the tip of the nose. This technique has a precedent in seventeenth-century calligraphic and en-graved decoration (Figure 4-78). Despite the spiral construction the head is perceived as if it were constructed of cross-section contours. Such technical tricks play on the limits of human visual perception.

explained by comparing the "natural" gradient of texture density with that of the "map" contour on a simple object such as a cylinder (Figures 4-81 and 4-82).

The naturally occurring gradient results from a regular pattern of texture on a surface. The evenly spaced vertical lines seen in Figure 4-81 are analogous to such a gradient. Initially these lines were drawn parallel and spaced equally on a sheet of paper, which was then wrapped around a cylinder. As seen on the cylinder, the lines are separated by an interval of space that appears to shorten as the surface turns from the viewer, thereby producing a "denser" textural effect on the sides than in the vertical center. The vertical lines in Figure 4-82, how-ever, are drawn differently than their counterparts in Figure 4-81. They represent the intersections of the cylinder by equally spaced imaginary planes at right angles to the line of sight—in short, they are like contours of a relief map. Sig-nificantly, the apparent variation of interval between the lines is much more pronounced than that seen in the "natural" density gradient, and creates a correspondingly stronger sense of relief. The effect observed in map contours is in a sense an exaggerated gradient of texture density, one that is well suited to the purpose of representing three-dimensional forms on a flat surface. Such an exaggerated gradient seems to compen-sate visually for the two dimensionality of the drawing surface and may account for the pronounced effect of relief seen in figures drawn in this way (Figure 4-80). Though it is effective in computer modeling (Figure 4-83), the relief map contour leaves much to be desired as a practical studio technique. The longitudinal slice is unwieldy to draw. Nevertheless the cross section is a useful drawing concept. When the cross section slices the form transversely as in Leonardo's *Anatomical Study* (Figure 4-67), the resulting contour is the basis for hatch modeling techniques.

STUDY 26:	**Contour Hatch Modeling**
materials:	❑ 36 × 24″ newsprint drawing pad
	❑ easel or straight-back chair
	❑ Masonite or plywood board and clamps
	❑ drawing crayon
reference:	❑ model
time:	❑ 30 minutes

---

resenting sculptural form (Figures 4-80). Such maps present a uniquely linear modeling of volumes without concessions to color or shadow factors.

Seen from a short distance, the individual lines in a contour body map seem to melt into an overall effect of relief mod-eling—darkening as surfaces turn, lightening on the flatter frontal surfaces. The contours' varying intervals become sharply denser on turned surfaces (i.e., the sides of the legs), denser in fact than might be expected in a naturally occurring density gradient. The reason for this difference of effect is

The term *hatching* contains a surprising metaphor, for it is derived from *hâchure,* a French word meaning "axing" or "chopping"—a brutal yet unforgettable way of visualizing the contours formed by the intersection of a body form with a plane. Fortunately both the intersection and the contour it describes are purely imaginary!

To begin your first study in hatch modeling, prepare a contour drawing of the model, developing the figure only as far as is needed to provide a frame of reference—ten minutes is sufficient for this phase of the study. Then, using the figure

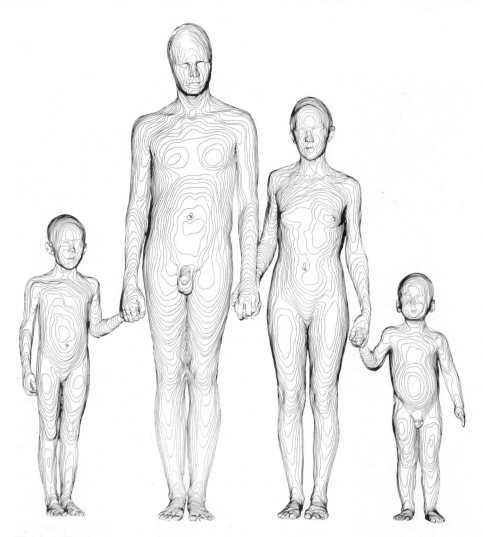

Figure 4-80. Dan McCoy, *Bodygram of a Family* (photogrammetric maps of a man, a woman, and two children) (photo © Dan McCoy/Rainbow).

Figure 4-81. Cylinder with equally spaced vertical lines on its surface. The regular spacing between the lines is comparable to a regularly repeating texture or pattern on the surface of an object. Such patterns in nature produce a gradient of texture density that serves as a visual cue in form perception.

Figure 4-82. Cylinder with vertical lines representing intersections of equally spaced planes. A comparison of the intervals between these lines with those in Figure 4-81 suggests that these may represent an exaggeration of naturally occurring gradients of texture density.

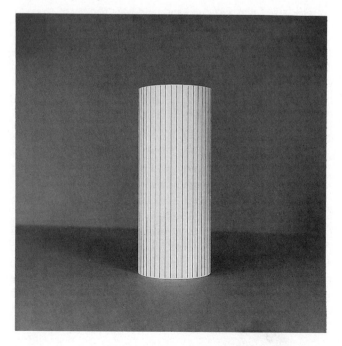

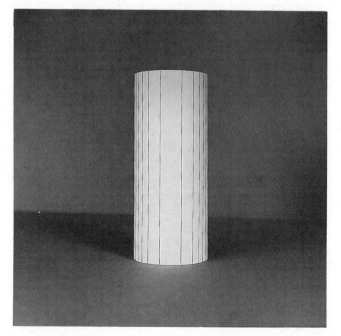

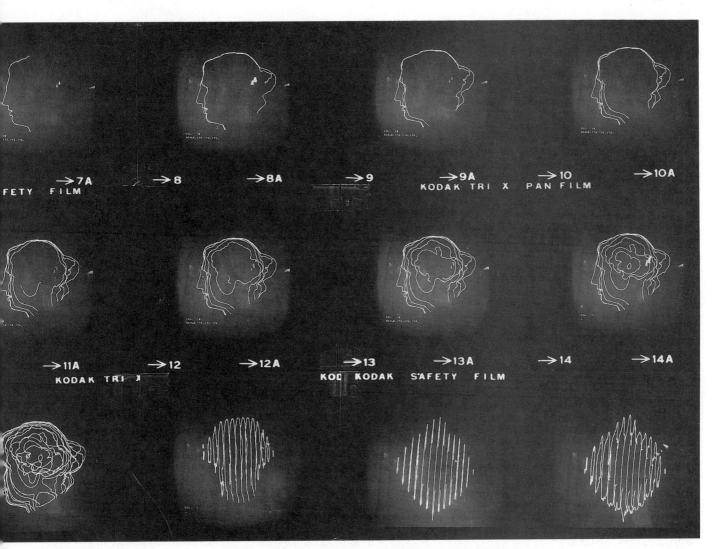

Figure 4-83. William Berry and Robert Tyndall, computer console displays. This series of photographs of the cathode display was taken at intervals as the computer image was generated and, in the lower three frames, "rotated" in "space." Upon the command of the operator the computer later directed a plotting machine to draw the image at lower left. The numerical data necessary for drawing the head was derived from photographs of a cast of the head of the Aphrodite of Melos similar to that in Figure 4-61.

drawing as a guide, draw cross-section contours as in Study 22, but do not complete them (Figure 4-84). In drawing each incomplete contour, or *hatch mark*, begin at the edge of the form and follow the rounded volume of the body, stopping when the contour straightens (that is, when the form you are drawing becomes relatively flat). By repeating this simple procedure, maintaining an approximately regular interval between them, the modeling process will begin. It is important to work slowly, giving each hatch mark the same attention and sensitivity you applied to the complete contours of Study 24. It is also important to space the hatch marks evenly, allowing a fairly wide interval between them. Beginners tend to crowd the marks, creating dark patches of tone that can

block further development of the drawing. Your previous experience with tonal modeling will help you decide where hatch modeling is needed in the figure. In the beginning it is best to reserve the contour hatch marks for parts of the figure where surfaces turn or recede sharply.

When a portion of the figure includes a general shift of direction (as in a flexed arm, for example), it is advisable to change the direction of the hatch. This can be accomplished by first imagining an intersection at a different angle and then drawing hatches to correspond to the new surface direction (Figure 4-85). In some areas of the figure you may wish to add a deeper tone within a previously modeled form. This can be accomplished by adding a second series of hatch marks,

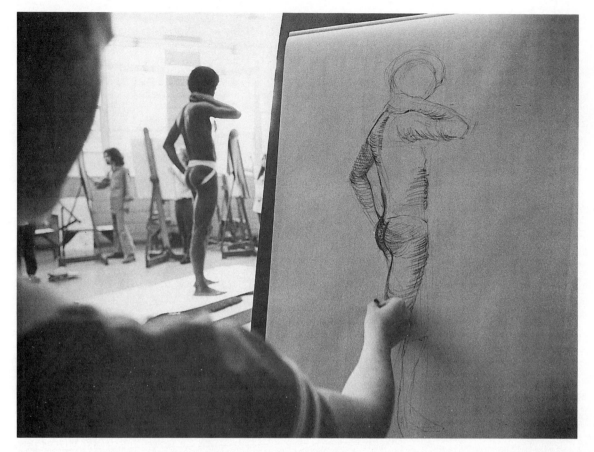

Figure 4-84. Modeling the figure with hatching over a preliminary contour drawing.

based on a different intersection, across those drawn earlier. Although this requires no new procedure, it has been given a separate name: *cross-hatching* (Figure 4-86).

With practice you will be able to draw hatch marks deftly without concentrating on each stroke. As you gain speed the arm motion may resemble that of an automobile windshield wiper (Figure 4-87). With large swinging hatch marks you can create forms of strongly modeled volumes, saving the shorter strokes for modeling the small forms (Figure 4-88). It is important that each hatch mark track an imaginary cross section. Drawn in this way hatch marks serve effectively as descriptors of form, and will not be mistaken for patterns on the model's skin (Figure 4-89). In skillful drawings contour hatching can produce such an effect of transparency that the individual hatching strokes go practically unnoticed.

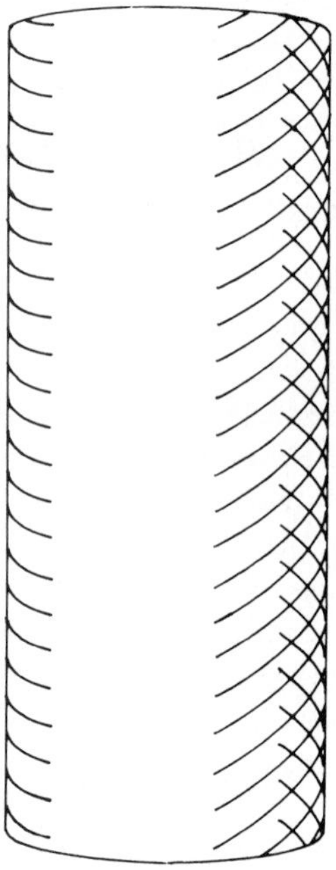

CONTOUR HATCHING AND SCULPTURE

The sculptural character of the hatch mark is borne out by analogous marks on the surfaces of some sculpture, especially clay and stone sculpture. In a terra cotta sketch from the sev-

Figure 4-85. Cylinder. Cross-hatching is executed by changing the angle of the imaginary plane on which the hatch contours are based. In this example, drawn mechanically, the cross-hatching is based on two different planes.

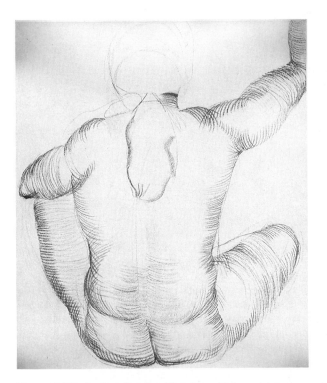

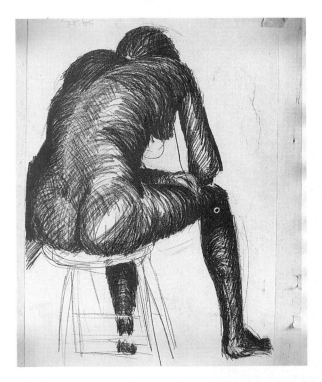

Figure 4-86. Student drawing. Modeling with incomplete cross-section contours. Crayon on newsprint paper. 36 × 24″. In this first attempt at hatch modeling the student varied the angle of the cross section in places, producing occasional cross-hatching effects, as in the lower left portion of the figure.

Figure 4-87. Student drawing. Figure modeled with hatching. Crayon on newsprint paper. 36 × 24″. With contour hatch marks drawn more rapidly than those in Figure 4-86, the modeling describes generalized large forms of the body.

Figure 4-88. Drawing from life with hatch modeling. Rather than modeling the entire surface of the figure, the student is employing hatching to model surfaces that appear to need articulation for structural clarity. The preliminary contour line representing the spine of the figure is helpful in constructing the figure.

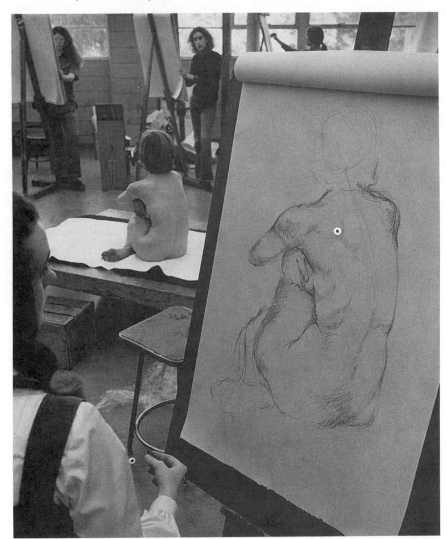

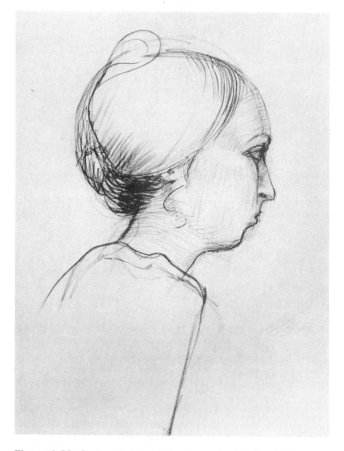

Figure 4-89. Student drawing. Life-size study of the head. Crayon on newsprint paper. 36 × 24".

Figure 4-90. Pupil of Giovanni Lorenzo Bernini (1598–1680), *Triton Bearing a Draped Woman on His Shoulder*. Terra cotta sketch (*bozzetto*). 19½" high. Cambridge, Fogg Art Museum, Harvard University. The effect of the actual volumes of these sculptured figures is given added emphasis by the hatchlike surface texture. Compare with Figure 4-91.

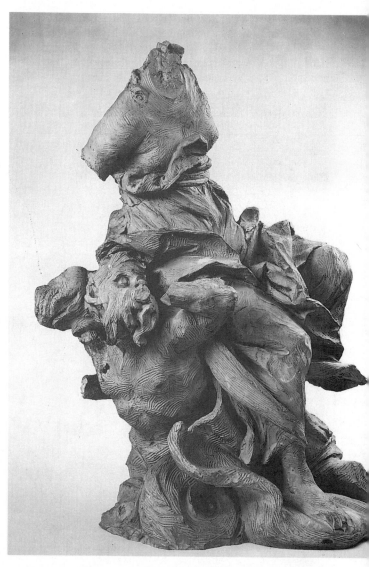

enteenth century (Figure 4-90), sets of lines were scratched into the clay by means of a modeling instrument with a saw-tooth edge. Because they are physically on the surface of the sculpture, they follow its contours in a way that can only be approached in drawing. They truly turn with the form and, thanks to their texture, heighten our awareness of the actual volume of the clay modeling. Similar hatching can be found in some stone sculpture, notably in the carved figures by Michelangelo. The claw chisel—a tool he preferred for carving the figure—left fine incised lines in marble that function remarkably like the contour hatching found in his pen and ink drawings.[24] His *Nude Study* in pen and ink offers an insight into this graphic analogy with carving (Figure 4-91). Beginning with a contour-line drawing of the figure—left bare of modeling in places—the artist modeled with small curving hatch strokes, adding layer upon layer, as seen especially in the torso. The richly textured modeling integrates anatomical structure with the gesture of the original contour drawing and virtually transforms the figure into sculpture.

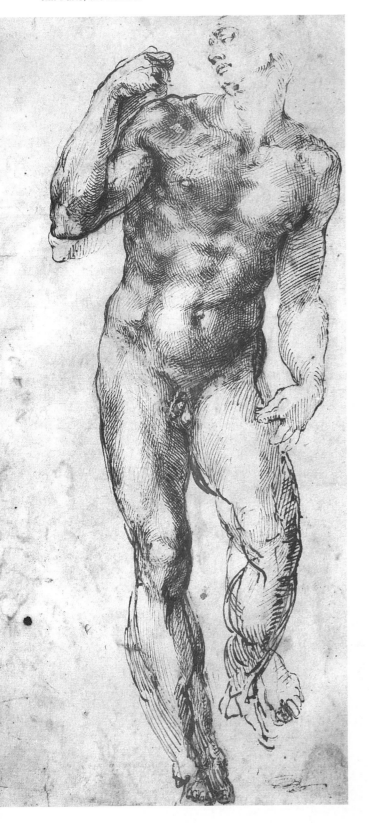

HATCHING AND FORM

Adding extra layers of hatching, à la Michelangelo, does not in itself guarantee the effect of volume in a figure drawing. In order to express three dimensionality, the hatching must be drawn in terms of an unifying structure, preferably one observed in the model. The importance of the structural factor in hatch modeling can be gauged by comparing a police drawing (Figure 4-92) with a *Self-Portrait* by Dürer (Figure 4-93). The police drawing consists of separate elements, assembled on the basis of the remembered appearance of individual facial features. Accurately reflecting the way it was made, the police drawing appears to be little more than an accumulation of isolated individual parts. We sense immediately the disconcerting lack of spatial (i.e., volumetric) coherence. The features appear to float as separate, positive constructs on a white ground, lacking sufficient integration to produce a sense of structural wholeness. The nose, for ex-

Figure 4-92. Newspaper reproduction of a composite drawing used in police investigation. Pieced together with the aid of eyewitnesses, the drawing lacks coherent spatial and structural organization; the individual parts remain isolated. Interesting for its naïveté of concept, the police drawing is the graphic opposite of the Dürer *Self-Portrait* (Figure 4-93).

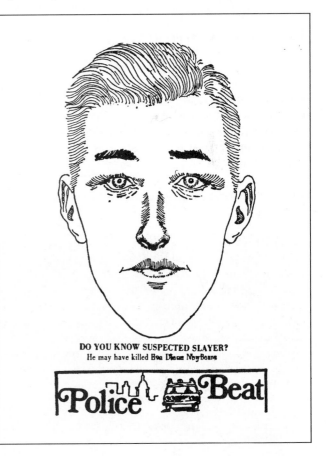

DO YOU KNOW SUSPECTED SLAYER?
He may have killed Boa Diaca NbyBoara

Police Beat

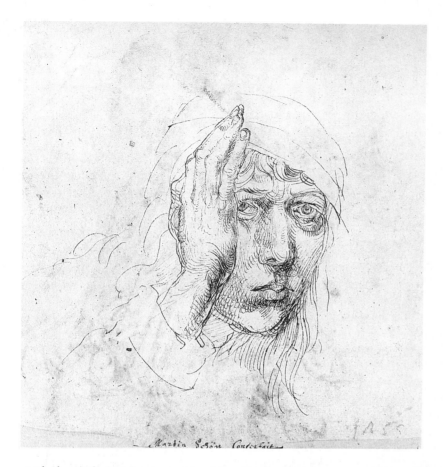

Figure 4-93. Albrecht Dürer, *Self-Portrait*, c. 1492–1493. Pen and ink. 5.86 × 5.55″. Erlangen, Universitätsbibliothek.

ample, has drifted oddly to one side of the other facial features. There is no hatch modeling at the bridge of the nose, a construction that plays an important role in articulating the features in Dürer's *Self-Portrait*—notably the relationship of the eyes and the nose. Likewise, the modeling that integrates the planes above and below the lips in the Dürer is mostly absent in the police drawing. In fact, such structural articulation is missing throughout the police drawing. To be fair we should point out that the police drawing is a composite by necessity and serves its intended purpose of visual identification surprisingly well.

Master Drawings and Contour Hatching

Contour hatching is an enduring approach to modeling in drawing. Since the time of Dürer succeeding generations of artists have managed to revive contour hatching and apply it creatively in their work (Figures 4-93, 4-95, and 4-96). Rembrandt in his *Reclining Nude* (Figure 4-94) employed contour hatching to model the figure, and to meld it with the setting or background—"overdrawing" until parts of the figure appear to merge with a near solid darkness. Despite the deep

Figure 4-94. Rembrandt, *Reclining Nude*, 1658. Etching. 3¼ × 6³⁄₁₆″. Amsterdam, Rijksmuseum.

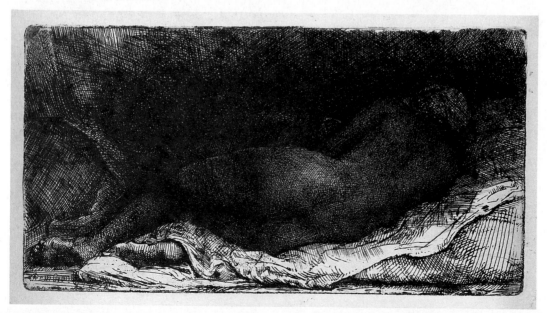

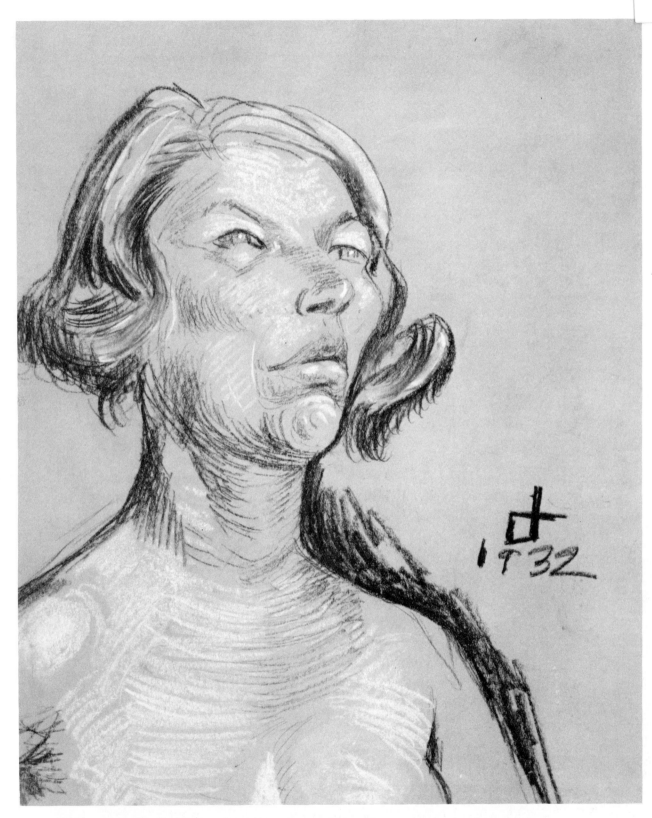

Figure 4-95. Otto Dix (1891–1969), *Head of a Woman*, 1932. Black and white chalk on brown ground paper. 22⅝ × 18½″. Cambridge, Busch-Reisinger Museum, Harvard University. With the brown paper serving as a middle value in the drawing, the artist used white chalk to model frontal surfaces of the figure with contour hatching, a technique also found in German Renaissance drawings.

values created by the many layers of hatching, the figure appears miraculously aglow in darkness.

Drawings by two twentieth-century artists demonstrate the versatility of contour hatching (Figures 4-95 and 4-96). In a masterful contour hatch drawing of the *Head of a Woman* (Figure 4-95), the German painter Otto Dix modeled with white and black crayons on a brown paper. With the brown paper serving as the middle value he modeled the projecting planes (i.e., as in the forehead) with the white crayon and the receding planes with the black crayon. Drawn with unflinching honesty of observation, Dix's *Head of a Woman* is in the graphic tradition of Dürer. Compare, for instance, the thorough contour hatch modeling of the neck with that of Dürer's drawing *Catherine* (Figure 1-1). The use of white hatch marks also has precedent in drawings by Dürer, as Dix was well aware. Yet the drawing is unmistakably modern in character.

It is instructive to examine how a modern sculptor used contour hatch to model figures in a composition (Figure 4-96). The drawing entitled *Coal Miners at Work* by the British sculptor Henry Moore is a technical tour de force with mixed media. Here, too, white hatching enlivens the modeling of the figures, but it has a different source. Instead of a white crayon the artist used *resist* technique. In brief the white contour hatch in the figures was obtained by marking the paper with a water resistant wax crayon or glue prior to toning the paper with wash. Later the artist drew dark lines of contour hatch over portions of the white. These later additions act in concert with the initial white hatch, reinforcing the sculptural description of the figures. As in the drawing by Dix, the highest values, as well as the darkest, are drawn with hatch. The Moore drawing exhibits a remarkable harmony of technique and subject. The dark cramped spaces of the coal mine appear as if carved out by hatch marks in the drawing. In keeping with the roughly hewn planes of the mine, straight line segments, not contour hatch, define the spaces and enframe the figures within the long rectangular format of the drawing. The Moore drawing thus mixes two types of hatching as well as media. Hatching with straight-line segments—called plane hatching—is itself a mode of drawing worthy of study.

Plane Hatching

Just as the continuous curves of the cross-section are the basis for contour hatching, so the planes of figure structure are the basis for another type of linear modeling: *plane hatching*. Plane hatch modeling will seem familiar if you have practiced the angular-line techniques discussed in Study 9 in Chapter 3, for it is based on the same principle: the artistic interpretation of rounded surfaces as imaginary flat planes. There is, however, an important difference. While in Study 9 lines represent only the angular intersections of planes, plane hatch modeling can

Figure 4-96. Henry Moore (1898–1986), *Coal Miners at Work*, 1942. Charcoal and wash with resist. 305 × 557 mm. Allen Memorial Art Museum, Oberlin College, Oberlin, Ohio, Charles F. Olney Fund, 1948.

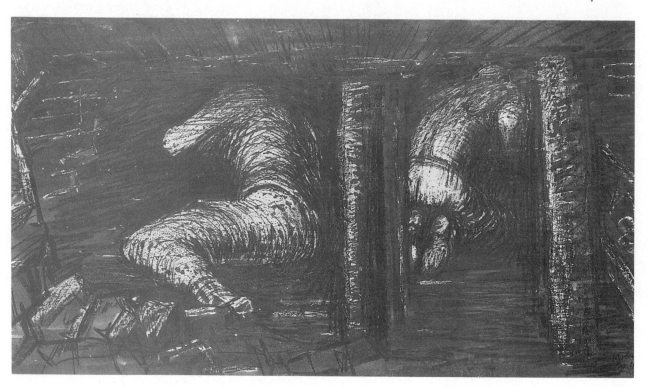

also represent the planes and their associated tones of light and dark (Figure 4-97). The direction of the hatch is suggested by the orientation of the planes as you see them on the model rather than by the imaginary intersection of a plane, as in contour hatch modeling.

An effect that is present in other types of modeling but is especially noticeable in plane hatching is *virtual line*, a contour that appears to be formed by the tip ends of hatch marks (Figure 4-98). Virtual lines are visible both at the edges of hatched planes terminating in white space and at the intersections of hatched planes. A device of great subtlety, the virtual line (also known as *implied contour*) can be used to suggest linear elements such as shadow contours.

STUDY 27: **Plane Hatch Modeling**

materials: ❏ 36 × 24″ newsprint drawing pad
  ❏ easel or straight-back chair
  ❏ Masonite or plywood board and clamps
  ❏ drawing crayon
reference: ❏ model
time: ❏ 30 minutes

If this is your first experiment with plane hatching, it is best to begin by drawing the figure using the angular measurement method outlined in Study 9 (Figure 4-99). Once the figure drawing is established in line by angular measurement, examine it in terms of the largest angular features which can be interpreted as intersections of planes. It is likely that some

Figure 4-97. Plane hatching. The angular intersection of body forms can be interpreted as simple linear angles (a) or as the intersections of planes (b). In the latter case straight hatch marks can effectively describe such planes (c).

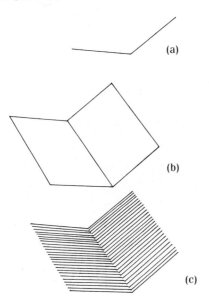

(a)

(b)

(c)

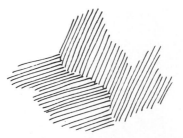

Figure 4-98. Virtual lines. Linear effect produced by the tips of hatch marks both at the intersection of the two planes and at the opposite sides of the planes. Such effects are referred to as implied contours or virtual lines.

intersections of planes will be marked by shadow contours (i.e., the terminator lines separating the illuminated forms of the body from those in shadow). For that reason plane hatching is especially effective for shadow modeling. A large area of shadow can be laid in with hatching oriented in the same direction (Figures 4-100 and 4-101). Smaller planes can easily be defined within the larger areas of hatching by means of cross hatch oriented in a different direction. With practice you will find planes of hatching can be laid in quickly and easily even though the resulting drawing effects may appear complex (Figures 5-30 and 6-25).

Precedents

Artists from various periods have found their personal expression using plane hatch modeling and adapting its elements to their own artistic temperaments. You can see a bold use of plane hatch modeling in Jacques Villon's engraving *Jeune Fille* (Figure 4-102). Few edges of form in the work are defined by line borders (enclosures): Instead, the artist has modeled the head in broad almost architectural planes by means of hatch marks that, though limited in direction, create effects of surprising complexity and subtlety. A slight thickening of the hatch marks, for example, appears to define areas such as the mouth without a change of hatching direction.

The severe, angular construction of the head by means of hatch planes, though based on observation, reveals Villon's interest in cubism, an art movement that stresses the formal, abstract aspect of visual reality and, in the words of Villon, "represents the object on every surface."[25] Given the importance of faceted surfaces in cubist art, modeling, in particular plane hatch modeling, was a logical choice for Villon in drawing and printmaking. Yet his graphic works are highly personal, as was his interest in cubism: ". . . I have not been a Cubist because of doctrine," he once remarked, "but because it suited me."[26] His work confirms the value of remaining faithful to one's artistic sensibility.

An equally personal use of plane hatching is seen in the *Self-Portrait* by Cézanne, the late nineteenth-century French

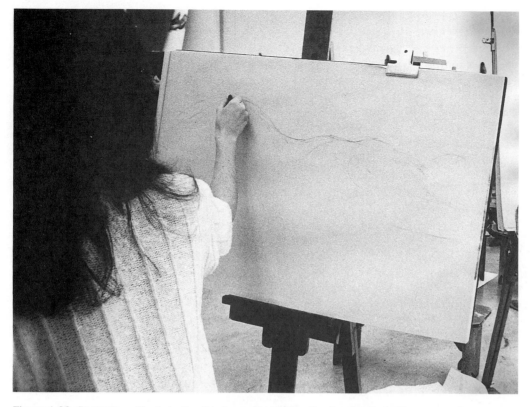

Figure 4-99. Beginning a life study. Careful observation yields a line drawing that will serve as a framework for hatch modeling. The medium is crayon.

Figure 4-100. Developing a life study. Modeling with plane hatching describes the figure structure implied in the preliminary line drawing.

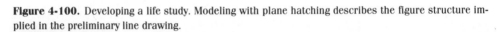

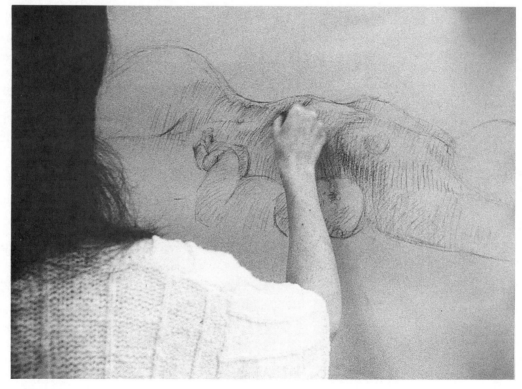

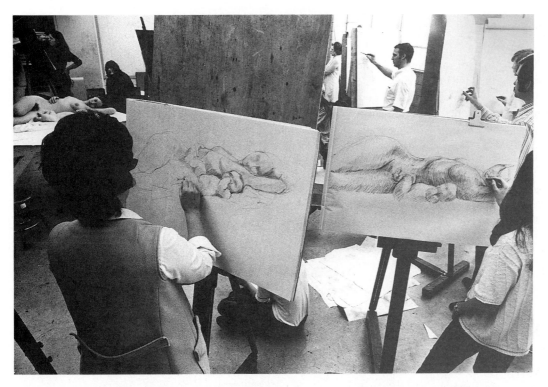

Figure 4-101. Drawing from life. The student on the left is using plane hatching to model the effects of light on the model; the student on the right is using plane hatching to describe form in a more arbitrary way. The earlier stages of the latter drawing are shown in Figures 4-99 and 4-100.

Figure 4-102. Jacques Villon, *Jeune Fille*, 1942. Engraving, artist's proof. 11⅜ × 8¹/₁₂″. Boston Public Library, Print Department.

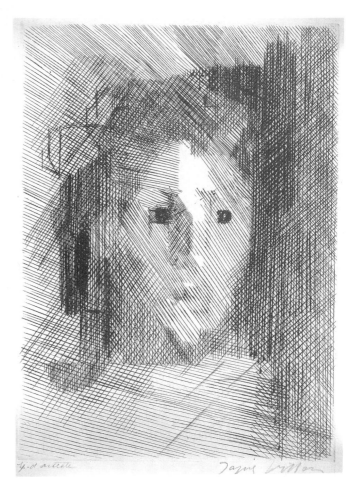

painter (Figure 4-103). Using lightly drawn contour lines as guides, Cézanne modeled this drawing selectively with plane hatch consisting of groups of short pencil marks that resemble brushstrokes. The surprising elegance of his drawing resides in this selective process; much of the drawing remains white. The quirky shadow contour on the forehead of his *Self-Portrait*, for example, preceded and helped place the single small patch of hatching above the brow—a key element

in modeling the ridge of the brow itself. Cézanne's plane hatching, though drawn with pencil, has an oddly chromatic "painterly" quality that is often seen in his paintings where the planes appear translated into colors. It can be said that even in black and white, he modeled in color.

Plane hatching is not, however, the exclusive domain of draftsmen-painters: Its effectiveness in modeling sculptural form is ably demonstrated by the contemporary Italian sculptor Emilio Greco. His drawing in pen and ink entitled *Dorso* is a powerful statement with plane hatch modeling in the relief mode: Receding forms grow dark with hatching (Figure 4-104). Though the artist's method is straightforward, the drawing is remarkably personal, with curious departures from the traditional method. The modeling of the hand, for example, is inexplicably heavy, as though the hatch was meant to cover up a passage of form that did not please the artist. Similarly, the head is modeled in an oddly wider stroke than the rest of the drawing. Unlike the relief modeling of the

Figure 4-103. Paul Cézanne, *Self-Portrait* (on a sheet with *Portrait of Cézanne's Son*). Pencil on white sketchbook paper. 8.5 × 4.9″. Courtesy of The Art Institute of Chicago. The initial stage of the drawing is evident in the delicate contour lines that appear to flow around the features. The contours serve not only to define the edges of the outer limits of form but also to mark the borders of shadowed planes, as in the contour across the area of the forehead. Cézanne applied plane hatching to the contour structure in a way that suggests both form and shadow.

Figure 4-104. Emilio Greco (b. 1913), *Dorso*, 1954. Pen and ink. 19.4 × 13.4″. Bath, Adams and Dart Publishers.

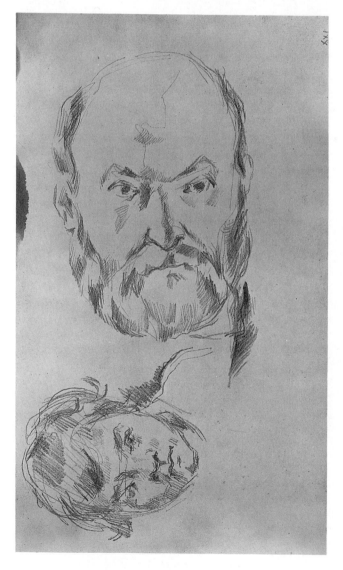

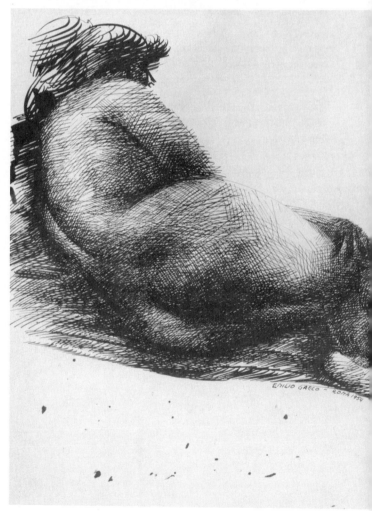

back the hatching of the thigh suggests shadow modeling. These minor inconsistencies, however, do not mar the surpassing solidity that marks this drawing as the work of a true sculptor. Indeed Greco carries on the tradition of Michelangelo, employing cross-hatching to evoke the chisel marks of stone carving (Figure 4-91).

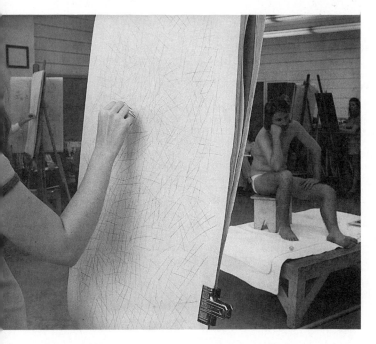

Figure 4-105. Drawing tone with random hatch marks.

Figure 4-106. Figure and ground study. Hatch marks in this study are limited to three directions: vertical, horizontal, and diagonal. The tonal ground defines the form of the figure and integrates it pictorially.

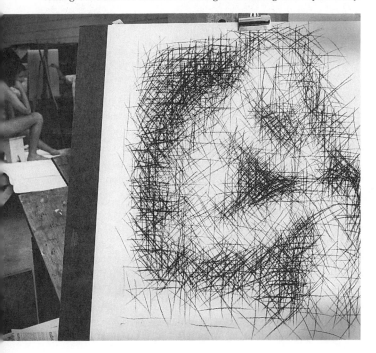

It is also instructive to compare Greco's *Dorso* with Rembrandt's etching *Reclining Nude* (Figure 4-94). The two works offer a similar view of the figure, and the graphic methods that produced them, though not identical, have much in common. Both artists modeled the figure in relief with hatching and cross-hatching, but made some concessions to effects of light and shadow. Both artists deliberately left tiny glowing white spots of unmarked paper in the areas of deepest tone, the result of near microscopic ground reversals of spaces between lines of hatch. A notable difference is seen in the way the two figures are integrated with their respective ground. Although both artists modeled the figure with deep tones of hatching, the Greco figure remains isolated against a white ground; the hatching serves primarily to model the figure, while the ground, with the exception of the cloth underneath the figure, remains unmarked by the artist's pen. Rembrandt, however, imposed even deeper hatching in the background, thereby defining the pictorial space and creating a subtle figure-ground relationship. As a result the darkly modeled figure appears to glow mysteriously against a cloth backdrop. The use of hatch to define and activate pictorial space in a drawing can be rewarding in life drawing. If you would like to experiment with this approach to the figure-ground relationship, the following study serves as a convenient introduction.

STUDY 28:	Hatching and the Figure-Ground Relationship
materials:	❏ 36 × 24″ drawing pad
	❏ easel or straight-back chair
	❏ Masonite or plywood board and clamps
	❏ drawing crayon
reference:	❏ model
time:	❏ 20 minutes

Without observing the model, first draw enough hatch marks to cover the drawing page with a light tone. Straight hatch marks of approximately the same length are suitable for this purpose (Figure 4-105) or, if you prefer, wiggly marks (Figure 4-107). They can be drawn either in random directions or in a few specific directions (i.e., vertical, horizontal, and diagonal) (Figure 4-106). After you have developed an even, light texture of hatch marks on the paper, you are ready to begin drawing the figure from the model. Instead of drawing the positive form of the figure as in previous studies, first draw the ground surrounding the positive form, continuing with the same type of hatch marks but making a darker tone. There is no need to press harder with the crayon in order to achieve the dark tone: It will occur naturally as the hatching strokes accumulate. Drawn in this way, the ground effectively shapes and models the figure thereby establishing a rich figure-ground relationship. The figure, instead of being conceived as an isolated positive form surrounded by empty (i.e., nega-

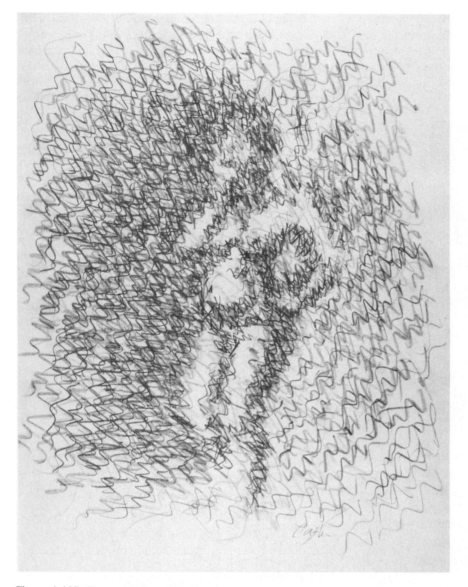

Figure 4-107. Figure and ground study with wavy hatch marks.

tive) space, will exist in a pictorial environment, which can itself be further modeled. The possibilities inherent in this approach are explored further in Chapter 7.

Precedents

The pictorial potential of hatching intrigued the American painter James McNeill Whistler, whose drawing *Study for Weary* (Figure 4-108) is an instructive example of crayon technique. His bold, slashing crayon strokes establish the pictorial space of the drawing, defining and leaving almost untouched the two high-key areas—the face and the hand of the figure. Departing from the approach seen in the rest of the drawing, the delicate modeling of the face seems almost out of keeping with the starker drawing of the hand, an in-

consistency that may border on sentimentality in the eye of the contemporary viewer. Within the dark areas, however, Whistler subtly varied the tonal values so that within what at first may appear to be uniform blackness emerges a cushion or pillow behind the head and the figure's dark dress half covered by a blanket—all as integrated elements within a pictorial space not unlike that of his painting.

The hatch found in prints by Goya is as rich in texture as that of Whistler or Rembrandt but plays a different role. In his *Disparate General* (in English, *General Absurdity*) the hatching crosses contour boundaries, sweeping over a group of huddled figures and weaving them together in a strange fabriclike texture (Figure 4-109). Edges of some forms are marked by shifts in value and by abrupt changes in hatch direction, strongly suggesting differences of color. Looming over the figures is a dark ground of granular texture (aquatint),

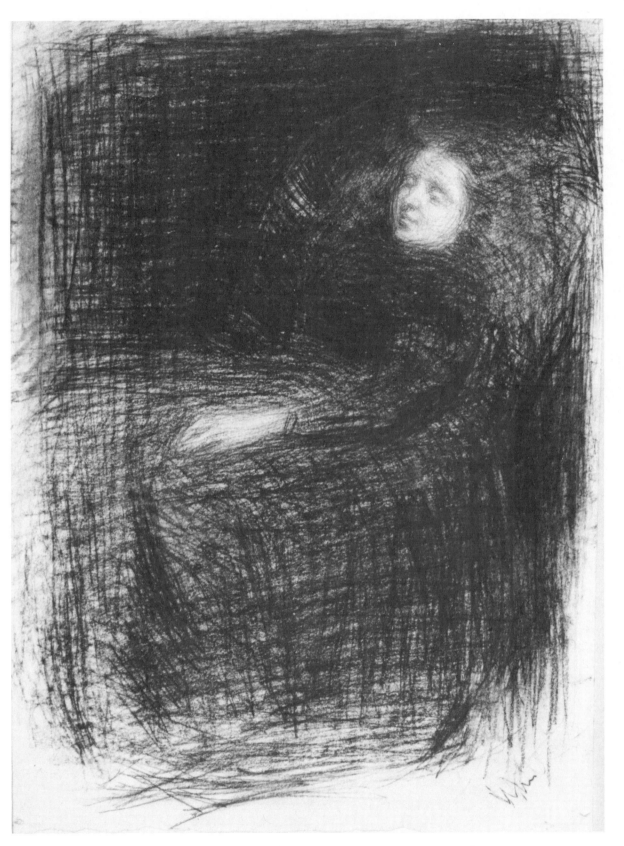

Figure 4-108. James Abbott McNeill Whistler (1834–1903), *Study for Weary.* Black chalk. 9⅝ × 6⅞″.
Williamstown, Massachusetts, Sterling and Francine Clark Art Institute.

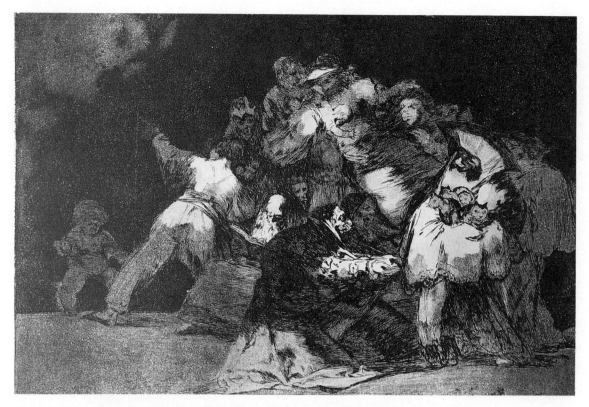

Figure 4-109. Francisco Goya (1746–1828), *Disparate General.* Etching and aquatint. 9.7 × 13.8″. Madrid, Museo del Prado.

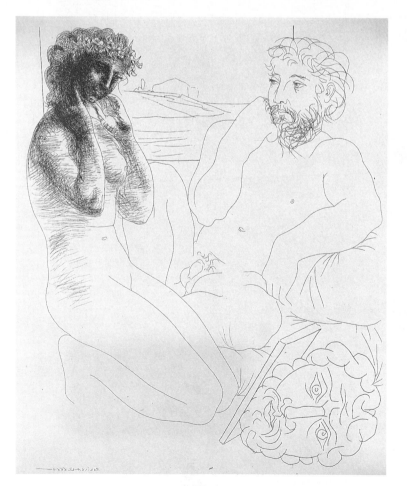

Figure 4-110. Pablo Picasso, *Sculptor with Kneeling Model.* April 18, 1933. Etching, printed in black, 14½ × 11¹¹/₁₆″. The Museum of Modern Art, New York. Purchase.

creating a dense atmospheric effect in keeping with the theme of absurdity. The eerie glow of Goya's hatching owes little to natural light and shadow or indeed to relief modeling. Instead it arises from the deliberately unnatural placement of light and dark areas in the context of a complex pictorial composition.

SUMMARY

The studies and master drawings in this chapter are arranged to focus clearly on specific modalities of modeling. Due to the complexity of the subject the functions of line as contour and as outline are considered separately in Chapters 2 and 3, but keep in mind that all drawing methods are part of an artistic continuum which has no such clear distinctions. Artists are sometimes able to fuse diverse techniques creatively in a single work. An example of such a fusion occurs in Picasso's etching *Sculptor and Model* (Figure 4-110), in which he combines classic line with hatch modeling. Although the two techniques have existed side by side for centuries, Picasso is one of the few artists to combine them successfully in a finished work of art. He did so by adding a darkly glowing passage of hatch modeling to line figures conceived in the classical mode. The contrast between the high-key effect of the line drawing and the dramatic emphasis of the modeled head has a freshness characteristic of highly original art. This work serves as a reminder of the creative uses of modeling that remain to be explored.

NOTES

1. Ulric Neisser, "The Processes of Vision," *Scientific American*, vol. 219, no. 3 (Sept. 1968), p. 205.

2. Leonardo da Vinci, *Treatise on Painting*, vol. 1, trans. A. Philip McMahon (Princeton, N.J.: Princeton University Press, 1956), p. 285.

3. In theory black is not a color but the absence of color. Since all pigments reflect some light, however, there are actually different blacks. Felt-tip pens are available in both warm and cool blacks.

4. Norma Brouse, "New Light on Seurat's 'Dot': Its Relation to Photo-Mechanical Color Printing in France in the 1800's," *The Art Bulletin*, LVI (Dec. 1974), p. 584.

5. Ibid., p. 581.

6. Ibid., p. 586.

7. Jeanne L. Wasserman, assisted by Joan M. Jukach and Arthur Beale, *Daumier Sculpture, A Critical and Comparative Study* (Cambridge, Mass.: Fogg Art Museum, Harvard University, 1969), p. 89.

8. The association of *drawing* with *design* is not superficial. Drawing almost always involves design in the modern sense, whether it be two or three dimensional. Although a distinction is made in the English language, in French and Italian the same word signifies both (i.e., *dessin*, *disegno*).

9. The early twelfth-century writer Theophilus, for example, explained how to depict a round tower by superimposing darker and lighter tones on a color of middle value, with a band of white painted in the middle of the tower from top to bottom. Darker bands of tones placed on each side of the white were intended to designate the roundness of the form turned from the viewer on each side. Paul Hills, *The Light of Early Italian Painting* (New Haven: Yale University Press, 1987), pp. 19–28.

10. James J. Gibson, *The Senses Considered as Perceptual Systems* (Boston: Houghton Mifflin, 1966), pp. 198–199.

11. Ibid., p. 191.

12. Renaissance artists of fifteenth-century Italy invented perspective, a geometrical system for representing the apparent diminution of size associated with distance. In traditional linear-perspective renderings, apparent size changes are projected along lines that radiate from imaginary vanishing points on a horizontal line. As a drawing method, linear perspective is a practical means of representing solid objects with geometrical surfaces such as architectural constructions but is not necessary for drawing the figure. Distance and the resulting apparent diminution of size generally play a lesser role in determining the appearance of the body than do the factors discussed in Chapter 5, such as surface orientation. For this reason perspective is not treated as a drawing method in this book.

13. Neisser, "Processes of Vision," p. 208.

14. Ingres, "Note for 'L'Age d'Or'," cited by Kenneth Clark in *The Nude* (Garden City, N.Y.: Doubleday, 1959), p. 219.

15. Leonardo da Vinci, *The Notebooks*, vol. 1, ed. Jean Paul Richter (New York: Dover, 1970), p. 281.

16. Julian E. Hochberg, *Perception* (Englewood Cliffs, N.J.: Prentice-Hall, 1964), p. 51. For an interesting discussion of the related phenomenon of color constancy see Jacob Beck, "The Perception of Surface Color," *Scientific American*, vol. 233, no. 2 (Aug. 1975), pp. 62–75.

17. Leonardo da Vinci, *The Notebooks*, p. 278.

18. Vilayanur S. Ramachandran, "Perceiving Shape from Shading," *Scientific American*, vol. 259, no. 2 (Aug. 1988), pp. 76–83.

19. The political nature of Käthe Kollwitz's art was not overlooked by the Nazis, who dismissed her in 1933 from her teaching post in the Berlin Academy, where she had taught master classes in graphic art since 1928. In 1936 they forbade an exhibition of her art. Earlier she had been the first woman ever elected to the Berlin Academy (Louis Kronenberger, *Atlantic Brief Lives* [Boston: Little, Brown, 1971], p. 436).

20. Surprisingly, drawing from casts was not practiced in the Ecole des Beaux-Arts during the nineteenth century. Instruction was limited to drawing from the live model, since cast studies were completed before admission to the Ecole (Albert Boime, *The Academy and French Painting in the Nineteenth Century* [London: Phaidon, 1971], pp. 24–25).

21. A specially prepared 35 mm slide is one means of demonstrating surface contours. The slide can be made from a small piece of kitchen aluminum foil cut neatly in half with a razor. Guiding the razor with a straight edge, cut two straight edges of foil. The edges should be separated very slightly to form a crack of about a hair's width or less. The two separated pieces can be held in position by an ordinary glass slide mount. If it is placed in a projector, such a slide creates a thin curtain of light, which behaves in the same way that a plane does when it intersects a solid object, producing a vivid effect of surface contour. It can be projected on a plaster cast as well as on a model.

22. "Exploring the Third Dimension with Camera and Computer," *Kodak Studio Light*, no. 1 (1975), p. 206.

23. *Surrealism* literally means "more than realism." As a twentieth-century school of art it attempts to re-create the fantastic dream imagery of the subconscious.

24. A more complete discussion of the claw chisel marks—known as *addentellati*—and their relation to Michelangelo's ink drawings is found in Rudolf Wittkower, *Sculpture Processes and Principles* (New York: Harper & Row, 1977), pp. 113—122.

25. Statement from the weekly Paris review *Arts*, April 26–May 2, 1961, quoted in Peter A. Wick, *Jacques Villon, Master of Graphic Art* (New York: October House, 1964), p. 24.

26. Ibid.

CHAPTER 5

The Skeleton

the structural framework of body forms

Now since the important thing in these arts is to draw a nude man and a nude woman well, and to remember them securely, one must go to the foundation of such nudes, which is their bones, so that when you will have memorized a skeleton you can never make a mistake when drawing a figure, either nude, or clothed; and this is saying a lot.

—BENVENUTO CELLINI

DIRECT OBSERVATION of external form was the basis of the previous drawing exercises. Your sense of structure, however, can be enhanced by studying the natural internal structure of the body, for the human body, unlike that of some other animals, depends on an interior bony framework—the skeleton—for its general external form.[1] If we were to remove the thighbone, as Stephen Peck, the anatomist, points out. "a thigh would have little more shape than a puddle of water."[2] Skeletal structure also affects the appearance of the body by governing movement and gesture: The bone formation at the knee joint, for example, largely determines the hingelike action of the leg and thigh (Figure 5-56).

Despite its key role in determining the form of the body, skeletal structure is not readily discernible in life (Figure 5-1). In order to perceive the skeleton in the model, it is necessary to have some prior knowledge of it. Seeing and knowing are closely linked; we tend to see only what we know.[3] Committing skeletal form to memory, as suggested by Cellini, is therefore a worthy project for the serious artist, for it enables us to see the form and structure of the human body more clearly by transcending the circular limitation of previous visual experience.

REFERENCE SOURCES

The best reference for studying the skeleton is the skeleton itself, ideally an articulated skeleton mounted on a stand (Figure 5-2). There is much to be learned from a mounted skeleton; however, the mounted skeleton with articulated joints is preferable, for it can be set in lifelike poses simulating those of the model (Figure 6-63). If an articulated skeleton is not available to you, you may be able to draw from one in a natural history museum or from a miniature plastic model, available in many stores.

Anatomical illustrations are another useful reference. Although no flat picture has the immediate three-dimensional clarity of a mounted skeleton, it can provide some visual information the skeleton cannot: For instance, an anatomical illustration is especially helpful in showing the relative position of the bones inside the body and their relationship to the muscles.[4] Anatomical plates are included here to assist you in studying skeletal and muscular structures. The appropriate illustrations are listed at the beginning of each study.

Another major source of information about the skeleton is the life model. Several key points of the skeleton lie just beneath the surface and can be detected by the eye as bumps

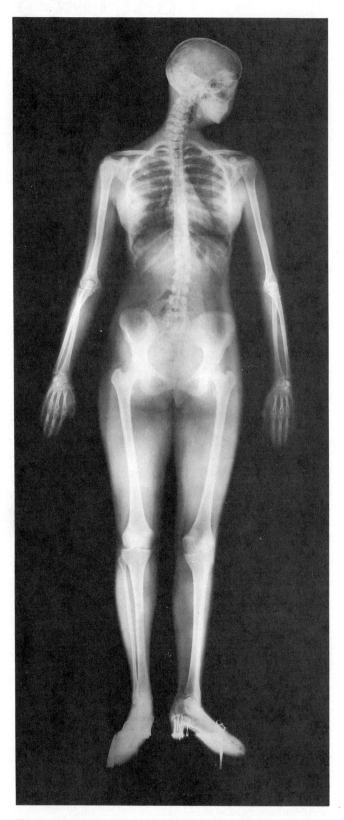

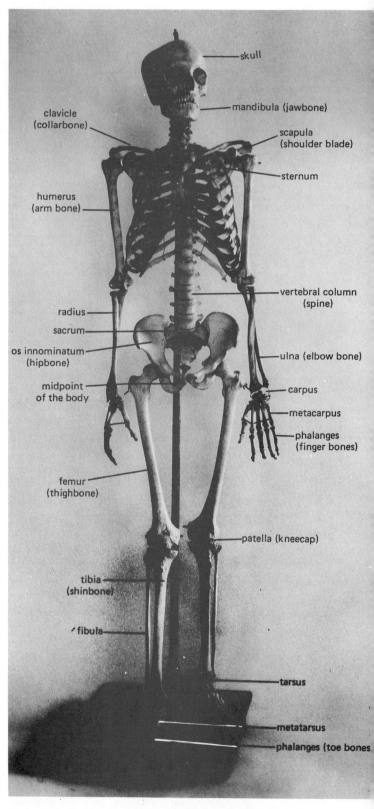

Figure 5-1. Radiograph of the female body (courtesy of Eastman Kodak Company). In an X-ray photograph the skeleton appears as a distinct pattern of white and gray, while the body tissues are seen as filmy tones ranging from near black to gray.

Figure 5-2. The male skeleton. A mounted and articulated skeleton is an excellent reference for studying skeletal forms. The dark parts of the rib cage represent softer cartilage, which does not retain its form when dry. Joints articulated with springs and bolts permit a variety of postures.

on the exterior of the body. In each study suggestions are provided for using anatomical clues of this sort.

STUDY 29   Introduction to the Skeleton

materials: ❑ 11 × 14″ bound sketchbook or bond paper held by a clipboard
              ❑ drawing pen (0.5 mm point) and India ink
              ❑ compressed charcoal pencil (optional)
reference: ❑ Figures 5-1, 5-2, 5-3, 5-4, and 5-5
time: ❑ 10–15 minutes for each drawing

A general introduction to skeletal forms can be gained by drawing directly from anatomical illustrations. Using the figures listed or a suitable anatomy book, make several ten- to fifteen–minute studies of the skeleton. Then try to repeat the same drawing from memory. After you have finished, you may make corrections by comparing your drawing with the illustration. In this exercise a rapid general rendering is preferable as a means of grasping the essential forms. Laborious copying of detailed anatomical illustrations may prevent you from concentrating on the more important larger forms, such as those of the rib cage, the skull, and the pelvis. When drawing the rib cage for example try to capture its egg-like general

Figure 5-3. The male skeleton, rear view. (Dr. J. Fau, *The Anatomy of the External Forms of Man* [London: Hippolyte Bailliere, 1849]. Courtesy of Countway Library, Harvard University.) Though lacking the three-dimensional clarity of a mounted skeleton, the anatomical illustration has the advantage of showing both the skeleton and its relationship to superficial forms of the body.

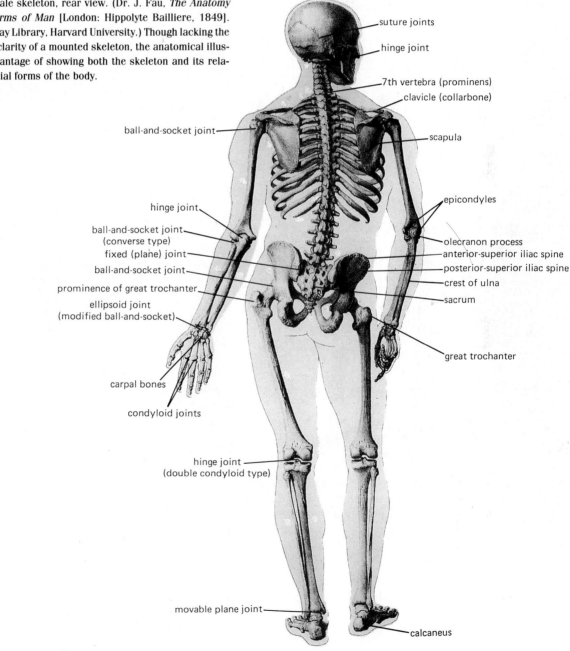

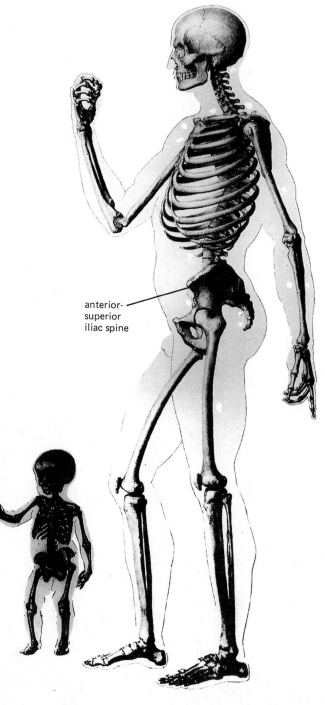

anterior-
superior
iliac spine

Figure 5-4. The male skeleton (side view) and the infant skeleton. (Dr. J. Fau, *The Anatomy of the External Forms of Man* [London: Hippolyte Bailliere, 1849]. Courtesy of Countway Library, Harvard University.)

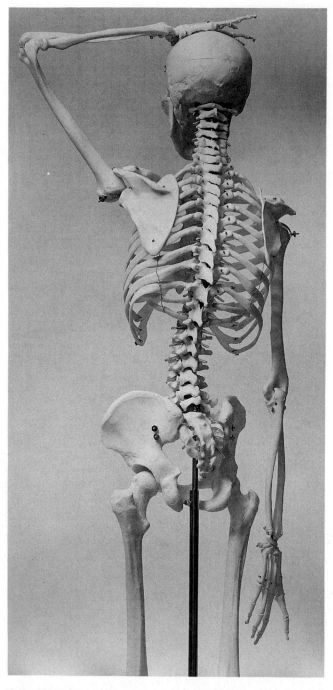

Figure 5-5. Three-quarter rear view of the mounted skeleton.

form, instead of the individual ribs. Your first efforts may not satisfy your desire for accuracy or completeness, but these qualities will come later with more experience in drawing the skeleton. Through this exercise, however, you will learn much of the basic structure, which can then be applied to studies relating the skeleton to the figure as a whole.

STUDY 30:   **The Model and the Skeleton**

materials: ❑ 36 × 24″ newsprint drawing pad
           ❑ easel or straight-back chair
           ❑ Masonite or plywood board and clamps
           ❑ drawing crayon (Nupastel or Conté) in two
              colors: black and sanguine recommended
reference: ❑ model and mounted skeleton or Figures 5-1, 5-2,
              5-3, 5-4, and 5-5
time: ❑ 40 minutes

Drawing from an actual skeleton in conjunction with the live model is perhaps the most direct way of comprehending the relationship of the bone structure with the exterior forms of the body. It is important the model hold a pose that can be simulated with the mounted skeleton. Place the mounted skeleton on the model stand in such a way that the model and the skeleton are in approximately the same pose (Figure 5-6). Allow yourself twenty minutes to make a contour drawing of the figure from the model, using a black or dark brown crayon. When the life drawing is completed, draw the skeleton inside the figure, using a sanguine or Venetian red crayon to distinguish the two drawings. While you are drawing the model, glance at the skeleton to see if you can locate skeletal features that are visible in the model. Collarbones, ribs, and cheekbones are a few skeletal parts that may be immediately apparent in the model, and closer comparison will reveal many others. For the purposes of this study Latin names of bones are irrelevant. Of special importance are any visible clues of the backbone, hipbone, and the rib cage. When you discover a clue to the skeleton such as the collarbone in the model, look for its counterpart on the other side of the body; then compare them for position. Is one higher than the other? Visually compare skeletal parts also for relative size. The beginner's tendency to exaggerate the head can be checked by comparing the skull with the rib cage (Figure 5-4). Visual comparison is vital for this study.

Figure 5-6. Drawing the skeleton within a life study. The mounted skeleton affords a means of visualizing the skeleton in the body. The student is interpreting the skeleton of the model by comparing the mounted skeleton with suggestions of the bony structure in the body.

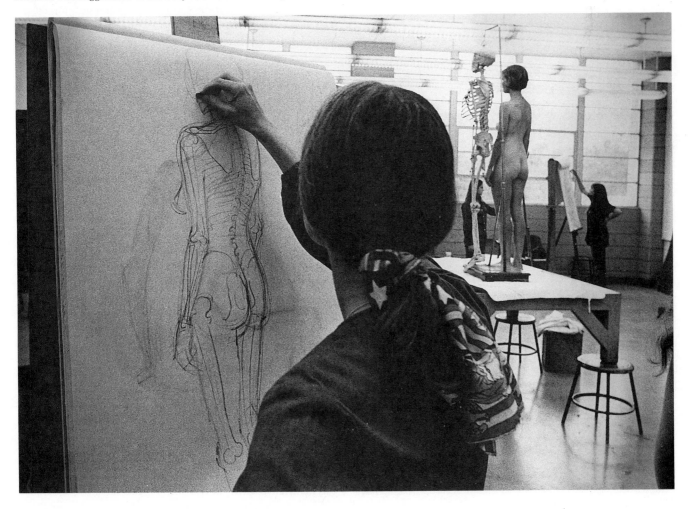

If a mounted skeleton is not available, you may wish to take your drawings of the model to a museum or laboratory in which a skeleton is on display and complete the study there. If no skeleton is available, anatomical illustrations are a good substitute.

Alternative Study

Making a Model of the Skeleton. The complexity of the skeleton demands the artist analyze skeletal forms and reduce them to simpler forms that are useful in drawing the figure. Making a model is one way of accomplishing this objective. It is important, however, that the model retain the essential character of the original skeletal forms. Traditional modeling media such as clay and wood are ill-suited to the subject of the skeleton. An unconventional but effective medium is suggested by Calder's brilliantly witty wire figures (Figure 3-38).

For ease of handling, pipe cleaner wire is recommended. It is available in 12-inch lengths that can be bent and twisted by hand, but is stiff enough to retain its form (Figure 5-7). As when drawing the skeleton with crayon, you will need to refer to the mounted skeleton in order to create the wire model. A practical part of the skeleton to model first in wire is the backbone (vertebral column).

Figure 5-7. Student model of the skeleton made of wire pipe cleaners. 14″ high.

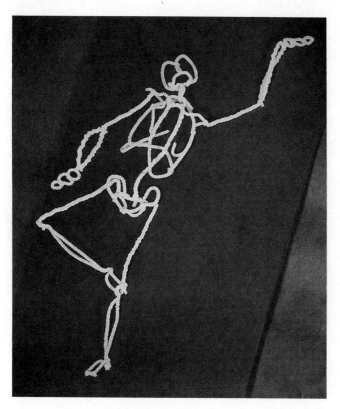

The fact that the vertebral column is not readily apparent in life and yet is of central importance in understanding the figure makes it worthy of special study.

STUDY 31:   **The Vertebral Column**

materials: ❑ 36 × 24″ newsprint pad
          ❑ easel or straight-back chair
          ❑ Masonite or plywood board and clamps
          ❑ drawing crayon
reference: ❑ model and mounted skeleton or Figures 5-1, 5-2, 5-3, 5-4, 5-5, 5-8, and 5-14
time: ❑ 5 minutes

Because this study focuses on the position and shape of the spine in the body, begin with a ten-minute contour study of the figure seen from the back or from the side. In drawing from life take care to indicate any visible suggestions of the vertebral column, such as the vertical groove of the back or bumps therein. A straight-on back view of the figure is best avoided in this study, as it does not permit observation of the spinal curves. After you have completed the life drawing of the back, indicate on it the general curves and position of the vertebral column (Figure 5-10), using anatomical illustrations or the mounted skeleton as a guide.

THE STRUCTURE OF THE VERTEBRAL COLUMN

As your study demonstrates, the vertebral column rises in a double S curve that begins with its two lowest parts, the sacrum and coccyx (Figure 5-9).[5] Above the sacrum the lumbar region of the spine is bowed forward.[6] The lumbar curve, which develops just before a child learns to walk, is in fact a by-product of our upright posture and is not generally found in animals that walk on all fours.[7] The lumbar curve is thus a peculiarly human characteristic that gives the figure its special grace and poise in the standing position.

Above the lumbar curve the spine continues its backward thrust until the less obvious dorsal curve appears, causing the upper spine to bend toward the front of the body. The dorsal curve accounts for the visible forward thrust of the neck. The uppermost seven cervical vertebrae, which make up the neck itself, curve backward again before terminating at the base of the skull. The lowest cervical vertebra is usually apparent as a bump on the back of the neck (hence the name *prominens*). On top of the curving form of the vertebral column the skull rests in a state of near perfect balance,[8] for the atlas vertebra, which supports the skull, joins it quite close to the head's center of gravity.[9]

The curving character of the spinal column, though apparent in anatomical illustrations of the skeleton, is seldom

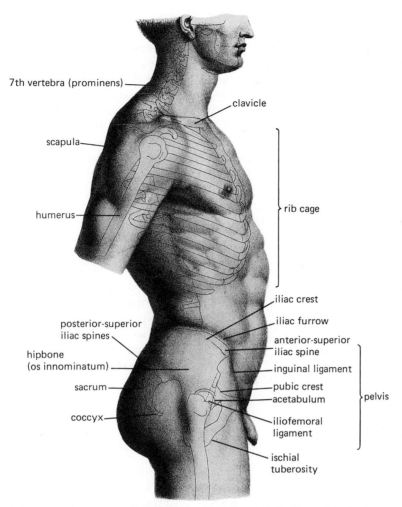

7th vertebra (prominens)

clavicle

scapula

humerus

rib cage

iliac crest

iliac furrow

posterior-superior
iliac spines

anterior-superior
iliac spine

hipbone
(os innominatum)

inguinal ligament

pubic crest

sacrum

acetabulum

coccyx

pelvis

iliofemoral
ligament

ischial
tuberosity

Figure 5-8. The axial skeleton in the figure: a structural assemblage that includes the vertebral column, the pelvis, the rib cage, the shoulder girdle, and the skull. (Dr. J. Fau, *The Anatomy of the External Forms of Man* [London: Hippolyte Bailliere, 1849]. Courtesy of Countway Library, Harvard University.)

Figure 5-9. *Left.* Line drawing of the vertebral column (after Gray's *Anatomy*). *Right.* Silhouette representing the spinal curves.

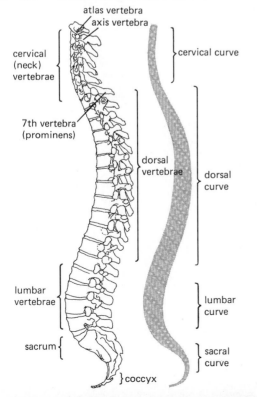

atlas vertebra
axis vertebra

cervical
(neck)
vertebrae

cervical curve

7th vertebra
(prominens)

dorsal
vertebrae

dorsal
curve

lumbar
vertebrae

lumbar
curve

sacrum

sacral
curve

coccyx

clearly visible in life, a fact that can mislead the uninformed draftsman. The reason for this is to be found in two features of human anatomy: (1) the spinous processes of the vertebrae (Figure 5-11) project outward to form a surface contour visible as a central groove on the back, which is less pronounced than the contour of overall form of the vertebral column (Figure 5-9); (2) two powerful sets of muscles (sacrospinalis), one on each side of the spinal column, tend to mask the lumbar curve, giving the back a straighter appearance in the lumber region (Figure 6-30).

The construction of the spine can be understood by examining the individual component bones, the *vertebrae.* Although there is considerable variation in size and shape among vertebrae, ranging from the generally smaller, lighter neck (*cervical*) bones to the large thick bones of the lower back (*lumbar*) region, certain features are common to almost all of them: the vertebral body, the arch, and the spinous process (Figure 5-11). The *vertebral body* is the solid, round, cylindrical part of the bone situated on the front (*anterior*) side of the spine. Like the drums of an architectural column, "the bodies of the vertebrae are stacked one upon the other, forming a

153

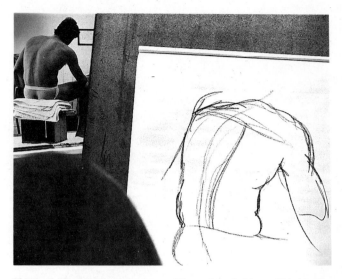

Figure 5-10. Drawing the curves of the vertebral column. This hastily drawn figure reveals two attempts at locating the spine. The first is represented by the darker line, which divides the figure equally. Just left of it is a second and more accurate line, which corresponds more closely with the groove of the model's back.

Figure 5-11. Dorsal vertebrae (after Gray's *Anatomy*).

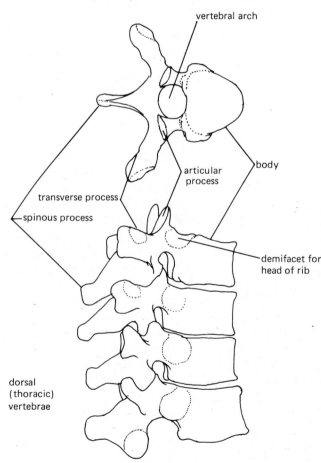

vertebral arch

transverse process

spinous process

articular process

body

demifacet for head of rib

dorsal (thoracic) vertebrae

strong pillar for the support of the cranium and trunk."[10] Sandwiched between the vertebral bodies are padlike disks of cartilage that are flexible enough to permit a certain degree of movement. Although the movement of the individual vertebra is very slight, together they add up to a remarkable range of turning and bending (Figures 5-12, 5-13, and 5-18).[11]

Located behind the body of the vertebrae is the *vertebral arch*, which forms a round opening through which passes the spinal cord. Projecting from the arch are a number of processes, the most visible of which is the *spinous process*, a knobby blade of bone extending backward and downward from the arch. The spinous process is also the most useful in drawing. In life it is familiar as a row of bumps along the vertical groove of the back, usually visible when the body bends forward. The most noticeable of these is that of the seventh (cervical) vertebra, mentioned earlier, known as the *vertebra prominens*. You can easily locate it by touching the back at the base of the neck. As a site for muscle and ligament attachments the spinous process provides leverage that facilitates movement of the vertebral bodies.

A vertebra generally has six other processes (projections) in addition to the spinous process. Four *articular processes*, located on the arch, connect other vertebrae with joints. The remaining two, called *transverse processes*, are winglike projections on the sides of the arch, which, like the spinous process, provide extra leverage for the muscles and ligaments attached

Figure 5-12. Movements of the vertebral column. *Left.* Extension. *Center.* Rotation. *Right.* Flexion. The zigzag lines represent tensed muscles. (Jean Galbert Savage, *Anatomie du Gladiator Combattant.* Courtesy of Countway Library, Harvard University.)

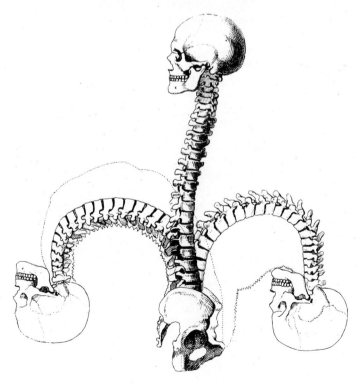

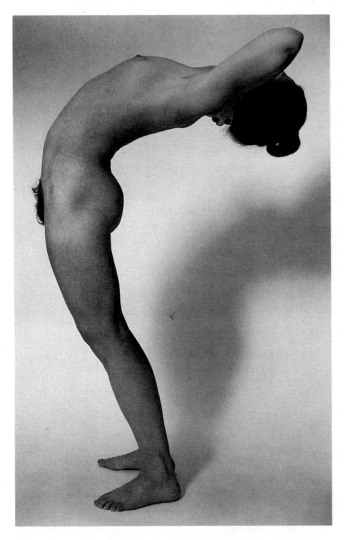

triangular sacrum fits between the hipbones, to which it is fixed by nonmovable joints. Beneath the sacrum is the coccyx, a small segmented bone that forms the vestigial tail of the vertebral column. The sacrum and coccyx together form a hooklike curve that turns inward at the lower end. In a standing figure the sacrum transfers most of the upper body weight to the pelvis (and thence to the leg bones). The sacrum's relationship to the pelvis can be better studied as a part of the axial skeleton proper.

STUDY 32:   Drawing the Axial Skeleton

materials: ❑ 14 × 11″ sketchbook
❑ drawing pen (0.5 mm point recommended)
❑ India ink
❑ 14 × 11″ pad of tracing paper
❑ HB drawing pencil
❑ eraser
❑ transparent (Scotch) tape

reference: ❑ model and mounted skeleton or Figures 5-5, 5-8, 5-14, 5-15, and 5-16

time: ❑ part 1: 15 minutes for each drawing of the model
❑ part 2: 30 minutes for each drawing of the skeleton

Figure 5-14. Frontal (anterior) view of the mounted skeleton.

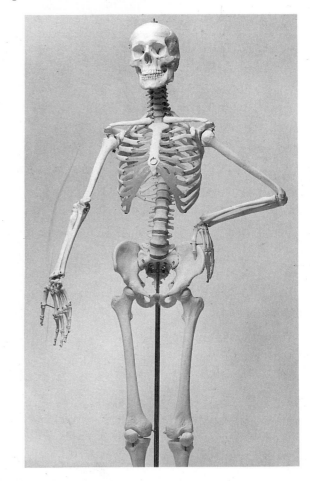

Figure 5-13. Extension of the vertebral column in a "stretching" gesture. The slight movement of each vertebra permits a wide range of movement of the vertebral column as a whole.

to them (Figure 5-11). Variations of these general features are noticeable in different regions of the spine.

The special construction of the top two vertebrae, the atlas, and the axis vertebra immediately beneath it makes possible the freedom of movement associated with the head. The axis vertebra features a vertical projection that acts as a pivot for the atlas vertebra above it, enabling the head to turn easily to the side (Figure 5-9). Further down the spine the *dorsal* vertebrae feature articular surfaces in the form of facets or half-facets that accept rib heads (Figure 5-11). Understandably, such facets are entirely lacking in the lumbar vertebrae (below the rib cage).

The lowest region of the spine appears so different from the rest that at first there seem to be no similarities. This is due to the fact that the vertebrae of this section fuse together early in life to form two connecting bones, the *sacrum* and the *coccyx*, which have their own distinctive shapes. The wide

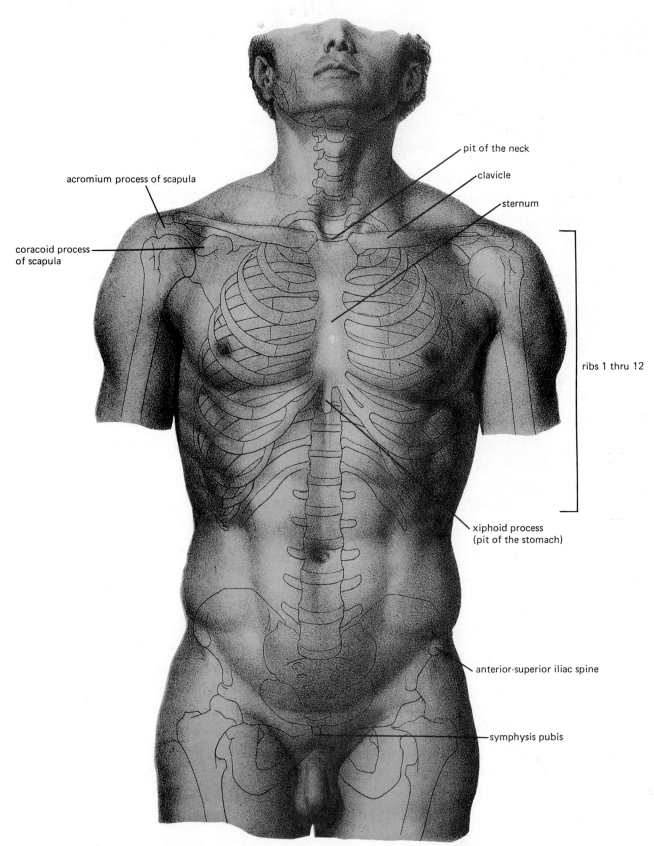

acromium process of scapula

coracoid process
of scapula

pit of the neck

clavicle

sternum

ribs 1 thru 12

xiphoid process
(pit of the stomach)

anterior-superior iliac spine

symphysis pubis

Figure 5-15. The axial skeleton and its relation to exterior form. (Dr. J. Fau, *The Anatomy of the External Forms of Man* [London: Hippolyte Bailliere, 1849]. Courtesy of Countway Library, Harvard University.)

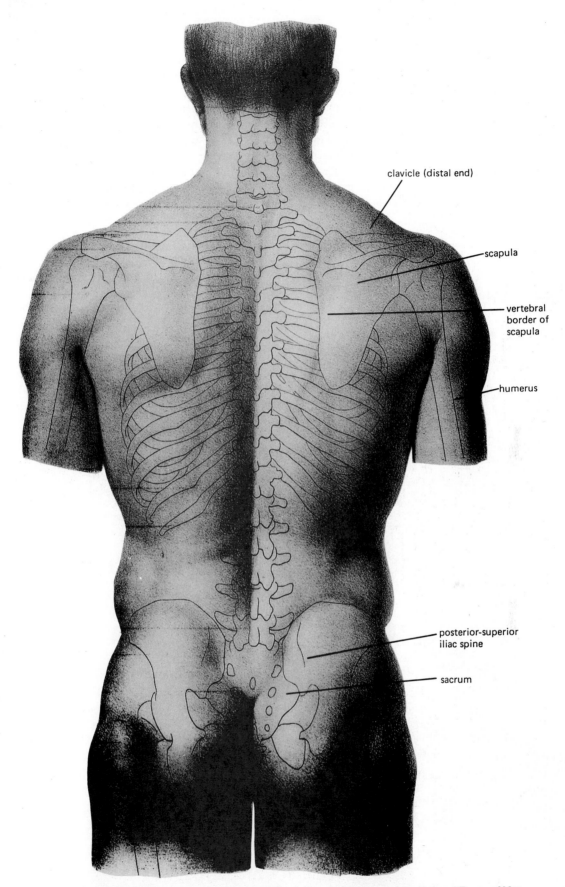

Figure 5-16. The axial skeleton, posterior view. (Dr. J. Fau, *The Anatomy of the External Forms of Man* [London: Hippolyte Bailliere, 1849]. Courtesy of Countway Library, Harvard University.)

Labels on figure:
clavicle (distal end)
scapula
vertebral border of scapula
humerus
posterior-superior iliac spine
sacrum

Part 1

For this study your drawings from the life model will serve as a means of visualizing the axial skeleton. With that in mind first execute a series of twleve pen-and-ink drawings of the nude model (Figure 5-17). You can use the rapid contour technique (described in Chapter 3) because the drawings need not be highly developed. In preparing them, however, reverse the procedure of the previous exercises; that is, indicate the position and curvature of the spine first, and then use this indication as the basis for visual measurements while you draw other features of the figure.

The vertebral column makes an almost ideal line of reference on which to base a drawing of the figure, for it is of central importance to the attitude and gesture of the body. The idea of an imaginary internal line as the basis for setting up a drawing is applicable to almost any subject[12] and is also very helpful in developing your skills. Certain other skeletal features of the figure can be drawn from life and can serve as references for drawing the skeleton later. These include bony

Figure 5-17. Drawing with pen and ink in the sketchbook. To ensure an uninterrupted flow of ink in the drawing pen, the sketchbook should be held at an oblique angle rather than perpendicular to the floor.

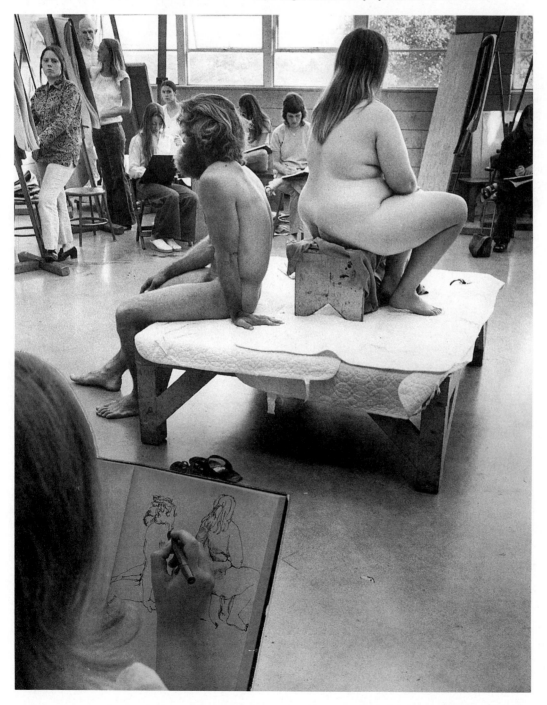

protrusions just under the skin that reveal the position of skeletal structures deeper inside the body. For example, the slight depression at the base of the neck, known as the pit of the neck (Figure 5-15), is usually visible in life. The bottom (or floor) of the pit marks the upper (superior) surface of the breastbone (*sternum*), as well as the inner (*medial*) attachments of the collarbones (*clavicles*). An indication of the pit of the neck in your life drawing, if your view of the model permits, indicates the correct placement for drawing the rib cage and the shoulder girdle of the same figure later. The pit of the neck is also important as a surface indicator of the body's line of lateral symmetry, being midway between the two shoulders.

In drawing a shoulder of the figure, compare it as you draw not only with neighboring forms but also with the position of the opposite shoulder. Does it lie above or below its counterpart? Are both at the same height in the figure? Your estimates can be marked simply with dots of the pen. An imaginery line can be drawn between the two shoulders to form the *shoulder axis*, a useful tool both for beginning a life study and for constructing the skeleton. The shoulder axis can be visualized conveniently in the skeleton by drawing a line between the outer (acromial) ends of the collar bones (clavicles). Readily apparent in the skeleton, the ends of the collar bones are often visible in life as bumps on the upper surface of the shoulders (Figures 5-15, 5-16, and 5-18). Critical to most gestures of the figure, the shoulder axis—together with the vertebral column—offers a key to visualizing the skeletal structure.

The most prominent visual clues in the pelvic region are two bony projections that you can easily feel on each side of your body just below the waist. Called the *anterior-superior iliac spines*, they may be visible on the body as slight bumps (Figure 5-8). In addition to revealing the position of the pelvis the two projections define a line known as the *pelvic axis*, which is useful in articulating the form of the trunk with that of the legs (Figures 5-15 and 5-18).

Pen and ink is recommended as the drawing medium for the life studies because it is clearly visible through translucent tracing paper, the material used in Part 2 of this study. The HB drawing pencil is also suitable, if you prefer a pressure-sensitive medium (Figure 5-21).

Figure 5-18. Black dots mark anatomical clues useful in visualizing the skeleton and its major axes: above, the pit of the neck and the acromial ends of the clavicles; below, the anterior superior iliac spines of the pelvis. The relationship of the two axes is a key to understanding figural gesture.

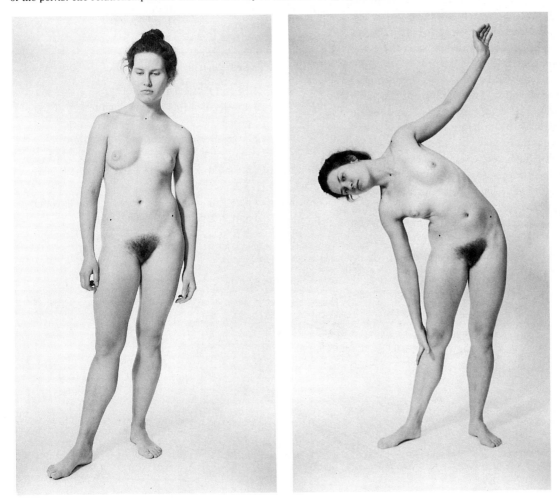

Part 2

From your series of drawings select six that you like best, and then cut rectangular pieces of tracing paper slightly smaller than the size of the sketchbook page (Figure 5-19). Place the tracing paper over the drawing and tape one edge of it to the sketchbook page. In this way the tracing paper is held in one position over the drawing but can be lifted if you wish to examine the original drawing underneath. The remaining five drawings should also be prepared with tracing paper overlays. By rendering the skeleton on the tracing paper overlays you can make anatomical studies without altering the original life drawings. Even if you decide to erase and start over, the original drawing remains untouched. After selecting one drawing for your first study try to visualize the skeleton as it might appear in the figure. Then review the anatomical illustrations in this book until you find a view of the skeleton that approximates your figure drawing. You may need to refer to more than one illustration to obtain the visual information necessary to render the axial skeleton in the attitude dictated by your original drawing.

As a first step, make an effort to visualize the position of the spine in your drawing and then sketch it lightly on the overlay. With the general position in place, you will find it easy to develop the curves of the vertebral column on the tracing paper overlay. The vertebral column will suggest the position of the skeletal forms to which it attaches—namely, the skull, the pelvis, and the rib cage. Work toward accuracy of placement and position rather than detail, using the eraser to clear away confusing mistakes.

Certain abstract forms may assist you in making the generalized drawing of the skeleton. The cranium of the skull, for example, can be visualized as an enormous egg, poised on top of the spinal column with the larger end in the back.[13] The rib cage also suggests an egglike form, but one in which the large end is cut off. Attached to the spine at its back, the rib cage projects forward from it, creating a hollow enclosure (Figures 5-42, 5-44, and 5-20). There is no need to be concerned with such details as the form of individual ribs in this study: Draw only the large general forms. When the general

skeletal forms are accurately rendered, the smaller units of form, such as ribs and individual vertebrae, fit readily into place. You may find it helpful, however, to indicate the position of the collarbones (clavicles) and shoulder blades (scapulae), which form part of the rib cage and determine the shoulder axis, as noted earlier. In addition include the femur bones, which join the pelvis at the hip, and the humerous bones, at the shoulders, for they can help you visualize the exact position of the axial skeleton (Figure 5-21).

In drawing the pelvis try not to lose sight of its essential three-dimensional character, which is that of a ringlike formation enclosing a round void—the pelvic cavity (Figure 5-22). The front center of the ring corresponds with the vertical midpoint of the body. The back of the ring joins the vertebral column by means of the sacrum, a joint that is suggested in life by the triangular plane between the hips in the lowest region of the back. Seen from the side, the ring shape of the pelvis appears to sag downward in the front somewhat as the ribs do in relation to the spine. From the front and back of a standing figure, however, the pelvis is seen aligned horizontally with the vertical of the spine. Even when the spine bends, the pelvis maintains a relatively fixed angular relationship with the lower spine, for the joint of the sacrum and the pelvis does not permit movement.

Some components of the axial skeleton that are treated broadly in this study—the skull, the rib cage, and the pelvis—are such important determinants of the body form, they merit separate examination.

STUDY 33:   Self-Portrait with the Skull

materials: ❏ 14 × 11″ tracing paper
  ❏ drawing pen (0.5 mm) or compressed charcoal pencil
  ❏ large dressing mirror and smaller mirror (optional)

reference: ❏ mounted skeleton or Figures 5-5, 5-14, 5-23, 5-24, and 5-25

time: ❏ part 1: 30 minutes to 1 hour for the life study
  ❏ part 2: 1 hour for the skull study

Figure 5-19. The sketchbook overlay. Tracing paper can be cut and taped over a figure drawing for a study of the skeleton.

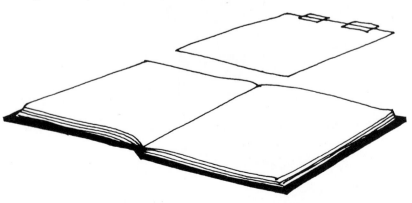

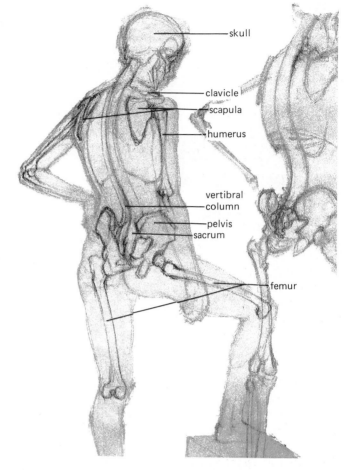

Figure 5-21. Student drawing. The figure drawn from life with an interpretation of the skeleton. Graphite and sanguine pencil on sketchbook paper and tracing paper overlay. 14 × 11″.

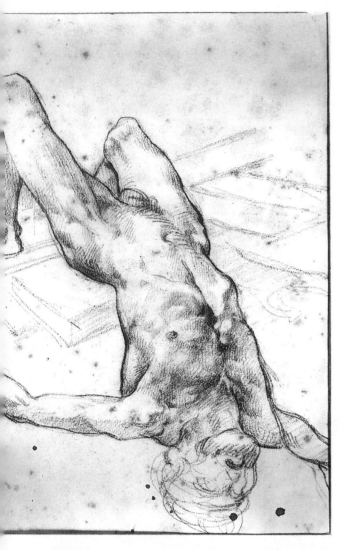

Figure 5-20. Théodore Géricault, *Study for* The Raft of the Medusa, 1818. Charcoal on white paper. 289 × 205 mm. Besançon, Musée des Beaux Arts. The lower edge of the rib cage and pelvic prominences are apparent in this superbly modeled life study.

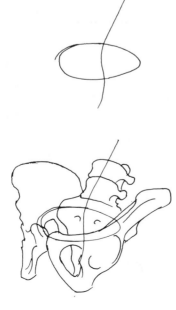

Figure 5-22. The oval void of the pelvis can serve as a basis for positioning a drawing of the pelvis.

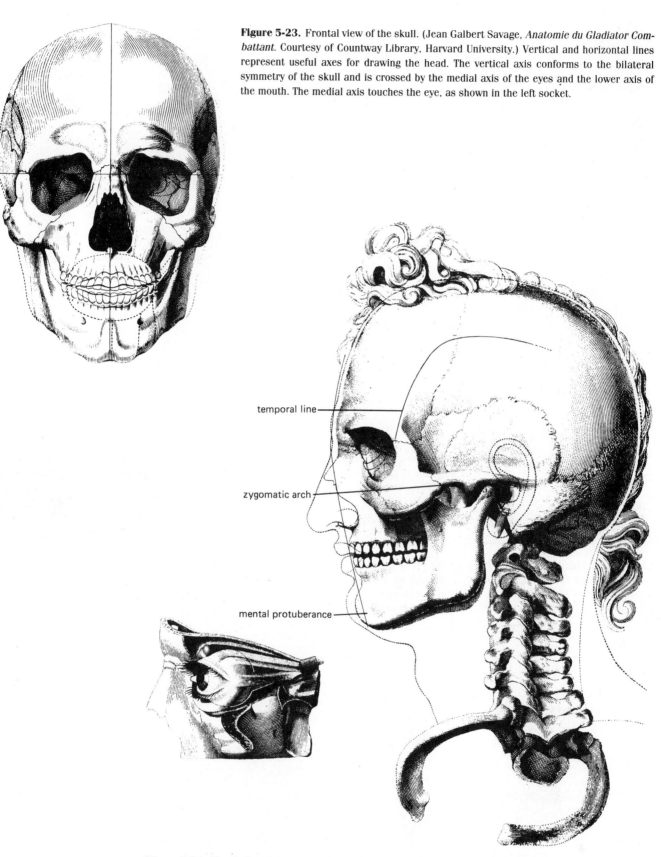

Figure 5-23. Frontal view of the skull. (Jean Galbert Savage, *Anatomie du Gladiator Combattant.* Courtesy of Countway Library, Harvard University.) Vertical and horizontal lines represent useful axes for drawing the head. The vertical axis conforms to the bilateral symmetry of the skull and is crossed by the medial axis of the eyes and the lower axis of the mouth. The medial axis touches the eye, as shown in the left socket.

temporal line

zygomatic arch

mental protuberance

Figure 5-24. The skull with the complete profile and the vertical axis. This skull features an unusually short cranium extension behind the spinal joint but is otherwise normal.

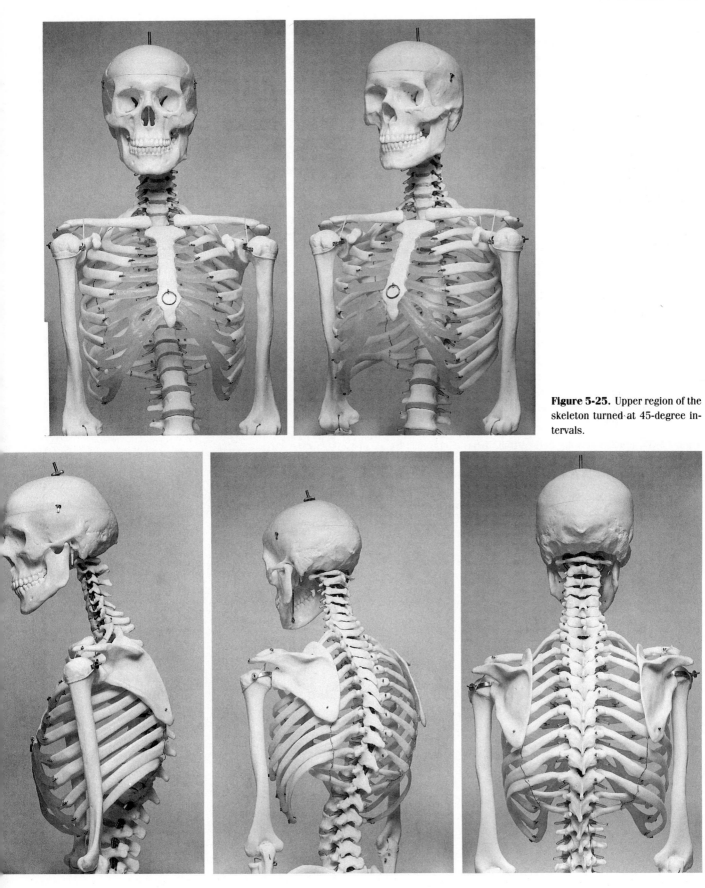

Figure 5-25. Upper region of the skeleton turned at 45-degree intervals.

Because the skull and the form of the head are closely related, the self-portrait is a convenient vehicle for studying this part of the skeleton. Luckily the skull also serves as a means to sharpen your skill in drawing the head, the overriding artistic objective. The self-portrait has the added virtue of economy, as it eliminates the expense of a model! All that is required is a good mirror, preferably of plate glass, adequate illumination, and one or two hours of uninterrupted time. With two mirrors at your disposal, however, it is possible for you to see yourself in an unreversed image, like what you have seen in clothing store mirrors. Although this is the way others see you, you may find it refreshingly unfamiliar, and a fresh point of view can be a decided advantage in drawing the self-portrait.[14]

Bear in mind the purpose of this self-portrait is to study the head's relation to the skull. Before you begin to draw take time to examine your reflected image for formal features that hint of the skull. Several such features are likely to be readily apparent, including the checkbones, the eye sockets (especially their upper rims), the temples on each side of the forehead, and the bridge of the nose, to mention a few. They are easily felt with your fingers. Compare them with the skulls illustrated in this chapter. If the skull is unfamiliar to you, its novelty—like that of the unreversed image—can offer a new way of seeing and drawing the head.

Figure 5-26. Student drawing. Self-Portrait. Nupastel crayon. 14 × 11″. The student chose to represent the more general forms of the head, yet a portrait quality is apparent. The more characteristic forms of the individual are often seen in larger shapes rather than in details.

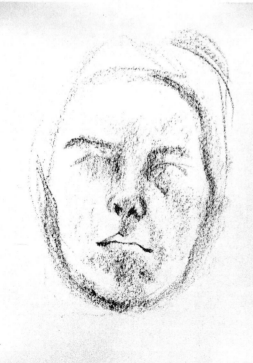

Part 1

Drawing the Self-Portrait. If this is your first self-portrait, a few suggestions are in order. Above all, draw yourself as you would draw a model, observing and drawing large forms and shapes first (Figure 5-26). The large formal characteristics, such as those just listed, are important in creating a convincing drawing of the head.

Visual measurement (of angles), as described in Study 9, offers a way of analyzing the form of the head. Ignoring the smaller facial features, try to describe the formal relationship between the neck and the big shape of the head. Look for the abstract relationship between the shapes created by the hair and the rest of the head. Then proceed to define features, such as the angle of the jaw, the planes of the cheeks, the forehead and temples (Figures 5-27, 5-28, 5-29, and 5-30). Even with the face left blank the character of the head will become apparent at this stage.

Figure 5-27. Student drawing of the head with emphasis on skeletal features. Graphite pencil on bond sketchbook paper. 14 × 11″. Drawn from life, this study records a search for exterior clues to the structure of the skull.

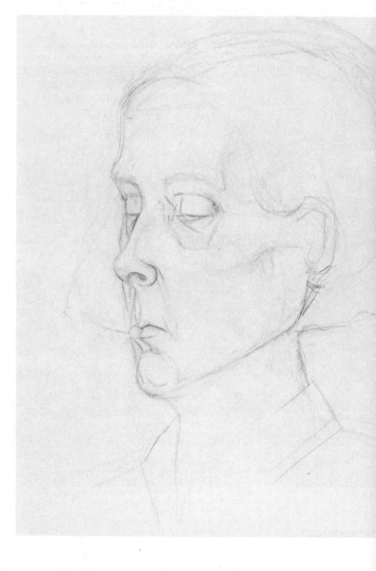

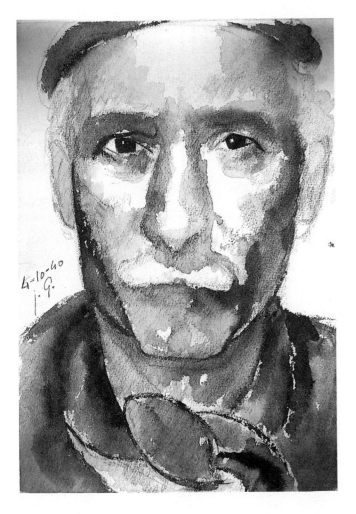

Figure 5-28. Julio Gonzalez (1876–1942), *Self-Portrait*, 1940. Wash and pencil. 9½ × 6¼″. Otterloo, Kröller-Müller National Museum. The Spanish sculptor adopted relief modeling in this self-portrait as a means of defining the form of the head in terms of broad planes suggestive of the underlying skull structure.

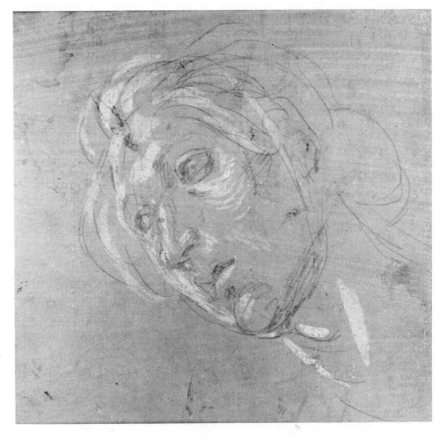

Figure 5-29. Filippino Lippi (attributed to), *Life Study of a Man's Head*, 1470–1480. Metalpoint and white on lilac-gray paper. 246 × 188 mm. Düsseldorf Kunstmuseum, Grafische Sammlung, Inv. Nr. Fp9 verso. This freely drawn study exhibits the use of arcs based on an ovoid concept of the head. Both the vertical medial arc and the arc connecting the eyes are apparent. The contours of the eyelids suggest the spherical form of the eyeball.

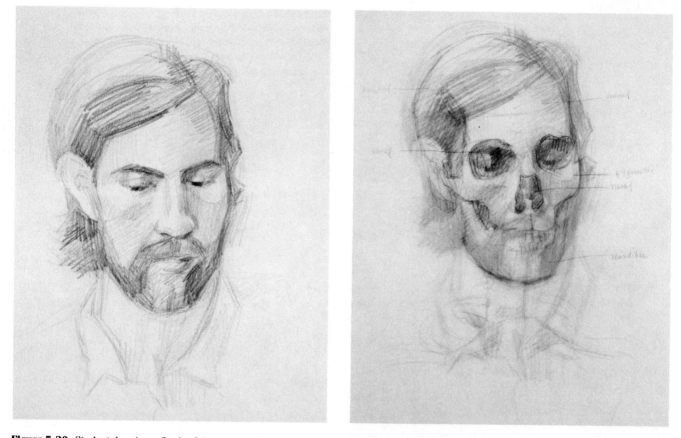

Figure 5-30. Student drawings. *Study of the Head and Skeletal Analysis Overlay.* Graphite pencil on bond sketchbook paper. 14 × 11″.

Smaller features will fit easily within the context of the larger forms. In drawing the form of the eyes, for instance, first analyze the larger form of the eye socket and the eyeball rather than attempt seductive details of the iris and pupil (Figure 5-27). The upper contour of the eye socket rises from the bridge of the nose and droops downward slightly toward the outer sides (Figure 5-23). The lower contour of the eye socket is often suggested by a slightly bluish coloration in that region, caused by the eye muscles and their associated blood vessels. Though only a small portion of the eyeball itself is normally exposed in life, its spherical form is often suggested by eyelids, which usually follow the form of the eyeball both above and below the exposed portion (Figure 5-27 and 5-29).

The completed self-portrait serves as the basis for drawing the skull. With a sheet of tracing paper taped over your self-portrait, try visualizing and then drawing a line that follows the vertical division of the head's symmetry. In a frontal view the line will be straight (Figure 5-23), but when the head is turned to the side, the line will describe a gently curving arc (Figures 5-29 and 5-33). Check your original drawing against this line. Are the facial features consistently spaced in relation to the line? If not, is the apparent asymmetry in your drawing intentional? Such questions may lead you to reevaluate and change your drawing.

The central curving line, also known as the *medial arc*, provides a visual reference for gauging the relative position of basic facial elements in a drawing of the head. It is comparable to the Greenwich meridian that divides the globe in half along the north-south axis. Once the medial arc is in place, visualize the basic features of the head, such as the eyes and the mouth, as lying on arcs similar to those that mark latitude on the globe. The projecting form of the nose, however, rises above the medial arc and can confuse the beginner. For this reason pay special attention to the construction of the lower portion of the nose, which lies on the medial arc. Like the eyes, the mouth can also be conceived as lying along a horizontal arc intersecting the medial arc.

Precedents

Since their initial formulation in the Renaissance, arc constructs appear to have played a part in the visual thinking of many artists, and in some master drawings the arcs are clearly visible.[15] The medial arc, for example, is apparent in a drawing of the head by the Italian artist Filippino Lippi (c. 1457–1504), as is the general ovoid form on which the arc is based (Figure 5-29). The horizontal arc construction appears in a drawing by Piero della Francesca (1420–1492) in which the head is represented as an ovoid, with the planes of each cross section tilted upward with respect to the viewer (Figure 4-73). Leonardo da Vinci used a similar formula to study the form of the skull by making both a vertical section of the entire skull and a horizontal section of the cranium (Figure 5-31). An intriguing example of the medial arc drawn in segments is seen in a superb study of the skull by Alberto Giacometti (1901–1966) (Figure 5-32).

Part 2

Drawing the Skull. The medial arc you have drawn on the tracing paper over your self-portrait can be useful in drawing the cranium. With anatomical illustrations as a reference, try drawing the ovoid form of the cranium within the outer lines of the self-portrait so the medial arc appears to lie in a

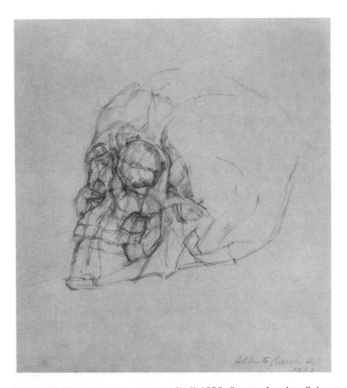

Figure 5-32. Alberto Giacometti, *Skull*, 1923. Crayon. London, Sainsbury Collection.

Figure 5-31. Leonardo da Vinci, *Anatomical Studies of Skulls*, 1489. Silverpoint. 18.1 × 12.9 cm. Windsor Castle, Royal Library. Leonardo's interest in the structure of the skull is evidenced by his careful proportional studies of its form. The vertical section of the bottom skull corresponds with the vertical axis of Figure 5-23.

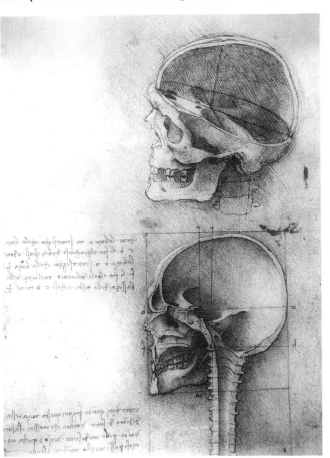

centered position on the ovoid. At this stage in the drawing it is vital to estimate the size of the cranium carefully, for it is a common error to draw the back portion of the head too small in proportion to the front. The reason for this recurring problem may be that this region of the head is usually concealed by masses of hair, making it difficult to visualize the cranial region. When the head is bald, however, the true form of the cranium is displayed (Figure 6-37). By drawing the cranium accurately on the overlay any discrepancy in this part of the drawing will become apparent, supplying helpful feedback for corrections.

The formal similarity of the cranium and the egg is not coincidental. In both cases the need to protect delicate contents dictated a form having maximum strength and minimum weight. Unlike the eggshell, however, the cranium is composed of eight platelike bones that are held together by nonmoving suture joints, visible as zigzagging cracks in the skull's surface.

The eye sockets can also be spaced by means of the medial arc. They form a symmetrical pattern, crossing the medial arc at a height roughly equal to the vertical middle of the head (Figures 5-23 and 5-33). A horizontal axis at this height can be helpful in locating their positions, for they are not aligned as on a flat plane, but conform to the curve of the skull. The eye sockets are thus turned slightly away from each other, a difference of alignment that is more pronounced in the skulls of lower animals. The eye sockets of the skull, also known as

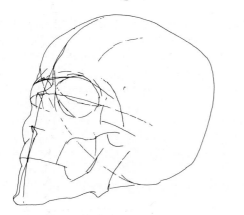

Figure 5-33. Linear reduction of Figure 5-32, indicating vertical and horizontal axes.

orbits, are round bony concavities housing the eyeballs and the surrounding muscles that move them. The outline shape of the orbits recalls the lenses of aviator-style sunglasses, a resemblance heightened by the linear joint at the bridge of the nose (Figure 5-24). While drawing the orbits of the eyes, compare them with the self-portrait underneath the overlay to see whether they conform to the symmetry dictated by the medial line. The orbits also provide a way of checking your drawing for accuracy, for they can serve as a frame of reference for visible portions of the eyeball.

On the outer side of the orbit of each eyeball is the cheekbone (*zygomatic bone*). Viewed from the side, it contributes to an irregular contour ridge, the *temporal line,* that extends along the left and right sides of the forehead, echoing the medial arc of the cranium (Figure 5-24). This contour originates near the ear and terminates almost imperceptibly on the upper side of the cranium. The lower edge of the zygomatic bone, a major determinant of the planes of the cheek, may be visible in life. Viewed from above, the zygomatic bone appears as part of an open bony arch. A slender band of muscle connects the outer surface near the arch with the side (angle) of the mouth. Called the *zygomaticus major,* it creates a characteristic transitional plane of the jaw (Figure 6-34).

The cartilage structure that gives the nose its projecting form is almost never preserved in the skull, which shows only the bridge between the eyes and the nasal cavity. This has the virtue of making the medial arc easier to visualize in the skull than it is in life, for it is not interrupted by the projection of the nose. Moreover, you can observe in the skull a fine suture joint above and below the nasal cavity that corresponds to the position of the medial arc. The same joint appears to divide the upper teeth into two symmetrical groups.

The teeth are the only part of the skeleton exposed to view in life, and they play a significant role in shaping the lower part of the head, a fact made sadly plain in people who are toothless. Though they are seldom exposed in portraits, the teeth make a fascinating study, as is demonstrated in a print (Figure 5-34) by the Spanish artist Jusepe de Ribera (1591–

1652). In this startling rendering of a gaping mouth, both upper and lower sets of teeth are shown. Those exposed in a smile, however, are usually the upper teeth, as they tend to overlap the teeth of the jawbone (*mandibula*).

The *mandibula* can be drawn with its center along the same medial arc as the rest of the skull, for, despite its well-known mobility, the jaw generally remains aligned with the arc. Distinguishing features of the mandibula are the angle at the back and the mental protuberance in front. In life the masseter muscle joins the mandibula with the zygomatic bone to form a plane that contributes much to the formal character of the head (Figures 6-34, 5-24, and 5-28).

Alternative Studies

a. The Life Study and the Skull. You can also accomplish the objectives outlined for the self-portrait by drawing a study of the skull over a life drawing of the head in your newsprint pad. A life-size drawing of the head will permit a more complete formal description of both the head and the skull. Perhaps your pad already contains a suitable study of the head drawn from the model. If not you may arrange for another student to sit as model in exchange for your sitting for him or her. If this arrangement is not feasible, a life-size self-portrait study will serve the purpose. Whoever the model, try limiting the drawing session to 25 minutes, bearing in mind that the goal is to create a convincing structure, taking into account any clues of the skull visible in life. The clues will help you visualize the skull, as you draw it directly over the life study (Figures 5-35 and 5-36). It is important that the sitter understand beforehand the anatomical purpose of the drawing, which, far from being a flattering portrait, will stress the bone structure of the skull!

Figure 5-34. Jusepe de Ribera (1591–1652), *Studies of the Mouth and Nose.* Engraving. Copenhagen, Royal Museum of Fine Arts.

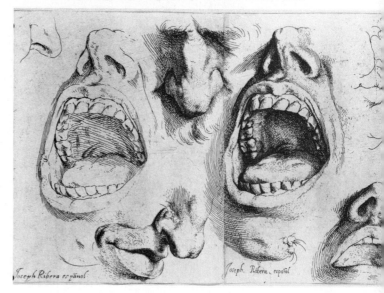

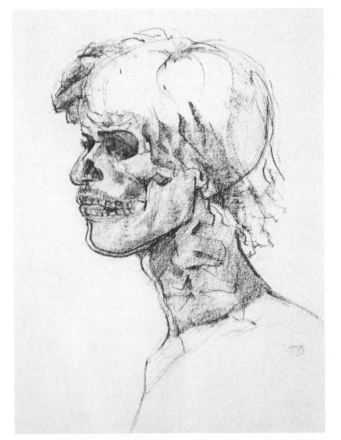

Figure 5-35. Student drawing. Study of the head and neck with skeletal analysis. Conté crayon on laid paper. 24 × 18″.

b. Memory Drawing of the Skull. After completing several skull studies with the head, you will be able to visualize the skull clearly in the model, for the bones lie very near the surface and directly determine the exterior form of the head. You may wish to test your knowledge of the skull by making a rapid overlay study from memory over a life drawing of the head. Visualizing the exterior structure of the skull can be of particular value in portraiture because it provides a coherent framework for rendering the expressive features of the face.

c. Multiple Studies of the Skull. Because the form of the head is determined in large measure by the skull, the skull itself can be made the focus of studies, without recourse to a life study of the head. If you have access to a mounted skeleton, arrange to draw studies of the skull viewing it from different vantage points. Following Giacometti's example, interpret the construction of the skull in line as much as possible before resorting to tonal modeling.

In drawing the skull, you will be participating in an artistic tradition with a long history. The skull is, of course, the traditional symbol of human mortality and as such appears in much medieval and Renaissance art. Some drawings of the skull are ranked very highly as independent works of art (Figures 5-31 and 5-32).[16]

Figure 5-36. Student drawing. Self-portrait with Three Skull Studies. Crayon on bond paper, 24 × 36″.

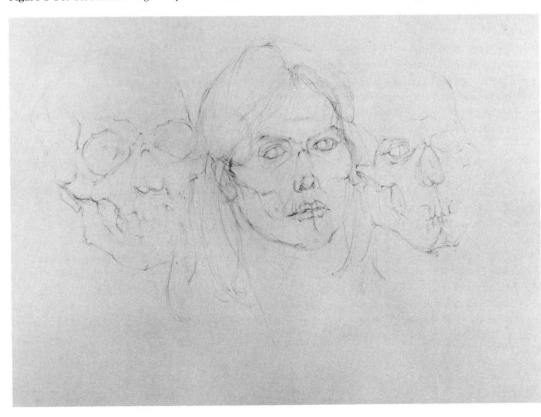

THE PELVIS

In contrast to the skull, the pelvis has little direct influence on the body's exterior form due to the abundance of tissues covering it. Indirectly, however, the pelvis determines the form of the lower trunk and influences many gestures of the body. Pelvic structure is therefore important in any serious study of the human form.

Comparable to the skull in height, the pelvis appears to be an irregular bony ring formed of two haunch bones (*os innominatum*) joined together in the front and united in the back by the triangular base of the vertebral column (the sacrum). In reality the haunch bone includes components that are fused together: (1) the ilium (flank bone), (2) the pubis, and (3) the ischium—names that will be useful for identifying anatomical landmarks of the pelvis (Figure 5-37). In the forward part of the ring the two pubis bones share a central cartilage joint known anatomically as the *symphysis pubis*. It is easily located in a standing figure, as the joint corresponds roughly with the vertical midpoint of the total height.[17] In the rear of the pelvis the sacrum resembles the keystone of an arch wedged, as it is, between the ilium bones, completing the pelvic ring (Figure 5-37).

The uppermost portion edge of the *ilium* forms a crest that terminates in a projection called the *anterior-superior iliac spine*, a helpful landmark in visualizing the position of the pelvis, as we noted previously. The same iliac crest continues on the posterior of the ilium to form a projection just above the joint with the sacrum—the *posterior-superior iliac spine*. In life this projection is suggested by two dimples that appear just above the hips on each side of their separation. If the dimples are visible, they are useful in determining the position of the sacrum, for they form a line that reflects the orientation of the pelvis (Figure 5-38).

The lower portion of the pelvis is the *ischium*, which extends downward from the ilium and curves forward as a tuberosity to join with the branch of bone above it, the pubis. The pubis and the ischial tuberosity unite to form the rounded opening visible on each side of the lower pelvis (the *obturator foramen*). This structure supports the body's weight in the sitting position.

The upper portions of the ischium and pubis are fused with the lower part of the ilium to form a cusp (the *acetabulum*) on the outer side of the pelvis. It is here that the round head of the thighbone (femur) articulates with the pelvis in a classic example of the ball-and-socket joint.

The pubis and the ilium form an irregular, jagged contour on the frontal surface, which is concealed in life by a powerful ligament connecting the anterior-superior iliac spine with the pubis: the *inguinal ligament*. The smooth curving line of the inguinal ligament creates the rounded contour along the lower abdominal region, a feature familiar in classical sculpture (Figure 6-54). This rounded contour, also known as the

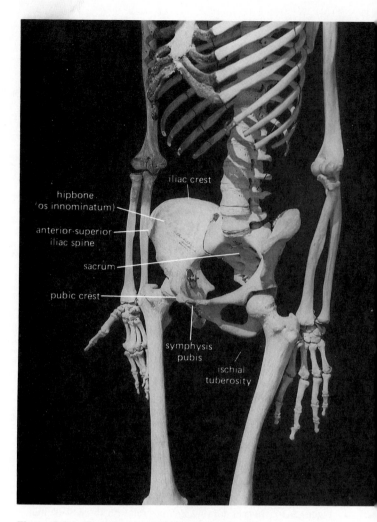

Figure 5-37. The pelvic region of the skeleton, three-quarter view.

groove of the groin, is less steep in the female, since the female pelvis is generally shorter and slightly wider than that of the male (Figure 5-39).

As the structural unit connecting the legs with the trunk, the pelvis exercises a special influence on the gestures of the body due to the way it transmits the weight of the upper body from the vertebral column to the legs. The special influence is explained by the differing types of pelvic joints. The pelvic joint with the spine is nonmoving. In terms of a specific gesture this means that when the pelvis tilts upward on the left side, for example, the lower portion of the vertebral column must tilt accordingly. The femur, however, is free to assume a relatively independent direction thanks to its ball-and-socket joint with the pelvis (Figure 5-40).[18] If the pelvic tilt is countered by an opposing tilt of the shoulder axis, as is natural in order to maintain equilibrium, the result is the contrapposto gesture of classic Greek sculpture (see Study 12).

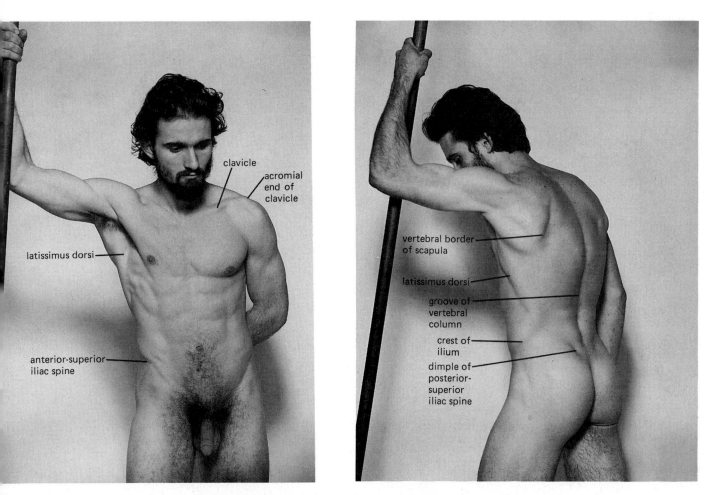

Figure 5-38. Muscle action. Against the resistance of a pole the arm pulls downward activating muscles of the arm and trunk, and also revealing external clues of skeletal structure.

STUDY 34:   Drawing the Pelvis

materials: ❏ 11 × 14″ sketchbook
❏ drawing pen (0.5 mm point recommended)
❏ HB drawing pencil
❏ tracing paper
❏ transparent (Scotch) tape

reference: ❏ model and mounted skeleton or Figures 5-1,
5-2, 5-3, 5-4, 5-5, 5-8, 5-14, 5-15, 5-16, 5-41,
5-42, 5-44, and 5-45

time: ❏ 30 minutes

Using a drawing from the model as the basis for your study, attach a tracing paper overlay, as in Study 33. Since the position of the pelvis in the figure may not be readily apparent, take time to examine your life study for any clues on the pelvic position.

Rather than draw the pelvis as an isolated element, begin by making a general indication of the axial skeleton, taking care to estimate the orientation of the pelvis in the figure. The most helpful anatomical clues for visualizing the pelvis in the figure are (1) the pubic joint (symphysis pubis), (2) the anterior superior iliac spines, which may be visible at the waist just below the flank pads, and (3) in a back view the dimples of the posterior iliac spines (Figure 5-38).

Figure 5-39. Composite of the female and male pelvis. The female pelvis (gray silhouette) is proportionately wider and shorter than the male pelvis (line).

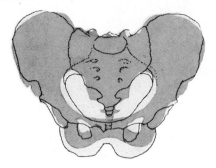

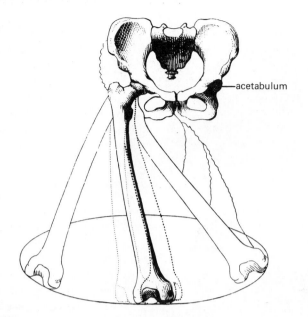

acetabulum

Figure 5-40. The action of the ball-and-socket joint of the hip. (Jean Galbert Savage, *Anatomie du Gladiator Combattant.* Courtesy of Countway Library, Harvard University.)

Figure 5-41. Back side of the female pelvis, seen from above and from below. (*Flaxman's Anatomical Studies,* engraving by Henry Landseer. Courtesy of Countway Library, Harvard University.)

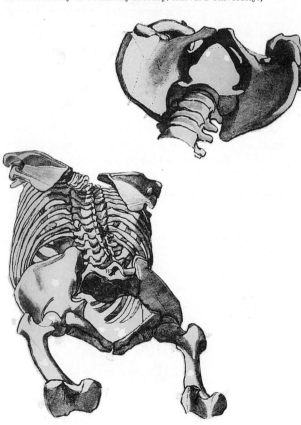

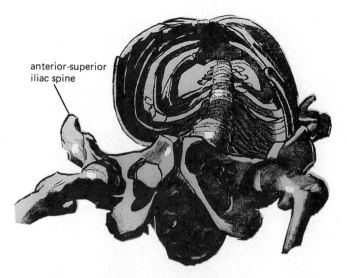

anterior-superior
iliac spine

Figure 5-42. Axial skeleton, seen from below. (*Flaxman's Anatomical Studies,* engraving by Henry Landseer. Courtesy of Countway Library, Harvard University.)

Figure 5-43. Student drawing. Life study with overlay study of the skeleton. Pen and ink on sketchbook paper. 14 × 11″.

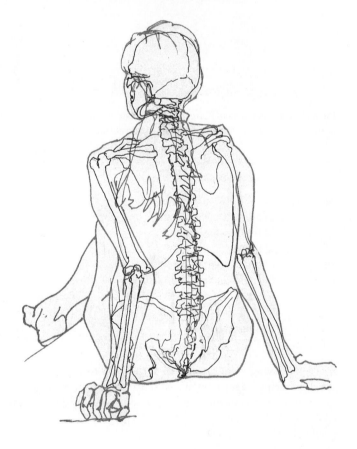

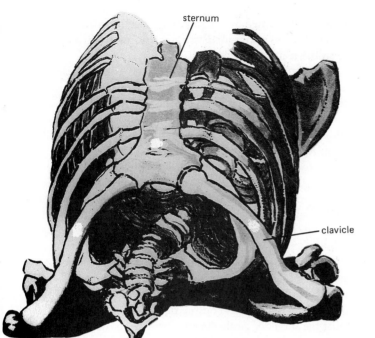

Figure 5-44. View of the rib cage, showing the bowlike construction of the clavicles and sternum. (*Flaxman's Anatomical Studies,* engraving by Henry Landseer. Courtesy of Countway Library, Harvard University.)

Due to the sculptural quality of the pelvis it is best to draw from a skeleton, but anatomical illustrations will serve the purpose. If you draw from anatomical illustrations, however, use illustrations of several views of the pelvis as a reference (Figure 5-45). A single illustration is unlikely to show the particular view required by your life drawing, while a variety of views will enable you to visualize the three-dimensional form of the pelvis quite accurately in the drawn figure (Figure 5-43).

Alternative Study

Making a Wire Model of the Pelvis. The important role of the pelvis in the skeleton coupled with the difficulty of seeing it in the body make the pelvis a worthy subject for a three-dimensional model in wire. Wire pipe cleaners—the suggested medium—are available in 12-inch lengths that can be bent easily by hand, but retain their form. See Alternative Study 30 for a discussion of wire as a means of making models (Figure 5-7). As when modeling the skeleton, refer to the mounted skeleton or anatomical illustrations (Figure 5-45). In preparation draw two or more views of the pelvis in line with the objective of reducing it to its essential structure, which can later be recreated in wire (Figure 5-46). A practical feature of the pelvis to model first in wire is the ringlike internal cavity (Figure 5-22).

Figure 5-45. The female pelvis with two lumbar vertebrae, five views.

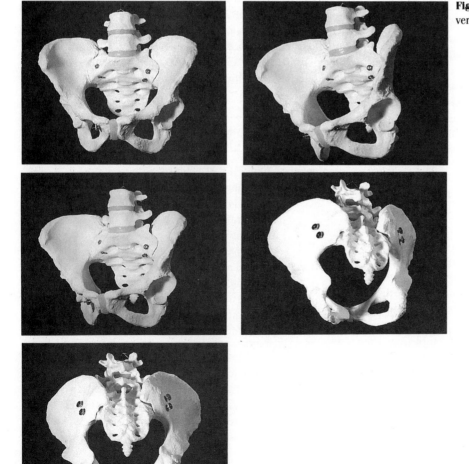

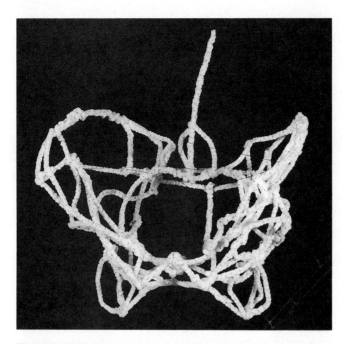

Figure 5-46. Student model of the pelvis constructed with wire pipe cleaners.

THE RIB CAGE
AND THE SHOULDER GIRDLE

The general eggshell form of the rib cage is suggestive of its role in protecting vital organs, such as the heart and lungs. The uniquely flexible construction of the rib cage allows it to change shape slightly, an action necessary for breathing. The rib cage also provides flexible attachment and support for the shoulder girdle, the bony structure that articulates with the arm bone (*humerus*). Such varied functions account for the relatively complex structure of the rib cage and the nature of its component parts—the ribs, the breastbone, the collarbones, and the shoulder blades.

Common sense might suggest that the ribs are simply a series of rings extending at right angles from the spine, which is how they frequently appear in Halloween decorations. In reality the ribs are more complex. Bladelike in form, the ribs curve downward from the vertebral column that supports them (Figures 5-8 and 5-25). Near their vertebral joints the ribs also arch backward, contributing a roundness of form to the back on each side of the groove of the spine. The oblique curves of the ribs continue in front as (costal) cartilage that joins the breastbone (*sternum*), thereby completing the rounded enclosure. A segmented bone resembling a necktie both in shape and position, the sternum is detected in the body by touching *the pit of the neck* (Figure 5-15), which reveals the bone's upper limit. The lower limit of the sternum (the *xiphoid process*) is visible only when the chest is expanded and the stomach drawn in. Then it appears at the top of the

pointed arch formed by the lower ribs (the *thoracic arch*). The xiphoid process corresponds with the position of the pit of the stomach in life (Figure 5-15).

The shoulder girdle (Figures 5-15 and 5-16), consisting of the collarbone (*clavicle*) and the shoulder blade (*scapula*), is the only skeletal structure linking the rib cage and the arm bone (*humerus*). Surprisingly, the shoulder girdle joins the rib cage only at the sternum. This juncture can be located by touch. If you feel the pit of your neck, you will notice slight elevations to the right and to the left. These bumps represent the joints of the proximal ends of the clavicles with the sternum. The clavicle is a relatively thin bone, and in general the shoulder girdle is a weak structure compared with the pelvic girdle, but it compensates for its lack of strength with greater mobility.

Although the individual joints of the shoulder girdle permit only limited movement, together they account for the broad range of movement associated with the shoulder. One consequence of the loose construction of the skeletal shoulder is that the shoulder girdle depends heavily on muscle attachments to hold it in place. This is especially evident in the scapula, a thin triangular bone that forms the major part of the joint with the humerus and glides freely over the back of the rib cage. The scapula is held in check by muscles attaching it firmly to the vertebral column and rib cage. An important feature of the scapula is its spine, the elevated ridge on its outer surface, which rises near the shoulder to form a knobby projection called the *acromium process*. The acromium process, together with the socket-type head of the scapula and its associated *coracoid process*, receives the head of the humerus at the shoulder. The clavicle, despite its proximity, does not form part of the joint with the humerus.[19]

STUDY 35: **Drawing the Rib Cage and the Shoulder Girdle**

materials: ❑ 11 × 14″ sketchbook
❑ drawing pen (0.5 mm point recommended)
❑ India ink
❑ HB drawing pencil
❑ tracing paper
❑ transparent (Scotch) tape

reference: ❑ model and mounted skeleton or Figures 5-3, 5-4, 5-5, 5-8, 5-14, 5-15, 5-16, 5-25, 5-41, 5-42, and 5-44

time: ❑ 15 minutes for the life study
❑ 45 minutes for the skeletal study

Due to special problems associated with drawing this part of the skeleton, it is advisable to make several life drawings that afford different views of the upper half of the figure. When drawing from the model be sure to indicate any visible anatomical landmarks associated with the rib cage (Figure 5-47).

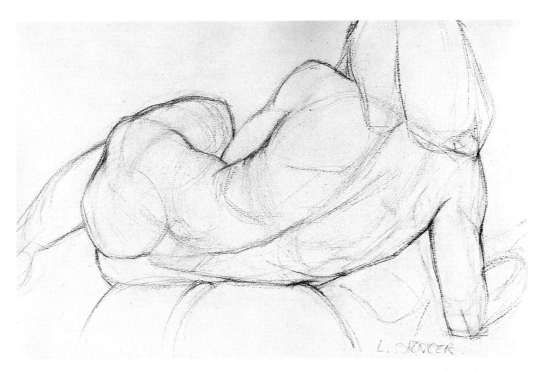

Figure 5-47. Student drawing. Life Study Based on Skeletal Forms. Crayon on newsprint paper. 18 × 24″. Lightly drawn preliminary lines suggest position of the rib cage, scapula, vertebral column, and the sacrum.

Figure 5-48. Student drawing. Life study of the model. Pen and ink on sketchbook paper. 10 × 8½″. The drawing includes indications of visible landmarks of the scapula and the spine.

Figure 5-49. Student drawing (Figure 5-48), with overlay study of the rib cage and the shoulder girdle. Graphite pencil. This study illustrates the displacement of the scapula when the arm is raised.

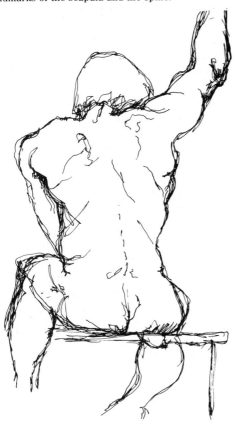

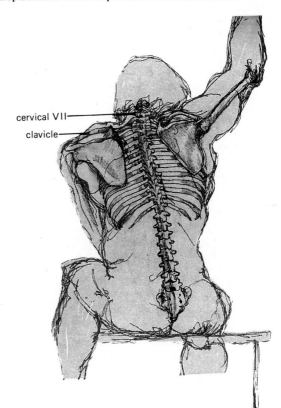

cervical VII

clavicle

Most useful are the pit of the neck, the pit of the stomach, and, depending on the pose, any suggestion of the clavicles and scapulas. Such indications simplify the skeletal study of this region, which is exceptionally changeable in appearance (Figures 5-48 and 5-49).

With a tracing sheet taped over your life study, begin the skeletal study by penciling in the curving form of the spinal column (as in Study 31). It is important to render its position accurately, for the vertebral column governs the orientation of the rib cage. At this point the anatomical landmarks we mentioned will be helpful. If the pit of the neck is indicated in your drawing from life, you can easily render the sternum and develop the truncated egg shape of the rib cage with respect to the position of the vertebral column. Even so, it is wise to check the sternum and the vertebral column for position. Remember that the sternum aligns with the spinal column *only* if the body is seen directly from the front. The individual ribs, though not essential to this study, can be delineated within the general form, if you wish a more detailed study (Figure 5-49).

THE APPENDICULAR SKELETON

The bones of the limbs, collectively known as the *appendicular skeleton*, have several features in common. Both the arm and leg are joined to the axial skeleton by single bones with rounded heads: the *femur* of the thigh and the *humerus* of the arm. Both bones are relatively long; the femur is "the longest, largest, and strongest bone in the skeleton, and almost perfectly cylindrical in the greater part of its extent (in a man six feet high it may measure eighteen inches—one-fourth of the whole body)."[20] The farthest (distal) ends of the femur and humerus flare out and form knobs called *condyles* that articulate with the outer limbs. Both the (lower) leg and the forearm have two bones: In the arm they are the *ulna* and the *radius*; in the leg, the *tibia* and the *fibula* (Figure 5-2). There is also a similarity of proportions: Both the (upper) arm and the thigh are proportionately longer than their respective lower member.

The differences in structure between the legs and the arms are related to differences in function. The assumption of upright posture has resulted in more specialized roles for the limbs.[21] The lower limb has evolved into a stronger but less flexible structure; the arm, no longer needed to support the body, has evolved into a lighter structure with a great range of movement. Illustrating this difference is the fact that we can easily rotate the forearm and the wrist about 180 degrees with moving the (upper) arm; the leg, however, can achieve only a small degree of rotation at the knee without turning the thigh as well. The reason for this contrast is revealed in the skeletal structure.

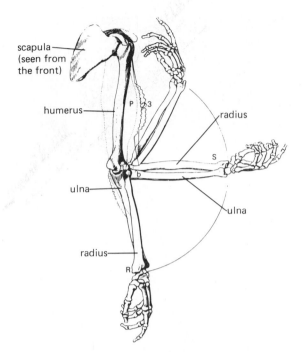

Figure 5-50. Movements of the arm, forearm, and hand. (Jean Galbert Savage, *Anatomie du Gladiator Combattant.* Courtesy of Countway Library, Harvard University.) The forearm swings along an arc dictated by the hinge joint of the ulna and the humerus. At the same time the wrist rotates from the supine position, seen at the top and middle, to the prone position, at bottom. The prone position requires that the radius cross the ulna, a movement made possible by the converse ball-and-socket joint of the radius and the humerus.

The two bones of the (lower) leg, the fibula and the tibia, form a nonmoving joint just below the knee. Although the knee has the largest movable joint in the body, it functions primarily as a hinge (Figures 5-52 and 5-56). The forearm construction is quite different: The two bones are formed so that one, the radius, can rotate around the other, the ulna (Figure 5-53). The proximal end of the radius features a rounded cusp that joins with the ball-like condyle[22] on the outer side of the humerus at the elbow (the *capitulum*). As the structure suggests, this joint permits rotation of the forearm. The distal end of the radius articulates with the wrist (*carpal*) bones: When the radius rotates, the wrist and hand also turn. Movements of the ulna, however, are more like those of the tibia, in that they are governed by a hinge-type joint at the elbow so that the ulna, unlike the radius, does not rotate when the hand turns. This fact may seem difficult to comprehend but is easily demonstrated in the skeleton (Figures 5-53 and 5-58). If the skeletal hand is lying palm up (*supine*), the radius and ulna do not cross but lie parallel; but if the hand is rotated so it is palm down (*prone*), the arm appears straight, but the radius crosses over the ulna. This movement, which so fascinated Michelangelo (Figure 6-52), naturally affects the po-

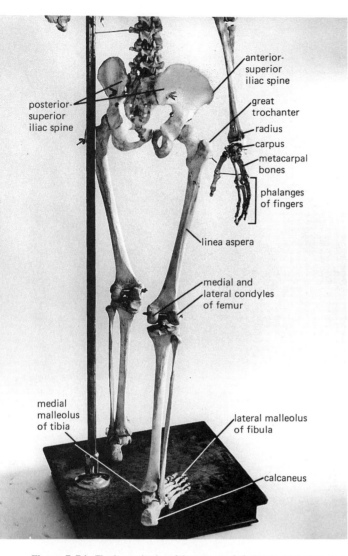

posterior-
superior
iliac spine

anterior-
superior
iliac spine

great
trochanter

radius

carpus

metacarpal
bones

phalanges
of fingers

linea aspera

medial and
lateral condyles
of femur

medial
malleolus
of tibia

lateral malleolus
of fibula

calcaneus

Figure 5-51. The lower limbs of the mounted skeleton, posterior view. The femurs form a characteristic angle with the tibia and the fibula in the standing position.

sition of the muscles that lie over these bones and thereby alters the appearance of the entire forearm. The hinge joint of the humerus and the ulna governs only the extension, or unbending, of the arm. The familiar tip of the elbow, visible when the arm is bent, is actually a projection of the ulna called the *olecranon* process (Figure 5-3). The condyle of this process glides in a groove of the humerus.[23] As the forearm extends, the olecranon process glides backward until it catches in a notch on the back of the humerus, terminating the extension of the forearm at an angle of about 180 degrees with the (upper) arm (Figures 5-14, 5-50, and 5-54).

STUDY 36:   **The Skeletal Arms**

materials: ❑ 11 × 14″ sketchbook
   ❑ drawing pen (0.5 mm point recommended)
   ❑ HB drawing pencil
   ❑ tracing paper
   ❑ transparent (Scotch) tape

reference: ❑ model and mounted skeleton or Figures 5-2, 5-3, 5-4, 5-5, 5-14, 5-50, 5-53, 5-54, and 5-58

time: ❑ 15 minutes for the life study
   ❑ 45 minutes for the skeletal drawing

Because movement of the arm bones causes the external forms of the arm to change, it is advisable to prepare a series of at least four drawings from life, with the model posed to display various gestures of the arm (Figures 6-43 and 6-44). It is particularly helpful to include poses that show the supine and prone attitudes of the hands (Figure 5-53). While drawing search out skeletal features visible in the arm. The distal end

Figure 5-52. The skeletal legs and feet. The structural difference between the distal ends of the tibia and the fibula causes the superficial ankles to appear noticeably higher on the medial (inner) side of the foot.

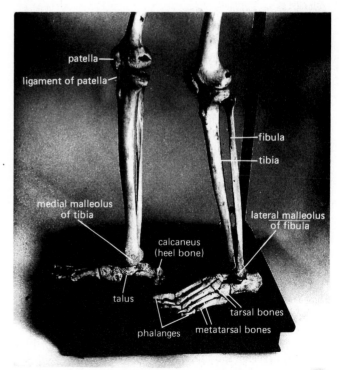

patella

ligament of patella

fibula

tibia

medial malleolus
of tibia

lateral malleolus
of fibula

calcaneus
(heel bone)

talus

tarsal bones

metatarsal bones

phalanges

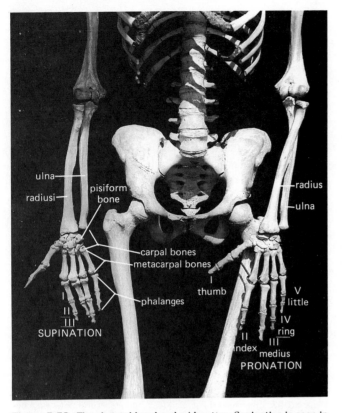

Figure 5-53. The skeletal hand and midsection. Supination is seen in the right hand, and pronation in the left hand of this mounted skeleton. The ulnar joint retains the same relative position with the femur in both cases.

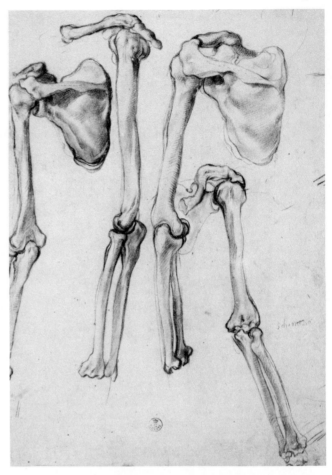

Figure 5-54. Jacopo da Pontormo, *Four Anatomical Studies of the Arm Bones and Shoulder Blade*, c. 1520. Red chalk. 29 × 20.1 cm. Florence, Galleria degli Uffizi.

of the humerus, for example, can be identified in life by the angular bump caused by the *epicondyle*[24] on the inner (medial) side of the elbow; likewise the tip of the elbow reveals the position of the proximal end (olecranon process) of the ulna. The wrist—when turned in the prone position—displays a bump (on the little finger side) marking the distal end of the ulna. Including such features in the life drawing will facilitate the skeletal study to be drawn later on the tracing paper overlay.

Alternative Study of the Arms

The importance of the arms in human gesture coupled with their ability to change in appearance has made them the subject of study by many artists, employing approaches that are still valid. Ingres, for example, studied the arm gestures of a single figure by drawing versions of the arms (Figure 5-55). So can you. You need only arrange for the model to move the arms to a new position while otherwise maintaining the same pose during the drawing session. In a thirty-minute

drawing session allow at least ten minutes for the new gesture of the arms. You may prefer to use the larger format of the newsprint pad instead of the sketchbook to accommodate this study (Figure 3-63).

STUDY 37: The Lower Limbs

materials: ❑ 11 × 14″ sketchbook
❑ drawing pen (0.5 mm point recommended)
❑ HB drawing pencil
❑ tracing paper
❑ transparent (Scotch) tape
reference: ❑ model and mounted skeleton or Figures 5-1, 5-2, 5-3, 5-4, 5-51, 5-52, and 5-56
time: ❑ 15 minutes for the life study
❑ 45 minutes for the skeletal drawing

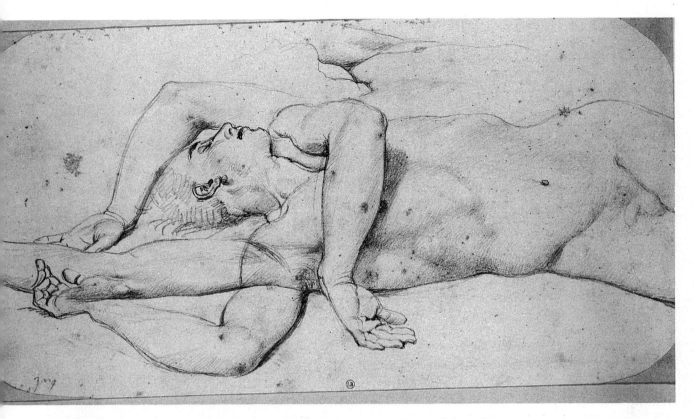

Figure 5-55. Jean-Auguste-Dominique Ingres, *Study for Acron.* Graphite. 15.5 × 30.8 cm. Bayonne, Musée Bonnat. The artist drew several gestures of the arms before deciding which to use for the figure for Acron in the painting *Romulus Conqueror of Acron.*

Part 1

Life drawings of the whole figure will serve well as the basis for your first studies of the lower limbs, for only the figure in its entirety can demonstrate the proportional relationship between the lower limbs and the rest of the body.[25]

As in the previous studies it is advisable to include any visible clues of the skeletal lower limb. One such clue is the prominence of the *great trochanter* outer side of the hip (Figure 5-51). The kneecap (*patella*) is another skeletal part often visible in life (Figure 5-52). In the leg proper[26] the shinbone (*tibia*) is often apparent in life as a curving ridge originating just below the kneecap and terminating with the shape of the inner ankle (*medial malleolus*). The thinner bone beside the tibia, known as the *fibula*, is usually not visible in life, but can be located by means of its heads. The proximal head of the fibula is responsible for a bump visible on the side of the leg just below the knee. The distal end of the fibula, called the *lateral malleolus*, produces the familiar bulge of the outer ankle. The inner ankle, or *medial malleolus*, is shaped by the end of the tibia and is slightly higher than the outer ankle.

Part 2

With indications of these superficial skeletal features in the life study, an overlay study of the skeletal leg will present little difficulty. The prominence of the great trochanter will reveal the position of the proximal end of the femur, which, with its stem and ball, somewhat resembles a pistol handle. The *patella*, a disklike bone connected by tendon with the proximal end of the tibia, indicates the knee joint it protects. Below the patella, the shinbone and inner ankle facilitate drawing the form of the tibia. The tibia and fibula bones have the appearance of an enormous safety pin (Figure 5-52).[27] Structurally, however, the fibula serves as a reinforcing buttress for the tibia.

If your study represents a standing figure, the orientation of the bones needs attention, for the characteristic alignment of the femur and the tibia is not obvious externally. Seen from the front the femur usually does not continue the vertical line of the tibia in the leg but rather inclines outward from the knee joint at a slight angle (Figures 5-1 and 5-2).[28] If the leg in the standing figure is viewed from the side, the tibia and femur also may not be in exact alignment but may form a slight angle along the front of the leg at the knee, an angle that varies from person to person. The degree of this angle (or extension) is determined by the ligaments of the knee joint rather than by skeletal structure in the strict sense.[29]

Ligaments and the Lower Limb

Although a detailed study of ligaments lies beyond the scope of this book, the structure of the leg is such that certain ligaments, which attach bone to bone, merit consideration. Among these is the patellar ligament we already noted (Figures 5-52 and 6-54). Since the patella has no joint with the rest of the skeleton, the patellar ligament should be rendered as part of the skeletal study. The iliofemoral ligament (Figure 5-8) is likewise of special interest. It joins the great trochanter and the neck of the femur with the pelvis (at the anterior-inferior iliac spine). This ligament joins no muscle tissues and thus causes no movement, but it does check the backward movement of the femur, effectively locking the joint when the femur lines up with the trunk. In this way it assists the body in standing erect with relatively little effort.[30]

THE EXTREMITIES: COMPARABLE STRUCTURES

The affinities of structure observed in the lower limb and the arm are paralleled by the structure of the *extremities*. Even a superficial inspection of the hand and the foot reveals a surprising similarity of construction—surprising chiefly because it is so well disguised in life by overlying tissue (compare the skeletal hand and foot in Figures 5-52 and 5-53). These structural parallels make it convenient to study the hand and the foot together.

Although the toes are much shorter than the fingers, the number of bones comprising each is the same—three. Moreover, the toe and finger bones diminish proportionately in length so the tips are the shortest. As if to underscore this similarity, the toe and finger bones have the same anatomical name—*phalanges*.[31] The shorter length of the toes renders them practically useless for grasping objects, but it enhances the action of the powerful muscles that pull the toe bones downward. This downward resistance of the toes is useful in running, for it effectively lengthens the leg and provides a spring of step well known to track athletes (Figures 5-56 and 5-57).

We do not ordinarily associate the big toe with the thumb, but the skeleton clearly demonstrates their common structure (compare Figures 5-58 and 5-59). Their different appearance in life is due primarily to the fact that the *metacarpal* bone of the thumb is physically separate from the other metacarpal bones of the hand. This arrangement permits the hand to

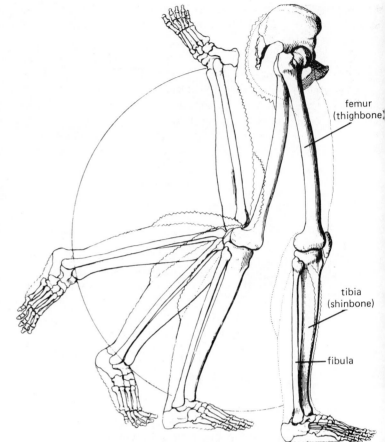

femur (thighbone)

tibia (shinbone)

fibula

Figure 5-56. Movements of the lower limb. (Jean Galbert Savage, *Anatomie du Gladiator Combattant.* Courtesy of Countway Library, Harvard University.) The hinge joint of the knee permits the leg to swing backward behind the thigh but not forward, since its movement is checked by ligaments that lock the joint in place. This feature enables the body to stand with little muscular effort of the leg. (Arthur Thompson, *A Handbook of Anatomy for Art Students* [New York: Dover, 1964], p. 291).

grasp—its most basic function. The corresponding *metatarsal* bone of the big toe is wedded by tissue to the rest of the metatarsal bones, assuring a firm platform to support the body.[32]

All of the metacarpal bones of the hand reveal a general affinity to the metatarsal bones of the foot. This is not the case, however, with adjoining *carpal* bones in the hand and *tarsal* bones in the foot (Figures 5-52 and 5-53). The eight carpal bones of the wrist and the seven tarsal bones of the foot have a similar masonrylike construction, but their differences are striking:[33] "The outstanding deviation of a foot is the enlargement and backward projection of its bone to form a heel."[34] This is the heel bone, or *calcaneus*. In addition to forming one end of the arch it provides the leverage necessary for the flexion of the foot—the action that enables ballet dancers to stand on their toes (Figure 5-59).

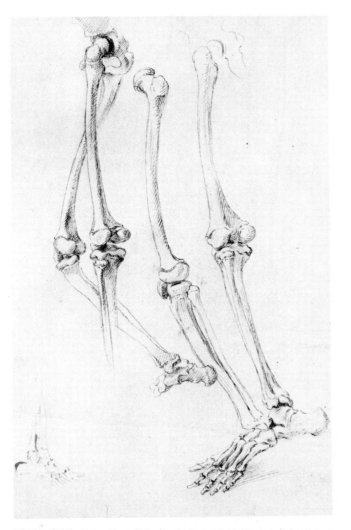

Figure 5-57. Peter Paul Rubens, *Studies of the Bones of the Lower Limb.* Pen and ink. 257 × 184 mm. Budapest, Museum of Fine Arts. Rubens's interest in representing movement noted in Figures 3-69 and 3-70 is also reflected in this study of the lower limbs.

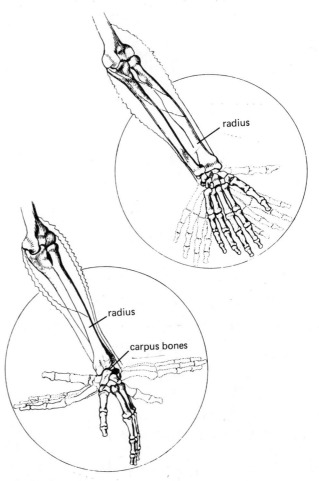

Figure 5-58. Movements of the wrist (carpus). (Jean Galbert Savage, *Anatomie du Gladiator Combattant.* Courtesy of Countway Library, Harvard University.) The carpus joins the radius in a ball-and-socket-type joint in which the ball is oblong and does not permit the vertical rotation observed in the humerus at the shoulder. Zigzag patterns indicate the muscles that cause the movement illustrated.

Despite their structural affinities, the hand and foot have a remarkably different history in visual art. Often depicted in portraits, the human hand also has been the subject of some of the finest drawings by artists of the past, while the foot by comparison has been neglected. The unequal treatment may be due in part to the hand's role in visual experience. Unlike the foot, the hand is used as a means of visual communication through gesture. Waving good-bye is an example of a common hand gesture in the West. In some cultures, however, hand gestures amount to a veritable language. Gestures of the hand communicate a "vocabulary" rich with specific meanings in classical dance and visual arts of India. In Italy, as in other Mediterranean countries, the hand is an important adjunct of speech, a fact that may account in part for the subtlety of gesture seen in Leonardo's studies of the hand. The special challenge of drawing the hand is implied by the number and

quality of drawings of this subject produced by major artists of the past and present (Figures 5-63, 5-64, and 5-65).

STUDY 38:   **The Hand and the Foot: Comparative Studies**

materials: ❑ 11 × 14″ sketchbook
            ❑ drawing pen (0.5 mm point recommended)
            ❑ India ink
            ❑ HB drawing pencil
            ❑ 36 × 24″ newsprint pad (optional)
            ❑ drawing crayon (optional)
reference: ❑ model and mounted skeleton or Figures 5-3, 5-4,
                5-5, 5-14, 5-50, 5-51, 5-52, 5-53, 5-58, and 5-59
time: ❑ 15 minutes for each life study
            ❑ 30 minutes for each skeletal study

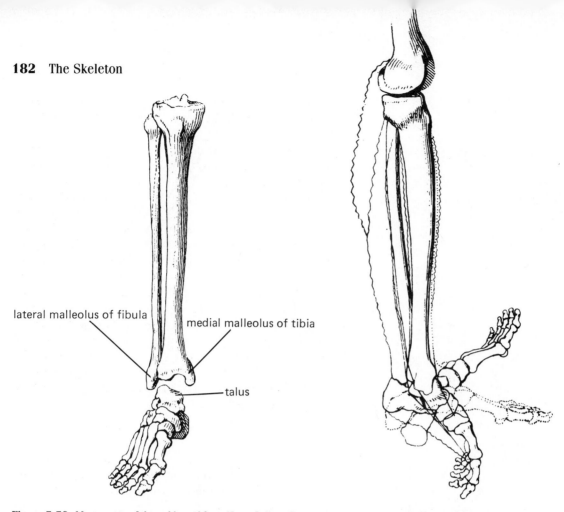

lateral malleolus of fibula

medial malleolus of tibia

talus

Figure 5-59. Movements of the ankle and foot. (Jean Galbert Savage, *Anatomie du Gladiator Combattant.* Courtesy of Countway Library, Harvard University.) The distal ends of the tibia and the fibula, together with the talus (anklebone), form the ankle joint. The ankle joint is superficially apparent in the protuberances of the lateral and medial malleoli. Activated by muscles of the calf, the foot points downward; the muscles in front cause the foot to point upward.

Part 1: Life Studies of the Hand and Foot

In drawing the extremities no model other than yourself is necessary. Given the complexity of form in the hand and foot, it is wise to make studies from a variety of viewpoints. If space permits, draw them on the same page, reserving the opposite page for skeletal studies (Figures 5-60, 5-61, 5-67, and 5-68). As in the other studies try to take note of external clues of skeletal structure. In the hand look for indications of the knuckles, for example; in the feet, the prominences of the heels and ankles (Figure 5-66).

Part 2: Skeletal Studies

(a) The Hand. From your drawings of the hand select two for a study of the skeletal structure. Then arrange the hand of the mounted skeleton in approximately the same gesture as your life study of the hand (Figure 5-61). If no mounted skeleton is available, review the anatomical illustrations listed for a skeletal hand in a similar view. Rather than make an overlay as in the previous studies, draw skeletal interpretations of the two hand studies on the opposite page of the sketchbook.

Comparing the skeletal hand with the life study, first make a rough indication of the radiating pattern of the phalanges and metacarpal bones as a practical way to begin your study. With this framework established, you can start to develop the form of individual bones. The lengths of the outer two phalanges will correspond with the creases under the last segments of the fingers. In each finger the largest phalanx extends inside the outer pad of the palm, joining with the metacarpal bone at the knuckle. This phalanx is therefore somewhat longer than the exterior suggests. As we noted, the phalanges diminish in size in approximately the same proportion for all fingers. You can use the indications of the knuckles in the original life study to estimate the position of the metacarpals. These bones converge from the knuckles to the carpals, the compact group of small bones that form the wrist. Little of the metacarpal and carpal bone structure is normally visible in the hand. Do not confuse the radiating pattern of the metacarpal bones with a similar but separate radiating pattern caused by

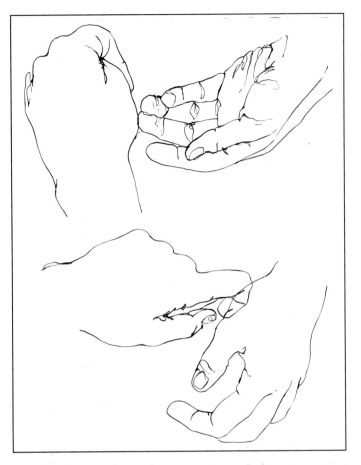

Figure 5-60. Student drawing. Study of the left hand. Compressed charcoal pencil on sketchbook paper. 11 × 8½".

the tendons attached to the tops of the knuckles (discussed in Chapter 6).

The carpal bones can be drawn as a single form; individually they have little effect on the external appearance of the hand. As a group, however, they form a rounded (ellipsoidal) surface articulating exclusively with the radius—the free-swinging joint of the wrist.

(b) The Foot. Although the skeletal foot presents a fairly complex structure, its general form is quite simple, resembling a wedge with a low arch on its underside (Figures 5-56 and 5-66). As in the preceding study, the mounted skeleton (or anatomical illustrations) can serve as a reference. Position yourself so your view of the skeletal foot matches what you saw in your life study of the foot. Compare the life study with the skeleton. Before rendering individual bones draw the general form of the bones. Check the position of the top of the arch, if visible, for appearances are especially deceptive in this region.[35] The rear portion of the arch terminates in the *calcaneus*, the round end of which contrasts with the wedgelike tapering of the bones at the other end of the foot. The top

of the arch features the *talus*, a large bone that provides a spool-shaped articular surface for the joint with the leg bone (*tibia*).

The ankle joint, which transmits the body's weight to the foot, also merits close attention. The bump of the inner ankle (*medial malleolus*) is caused by the distal end of the tibia, which articulates with the spool-shaped articular surface of the *talus*. The fibula rests on the outer side of the talus, creating the form of the outer ankle (*lateral malleolus*). The tibia and fibula combine to hold the spool of the talus on the sides in a pincerlike grip, which prevents the joint from slipping to the sides while permitting the extension and flexion of the foot (Figure 5-59). Situated beneath the talus is the calcaneus in the rear and the other tarsal bones in the front. The joint of the tarsals with the metatarsals, about midway on the top of the foot, may be visible as a slight bump. The phalanges of the toe continue the radiating pattern that originates in the metatarsals. The phalanges of the big toe bend slightly, however, in the direction of the other toes, giving the foot its unique sole shape (Figure 5-62).

Figure 5-61. Student drawing. Study of the skeletal hand, forearm, and the pelvis. Ballpoint pen on sketchbook paper. 14 × 11".

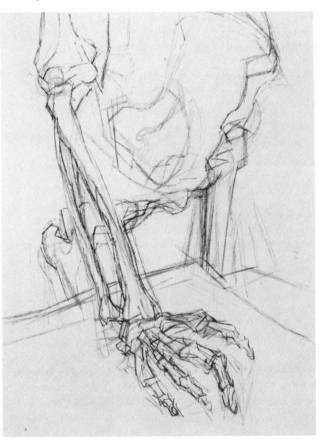

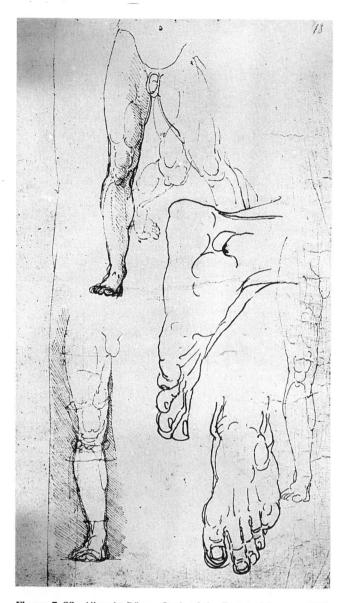

Figure 5-62. Albrecht Dürer, *Study of the Feet and Legs*, c. 1500. Page from *The Dresden Sketchbook*. Pen and ink. 294 × 206 mm. Dresden, Sächsische Landesbibliothek. Though simply drawn in contour, Dürer's studies of the foot describe prominences at such places as the heel and ankle that clearly suggest the underlying skeletal structure.

Alternative Study of the Skeletal Hand and Forearm

As you can see in master drawings of the hand (Figures 5-63, 5-64, and 5-65) many of its gestures are more complete and hence more meaningful when the drawing includes the wrist and forearm. The same may be said for studies of the skeletal hand. With that objective in mind, arrange the mounted skeleton so its hand rests naturally, on a table, or on

the skeleton itself. No other model is needed. The abstract complexity of the skeletal hand invites the use of line with visual measurement (Figure 5-61). Because of their role in gesture the articulations of the joints merit special attention in this study.

Alternative Study of the Foot and Leg

You can test your knowledge of the skeletal structure of the lower limb and foot without resorting to an overlay drawing of the bones. Drawing from life, try to discover and draw

Figure 5-63. Leonardo da Vinci, *Study of a Woman's Hands*, c. 1474. Silverpoint on a prepared pink ground. 21.5 × 15 cm. Windsor Castle, Royal Library.

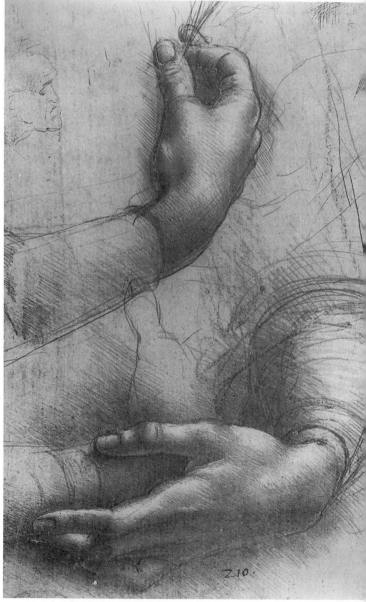

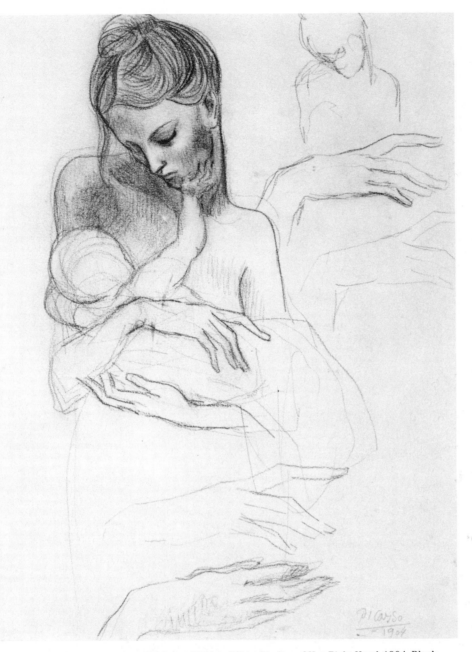

Figure 5-64. Pablo Picasso, *A Mother Holding a Child and Four Studies of Her Right Hand*, 1904. Black crayon. 13½ × 10½″. Cambridge, Fogg Art Museum, Harvard University. Bequest of Meta and Paul J. Sachs.

some of the skeletal clues that are evident on the surface, notably those of the joints, such as the malleolus of the tibia at the ankle and the patella at knee. Drawing from the model will provide a more familiar view of the foot and leg, but drawing your own legs and feet in a necessarily foreshortened view is an added challenge (Figure 5-68). Perhaps that was what induced the young Degas to draw a sketchbook study of his left leg and foot[36] (Figure 5-67). For a review of foreshortening and visual measurement see Study 9.

STUDY 39:   Comparative Studies: The Animal Skeleton

materials: ❑ 11 × 14″ sketchbook
❑ drawing pen (0.5 mm point recommended)
❑ India ink

reference: ❑ mounted skeleton of an animal and anatomical illustrations of the human body

time: ❑ 30 minutes for each study

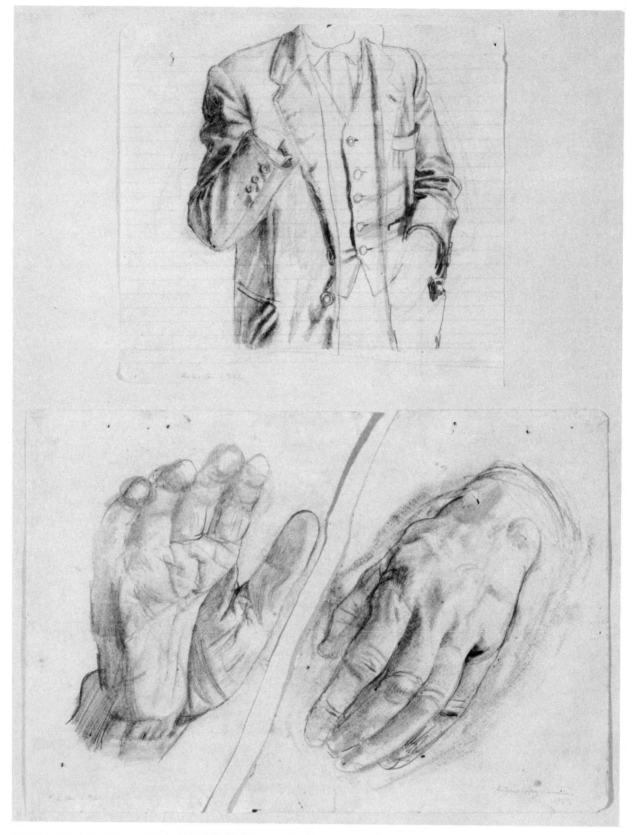

Figure 5-65. Antonio Lopez Garcia (b. 1936), Two sheets of sketches. Graphite pencil. 20.5 × 22 cm. and 20.4 × 22 cm (photo courtesy Galerie Herbert Meyer-Ellinger, Frankfurt am Main).

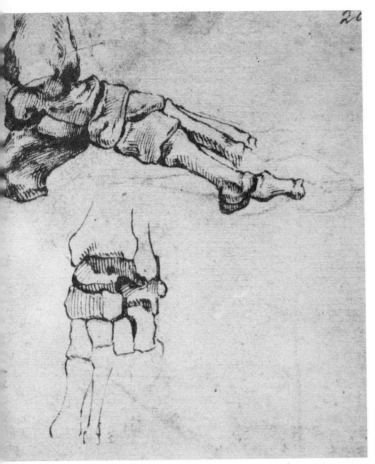

Figure 5-66. Michelangelo, *Studies of the Skeletal Foot.* Crayon, pen and ink. Florence, Casa Buonarroti (photo courtesy of Alinari). A faint crayon drawing of the foot encloses the larger study in ink.

Studies of animal skeletons are not only of assistance in drawing animals but also enhance your awareness of the unique characteristics of the human skeleton and, ultimately, of the human form. Though they are not found in art schools or art museums, displays of animal skeletons are available in most natural history museums and frequently in zoology departments of colleges and universities. Once you have located such a display as a model, take your sketchbook there and draw from it. Leave the page opposite the drawing blank and with the aid of an anatomy book (or a mounted skeleton), render the human skeleton in a comparable position and scale later. Skeletons of other primates (apes, monkeys, chimpanzees) offer intriguing subjects owing to their subtle differences from the human frame (Figures 5-69 and 5-70).

STUDY 40:   Drawing the Skeleton from Memory

materials: ❏ 36 × 24″ newsprint drawing pad
❏ easel or straight-back chair
❏ Masonite or plywood panel and clamps
❏ Sanguine and black or brown drawing crayons
reference: ❏ model and mounted skeleton or anatomical illustrations
time: ❏ 35 minutes

With this study you will be able to apply what you have learned, by visualizing the skeleton in the human figure without the assistance of a mounted skeleton or an anatomy book. It is not intended as a test of your knowledge of the skeleton, but rather a way of further investigating the interaction of the skeleton and the human form.

Start by developing a drawing of the figure from the model—a fifteen-minute session should be sufficient. Observe the model carefully for skeletal landmarks, such as the sternum, clavicles, anterior iliac spines of the pelvis, and

Figure 5-67. Edgar Degas (1834–1917), *Study of the Leg,* 1855. *Notebook 3,* page 47. Soft pencil. Paris, Bibliothèque Nationale.

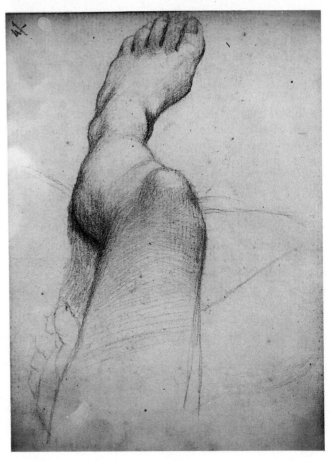

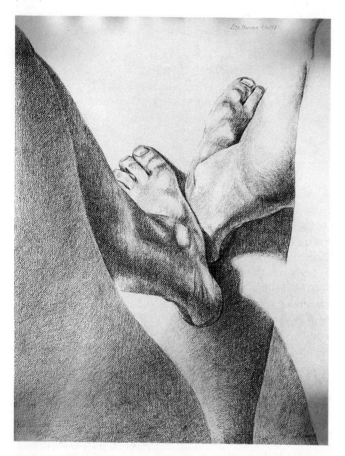

Figure 5-68. Student drawing. Studies of the Artist's Feet and Legs. Conté crayon on laid (Canson) paper. 25 × 19″.

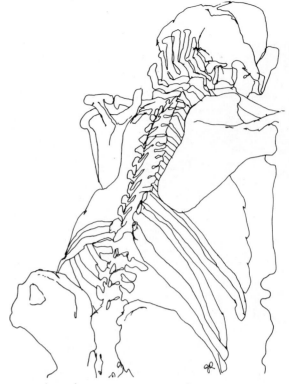

Figure 5-69. Student drawing. Comparative Study of the Ape Skeleton. Pen and ink on sketchbook paper. 14 × 11″. The special affinity between ape and human skeletons makes them an interesting subject for comparison. The lowered skull and projecting spinous processes of the ape are reminders of its four-footed posture.

Figure 5-70. Student drawing. Comparative Study of the Human Skeleton. Pen and ink on sketchbook paper. 14 × 11″. After completing the study of the ape skeleton (Figure 5-69) the student drew this similar view of the human frame, thereby inviting close comparison.

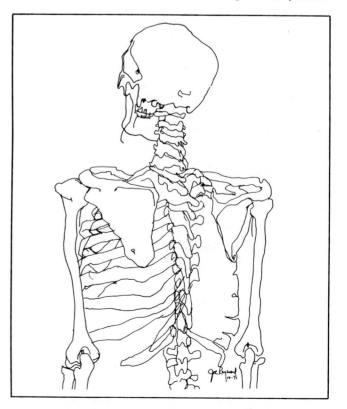

groove of the spinal column. You may be surprised at the number of skeletal features you can identify through clues of surface anatomy. You may even be able to visualize the entire rib cage in the model. If you have learned the skeleton well, you may experience, as have other artists, an almost shocking recognition of the entire skeleton.

Referring back to the model as you work, draw the skeletal form within the drawing of the figure. You may wish to use a different colored crayon in order to distinguish the skeletal drawing from that of the figure. As in the sketchbook studies, it is helpful to generalize the most complex forms at first. This is particularly true of the rib cage. Smaller forms, such as the ribs, can be drawn later within the general forms (Figure 5-71). No more than twenty minutes should be allotted to drawing the skeleton, for more time would tempt you to embellish with unnecessary and possibly inaccurate detail.

When the study is complete, compare your analysis with the skeleton (or anatomical illustration). Correct the drawing on the spot in order to resolve problems while they are still fresh in your mind and the model is in front of you. You may find your drawing of the skeleton does not match the anatomical clues of the figure drawing. If this is the case, check

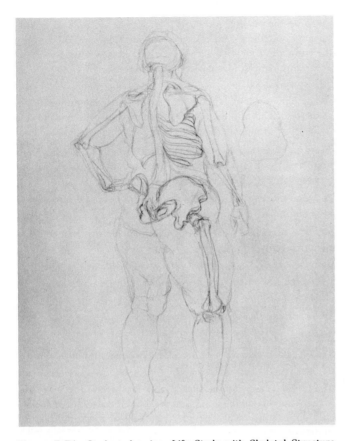

Figure 5-71. Student drawing. Life Study with Skeletal Structure Drawn from Memory. Crayon on newsprint paper. 24 × 18″. Smaller forms, such as the ribs, were drawn after the larger form of the rib cage was constructed.

your drawing carefully against the model, for the error may reside in the drawing of the figure rather than in that of the skeleton if the latter is rendered accurately. Repeat this exercise at least once a week until you develop a clear mental image of the skeleton applicable to the figure in many positions.

Drawing the skeleton from memory reveals both the strengths and the weaknesses of your understanding of skeletal form, and it may do the same for your drawing of the figure, suggesting areas that need further study. This is perhaps the most important of the anatomical studies, for your newly acquired ability to see skeletal structure in the body will almost certainly be reflected in a greater sense of interior structure in your drawings of the figure.

SUMMARY

The chief purpose of skeletal studies is to give you insight into the solid framework of the body with attention to those aspects that are useful in visualizing and drawing the figure. The skeletal structure alone, however, represents only one aspect of the human form, for it operates as part of a system activated by the energy of muscles. Although it is convenient to study the skeleton by itself initially, it is the interaction of the skeleton and the muscles that determines the appearance of the body. For the visual artist the interaction is of special interest, for "... the notion of the body as a complex of thrusts and tensions, whose reconciliation is one of the chief aims of the figure arts, remains eternally true."[37]

NOTES

1. Certain classes of creatures, such as insects and crustacea, possess external skeletons. The key to their structure for drawing purposes is the superficial appearance of their forms rather than the internal structure, as is the case with the human body.

2. Stephen Rogers Peck, *Atlas of Human Anatomy for the Artist* (New York: Oxford University Press, 1951), p. 2.

3. Psychologists remind us that "visual perception is as much concerned with remembering what we have seen as with the act of seeing itself." Ralph Norman Haber, "How We Remember What We See," *Scientific American*, vol. 222 (May 1970), p. 104.

4. For a list of recommended anatomy books for artists see the bibliography.

5. *Coccyx* mens "cuckoo" in Greek, and the coccyx of the spinal column is so named because of its supposed similarity to the cuckoo's beak (Henry Gray, *Anatomy, Descriptive and Physical* [Philadelphia: Running Press, 1974], p. 50).

6. *Lumbar* refers to the region of the body between the hipbone and the lowest ribs (i.e., the loins).

7. Arthur Thomson, *A Handbook of Anatomy for Art Students* (New York: Dover, 1964), p. 3.

8. The atlas vertebra, which supports the globelike cranium of the skull, derives its name from the mythical Atlas, who supported another globe—the earth—on his back (Gray, *Anatomy*, p. 36).

9. The balance is not quite perfect. If a person falls asleep sitting up, the head tends to fall forward.

10. Gray, *Anatomy*, pp. 34–35.

11. The term "vertebra" is derived from the Latin *vertere*, "to turn" (Gray, *Anatomy*, p. 34).

12. "When you draw take care to set up a principal line which you must observe all throughout the object you are drawing; everything should bear relation to the direction of this principal line" (Leonardo da Vinci, *The Notebooks*, vol. 1, ed. Jean Paul Richter [New York: Dover, 1970], p. 260).

13. Certain artists have found the visual analogy between the head and the egg to be useful imagery in their work. Among these is the surrealist Giorgio de Chirico (b. 1888), who depicts the head of a figure as an egglike form in several of his compositions.

14. The mirror is also useful as a means of inspecting the drawing itself, for a reversed image can sometimes provide an insight into your own work. This use of the mirror by artists was noted in Ren-

aissance times by Leonardo da Vinci, whose *Treatise on Painting* advised, "When you wish to see whether the general effect of your picture corresponds with that of the object presented by nature, take a mirror and set it so that it reflects the actual thing, and then compare the reflection with your picture and consider carefully whether the subject of the two images is in conformity with both, studying especially the mirror." Before Leonardo, the artist and theoretician Alberti also recommended the use of the mirror. (Quoted in Robert Goldwater and Marco Treves, *Artists on Art* [New York: Pantheon, 1945], p. 54.)

15. Anthropologists prefer to reduce the medial arc to a straight line for purposes of angular measurement against the central axis of the cranium. The *facial angle*, as it is called, is "made by the intersection of the [vertical] axis of the face with the [central] axis of the skull" (*Webster's New Collegiate Dictionary* [Springfield, Mass.: Merriam, 1951]).

16. In the view of Kenneth Clark, a noted authority on Leonardo, the artist "never surpassed the rendering of light passing curved surfaces in the studies of skulls dated 1489 [Figure 6-27]" (Kenneth Clark, *Leonardo* [Baltimore: Penguin, 1959], p. 77).

17. The vertical midpoint is generally slightly higher in the female figure than in the male. Peck, *Atlas of Human Anatomy*, p. 60.

18. The ball-and-socket joint is capable of rotation in addition to the hinge movements of other free-moving joints. Movement at joints is facilitated by *synovia*, an oily fluid produced by a membrane lining the inner surface of the joint's ligaments (Thomson, *Handbook of Anatomy*, p. 28).

19. The bony bump you can feel on the top of your shoulder is not the acromium process of the scapula but the prominence of the outer end of the clavicle. The acromium process of the scapula extends beyond the prominence of the clavicle to the tip of the shoulder.

20. Gray, *Anatomy*, p. 183.

21. Anthropoid apes have thumbs on both hands and feet, reflecting the unspecialized use of these members.

22. *Condyle* is defined as "an articular prominence on a bone," often appearing in pairs (i.e., on the distal end of the humerus and femur). The word also refers to any smooth surface of a joint (*Webster's Third New International Dictionary* [Springfield, Mass.: Merriam, 1971]).

23. The term *funny bone* is defined as "the place at the back of the elbow where the ulnar nerve rests against the medial condyle of the humerus: olecranon." Although the terms *funny bone* and *humerus* suggest a pun, there is no link between them. Humerus derives from the Latin word for shoulder (*Webster's Third New International Dictionary* [Springfield, Mass.: Merriam, 1971]).

24. *Epicondyle* literally means "on or beside the condyles" and refers to a knobby swelling of the bone extending beyond both condyles at the distal end of the humerus. The inner (medial) epicondyle is much more prominent than the outer (lateral) epicondyle. Ibid.

25. The lower limb is approximately half the body height, measured from the greater trochanter. (Thomson, *Handbook of Anatomy*, p. 428).

26. The word *leg* in anatomy is used only to refer to that part of the lower limb from the knee to the ankle.

27. The word *fibula*, in fact, originally denoted the ancient equivalent of a safety pin.

28. The angle of inclination in the femur is usually greater in the female skeleton due to the greater width of the female pelvis (Gray, *Anatomy*, p. 183).

29. Thomson, *Handbook of Anatomy*, p. 291.

30. Ibid., p. 259.

31. *Phalange* is derived from the Greek *phalanx*, meaning "a line of soldiers."

32. *Carpal* is derived from *karpos*, Greek for "wrist." Likewise *tarsus* is Greek for "flat of the foot," and *meta* simply means "after." As an anatomical term *metatarsal* thus designates the bone's relative position in the skeleton.

33. The difference in the number of bones in the tarsus and in the carpus is believed to be due to the fusion of two bones in the former, causing the tarsus to have one bone less than the carpus (Thomson, *Handbook of Anatomy*, p. 15).

34. Peck, *Atlas of Human Anatomy*, p. 78.

35. The Achilles tendon of the heel conceals the length of the calcaneus in life.

36. The sketch by Degas of a man's leg is "undoubtedly the artist's. . . ." Theodore Reff, *The Notebooks of Edgar Degas*, vol. 1 (New York: Hacker, 1985], pp. 42–43.

37. Kenneth Clark, *The Nude* (Garden City, N.Y.: Doubleday, 1956), p. 453.

CHAPTER 6

The Muscles

the dynamics
of the human form

To draw the human figure it is necessary to know as much as possible about it, about its structure and its movements, its bones and muscles, how they are made, and how they act. . . .

—THOMAS EAKINS

IT WOULD BE POSSIBLE to imitate body movement by attaching strings to a skeleton and operating it as if it were a puppet, with each string producing a leverlike movement of the bone to which it is fastened. In life the bones of the skeleton also move like a series of levers by means of a pulling action. The pulling action in the body, however, is caused internally by means of muscle tissues consisting of elongated fibrous cells that can suddenly change length.[1] When the muscle cells are at their longest, they are said to be *relaxed*; when *tensed*, some muscle fibers contract to as little as one-half their original length.[2] The pull resulting from this contraction is transmitted by means of *tendons*, which consist of tough elastic material that forms at the ends of muscle fibers and is attached to bone or to other tissues, enabling many muscle fibers to combine and perform a common function. Such a unit of muscle fibers and tendons constitutes the muscle proper and gives the "typical" muscle a spindle (*fusiform*) shape (Figure 6-1). The word itself suggests a more vivid image, for it is derived from the Latin *musculus*, which literally means "little mouse"[3] and refers not only to the form of the muscle, with its thick body and tail-like tendons, but also to the crawling motion that it can produce as it contracts.

The locations of the muscle's attachments with the skeleton determine the muscle's action. If the attachments are with two bones that have a common movable joint, the muscle can produce a lever-type action comparable to the movement of a screen door pulled shut by a common door spring. The brachialis, an arm muscle, offers an example of this type of action (Figure 6-2). When the brachialis contracts the arm bends forward (*flexes*). With such flexion the forearm usually moves more than the upper arm, for the latter is anchored at the shoulder by the weight of the body. For this reason anatomists distinguish between the attachments of muscles, calling those that tend to move less *origins* and those that are more mobile *insertions*. As a rule the classification of two attachments of a muscle can be determined by considering which is nearer the greater mass of the body.

Not all muscles produce a *direct action* of the kind generated by the brachialis, for many are attached to bones that are separated by intervening bones. The biceps muscle of the arm (Figure 6-3), for example, originates in the bones of the shoulder girdle and inserts with bones of the forearm, skipping the intervening humerus bone entirely. This arrangement results in an *indirect action*, whereby contraction can cause not only flexion of the forearm, as does the brachialis, but also effect the raising of the entire arm. *Antagonistic muscles*, on the opposite side of the arm, operate by the same principle, though they serve to bend back (*extend*) and lower the fore-

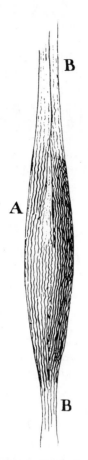

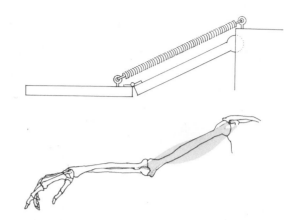

Figure 6-3. Indirect action of muscles. Although the biceps muscle lies over the ulna, it does not attach to it. The biceps attaches instead to the adjoining bones, an arrangement that enables it to flex and raise the arm—indirect actions. When the biceps flexes the arm, the humerus is held steady by *synergist* muscles. In addition *fixation* muscles act to hold the scapula steady as a base for the humerus.

Figure 6-1. Muscle components. The fusiform type of muscle consists of a fleshy body (A), which contracts and relaxes, and tendons (B), which lead to attachments with bones. This muscle has two upper tendons and one lower.

Figure 6-2. Direct action of muscles. The action of a spring pulling a door shut is similar to the direct action of muscles pulling against bones that are connected with a hinge-type joint, such as the elbow joint of the humerus and ulna. The brachialis muscle (in gray) causes the arm to flex.

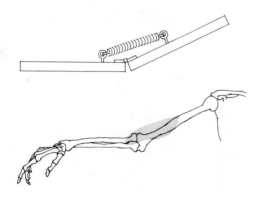

arm. Such direct and indirect muscle actions are common throughout the skeletomuscular system and account not only for flexion and extension of the limbs but for *rotation* as well. Rotation, however, differs from the other skeletal movements in that it requires a special ball-and-socket type of joint, such as that seen in the shoulder, while flexion is possible within the limitations of a hinge-type joint, as seen in the knee. Another requirement for rotation is that the tendon of the muscle involved must attach to the far side of at least one of the bones to which it is joined. When the muscle contracts, a twisting action results, similar to the torque produced by the string that spins a toy top. Perhaps the clearest examples of such rotation occur in the shoulder and elbow joints.

The relaxation of muscles also plays a vital role in producing motion.[4] As the muscles on one side of a limb contract, those on the other side must relax if the limb is to move. Equal tension on both sides results in no motion at all, as the pull of the muscles on one side opposes and neutralizes that of the other. Such *isometric* tension is most visible in the strained but static poses of weight lifters. The same kind of tension, though perhaps less marked, enables the artist's model to hold a pose. The fact that the model tires quickly from holding a standing pose attests to the muscular activity involved. While holding a fixed standing position the skeleton and muscles work in a way analogous to structures such as radio transmission towers (Figure 6-4). The tower girders, like the bones of the skeleton, are incapable of standing erect by themselves. With the help of the tension created by the surrounding cables, however, the girders are held upright, reaching heights far beyond their independent capabilities. In a similar way the tension of the muscles, aided by ligaments of the joints, maintains firm posture.[5]

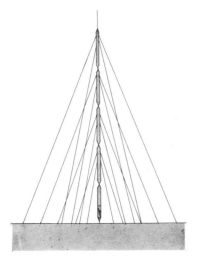

Figure 6-4. Radio tower. A typical broadcast tower depends on the tension between cables and rigid beams for support. A comparable tension between antagonistic muscles plays an important role in maintaining body posture and position.

The tensions and thrusts of the body that have excited the imagination of many artists thus have a physical basis in the skeletomuscular system. For this reason the integral system merits study as a way of deepening our understanding and appreciation of these forces and their influence on the form and appearance of the body. Though the muscles are partially visible on the body surface, their interaction with the skeleton is not readily apparent in most cases. A systematic method of anatomical study similar to that employed in Chapter 5 for the skeleton is recommended.

METHODS, MATERIALS, AND REFERENCES

A practical way of studying the skeletomuscular system is to draw the figure from life, using pen and ink and a sketchbook, and then to draw a skeletal analysis of the life drawing on an overlay in pencil, as described in Chapter 5. The final step, which is unique to this exercise, is to draw an interpretation of the muscles on a second tracing paper overlay (Figure 6-5). A sanguine pencil is an excellent medium for drawing a study of the muscles, for it produces a rusty-red color suggestive of muscle tissues and is not easily confused with the tones of the drawings underneath. An effective technique for modeling muscle tissues in pencil is found in anatomical studies by Paul Klee and George Grosz, who used pencil line to describe the direction of the muscle fibers (Figures 6-21 and 6-22).

The illustrations in this chapter are adequate for the suggested studies. In addition to anatomical illustrations an *écorché* (Figure 6-6),[6] a plaster cast showing the muscles, can be helpful. This cast provides a three-dimensional representation of muscle structure and is particularly useful when it can be compared with the live model, for it represents the figure without the superficial tissues that tend to disguise the muscle forms in life.

Much can be learned about the muscles by direct observation of the human body itself without recourse to an écorché, for specific gestures can bring specific muscles into play. When the arm, for example, is raised from the side of the body to a horizontal position, the shoulder muscle (deltoid) tenses, thus revealing its function. By raising your arm you can feel how the deltoid changes from a soft mass to a hard tense form, as suggested in a drawing by Michelangelo (Figure 6-7). The muscles underneath the arm, which can oppose such an action, remain relaxed, a fact that you can verify by feeling the lower side of the raised arm. Quite the contrary occurs when the arm is pulled downward and meets the resistance, say, of a tabletop: The deltoid muscle relaxes and the underarm muscles become tense.

When a muscle is tensed, it generally reveals its form on the surface of the body more clearly than it does in a relaxed state (Figure 6-8). A gesture or action of the body is expressed externally by clear muscle forms in the region(s) of the body involved in the action. An artist familiar with muscle anatomy can afford to be selective, emphasizing only those muscles that express the action, for, as Leonardo reminds us, there is no point in drawing all the muscles of the figure unless

Figure 6-5. Sketchbook with overlay sheets. A life drawing (1) in a sketchbook can serve as the subject of anatomical studies executed on tracing paper sheets (2, 3) taped over the original drawing.

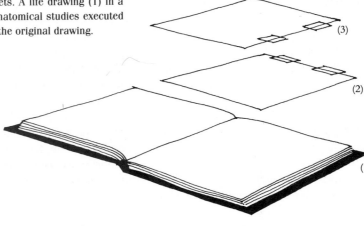

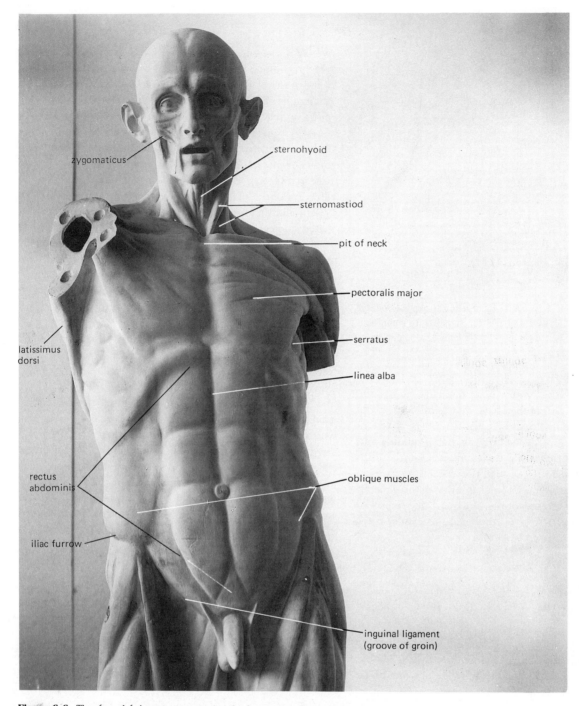

zygomaticus

sternohyoid

sternomastiod

pit of neck

pectoralis major

serratus

linea alba

latissimus
dorsi

oblique muscles

rectus
abdominis

iliac furrow

inguinal ligament
(groove of groin)

Figure 6-6. The *écorché*. A cast representing the figure with the skin removed, the écorché displays the superficial muscle structure more clearly than is possible in life.

they are exerting great force. Do not try to make all the muscles of your figures apparent because even if they are in the right places, they do not show very clearly unless the parts in which they are located are exerting great force or are greatly strained; the muscles of those parts which are unexercised should not show. If you do otherwise, you will make something that looks more like a bag of nuts than a human figure.[7]

If a specific set of muscles is the subject of a study, however, you may prefer to obtain a clearer view by having the model tense them, whether or not they are involved in the gesture of the pose. This can be particularly helpful in studying parts of the body with relatively complex muscle forms, such as the limbs. The arm muscles in a life study by Degas (Figure 6-9) are so well defined, it is probable the model tensed them in order to better display their structure. Generally, however, it is advisable to follow Leonardo's suggestion and to emphasize only those muscle forms that are visibly active in a gesture. Muscle forms that are not apparent in the model can later be drawn on the overlay study by referring to anatomical illustrations.

194

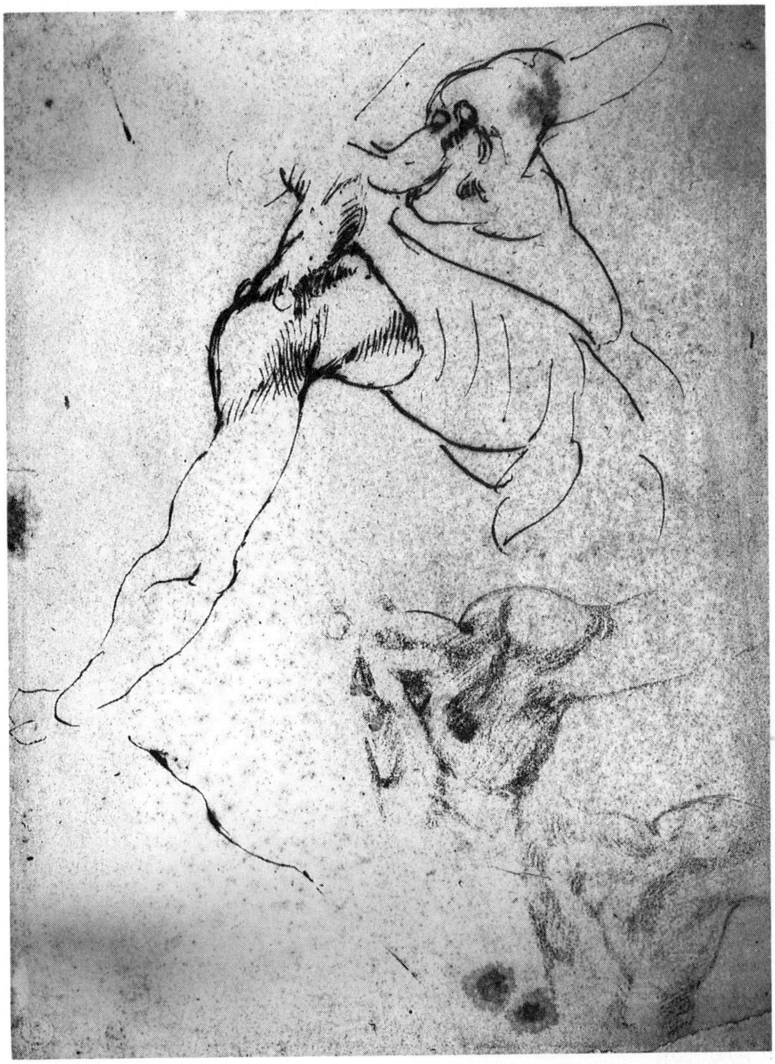

Figure 6-7. Michelangelo, *Anatomical Studies*, c. 1504–1506. Ink and black chalk. 28.4 × 21 cm. Florence, Galleria degli Uffizi. In these studies of the shoulder Michelangelo vividly conveys the muscular tension that is created when the arm is raised.

Figure 6-8. Eadweard Muybridge (1830–1904), *Man Heaving a 75-Pound Boulder*, 1884–1885. Serial photograph. Washington, D.C., Smithsonian Institution. The muscle forms of the leg and abdomen become clear as they are tensed for throwing; afterward they become less conspicuous, as seen in the lower right frame.

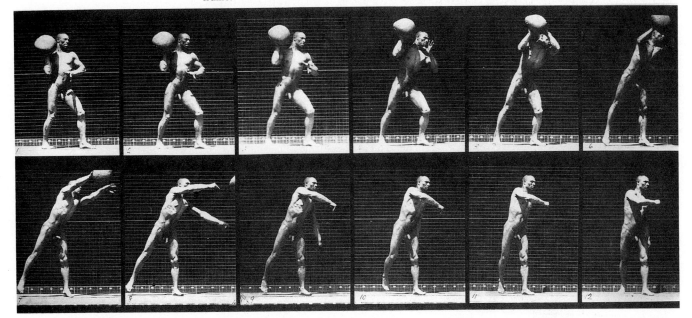

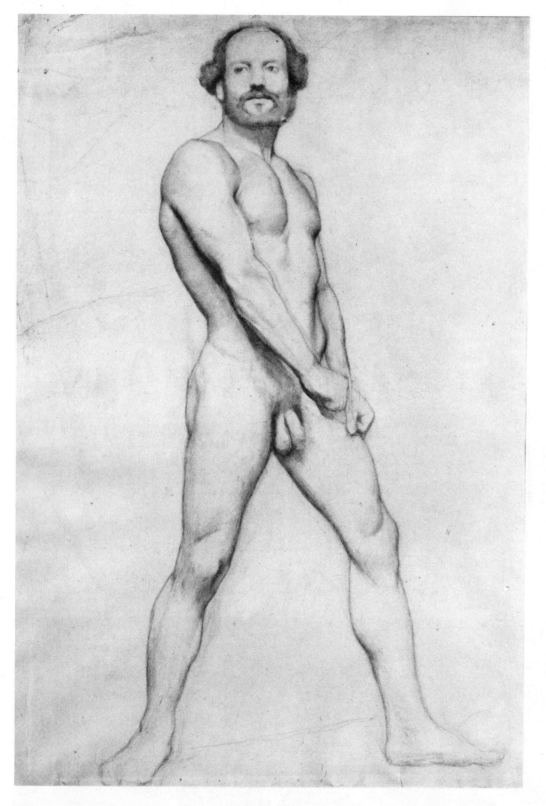

Figure 6-9. Edgar Degas, *Academic Study of a Nude Man*, 1856–1858. Charcoal on pale gray paper. 24 × 18⅜″. Boston, Museum of Fine Arts. Gift of W. G. Russell Allen. This study was executed roughly ten years before Degas began working in the mature impressionist style for which he is best known. The skill and knowledge necessary to produce the later drawings were gained in part through life studies such as this.

Whether or not a muscle is tensed, its tendons remain the same length. The proportion of tendon to muscle body, however, varies with the individual and accounts for differences of build that are not due to athletic training or the lack of it. In some people "... the muscular fibers are long and the tendinous portions are relatively short ... in others the fleshy belly of the muscle is short and the tendons long."[8] Observed differences of muscle build between the sexes are surprisingly slight; most are simply due to the protective fatty tissues that usually characterize the female body (Figures 6-10 and 6-11): "This augmented investment amply fills the hollows and crevices of deeper structures and accounts for the smoothness and the flowing line of surface form."[9]

Despite differences of build, the body's bilateral symmetry earlier noted in the skeleton is also reflected in muscle structure. A muscle on the right side of the trunk is matched by a similar one on the left. The line of symmetry dividing the trunk is generally marked by a slight furrow running vertically from the pit of the neck to the pubis. In the cadaver the furrow is visible as a band of tendinous tissues, whose whitish color gives it the name *linea alba* (Figures 6-6 and 6-12).[10] A similar line of symmetry is apparent in the groove of the spine on the back of the trunk (Figure 6-27). The muscles appear as a symmetrical pattern only when the body is viewed directly from the front or back (Figures 6-13, 6-14, 6-21, 6-25, 6-26, and 6-27). The *structural* symmetry of the muscles, however, does not change when the view of the body changes, for the muscle origins and insertions retain their bilateral structure in relation to the skeleton. The muscle attachments are therefore a key to understanding and interpreting the appearance of the muscles as a part of the unchanging symmetrical structure of the body. The symmetry of muscle structure is most apparent in the trunk, the subject of the following study.

Figure 6-10. The female model and the skeleton. Surface forms of the female figure, though generally displaying subtler transitions than those of the male, nevertheless contain the same skeletal and muscular features. The skeleton and the model are being compared by the student.

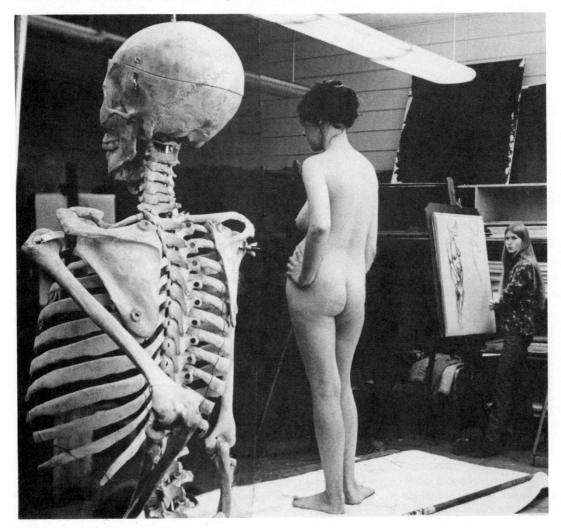

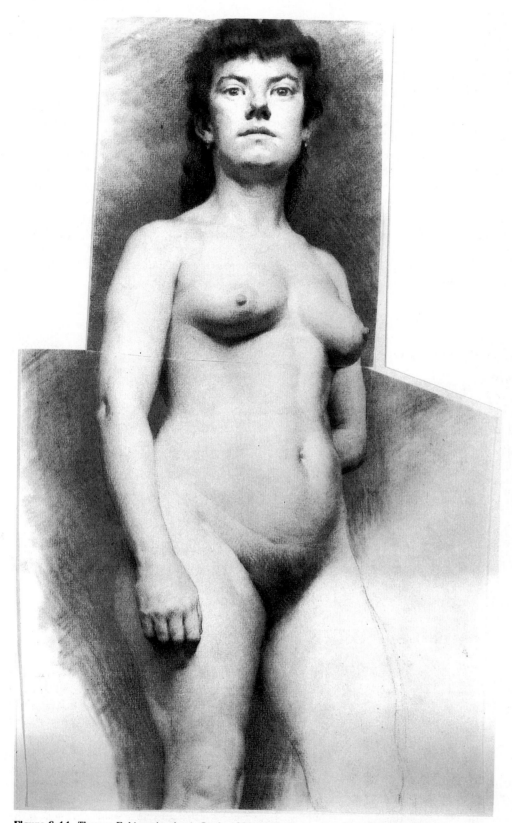

Figure 6-11. Thomas Eakins, *Academic Study*, 1866–1869. Charcoal on French paper. Cambridge, Fogg Art Museum, Harvard University. (Courtesy of Seiden and de Cuevas, Inc.) This study, drawn while Eakins was a student in Paris, was cut apart in order to pass through American customs, which in the nineteenth century censored drawings of nudes. The piece representing the figure below the knee is apparently lost.

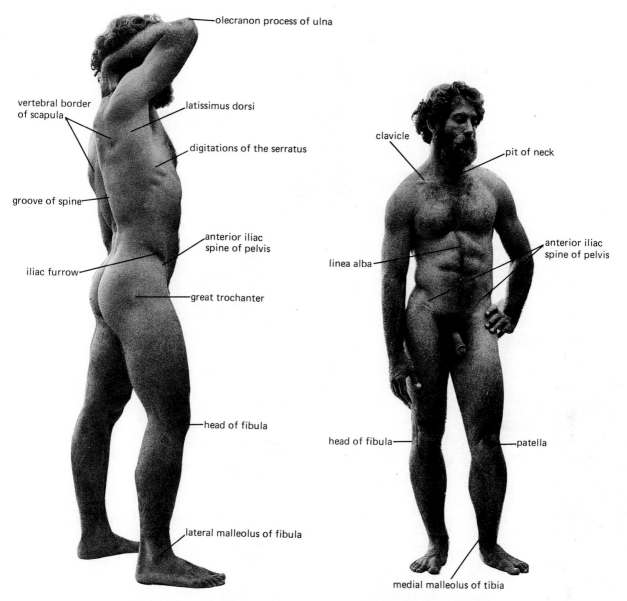

Figure 6-12. Skeletal landmarks on the body. The presence of the skeleton in the body is revealed by prominences (bumps) and other surface discontinuities caused by bones just beneath the skin. The iliac furrow, for example, reveals the position of the anterior iliac spine of the pelvis. Such skeletal landmarks are also helpful in visualizing muscle origins and insertions.

STUDY 41:   The Muscles of the Trunk: Front View

materials: ❏ 14 × 11″ sketchbook
  ❏ drawing pen and ink (0.5 mm point)
  ❏ India ink
  ❏ HB drawing pencil, sanguine pencil, tracing paper

reference: ❏ Figures 6-6, 6-12, 6-13, and 6-19 or the écorché

time: ❏ 15–20 minutes for each life study
  ❏ 30 minutes for the overlay drawing of the skeleton
  ❏ 30 minutes for the overlay drawing of the muscles

A figure study drawn previously can serve as the basis for this study, or you may prefer to start fresh by making three or more studies that show the front side of the trunk. It is helpful to indicate the bony landmarks of the body (such as the pit of the neck, the clavicles, and the spines of the pelvis) accurately in preparing the life study (Figure 6-12). They are useful not only in structuring the skeletal study on the first overlay drawing, but also in visualizing sites of muscle attachments (Figures 6-15 and 6-16). The pit of the neck, for example, suggests the origins of chest and neck muscles as well as the location of the sternum. The linea alba, which lies over the sternum, can also be traced down the trunk as a means of locating muscles in the abdominal region (Figure 6-17).

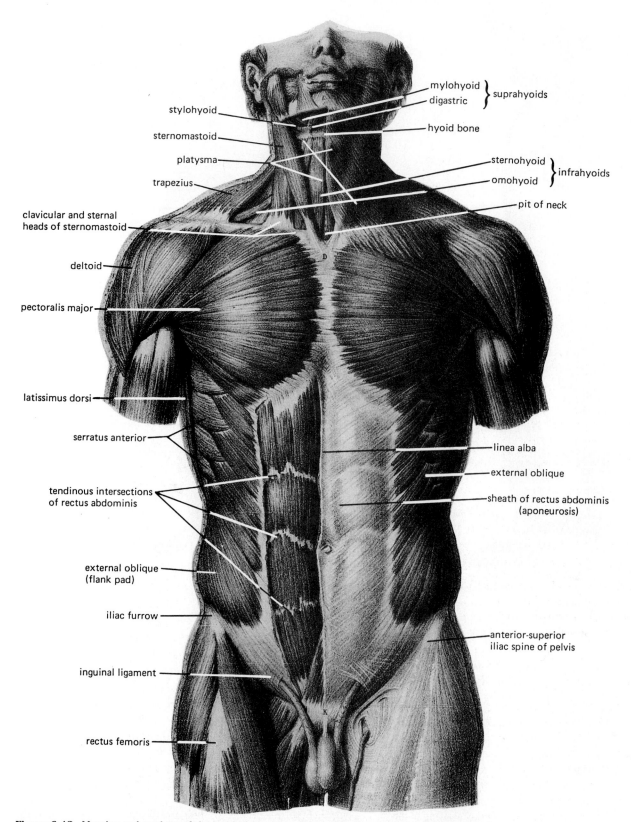

mylohyoid
digastric
} suprahyoids

stylohyoid

hyoid bone

sternomastoid

platysma

trapezius

sternohyoid
} infrahyoids
omohyoid

clavicular and sternal
heads of sternomastoid

pit of neck

deltoid

pectoralis major

latissimus dorsi

serratus anterior

linea alba

external oblique

sheath of rectus abdominis
(aponeurosis)

tendinous intersections
of rectus abdominis

external oblique
(flank pad)

iliac furrow

anterior-superior
iliac spine of pelvis

inguinal ligament

rectus femoris

Figure 6-13. Muscles and tendons of the trunk, front view. (Dr. J. Fau, *The Anatomy of the External Forms of Man* [London: Hippolyte Bailliere, 1849], plate 10. Courtesy of Countway Library, Harvard University.) The white sheath of tendinous tissue (aponeurosis) that clothes the abdominal muscles is removed on the figure's right side.

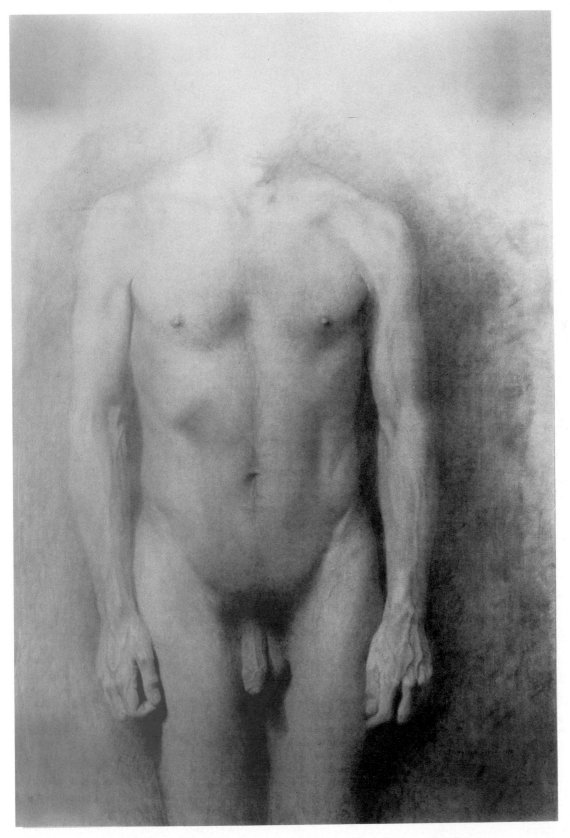

Figure 6-14. Francisco Lopez (b. 1932), *Male Nude*, 1973. Graphite. 98 × 66 cm (photo courtesy Galerie Herbert Meyer-Ellinger, Frankfurt am Main).

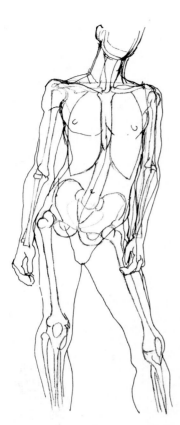

Figure 6-15. Student drawing. Life sketch and skeletal study. Ink and graphite pencil on sketchbook bond paper. 11 × 8½″.

Figure 6-16. Student drawing. Arm and trunk muscles. An overlay taped on the study shown in Figure 6-15 provides the surface for an additional study, drawn in sanguine pencil.

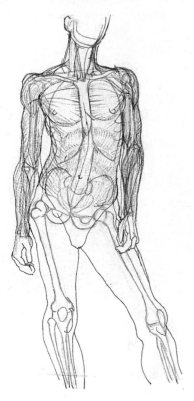

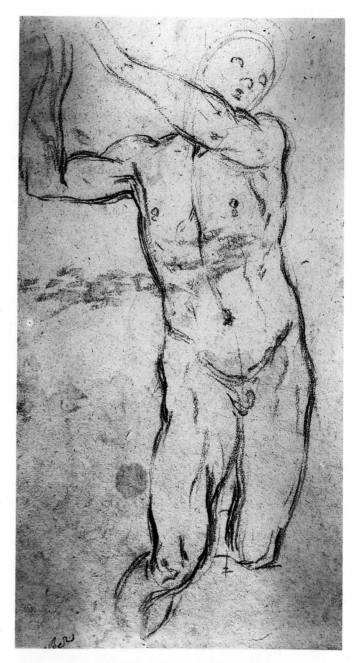

Figure 6-17. Giovanni Lorenzo Bernini, *Study of the Nude,* c. 1655. Red crayon on gray paper. 386 × 212 mm. Leipzig Museum der Bildenden Künste. The light preliminary lines in this drawing, a study for a sculptured figure of Daniel, include a rendering of the linea alba.

TRUNK MUSCLES: FRONT SIDE

In the upper part of the trunk the linea alba separates the two sets of pectoral muscles, the *pectoralis major.* The largest and most visible of these originates from the sternum and the clavicle (Figures 6-13 and 6-19). The fibers of the pectoralis major are drawn together near the shoulder, where they disappear from view under the deltoid to insert with a ridge on the front side of the arm bone (humerus) near the upper end. When the pectoralis major contracts, it pulls the arm forward toward the trunk. The pectoralis major also assists in rotating the arm (inward) and in pulling the arm down after it has been raised.

The lower border of the pectoralis major terminates in the abdominal sheath, a blanket of tendinous fascia[11] that encases a group of muscles directly below it called the *rectus abdominis* (compare Figures 6-13 and 6-14). Inserted with the cartilage of the fifth through the eighth ribs (counting from the top), the abdominal sheath extends all the way down to the pubis. Inside the sheath are the padlike divisions of the rectus abdominis muscles, which join each other by means of the tendinous intersections. The reason for the small length of the divisions is that smaller fibers are more powerful than long muscle fibers.[12] Since the rectus abdominis must provide great strength, it evolved in a segmented form that permits the muscles to be short but also to cover a relatively great length. A common function of the rectus abdominis is easily demonstrated by lying on your back and raising your legs. In this position you can feel that the rectus abdominis muscles immediately contract, even though they play no direct part in raising the legs.[13] The muscles directly responsible for raising the legs—the *prime movers*, as they are termed by anatomists—are the powerful muscles in front of the thigh, which also contract in this action. The rectus abdominis holds the pelvis steady while the thigh muscles, which originate with the pelvis, lift the leg. By stabilizing the origin of the prime mover the rectus abdominis functions as a *fixation* muscle.

The lower reaches of the abdominal sheath extend from the iliac crest to the pubis, forming the *inguinal ligament* that is visible in life as the groove of the groin (Figure 6-6). The lateral edges of the abdominal sheath serve as an insertion for the *external oblique muscles*, or the flank pads, which also insert with the iliac crest of the pelvis (Figures 6-13, 6-14, 6-18, and 6-19). In the latter insertion the external oblique muscle slightly overlaps the iliac crest. In the male figure this feature, known as the *iliac furrow*, is apparent as a contour that marks a division between the lower abdomen and the thigh (Figures 6-12, 6-13, 6-14, and 6-18).[14] The external oblique muscles reach upward diagonally from the abdominal sheath to their origins with the fifth through the twelfth ribs.[15] In order to attach to individual ribs, the external oblique muscles separate into fingerlike bunches of muscle fibers, called *digitations*.

The top four digitations slip between similar digitations of a neighboring muscle, the *serratus*, giving rise to a characteristic row of bumps along the sides of the chest (Figures 6-12 and 6-20). The remainder of the fan-shaped serratus disappears under the latissimus dorsi, slipping between the scapula and the rib cage to its hidden insertion along the medial edge of the scapula, an arrangement that enables this muscle to draw the scapula forward around the rib cage.

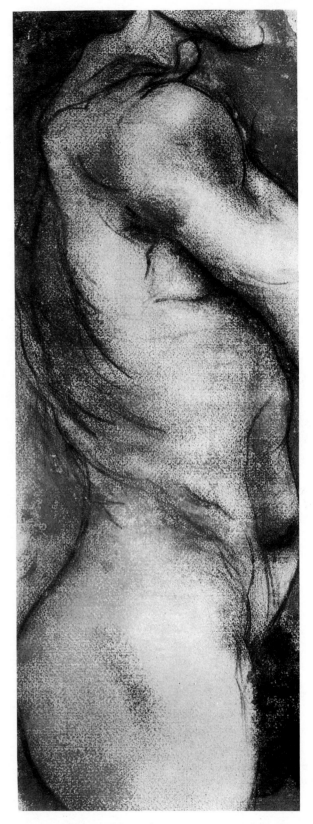

Figure 6-18. R. B. Kitaj (b. 1932), *Male Nude,* 1979. Pastel and crayon. London, British Museum.

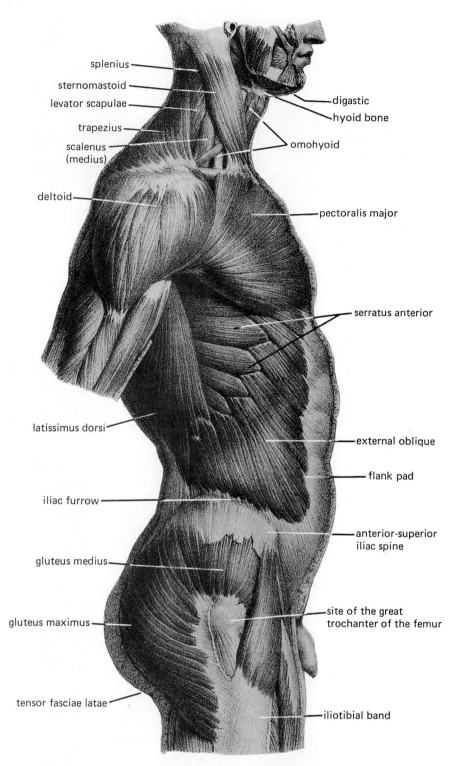

splenius

sternomastoid

levator scapulae

trapezius

scalenus
(medius)

deltoid

latissimus dorsi

iliac furrow

gluteus medius

gluteus maximus

tensor fasciae latae

digastic

hyoid bone

omohyoid

pectoralis major

serratus anterior

external oblique

flank pad

anterior-superior
iliac spine

site of the great
trochanter of the femur

iliotibial band

Figure 6-19. Muscles and tendons of the trunk, side view. (Dr. J. Fau, *The Anatomy of the External Forms of Man* [London: Hippolyte Bailliere, 1849], plate 12. Courtesy of Countway Library, Harvard University.)

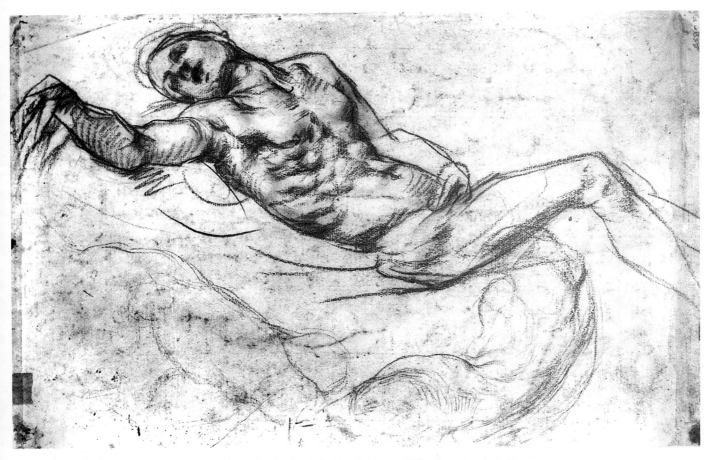

Figure 6-20. Jacopo da Pontormo, *Study for St. John, Dublin Pietà,* c. 1518. Natural red chalk. 392 × 262 mm. Florence, Galleria degli Uffizi. The muscle structure of the shoulder and the trunk is especially clear in this study, suggesting the interweaving digitations of the serratus and the external oblique muscles on the side of the chest as well as the iliac furrow at the juncture of the lower abdomen and the upper thigh. Compare Figure 6-19.

The *deltoid,* an important muscle of the shoulder, also attaches with the scapula. This attachment—one of the deltoid's two origins—is located on the projecting spine and acromium process of the scapula. The deltoid's other origin is with the outer (lateral) end of the clavicle. The deltoid rises in a rounded triangular shape, which inspired early anatomists to name it after the Greek letter *delta.* This muscle inserts at only one place: the raised surface on the outer side of the humerus known as the deltoid tuberosity.

The deltoid shares the scapular spine and the clavicle's lateral end with another muscle, the *trapezius,* which has insertions in both places (Figure 6-32). In a frontal view of the trunk (Figure 6-13) the upper portion of the trapezius reaches from the shoulder diagonally to the neck and its highest origin, the occipital protuberance, a bump in the lower back of the skull. The upper trapezius governs the attitude of the head, drawing it backward and rotating it.

STUDY 42:   The Latissimus Dorsi

materials: ❏ 11 × 14″ sketchbook
❏ drawing pen (1.5 mm)
❏ India ink
❏ HB drawing pencil
❏ sanguine pencil
❏ 11 × 14″ tracing paper

reference: ❏ model and écorché or Figures 6-12, 6-19, 6-21, 6-22, and 6-27

time: ❏ 15–20 minutes for the life study
❏ 30 minutes for the overlay drawing of the skeleton
❏ 20 minutes for the overlay drawing of the muscle

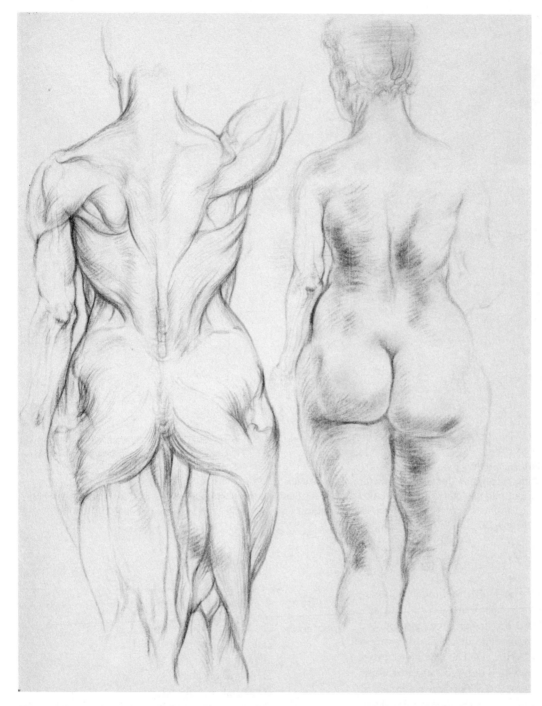

Figure 6-21. George Grosz, *Anatomical Study of a Female Nude.* Crayon. Peter Grosz collection.

Another major back muscle is often partially visible from the front just below the armpit—the *latissimus dorsi.* This muscle, which literally means "broadest muscle of the back," merits a separate study, not merely because of its unusual size but also because of its concealed insertion in the shoulder.

For this study draw the model from the side, preferably with the arm raised, a gesture that fully displays the latissimus

dorsi muscle. The study of the skeleton can be drawn in pencil on a tracing paper overlay (Figure 6-23). In addition to the axial skeleton the study should include the humerus of the arm, on which the insertion of the latissimus dorsi is located. The second overlay study (Figure 6-24) can be devoted entirely to the latissimus dorsi itself. The life study may suggest the muscle's position, for its lateral border is often visible as a

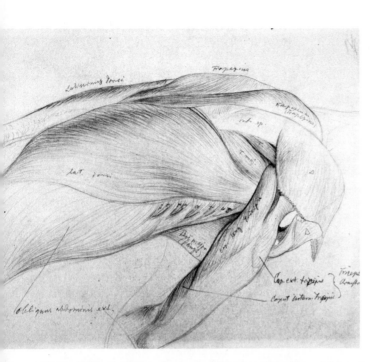

Figure 6-22. Paul Klee, *Anatomical Drawing of the Musculature of the Shoulder,* c. 1902. Graphite pencil. 17.3 × 21.4 cm. Foundation Paul Klee—Museum of Fine Arts Bern. Labeled in the artist's script are the latissimus dorsi, trapezius, oblique, infraspinatus, teres major, deltoid, triceps, and pectoralis major muscles.

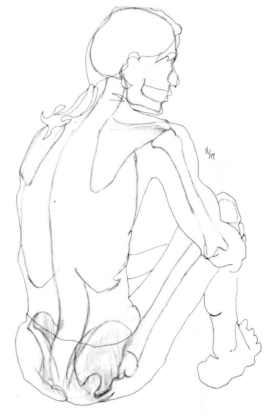

Figure 6-23. Student drawing. Life study with tracing overlay showing major skeletal forms. Pen and ink and pencil on sketchbook bond paper. 11 × 8½″.

Figure 6-24. Student drawing. Overlay study (over Figure 6-23) of the latissimus dorsi. Sanguine pencil on tracing paper. 11 × 8½″.

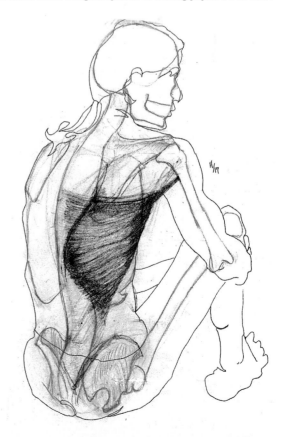

ridgelike discontinuity just beneath the armpit (Figure 6-12).

The origins of the latissimus dorsi are invisible on the body surface, as the muscle forms a broad, flat, tendinous sheath (*aponeurosis*) on the back before attaching to the spines of the vertebral column from the sacrum up to the middle of the rib cage.[16] Moreover, the upper portion of the muscle is partially covered by the trapezius muscle (Figure 6-27). From these origins, the latissimus dorsi sweeps laterally around the sides of the rib cage, covering the lower part of the scapula and holding it in place against the rib cage. Continuing around the rib cage, the muscle overlaps the serratus, inserting with the front side of the humerus near its head (Figures 6-19, 6-21, and 6-22).

If you imagine its insertion free of overlapping muscles, the function of the latissimus dorsi is not difficult to comprehend. As the muscle contracts, it pulls the arm backward and toward the trunk. The forward insertion on the humerus enables it to twist the arm, causing the limb to rotate inward.[17] The form of the latissimus dorsi is visually important in drawing the figure, as it helps articulate the arm with the trunk (Figures 8-8 and 8-14).

Studies of an individual muscle, such as the latissimus dorsi, are advisable if its function is obscured by overlapping muscles or other tissues, but it is usually most helpful to study muscles together as they appear in life. The remaining muscles of the back are considered in a single study.

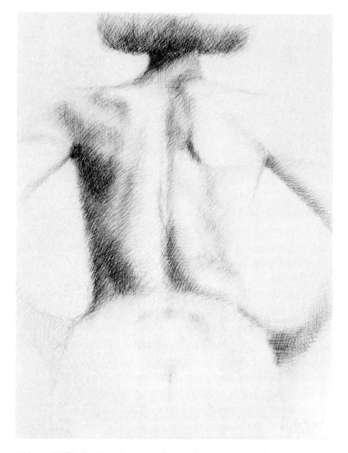

Figure 6-25. Student drawing. *Study of the Back.* Conté crayon on laid paper. 24 × 18″.

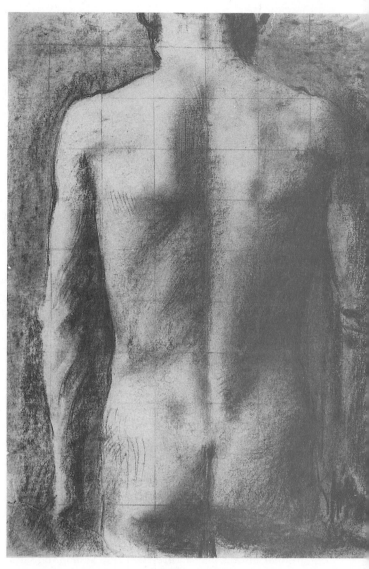

Figure 6-26. Antonio López-Garcia (b. 1936), *Male Nude Back,* 1963. Charcoal. 26.5 × 19.5 cm (photo courtesy Galerie Herbert Meyer-Ellinger, Frankfurt am Main).

STUDY 43:   The Muscles of the Trunk: Back View

materials: ❑ 11 × 14″ sketchbook
❑ drawing pen (0.5 mm point)
❑ India ink
❑ HB drawing pencil
❑ sanguine pencil
❑ 11 × 14″ tracing paper
❑ transparent tape
reference: ❑ model, Figures 6-19, 6-21, and 6-27, or écorché
time: ❑ 15–20 minutes for each life drawing of the skeleton
❑ 30 minutes for the overlay study of the muscles

If you do not already have a suitable pen-and-ink drawing of the back of the figure in your sketchbook, you may wish to prepare first several contour drawings of the model seen from behind. Allow no more than twenty minutes for each drawing. Select one of these for your study (Figure 6-28). After attaching an overlay sheet of tracing paper to the drawing,

render the skeleton on the overlay in pencil as before so that it corresponds to the gesture of the figure in the life drawing. After attaching a second overlay you are ready to begin a study in sanguine pencil of the muscles of the back (Figure 6-29).

The latissimus dorsi is a convenient place in the figure to begin drawing the back muscles, for you are likely to find traces of it in contours of your study from life. The lower region of the latissimus dorsi may reveal the rounded forms of the deeper *sacrospinalis* muscles on either side of the vertebral column. The tension produced by these powerful muscles is suggested clearly in a life study of the back by Michelangelo (Figure 6-30). The groove of the spine that separates the two sets of sacrospinalis muscles is most evident in a standing pose (Figures 6-25, 6-26, and 6-51). When the

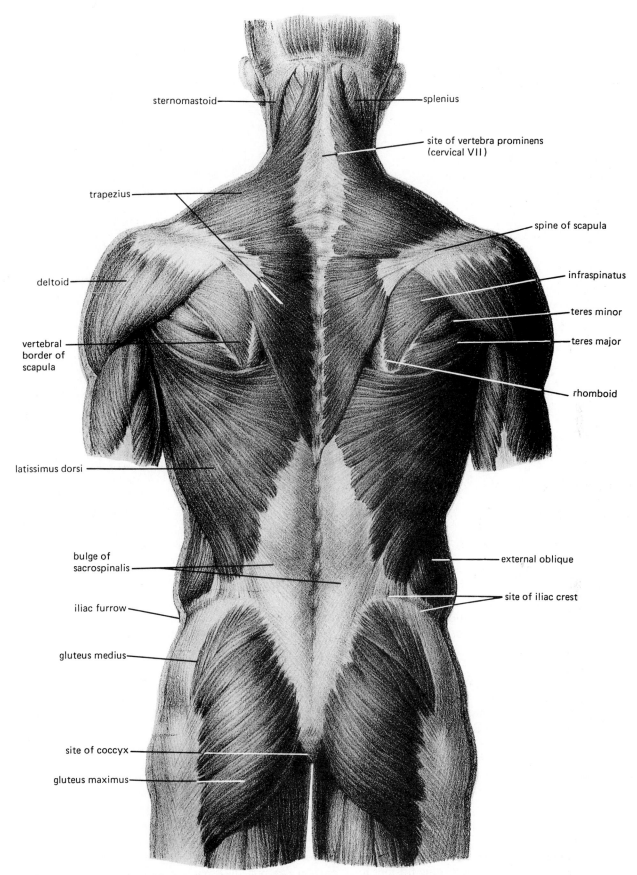

Figure 6-27. Muscles and tendons on the back. (Dr. J. Fau, *The Anatomy of the External Forms of Man* [London: Hippolyte Bailliere, 1849], plate 11. Courtesy of Countway Library, Harvard University.)

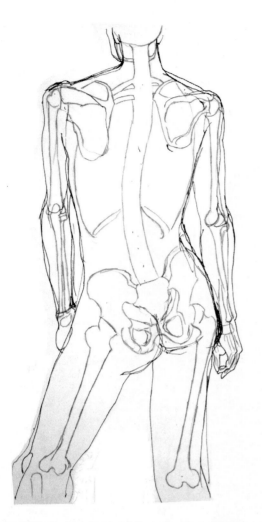

Figure 6-28. Student drawing. Life study with skeletal forms. Pen and ink and pencil on sketchbook bond paper. 11 × 8½″.

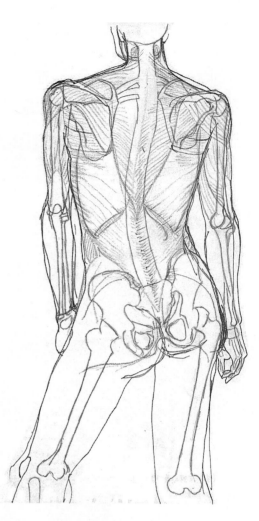

Figure 6-29. Student drawing. Overlay study (over Figure 6-28) of back muscles. Sanguine pencil on tracing paper. 11 × 8½″.

life model bends forward slightly, the groove disappears and is replaced by a row of bumps caused by underlying vertebral spines (Figure 6-31).

TRUNK MUSCLES: BACK SIDE

As the name suggests, the sacrospinalis muscles extend from the sacrum and the pelvic region up the length of the spine, attaching to vertebral spines and to ribs. The upper reaches of these muscles insert with neck vertebrae, though they are not visible in this region due to overlapping muscles. The sacrospinalis is also known as the *erector spinae*, for it holds the spine erect by pulling it backward in opposition to the rectus abdominis muscles. The sacrospinalis performs another vital function, which you can feel in your lower back while walking. The muscle tenses on the side of the raised foot, fixing the position of the pelvis and thereby permitting the foot to be raised.[18]

The upper-central portion of the latissimus dorsi is covered by the lower portion of the trapezius muscle, mentioned earlier in connection with the neck (Figure 6-27). Named after the trapezium, an irregular four-sided shape, the form of this muscle is elegantly subtle, changing according to the body's gesture. As the trapezius is seldom completely visible on the surface, its form is best visualized by reviewing its attachments, all of which are uncovered. The trapezius originates in the part with the occipital protuberance at the base of the skull and along much of the spinal column, including the *nuchal ligament* at the nape of the neck, the vertebra prominens, and all the dorsal vertebrae.[19] As we noted previously the trapezius finds insertion on the shoulder with the lateral end of the clavicle, the scapular spine, and the acromium process (Figure 6-27). The trapezius muscle can thus be visualized as consisting of two opposing parts, for the upper portion can pull the scapula toward the spine or upward, while the lower portion can draw it downward. When both

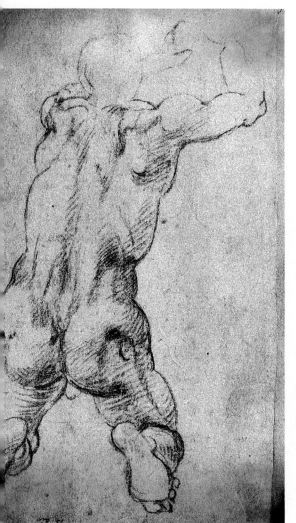

Figure 6-30. Michelangelo, *Study for* The Last Judgement, 1534–1541. Black chalk. 25.8 × 15.7 cm. Florence, Casa Buonarroti. The actions of the sacrospinalis and gluteus muscles are important in the gesture of this figure.

Figure 6-31. Student drawing. Study of the back. Crayon on newsprint paper. 24 × 18″. Skeletal forms of the rib cage, scapula, iliac crest, and prominences of the vertebral spines are integrated with muscle forms in this study.

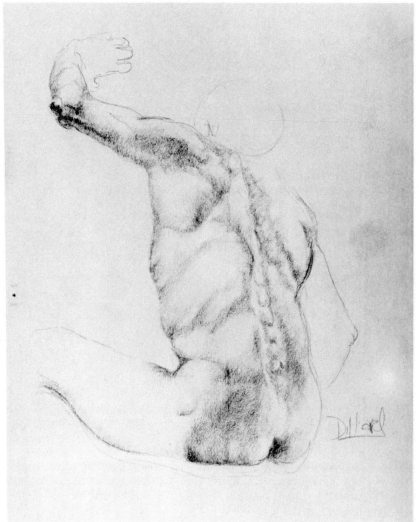

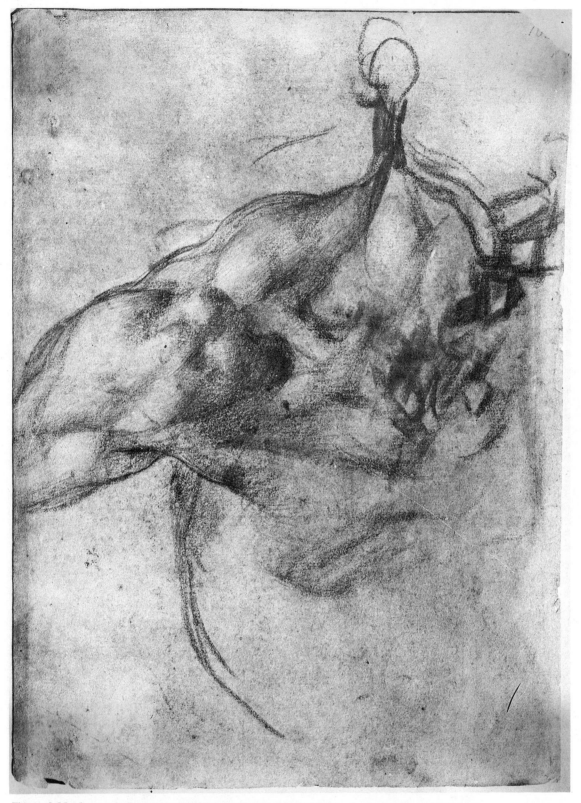

Figure 6-32. Jacopo da Pontormo, *Page from a Sketchbook, Right Side of a Nude Bust*, c. 1517–1520.
Red chalk on pink prepared paper. 21.8 × 15.9 cm. FC 132 recto. Rome, Istituto Nazionale per La Grafica.
This spirited study accurately integrates skeletal and muscle forms of the shoulder. The relationship of
the clavicle and the scapula to the deltoid and trapezius muscles invites comparison with Figure 6-19.

portions are tensed, however, the trapezius serves as a fixation muscle for the scapula.

Originating on the same scapular spine with which the trapezius inserts is the back portion of the deltoid (Figure 6-32). Though considered earlier as an arm muscle, it should be included in a study of back muscles because of its common attachment with the trapezius on the scapula.

In addition to the trapezius and the deltoid there are three other muscles that operate the scapula: the *infraspinatus*, the *teres minor*, and the *teres major* (Figure 6-27). Because they appear close together and are only partially exposed, they can be studied as a group. The infraspinatus, as its name suggests, originates just below the raised spine of the scapula.[20] Viewed without the deltoid that covers its outer reaches, the infraspinatus extends around the back of the humerus, inserting on the outer side of the bone near its head (at the major tubercle). This insertion enables the infraspinatus to rotate the arm outward when the muscle contracts (opposite to the rotation caused by the latissimus dorsi). The teres minor, originating on the lateral margin of the scapula, shares the infraspinatus's insertion on the humerus and assists it in rotating the arm outward. The straplike teres major, though also originating with the scapula (at the lower tip) has a different insertion and consequently a different function. The teres major follows the same route as the latissimus dorsi: It turns in between the humerus and the rib cage before inserting on the front of the humerus just below and behind[21] the insertion of the latissimus dorsi. As a result, when the teres major contracts it can rotate the arm inward and pull it downward, a function similar to that of the latissimus dorsi.

Figure 6-33. Deep muscles of the neck.

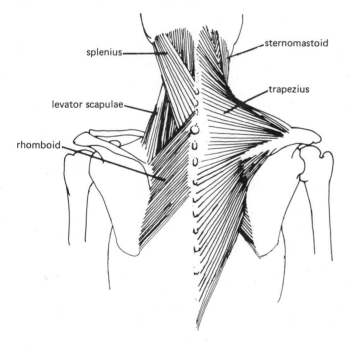

splenius—

sternomastoid

levator scapulae—

trapezius

rhomboid—

If you wish to make a more complete study of the back muscles, try omitting the trapezius muscle on one side of the sanguine drawing and rendering in its place the series of muscles it usually covers (Figure 6-33). Among these are the *major* and *minor rhomboids* and the *levator scapulae*, which contract to pull the scapula upward and toward the middle of the back, ". . . assisting the trapezius in bearing weights or in shrugging the shoulders."[22] Other hidden muscles are considered in connection with the neck region.

STUDY 44: Muscles of the Neck

materials: ❑ 11 × 14″ sketchbook
  ❑ drawing pen (0.5 mm point)
  ❑ India ink
  ❑ HB pencil
  ❑ sanguine pencil

reference: ❑ model (optional) and Figures 6-6, 6-13, 6-19, 6-27, 6-33, and 6-34

time: ❑ 15–20 minutes for each life study
  ❑ 30 minutes for each overlay study of the neck

The neck region can be studied either by preparing new life drawings limited to the upper region of the body or by simply adding to the overlay studies already made in connection with the trunk (Studies 41, 42, and 43 and Figures 6-16 and 6-23). If you opt for the latter approach, you can begin by adding one bone, the hyoid (Figure 6-34), to the overlay drawing of the skeleton. This U-shaped bone is held in place above the Adam's apple by muscles and tendons, somewhat as the patella is held in the knee; it has no joints with other bones.[23] You may also wish to add to the skeletal study the *Adam's apple*, an angular structure of cartilage that is plainly visible as a bump in the neck below the chin (Figures 6-35 and 6-36). Also known as the *thyroid cartilage*, the Adam's apple is generally larger in the male than in the female.[24] Below the Adam's apple is a smaller bump caused by the thyroid gland proper.

The neck muscles can be drawn with a sanguine pencil on a second sheet of tracing paper attached to the sketchbook page over the skeletal analysis. With a life drawing representing a frontal or three-quarter view of the neck (Figure 6-15), you can begin by rendering the *sternomastoid* muscles. Using the top of the sternum[25] in your skeletal overlay as a guide, draw the V-shaped juncture of the sternomastoids' origins with the sternum (Figure 6-35). Check the position of the insertions with the skull, the *mastoid processes*, which can be felt as bumps just behind the ears (Figure 6-34). The sternomastoid muscle has a secondary origin with the clavicle (Figure 6-13). The small space between the two origins creates a triangular "window" that is often visible in life, especially when the head is turned. With the sanguine pencil you can easily trace the diagonal sweep of the sternomastoid muscles from the sternum to the mastoid processes. Once rendered, this muscle can serve as a frame of reference for the remaining muscles of the neck.

THE NECK MUSCLES

The sternomastoid muscles work together to turn the head to the side. When the head turns toward the left side, for example, the sternomastoid muscle on that side relaxes while the muscle on the right contracts, pulling the left side of the head forward and rotating it in the direction of the left shoulder (Figure 6-35). With the head turned to one side, the tense sternomastoid in front appears to rise almost vertically from the sternum, an indication of how much the contraction shortens the muscle. Its secondary origin on the clavicle is also clearly visible. A more subtle function of the sternomastoid muscles is to raise the head while the body lies in a prone position.[26] The muscles are highly visible and tense in performing this action, a clear indication of their involvement.

A life drawing of the side or back of the neck usually takes into account the upper portion of the trapezius muscle (Figures 6-37 and 6-38). This large flat muscle accounts for the almost unbroken contour of the neck and the back. The up-

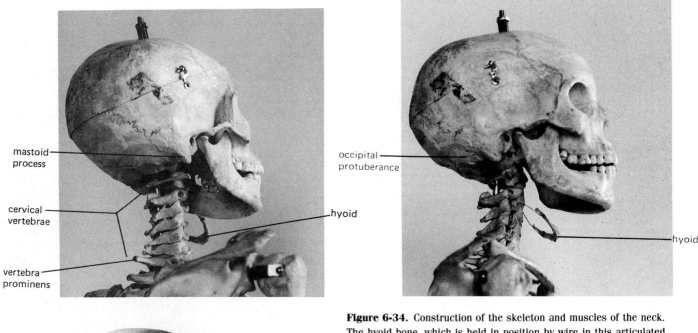

Figure 6-34. Construction of the skeleton and muscles of the neck. The hyoid bone, which is held in position by wire in this articulated skeleton, is supported (in a slightly higher position) by muscles in life. One set of these muscles, the sternohyoids, is seen in the écorché below.

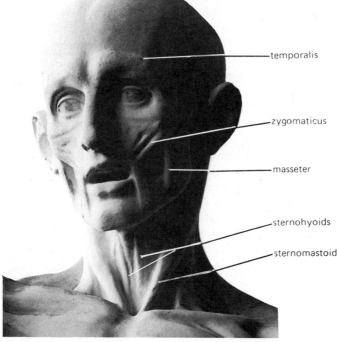

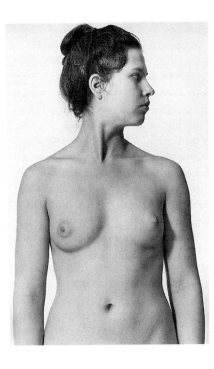

Figure 6-35. The sterno-mastoid and the trapezius are active in rotating the head. The sternal head of the sterno-mastoid is clearly displayed when the head is turned to the side.

Figure 6-36. Jacopo da Pontormo, *Page from a Sketchbook, Muscular Neck and Head Looking Up*, c. 1517–1520. Red chalk on pink prepared paper. 21.6 × 15.4 cm. FC 151. Rome, Istituto per La Grafica.

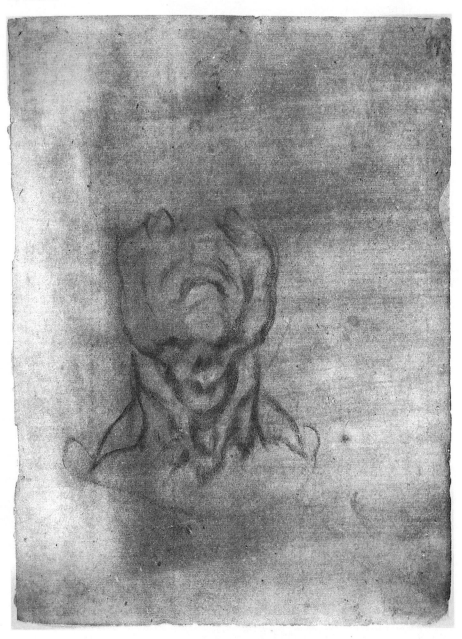

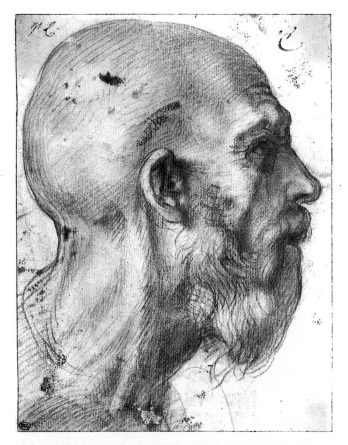

Figure 6-37. Andrea del Sarto (1486–1530), *Study of the Head.* Natural red chalk. 19.5 × 15 cm. Paris, the Louvre. This powerfully modeled drawing reveals surface forms of neck muscles, particularly the sternomastoid, with its insertion behind the ear, and the trapezius, visible on the posterior side of the neck. Between the two muscles can be seen the diagonal forms of the scalenus and levator scapulae muscles.

per cervical vertebrae have short spines and do not affect the trapezius's outer surface. The seventh vertebra of the neck (vertebra prominens), however, has a very long spine, which appears as a bump on the back of the neck (Figure 6-27), the only place where the vertebral column is apparent on the neck's surface.

Although the sets of sternomastoid and trapezius muscles dominate the exterior of the neck, intervening spaces make it possible to glimpse portions of other muscles that play a role in the structure and movement of the neck. Two such muscles are partially exposed between the sternomastoid and the trapezius: the *scalenus medius* and the *splenius* (Figure 6-19). The scalenus medius muscles, which originate with the transverse process of the cervical vertebrae (II–VII) and insert with the uppermost rib, pull the neck sideways toward the rib cage. When both the left and right scalenus muscles contract, however, the neck flexes forward. The splenius rises diagonally from its origin with vertebrae of the neck and chest to its

insertion with the occipital bone of the skull, a site shared with the sternomastoid, its opposing muscle (Figure 6-33).

Between the two sternomastoid muscles are two groups of muscles that control the hyoid bone (Figure 6-13). Their names reveal their location: Those above the bone are known as the *suprahyoid* muscles; those below, the *infrahyoid* muscles. When the neck muscles are tensed as you swallow, it is possible to feel the two sets of infrahyoids: the *sternohyoids* and the *omohyoids*. Both of these muscles insert with the hyoid bone, though they have different origins (Figure 6-34). The sternohyoid originates with the inner surface of the upper end of the sternum; the omohyoid, reaching under the sternomastoid on the side, finds origin with the scapula.[27] The omohyoid is also partly visible between the sternomastoid and the trapezius (Figure 6-19). Among the suprahyoids the most prominent externally is the *digastric* muscle. The anterior belly of the digastric muscle connects with the hyoid by means of a fibrous loop and extends to the inner side of the jawbone at the chin (symphysis of the mandible). The posterior belly of the digastric muscle extends backward to the mastoid process.

Figure 6-38. Andrea del Sarto, *Study for the Head of St. Elizabeth in the Painting* Madonna with St. Elizabeth and the Infant St. John, c. 1528. Natural red chalk. 25 × 18.6 cm. Oxford, Ashmolean Museum. Modeling of the neck region suggests complex muscle structure.

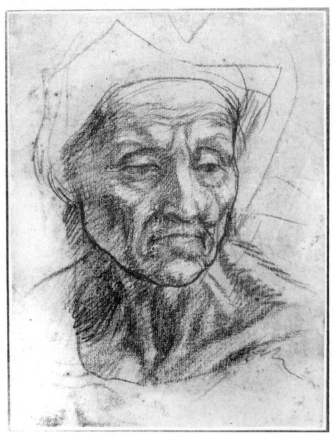

Last and in some ways least of the neck muscles is the *platysma*, a thin sheath that usually covers the entire front of the neck. It is generally visible only in times of physical duress, but in older persons it may always be apparent (Figure 6-38). Originating from a covering tissue (fascia) of the pectoralis, deltoid, and trapezius muscles, the platysma inserts with the lower jaw (mandibula) from the chin to the angle below the ear. This peculiar and seldom used muscle need not be included in your study, for its form is derived from the thicker, more active muscles situated beneath it.[28]

The Muscle Forms of the Limbs and Symmetry

Psychologists have found that "there is a general tendency to perceive any shape with the maximum degree of simplicity, regularity, and symmetry."[29] This tendency is expressed all too often in life drawings, in which the individual limbs may resemble forms turned on lathes. In life the limbs, though sharing in the bilateral symmetry of the body, are not individually symmetrical. The apparent asymmetry of the limbs can be understood by studying their muscular and skeletal structure.

Figure 6-39. Student drawing. Life study with tracing overlay showing skeletal arm. Graphite pencil on sketchbook bond paper. 14 × 11″.

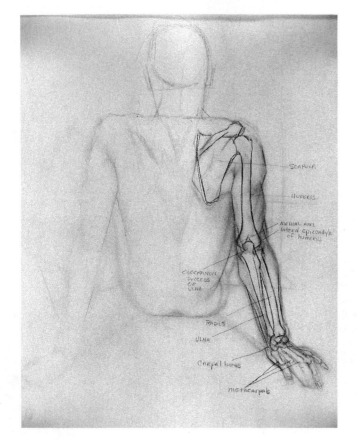

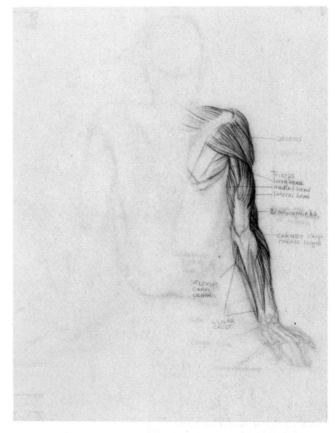

Figure 6-40. Student drawing. Life study with tracing overlay showing arm musculature. Graphite pencil on sketchbook bond paper. 14 × 11″.

STUDY 45:   The Arm Muscles

materials: ❑ 11 × 14″ sketchbook
❑ drawing pen (0.5 mm point)
❑ India ink
❑ 11 × 14″ tracing paper
❑ HB pencil
❑ sanguine pencil
❑ transparent tape
reference: ❑ model and Figures 6-41, 6-42, 6-43, 6-44, 6-45, 6-46, 6-47, 6-48, 6-49, 6-50, 6-52, and 6-53
time: ❑ 15–20 minutes for each life study
❑ 20 minutes of each overlay study of the skeletal arm
❑ 30 minutes for each overlay study of the muscle

In view of the complexity of the muscle structure in the upper limb, make six or more life drawings, showing the arm, forearm, and shoulder as large as conveniently possible on the sketchbook page. For a complete study of the arm muscles

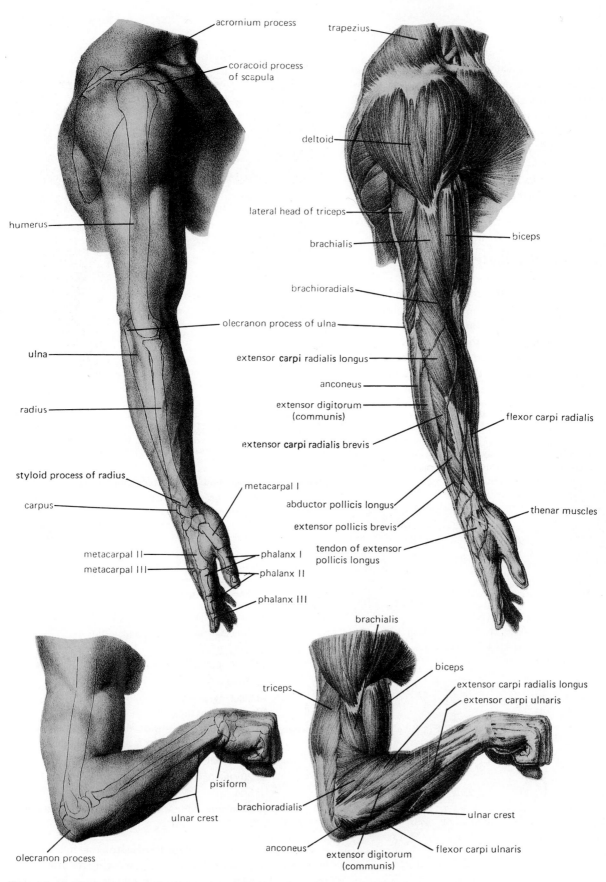

Figure 6-41. Muscular and skeletal structure of the arm extended and supinated (*above*), flexed and pronated (*below*), viewed from the side. (Dr. J. Fau, *The Anatomy of the External Forms of Man* [London: Hippolyte Bailliere, 1849], plate 15. Courtesy of Countway Library, Harvard University.)

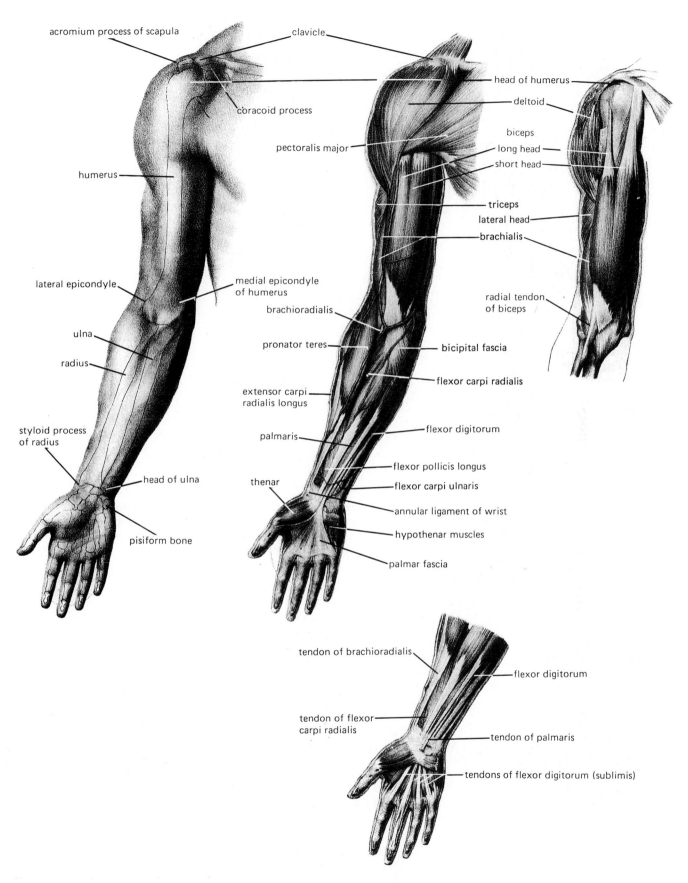

Figure 6-42. Muscular and skeletal structure of the extended and supinated arm, seen from the front. (Dr. J. Fau, *The Anatomy of the External Forms of Man* [London: Hippolyte Bailliere, 1849], plate 13. Courtesy of Countway Library, Harvard University.)

219

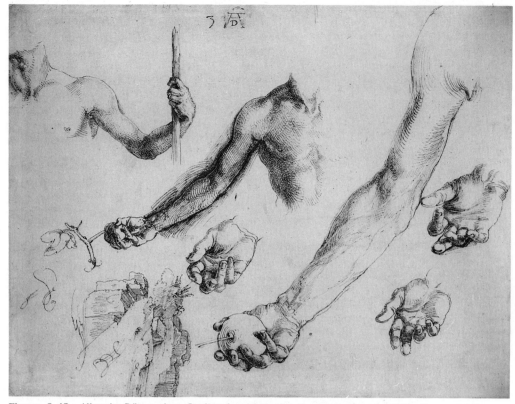

Figure 6-43. Albrecht Dürer, *Arm Studies for Adam* (for the engraving of 1504). Pen and ink. 8½ × 10⅞″. London, British Museum. The slight angle between the arm and extended forearm, evident in the two central arm studies, is characteristic of supination.

Figure 6-44. Paul Klee, *Arm Studies*, 1903. Graphite pencil. 27.7 × 37.1 cm. Foundation Paul Klee— Museum of Fine Arts Bern. The gesture of pronation is accurately drawn in the extended arms of this elegantly modeled study. In the lower left drawing of the raised and flexed arm the ulnar crest is shown connecting the tip of the elbow with the styloid process of the ulna at the wrist.

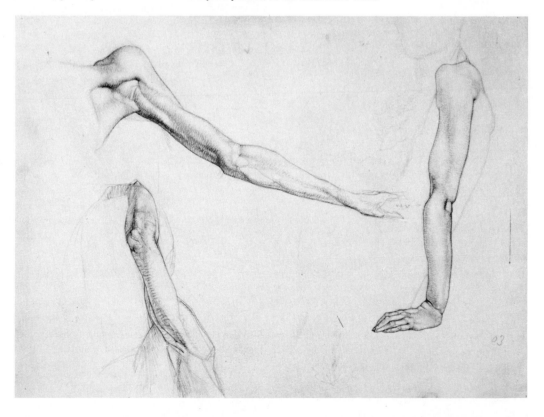

you need drawings of both sides of the arm and at least one view with the palm downward, or turned toward the back (in pronation), and another with the palm up or turned forward (in supination). The drawings will enable you to study the different appearance of the arm in those two positions (Figures 6-43 and 6-44), a difference due to the skeletal and muscular structure of the forearm.

When the life drawings are completed, tape two sheets of tracing paper over the drawing selected for anatomical study. The first overlay can be dedicated to the bones; the second, to the muscles of the arm (Figures 6-39 and 6-40). By making a skeletal study of the arm, forearm, and shoulder you can visualize the framework that provides the attachments for the muscles. For that reason the forearm bones should be drawn carefully to reflect the gesture. With the hand in pronation, the radius crosses over the ulna, but in supination the two bones are parallel (Figure 5-53). Other skeletal aspects that warrant attention are the knobs on the lower end of the humerus, known as the medial (inner) and lateral (outer) epicondyles (Figures 6-42, 6-45, and 6-46). In the forearm the wrenchlike head of the ulna displays two processes (projections), the olecranon at the tip of the elbow and the coronoid process on the opposite side (Figure 6-45), which are sites of muscle attachments. Other key sites of attachments are two bumpy projections at the far end of the forearm bones: the styloid process of the ulna (Figure 6-45), a spur that projects on the same side of the wrist as the little finger. Your life drawing may include already a major feature of the ulna: The ulnar ridge or crest that appears on its lower side and is usually visible in life (Figures 6-41 and 6-47). When the skeletal arm study is complete, it can serve as a guide for the second overlay drawing—a sanguine pencil study of the muscles, based on the anatomical illustrations in this chapter. As a prelude to your study, review the muscles of the arm and forearm and their attachments with the skeleton.

THE ARM MUSCLES

Consider first the frontal view of the upper arm as it appears with the palm turned outward in supination (Figure 6-42). The fleshy mass of the frontal region just below the deltoid is the biceps (literally, "two heads") muscle, which appears as a single semicylindrical form running almost parallel with the humerus. When the shoulder muscles that cover the upper fibers and tendons are removed (Figure 6-42, upper right), it is possible to see the two heads of the biceps, which find their origins with two places on the scapula. One head shares its attachment on the coracoid process with the pectoralis minor; the other tendon extends over the head of the humerus to reach a bump (tuberosity) on the scapula above the cusp joint (glenoid fossa) with the humerus. It is notable that the biceps has no attachment with the bone it covers, the humerus.[30] The biceps inserts with the radius and a ribbon of tendon

called the *bicipital fascia* (Figure 6-42). The latter remains on the surface and wraps around the forearm muscles just below the medial epicondyle of the humerus. The attachment of the biceps with the radius gives this muscle the dual function of flexing the arm and turning the lower arm to a supine position, a task assisted by lower arm muscles.

Immediately behind the biceps are the visible portions of a thicker, flatter muscle, the *brachialis*. With its origin on the front side of the lower half of the humerus and its insertion on the upper, anterior end of the ulna,[31] the brachialis assists the biceps in flexing the forearm (Figure 6-41). On the other side of the upper arm is the *triceps* muscle, which performs the opposing action of extending the arm. When the flexor and extensor muscles of the arm are tensed, they seem separated by a vertical ridge below the deltoid. The long straplike tendon of the triceps, which inserts with the olecranon process of the ulna, stretches along the almost flat surface of the arm's backside to the fleshy body of the triceps, with its characteristic swell, which appears halfway up the arm. True to its name, the triceps is divided into three heads: the *lateral* head, visible under the deltoid of the side; the *long* head, on the backside; and the *medial* head, on the inner side of the arm (Figure 6-46). The lateral and long heads are often visible in life when stressed and form an inverted V shape with their common flat tendon. Both have origins on the posterior side of the upper humerus (Figures 6-46, 6-48, and 6-49). The long head of the triceps originates with the scapula just below the hollow of the scapular joint with the humerus.

The simple gesture of raising the arm results in a dramatic change of the position of the scapula and the muscles attaching to it (Figure 6-50). The change, which begins when the arm is raised more than 30 degrees from the side of the body, is especially noticeable with the vertebral border and spine of the scapula. The scapular origin of the deltoid is sharply defined in the raised arm, when viewed from behind (Figure 6-51) or from the side (Figure 6-52).

The raised arm gesture seen in a frontal view (Figure 6-53) reveals not only the medial head of the triceps but also the *coracobrachialis*, a muscle wedged between biceps and the triceps near the armpit. Named after its origin with the coracoid process of the scapula, a site of attachment it shares with the pectoral minor muscle,[32] the coracobrachialis inserts with the inner side of the humerus at about the same height as the insertion of the deltoid on the other side. These attachments combine to enable the coracobrachialis to pull the arm toward the center and front of the body.

A special arrangement of muscle and tendon accounts for the characteristic tapering form of the forearm. The relatively thin tendons occupy most of the distal half of the forearm; the bulkier muscle bodies lie nearer the elbow joint. Arthur Thomson[33] points out that this arrangement frees the hand from the bulk of the large muscles. It also places less weight at the end of the arm, permitting a more efficient lever mechanism. The forearm appears to be a particularly clear instance

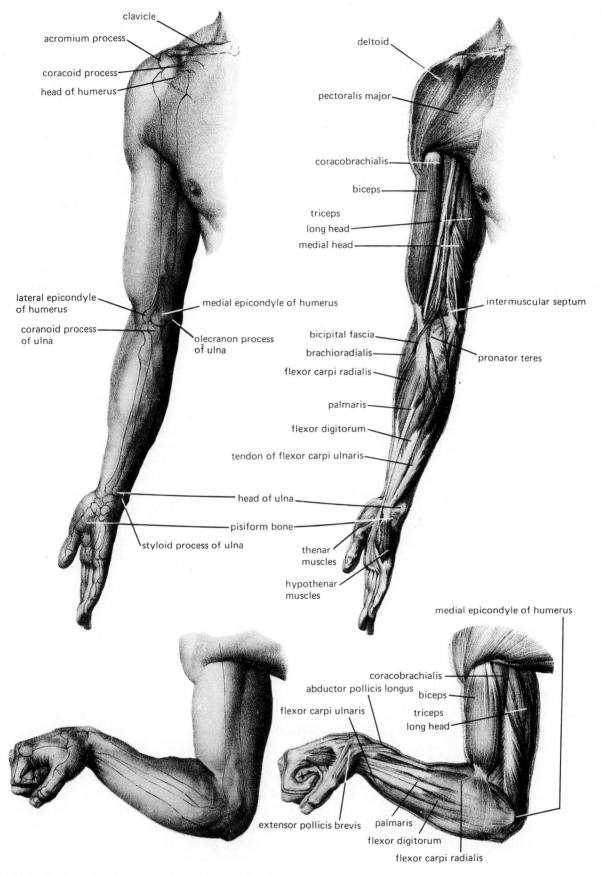

clavicle

acromium process

coracoid process

head of humerus

deltoid

pectoralis major

coracobrachialis

biceps

triceps
long head
medial head

lateral epicondyle
of humerus

medial epicondyle of humerus

intermuscular septum

coranoid process
of ulna

olecranon process
of ulna

bicipital fascia

brachioradialis

flexor carpi radialis

pronator teres

palmaris

flexor digitorum

tendon of flexor carpi ulnaris

head of ulna

pisiform bone

styloid process of ulna

thenar
muscles

hypothenar
muscles

medial epicondyle of humerus

coracobrachialis

abductor pollicis longus

biceps

flexor carpi ulnaris

triceps
long head

extensor pollicis brevis

palmaris

flexor digitorum

flexor carpi radialis

Figure 6-45. Skeletal and muscular structure of the inner side of the arm extended and supinated (*above*), flexed and pronated (*below*). (Dr. J. Fau, *The Anatomy of the External Forms of Man* [London: Hippolyte Bailliere, 1849], plate 16. Courtesy of Countway Library, Harvard University.)

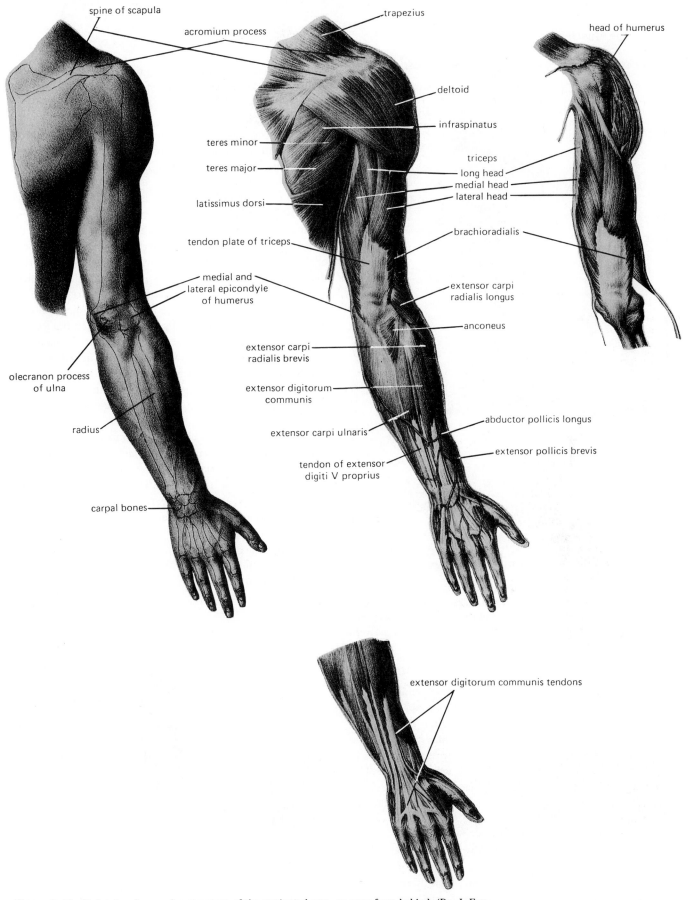

Figure 6-46. Skeletal and muscular structure of the supinated arm, as seen from behind. (Dr. J. Fau, *The Anatomy of the External Forms of Man* [London: Hippolyte Bailliere, 1849], plate 14. Courtesy of Countway Library, Harvard University.)

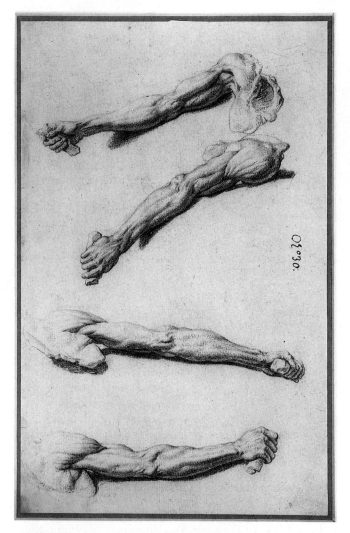

Figure 6-47. Jacob de Gheyn II (1562–1629), *Study of Arms,* c. 1600. Black chalk. 36 × 23.1 cm. Amsterdam, Rijksmuseum, Print Room. An accurate portrayal of the muscles of the arm in pronation, this series of drawings appears to be based on the flayed arm of a cadaver. Compare the ulnar crest in Figure 6-41.

elbow, with the inner being more prominent. A muscle originating on the outer (lateral) epicondyle and inserting with the radius on the side of the thumb can thus cause the distal end of the radius to turn over to the outer side of the ulna. This action in turn causes the hand to rotate to a supine position, for the wrist bones join exclusively with the radius. An extensor muscle of the same group bends back (extends) the hand.

The most superficial muscle of the extensor supinator group is the *brachioradialis,* which extends from its origin along the lower third of the humerus (on the lateral ridge) to the far end of the radius, where it inserts with the styloid process of the radius at the wrist (Figures 6-41 and 6-42). The relatively high origin of this muscle contributes a subtle and characteristic asymmetry to the forearm. The primary function of the brachioradialis is to flex the forearm. The diagonal twist of the brachioradialis, especially noticeable when the forearm is prone, indicates that this muscle can supinate the hand, but it also assists in pronation, when the arm is flexed. In other words the brachioradialis acts "... to throw the forearm and hand into the position they naturally occupy when placed across the chest; a position midway between supination and pronation."[34]

The brachioradialis is closely related to its companion supinator muscle, the *extensor carpi radialis longus,* which originates with the lateral ridge of the lower humerus and inserts with the metacarpal bone of the index finger on the radial side of the wrist. This muscle extends and abducts the wrist and with it the hand. Like the brachioradialis, it flexes the

Figure 6-48. Paul Klee, *Anatomical Drawing of the Arm Musculature,* 1902. Graphite pencil. 17.3 × 21.4 cm. Foundation Paul Klee— Museum of Fine Arts Bern.

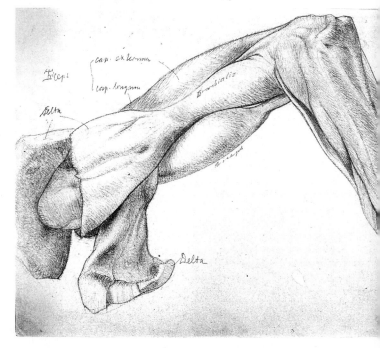

of anatomical form following function. An examination of the forearm's structure reveals two muscle groups with opposing functions: (1) the *extensor* and *supinator* muscles and (2) the *flexor* and *pronator* muscles. The ulnar crest makes a convenient landmark for studying the forearm muscles, for it marks the separation of the two groups of antagonist muscles. Seen from the side, the extensor supinator muscles appear on the top (dorsal) side above the ulnar crest; the pronator flexors lie below the ulnar crest on the inner (medial) side of the forearm (Figure 6-41, lower right).

Muscles that supinate or pronate the forearm attach either directly or indirectly to the radius, for it is the only forearm bone capable of true rotation. The mechanical leverage required for such rotation is provided by the epicondyles of the humerus, which project on both inner and outer sides of the forearm and assists with supination (when the forearm is extended) and pronation (when the forearm is flexed). Adjacent to the extensor carpi radialis longus is the *extensor carpi radialis brevis*. Although it originates with the lateral epicondyle of the humerus and appears to run somewhat diagonally across the arm, this muscle inserts with the base of the metacarpal bone of the middle finger, providing little or no mechanical leverage to rotate the hand, and consequently its chief function is to assist the extensor carpi radialis longus in extending and abducting the hand.

Situated just below the extensor carpi radialis brevis are two forearm muscles known as the *abductor pollicis longus* and the *extensor pollicis brevis*.[35] Their twisting configuration correctly indicates that they assist in supinating the forearm. Both originate with the back of the radius, though the abductor pollicis has an additional origin with the back surface of the ulna. The two muscles insert with the thumb bones, the abductor pollicis longus with the base of metacarpal bone I and the extensor pollicis brevis with phalanx I of the thumb (Figure 6-41). Both muscles abduct the thumb (that is, pull it away from the midline) and pull it up toward the back of the hand, helping with the action of supination. The extensor pollicis brevis inserts with the base of the first thumb phalanx and also extends the thumb.[36] The tendons of these muscles are indistinguishable in the metacarpal area, but there is a more visible tendon close by, which stands out when the thumb is raised. This tendon belongs to the *extensor pollicis*

Figure 6-49. Paul Klee, *Anatomical Drawing of the Upper Arm Musculature*, 1902. Graphite pencil. 17.3 × 21.4 cm. Foundation Paul Klee—Museum of Fine Arts Bern. With the deltoid removed, the origins of two heads of the triceps are displayed. Also exposed is the origin of the brachioradialis along the lower humerus.

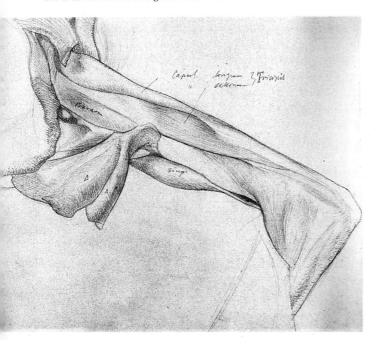

longus, which is covered by the other extensors of the wrist (Figure 6-41). Arising from its origin with the shaft of the ulna, the extensor pollicis longus inserts with the thumb's second (distal) phalanx. The chief action of this muscle is to adduct the thumb, though it, too, assists with supination.

The radiating tendons conspicuous on the back (dorsal) of the hand belong to a set of muscles called *extensor digitorum communis* (Figure 6-46). Its origin with the lateral epicondyle of the humerus is concealed by the brachioradialis and the extensor carpi radialis longus. Inserting with the phalanges of all fingers except those of the thumb, the extensor digitorum is a powerful extensor of the hand and fingers (II–V). The extension of the little finger is assisted by a separate but closely related muscle that parallels the extensor digitorum in its upper reaches, the *extensor digiti V proprius* (Figure 6-46). Differing only in its insertion, this muscle is essentially a part of the extensor digitorum, which separates above the wrist to form the distinct tendon of the little finger. Close to the extensor digitorum is the *extensor carpi ulnaris*, an extensor of the hand. It also pulls the hand toward the ulnar side of the arm. Leverage for these functions is provided by its origins with the lateral epicondyle of the humerus and the dorsal surface of the ulna. It inserts with metacarpal V of the little finger. Near the proximal end of the extensor carpi ulnaris and just below the elbow is the *anconeus*, a small muscle that slips diagonally from its origin with the lateral epicondyle of the humerus to its insertion with the dorsal surface of the ulna at the proximal end. At this point it appears as a continuation of the ulnar crest noted earlier. The anconeus assists the triceps in extending the forearm.

All of the superficial flexor pronator muscles of the forearm have prime origins with the medial epicondyle of the humerus, a knob that projects further than the lateral epicondyle on the other side of the humerus. The additional projection provides the flexor pronator muscles with the mechanical advantage that is apparent in the grasp (or flexion) of the human hand. The weaker action of extension is thought to be a consequence of the relatively poor leverage of the shorter lateral condyle.[37] The flexor pronator muscles are situated largely on the medial side of the forearm below the ulnar crest; when the hand lies in the prone position, they form the underbelly of the forearm (Figure 6-41, lower right).

The muscle immediately below the ulnar crest in the pronated forearm is the *flexor carpi ulnaris*, the lateral border of which runs along the ulnar crest just opposite the extensor carpi ulnaris. The muscle arises from two heads, one attaching with the medial condyle of the humerus and the other with the inner margin of the olecranon. By means of tendinous fascia the flexor carpi ulnaris also has an origin with the upper portion of the posterior border of the ulna. The lower half of the muscle consists of a tendon that inserts with the pisiform bone of the wrist (Figure 6-41), enabling the muscle to flex the wrist.[38] The action of the flexor carpi ulnaris is apparent when the little finger presses downward against a surface

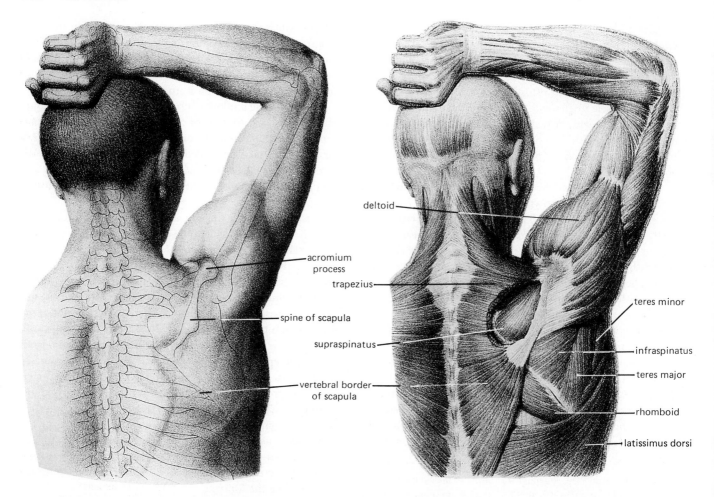

Figure 6-50. Skeletal and muscular structure of the shoulder and arm (flexed and pronated) as seen from behind. (Dr. J. Fau, *The Anatomy of the External Forms of Man* [London: Hippolyte Bailliere, 1849], plate 17. Courtesy of Countway Library, Harvard University.)

while the hand is prone. The resulting tensed muscle raises the tendon on the side of the wrist beneath the ulna.

When the hand is flexed against resistance, another tendon may be visible near the center of the wrist on the palm side. This belongs to a long muscle called the *palmaris*, which inserts with the aponeurosis of the palm (thus its name). Like other pronating and flexing muscles, the palmaris originates with the medial epicondyle of the humerus.[39]

Beside the palmaris is another pronator flexor muscle with the same origin, the *flexor carpi radialis* (Figure 6-42). It runs the entire length of the forearm and forms a groove with the brachioradialis. The long tendon of this muscle disappears from view at the wrist beneath the annular ligament to reach its insertion with the base of metacarpals II and III. The muscle's name derives from its function as a flexor of the radial side of the wrist; it is clearly visible at this point when tensed.

Situated between the flexor carpi radialis and the brachioradialis is the *pronator teres*, a muscle that runs diagonally from its origins at the medial epicondyle and the coronoid process of the ulna to its insertion as a flat tendon with the middle of

the outer surface of the radius. By means of these attachments the pronator teres is able to rotate the radius over the ulna, causing pronation, and when the radius is fixed, assist in flexing the forearm.

Two other muscles of the inner forearm that function primarily as flexors of the wrist are the *flexor digitorum* (*sublimis*) and the *flexor pollicis longus*. Both muscles contribute to shaping the contour of the inner side of the forearm, a contour that is smooth and regular in comparison with that of the dorsal side (Figure 6-43). The flexor digitorum originates with the medial epicondyle of the humerus, the ulnar tuberosity, and the anterior surface of the radius (Figure 6-42). In its lower reaches it splits into four separate bands of muscle, which join with tendons. These tendons, tightly gathered at the wrist, pass under the carpal bones to their insertions in the middle phalanges of the fingers (but not the thumb). Despite the breadth of the flexor digitorum it is more important for its effect on the total shape of the inner forearm than for its superficial aspect, for it is mostly covered by other muscles. The flexor pollicis longus, which assists in flexing the hand *hypothenar* muscles on the ulnar side of the palm (Figure 6-42). These two groups, which consist of seven smaller muscles, form the padlike bodies on the outer and inner sides of the palm. Both groups have origins in the carpal ligament (the front portion of the annual ligament that encircles the wrist). The thenar group inserts with the thumb at metacarpal I and at the first phalanx; the hypothenar group, with the little finger at the base of its first phalanx and the metacarpal V. With these attachments the thenar and hypothenar muscle groups are well situated to flex the thumb and the little finger, respectively, a function that produces some of the superficial folds of the palm (Figure 6-43).

THE LOWER LIMB MUSCLES

The lower limb generally presents a stronger but less mobile structure of bone and muscle than that observed in the arm. Despite similarities of skeletal structure in the two limbs there are significant differences, particularly in the joints of the

Figure 6-52. Michelangelo, *Study of Arms*, c. 1527. Natural red chalk with touches of black. 13 × 10⅛″. Oxford, Ashmolean Museum. Believed to be drawn from life, these studies were probably preparations for the allegorical sculpture of *Victory* in the Palazzo Vecchio, Florence. The arm is shown flexed and supinated. The projecting forms at the elbow and wrist provide a skeletal basis for the modeled contours of the muscles. The solid rendering of the elbows reveals the olecranon process of the ulna and the epicondyles of the humerus.

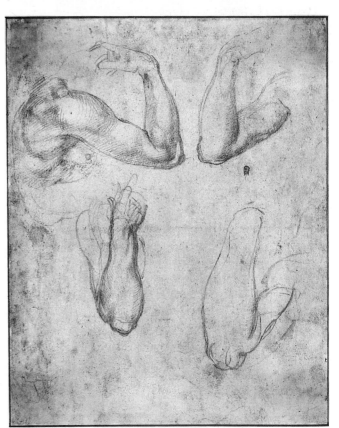

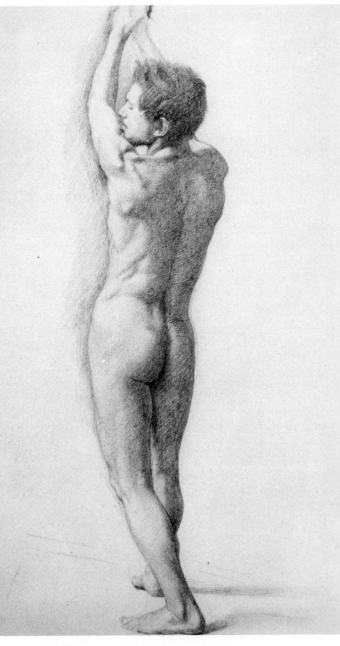

Figure 6-51. Edgar Degas, *Study of the Nude, Backview*, c. 1856–1858. Graphite pencil. 30 × 19.5 cm. Private collection. The structural richness of this drawing can be gauged by comparing it with Figures 6-27, 6-50, and 6-62.

and raising the thumb, is largely covered by other muscles but contributes indirectly to the form of the muscles that lie over it (Figure 6-42).

The individual muscles situated in the hand are of doubtful importance for drawing purposes. Many are either very small or covered by tendons, as is the case with the back of the hand. Two muscle groups of the palm, however, do merit the artist's attention: the *thenar* muscles of the thumb and the bones, which account for the visible distinctiveness of the limbs. The sturdy hip joint of the femur and the pelvis does not permit the degree of free-ranging movement observed in the shoulder joint with the humerus and the scapula. The leg's fibula also lacks the cusp-type joint that enables its counterpart in the arm, the radius, to rotate around the ulna. The consequences of these skeletal differences will become clearer as you examine the nature and functions of lower limb musculature.[40]

Figure 6-53. Skeletal and muscular structure of the shoulder and arm (flexed and pronated) front view. Compare with Figure 6-50. (Dr. J. Fao, *The Anatomy of the External Forms of Man* [London: Hippolyte Bailliere, 1849], plate 17. Courtesy of Countway Library, Harvard University.)

STUDY 46:   The Muscles of the Lower Limb

materials: ❑ 11 × 14″ sketchbook
❑ drawing pen (0.5 mm point)
❑ India ink
❑ HB pencil
❑ sanguine pencil
❑ 11 × 14″ tracing paper
❑ transparent tape

reference: ❑ model and Figures 6-54, 6-55, 6-56, 6-57, 6-58, 6-59, 6-60, 6-61, and 6-62

time: ❑ 15–20 minutes for each overlay study of the skeletal leg
❑ 30 minutes for each overlay of the muscles

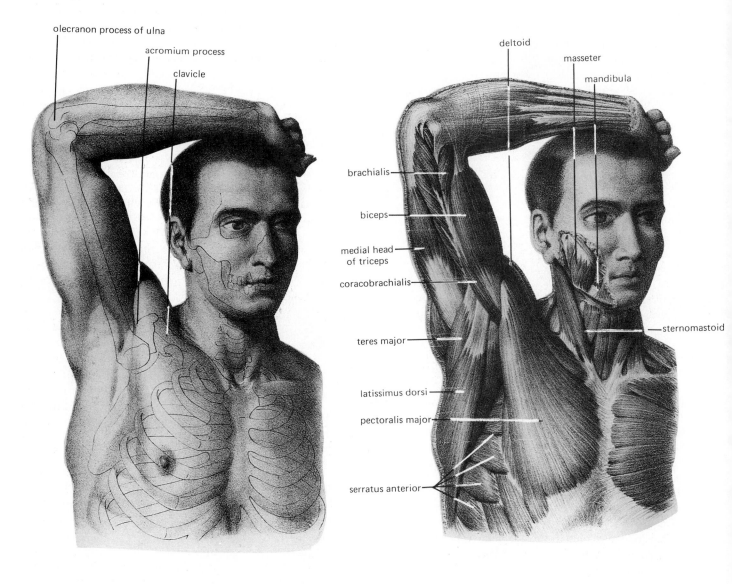

In order to gain a clear idea of the muscle structure of the lower limb, first prepare a series of life studies that provide several different views of the lower limb. Although these need not be highly developed drawings, they should include views of the front, the back, and the side. In drawing from life try to observe and draw any superficial landmarks that reveal skeletal structure on the lower portion of the body (Figure 6-12). For example, the points of the pelvis (the anterior-superior iliac spines), if drawn, can be used later as references not only in the skeletal study but also in the muscle study, for they are sites of important muscle attachments in the lower limbs. The same is true for the prominences of the great trochanters on the sides of the hips. Further down the limb are other skeletal landmarks, among them the kneecap (*patella*), the head of the fibula, the heel bone (*calcaneus*), and the ankles (*lateral* and *medial malleoli*). From your previous studies of the skeleton you will recall these and other bony landmarks and, more important, the skeletal structure they imply.

From this series of drawings select three that best illustrate different views of the lower limb. Tape two sheets of tracing paper over each of the selected drawings: one for a skeletal analysis of the lower limb in the life study; another for a study of the muscles of the same. The tracing paper overlay serves as the surface for a pencil rendering of the bones of the lower limb as they would appear in the original life study. In addition to drawing the bones of the lower limb proper it is important to render the pelvis and a general suggestion of the bones of the foot. Pay special attention to the bony formation of the joints, where the raised surfaces of epicondyles and tuberosities form important sites of muscle attachments. After completing the overlay drawings of the skeletal lower limb you are ready to begin studies of the muscles on a second tracing paper overlay. For this purpose the anatomical illustrations of the lower limb in this chapter are especially useful, as they show the skeletal and muscle structure in the context of an external view of the body. To clarify your understanding of the muscles represented in the illustrations it is helpful to consider their attachments and functions.

MUSCLES OF THE LOWER LIMB: GROUPS AND FUNCTIONS

The Thigh

The study of the lower limb muscles is simplified by a natural division into distinct groups with special functions. Viewed directly from the front, the thigh displays two basic muscle groups: the *extensors*, located on the front (anterior) side; and the *adductors*, on the inner (medial) side (Figure 6-54).

The four extensor muscles of the thigh share a common insertion with the kneecap (patella) and can be visualized as one muscle with four heads (*quadriceps*). Together they pull the kneecaps upward. The force of this movement is transmitted by the patellar ligament to the front of the tibia, resulting in a forward swing of the leg, used, for example, in kicking.

Foremost in the extensor group is the *rectus femoris*, an elongated muscle rising from a band of tendon that attaches to the patella and indirectly with the tuberosity of the tibia (Figure 6-54). It finds origin on the pelvis near the acetabulum at the anterior-inferior iliac spine, a site shared with the iliofemoral ligament. The pelvic attachment, unique in this extensor group, endows the rectus femoris with the special function of flexing and abducting the thigh (i.e., raising and drawing the femur outward) as well as that of extending the leg. The rounded bulk of the muscle is largely superficial and contributes directly to the profile contour of the front of the thigh.

The rectus femoris lies over the three adjoining vastus muscles, two of which are visible on each side of the former: the *vastus medialis* on the inner side of the thigh and the *vastus lateralis* on the outer. They and their companion muscle, the *vastus intermedius*, which lies hidden beneath the rectus femoris, originate with the femur. Seen as a group, the vastus muscles and the rectus femoris have a characteristic teardrop form (Figure 6-54, center).

Between the extensor group and the adductor group is a muscle that belongs to neither category, the *sartorius*. This straplike muscle, clearly seen in a drawing by Michaelangelo (Figure 6-55), is the longest muscle of the body.[41] Originating with the anterior-superior iliac spine of the pelvis, it reaches down around the inner side of the thigh before inserting on the upper medial surface of the tibia. This curious arrangement enables the sartorius to rotate the thigh as well as to flex and abduct it, thus assisting in crossing the legs.[42]

Beyond the sartorius on the inner side of the leg next to the crotch is a group of muscles responsible for the adduction of the thigh (that is, pulling the thigh inward toward the midline of the body). As a group the adductors of the thigh extend from the inner side of the femur to parts of the pelvis near the midline of the body (i.e., the pubic ramus and the tuberosity of the ischium).[43] Individual muscles of this group are seldom apparent in life, but together they make a continuous rounded form on the inner side of the thigh above the sartorius (Figure 6-54). The innermost of the adductor group is the *gracilis*, a muscle that descends from its origin with the lower surfaces of the pubis and the ischium to its insertion with the tibia immediately behind the tendon of the sartorius. Other muscles of the groups are the *adductor magnus*, the *adductor longus*, and the *pectineus*. These muscles fan out from origins with the front of the pelvis on either side of the symphysis pubis in the direction of their respective insertions with the femur.[44]

Certain muscles of the thigh are more fully displayed when the lower limb is viewed in profile from the outer side (Fig-

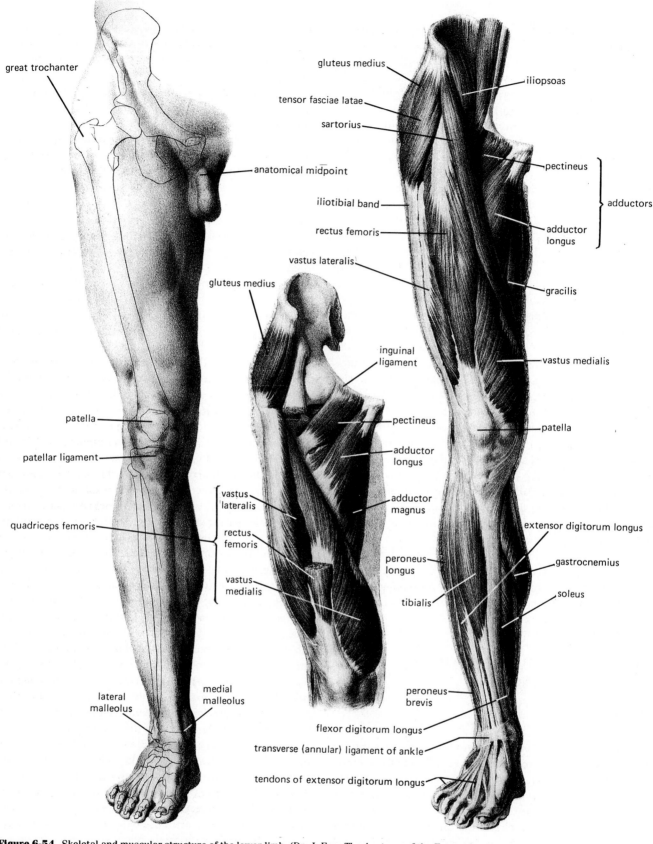

Figure 6-54. Skeletal and muscular structure of the lower limb. (Dr. J. Fao, *The Anatomy of the External Forms of Man* [London: Hippolyte Bailliere, 1849], plate 18. Courtesy of Countway Library, Harvard University.) The rectus femoris, sartorius, and gracilis muscles are excised in the central illustration in order to expose the deeper muscle forms, such as the vastus and the adductor muscles. The rendering of the femur (*left*) reveals the characteristically off-center diagonal thrust, which is reflected in the muscle structure of this region. Compare with Figure 6-55.

The wide band conveys the force of both muscles to the lateral condyle of the tibia. A visual side effect of the tension of the iliotibial band is the compressing or flattening of the muscles on the side of the thigh, in particular the vastus lateralis (Figure 6-57). Contraction of the tensor fasciae latae alone can assist in flexing the thigh as well as in abducting and rotating it inward.

Situated on the other side of the band, the gluteus maximus works in opposition to the tensor fasciae latae by extending the thigh backward, adducting it, and rotating it outward. The gluteus maximus inserts not only with the iliotibial band but also with the femur, where it has extensive attachments on the posterior surface below the great trochanter. Through these attachments the muscle acts as a powerful extender of the thigh. When we rise from a sitting position, the gluteus maximus helps straighten the thigh, enabling the body to assume an erect posture. Like the sacrospinalis, the gluteus maximus "plays an important part in the act of walking, as it supports the trunk on the limb which is in contact with the ground during the same time that the opposite foot is uplifted."[46]

In drawing the gluteus maximus on the overlay you may notice its lower border does not correspond closely with the crease below the buttock observed in life (Figure 6-62). The crease, or *gluteal furrow*, tends to be more horizontal in the standing figure, while the border of the muscle is on a diagonal with the thigh. This is due to the accumulation of fat that generally pads the lower medial border of the muscle and to the gluteal band of fascia supporting the fat. The space between the gluteus maximus and the tensor fasciae latae exposes part of another muscle of the buttock: the *gluteus medius*.

The gluteus medius lies over most of the back of the hipbone. From its tendinous insertion with the great trochanter the gluteus medius spreads in a radiating pattern to its origins along the back of the ilium of the pelvis, extending from a position near the posterior-superior iliac spine in the back to the anterior-superior iliac spine in the front (Figure 6-56).[47] The pelvic origins of the gluteus medius define the iliac crest, an important formal division of the figure visible in life (Figure 6-51). Because of its insertion with the outer side of the great trochanter the gluteus medius is an abductor of the thigh, capable of drawing the legs apart. While the muscle is in use or tensed, it is visible in the body. In a study by Michelangelo the tensed gluteus medius appears as an elevation above the region of the gluteus maximus (Figure 6-59).

The posterior profile contour of the thigh is formed by the *biceps femoris*, one of a group of three flexors of the leg (Figure 6-56). From a single insertion with the head of the fibula on the outer side of the leg the muscle rises up the back of the thigh. The tendon of insertion is easily detected near the knee when the biceps femoris is tensed. Like the biceps of the arm, the biceps femoris has two heads, each with a different origin. The long head of the biceps femoris, superficial for most of its length, disappears from view under the

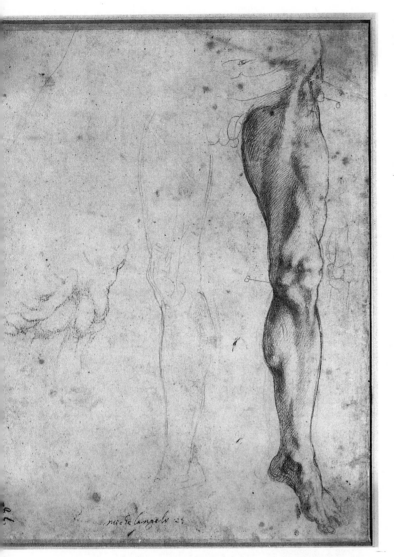

Figure 6-55. Michelangelo, *Studies of a Man's Leg*, 1515–1520. Natural red chalk. 28.3 × 21.2 cm. Oxford, Christ Church. The pelvic attachments of the sartorius and the tensor fasciae latae muscles are especially clear in this study. Compare Figure 8-8. In the modeled study of muscles of the thigh and leg the artist took care to point out clues to underlying skeletal structure with pinlike symbols. One symbol marks the knee joint, specifically the medial epicondyles of the femur and the tibia (elaborated in a line study to the right); another symbol points to superficial bumps (protuberances) of the great trochanter.

ures 6-56 and 6-58). Among these is the *tensor fasciae latae*, a short thick muscle that branches upward diagonally from the top of a wide strap of fascia called the *iliotibial band*.[45] Rising diagonally from the back portion of the band is the *gluteus maximus*, the hip muscle that originates with the lower side of the sacral triangle—the border of the sacrum and coccyx and the lateral surface of the ilium (Figure 6-62). The fascial strap spans most of the side of the thigh down to its insertion with the tibia on the outer tuberosity near the knee joint.

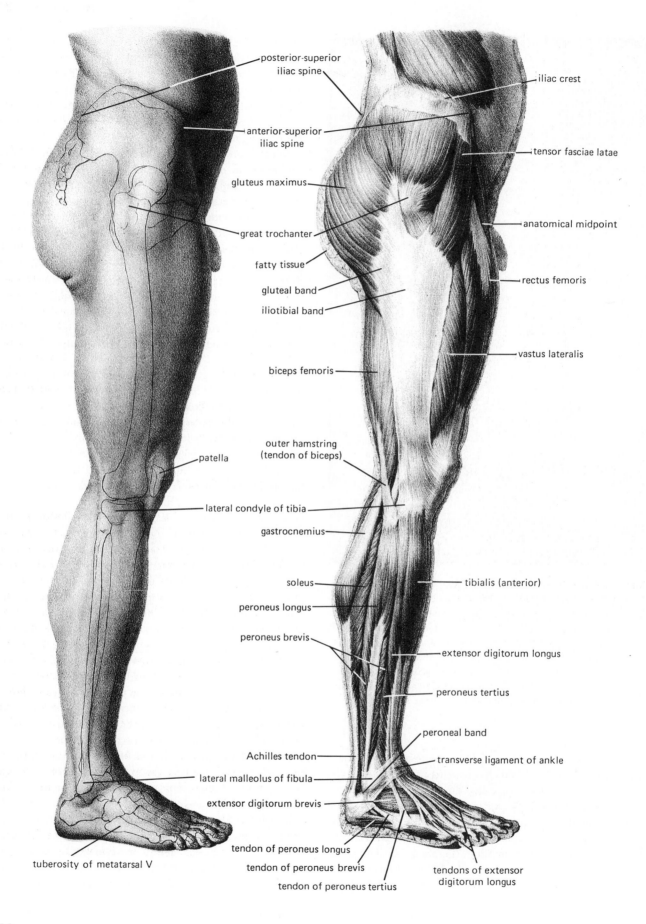

posterior-superior
iliac spine

iliac crest

anterior-superior
iliac spine

tensor fasciae latae

gluteus maximus

anatomical midpoint

great trochanter

rectus femoris

fatty tissue

gluteal band

iliotibial band

vastus lateralis

biceps femoris

outer hamstring
(tendon of biceps)

patella

lateral condyle of tibia

gastrocnemius

soleus

tibialis (anterior)

peroneus longus

peroneus brevis

extensor digitorum longus

peroneus tertius

peroneal band

Achilles tendon

transverse ligament of ankle

lateral malleolus of fibula

extensor digitorum brevis

tuberosity of metatarsal V

tendon of peroneus longus

tendon of peroneus brevis

tendons of extensor
digitorum longus

tendon of peroneus tertius

232

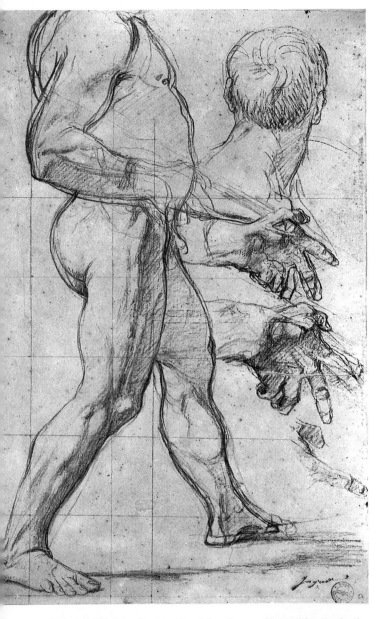

Figure 6-57. Jean-Auguste-Dominique Ingres, *Sheet of Studies for the Painting* The Martyrdom of Saint Symphorien, c. 1830. Graphite pencil. 40.5 × 26.8 cm. Bayonne, Musée Bonnat. Muscles of the lower limb appear "set" in tension in this vigorous life study. Compare with Figure 6-56.

Figure 6-56. Side view of the skeletal and muscular structure of the lower limb. (Dr. J. Fao, *The Anatomy of the External Forms of Man* [London: Hippolyte Bailliere, 1849], plate 21. Courtesy of Countway Library, Harvard University.) The characteristic tapering of the leg is due to the preponderance of muscle bodies in the calf region and the less bulky tendons of these bodies in the lower region. Compare with tapering of the forearm (Figure 6-42).

lower border of the gluteus maximus, beneath which it joins the pelvis at the ischial tuberosity below the acetabulum. The short head, visible only in the lower part of the thigh, tucks under the vastus lateralis before reaching its origin with the back of the femur along a ridge called the *linea aspera*, or rough line (Figure 6-62). The short head is the smaller muscle of the biceps. With its double origin, the biceps femoris is capable of assisting in a variety of actions: flexion of the leg, adduction of the thigh, extension of the thigh backward, and, by virtue of its insertion on the outer side of the tibia, rotation of the leg outward.

The columnar verticality of the flexor muscle group to which the biceps femoris belongs contrasts with the convex muscle formation of the front of the thigh. The flexor group appears as a pair of muscles that runs along the length of the posterior thigh but separates above the knee into tendons that reach opposite sides of the leg, where they insert with the tibia and the fibula. The inner flexor is the *semitendinosus* (so called because its lower half consists of tendon), which inserts with the tibia at the medial inner condyle. The semitendinosus lies directly over another flexor of the leg, the *semimembranosus*. Narrow portions of the latter, however, are visible on either side of the overlapping semitendinosus (Figure 6-62). The tendon of the semimembranosus reaches downward to its insertion with the inner tuberosity of the tibia, next to the insertions of the sartorius and the gracilis.

Muscles of the Leg and Foot

The insertion tendons of the flexors are called *hamstrings* after the *ham*, the hollow space behind the knee between the tendons.[48] The ham becomes evident when the knee is bent. When the knee is straightened, however, the hollow disappears, replaced by a bump or swelling caused by fatty tissues behind the knee. There a horizontal band of fascia[49] wraps around the back of the knee, somewhat like a natural garter strengthening the knee joint. The fascial band corresponds roughly to the crease that crosses the ham, usually visible on the back of the knee. (The slight bump above the fascia is caused by the inner portion of the semimembranosus.) Note that the flexor group flexes the leg, not the thigh. The flexor muscles can affect flexion at the hip joint: A person with tight hamstrings may not be able to touch the toes without bending the knees.[50] The flexor muscles, however, do assist the gluteus maximus in extending the thigh backward. Extension of the thigh is an indirect action on the part of the muscles,[51] which, except for the short head of the biceps femoris, are not attached to the femur.

Unlike the flexor muscles in the thigh, the flexors in the leg dominate the form of this part of the limb and contrast markedly with the leg's bony anterior surface. The most

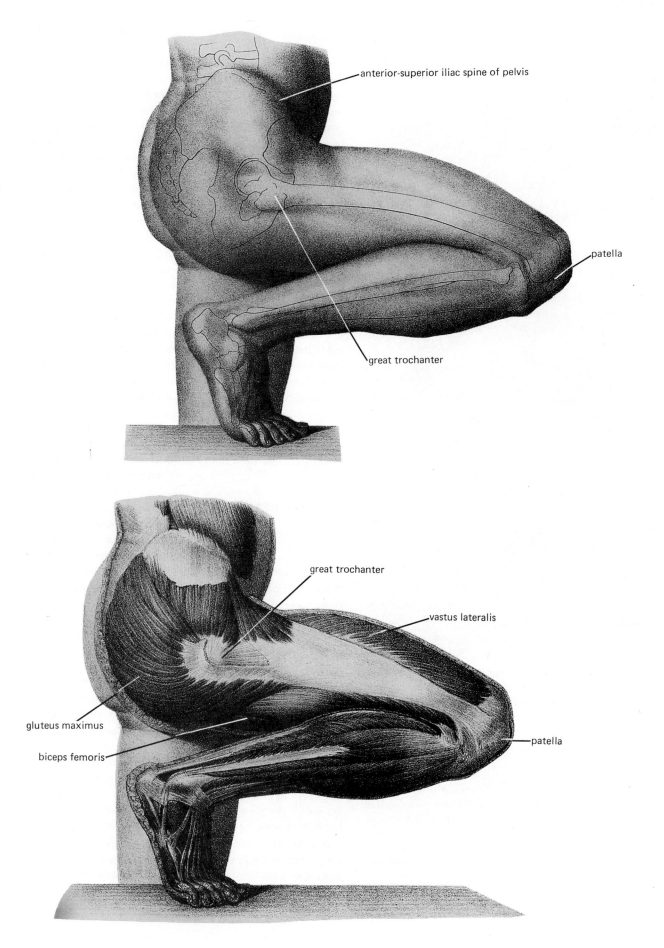

anterior-superior iliac spine of pelvis

patella

great trochanter

great trochanter

vastus lateralis

gluteus maximus

biceps femoris

patella

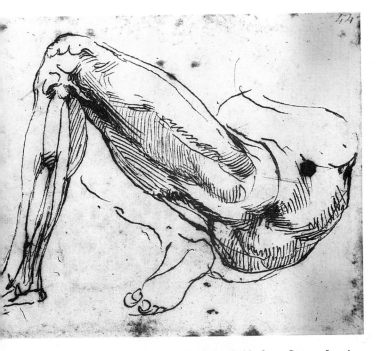

Figure 6-59. Michelangelo, *Study* (probably for a figure of a river god), c. 1525–1530. Pen and ink. 5⅝ × 3⅜″. Florence, Casa Buonarroti.

prominent and superficial of the leg flexors is the *gastrocnemius*, or calf muscle.[52] The two bodies of this muscle give rise to two heads, which disappear under the hamstrings to their origins above the lateral and medial condyles of the femur (Figure 6-62). The lower edges of the two muscle bodies form the straplike *Achilles tendon*, which inserts with the calcaneus (heel bone). Considered the strongest tendon in the body,[53] the Achilles tendon is shared with another flexor, the *soleus*, a flat muscle that lies under the gastrocnemius and originates with the upper third of the tibia and the fibula. Some texts consider the soleus and the gastrocnemius to be merely different heads of a single muscle.[54] Visually, however, they seem quite separate. Seen from the lateral side in a study by Michelangelo (Figure 6-59), the gastrocnemius appears as a distinct profile contour over the soleus. Viewed from the back (Figure 6-62), the bodies of the gastrocnemius exhibit a characteristic asymmetry, with the prominence of the medial head slightly lower than that of the lateral head. Contraction of the gastrocnemius and the soleus can result in a simple lever action in which the calcaneus pivots on the fulcrum of the ankle, causing the front of the foot to flex downward (*plantarward*) in an attitude familiar in classical ballet. Because the

←

Figure 6-58. Skeletal and muscular structure of the flexed leg and thigh. (Dr. J. Fao, *The Anatomy of the External Forms of Man* [London: Hippolyte Bailliere, 1849], plate 22. Courtesy of Countway Library, Harvard University.) Compare with Figure 6-59.

gastrocnemius originates with the femur, it is also able to flex the leg, an indirect action.

In order to complete a survey of the major leg muscles, consider the view from the front of the lower limb (Figure 6-54). The tibia is an invaluable reference for structuring a drawing of these muscles. The front medial facet of the bone shaft is bare of muscles, and the bone lies just beneath the skin. The lateral facet of the tibia, however, is covered with a muscle appropriately named the *tibialis*. The head of this muscle originates at the upper tibia, the lateral condyle of the tibia, and with the fascial membrane between the tibia and the fibula. The long tendon of the tibialis is visible midway down the leg, extending downward and inward to the inner side of the foot, where it curves under to insert with the inferior surfaces of the foot bones (specifically, cuneiform I and the base of the metatarsal I of the big toe). The attachments enable the tibialis to flex the foot. If you raise (flex) the front of your foot upward, for example, you can easily locate it by touching the front-most part of your leg. With its insertion on the inner side of the foot, the tibialis also inverts the foot, acting as an antagonist to a set of muscles with tendons that reach around the opposite (outer) side of the foot: the peroneus muscles.

The two main peroneus muscles—longus and brevis— appear on the outer (lateral) side of the calf next to the soleus (Figure 6-56). When the leg is extended (straight), the tendinous origin of the *peroneus longus* with the head of the fibula appears to be a linear continuation of the hamstring tendon of the biceps above it. The peroneus longus has a second origin with the upper lateral surface of the fibula. The lower lateral surface of the fibula serves as the origin of the *peroneus brevis*, a smaller muscle that is almost completely covered by the peroneus longus. The insertion tendons for both peroneus muscles are strung around the back of the lateral malleolus (the outer ankle) and strapped in place by a band of fascia (the *peroneal band*), one of several annular (ring-shaped) ligaments in this region (Figure 6-56). Beyond the outer malleolus, however, the tendons turn forward, forming an angle with each other before reaching their separate insertions with the underside of the foot. This arrangement enables the peroneus muscles to assist the gastrocnemius in flexing the foot (downward). The peroneus longus slips under the foot to reach its insertions with bone surfaces on the sole (*plantar*) of the foot, specifically with the internal cuneiform and the base of the metatarsal bone of the big toe. The peroneus brevis joins with a tuberosity of metatarsal V (of the little toe). These insertions enable the peroneus muscles to lift (evert) the outer side of the foot.[55] If you raise the outer side of your foot, you can see the peroneus muscles are tense and raised on the lateral side of the leg and the tendons are visible below the outer ankle. This tension opposes that produced by the tibialis, the antagonist of the peroneus. When both the tibialis and the peroneus muscle are tensed, their antagonism helps to support the foot's arch as well as to fix the position of the leg upon the foot, especially when the body rests on only one foot.[56]

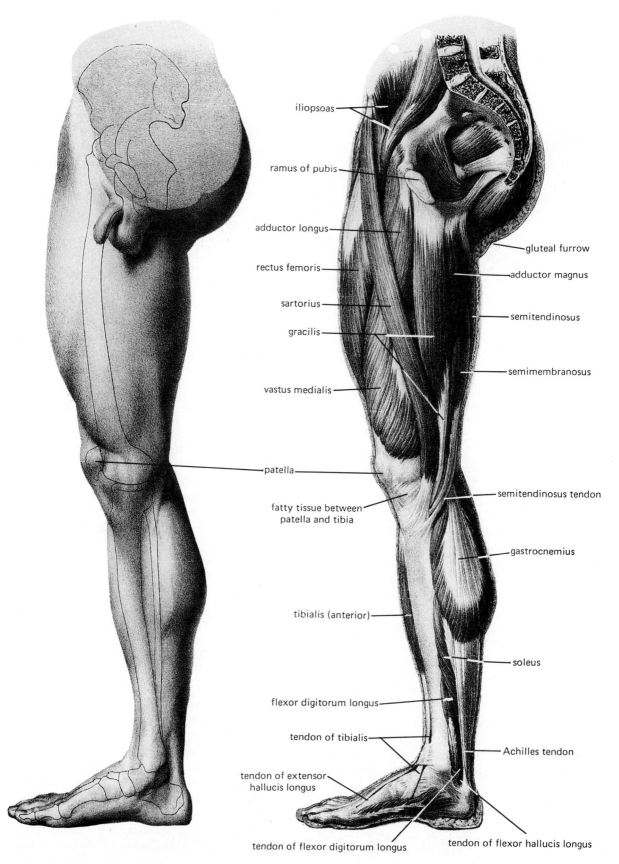

iliopsoas

ramus of pubis

adductor longus

rectus femoris

sartorius

gracilis

vastus medialis

patella

fatty tissue between
patella and tibia

tibialis (anterior)

flexor digitorum longus

tendon of tibialis

tendon of extensor
hallucis longus

tendon of flexor digitorum longus

gluteal furrow

adductor magnus

semitendinosus

semimembranosus

semitendinosus tendon

gastrocnemius

soleus

Achilles tendon

tendon of flexor hallucis longus

Figure 6-60. Muscular and skeletal structure of the lower limb, medial profile. (Dr. J. Fao, *The Anatomy of the External Forms of Man* [London: Hippolyte Bailliere, 1849], plate 20. Courtesy of Countway Library, Harvard University.)

236

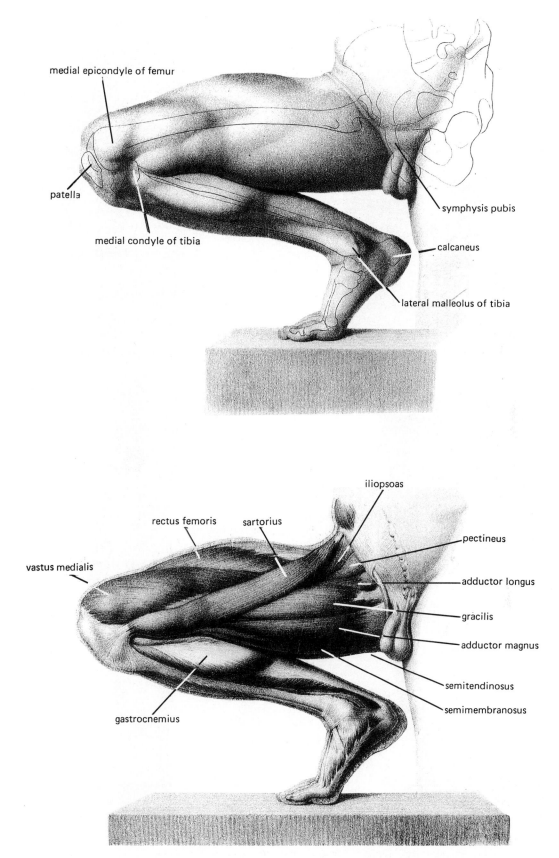

Figure 6-61. Medial view of the flexed lower limb. Compare with Figure 6-58. (Dr. J. Fao, *The Anatomy of the External Forms of Man* [London: Hippolyte Bailliere, 1849], plate 19. Courtesy of Countway Library, Harvard University.)

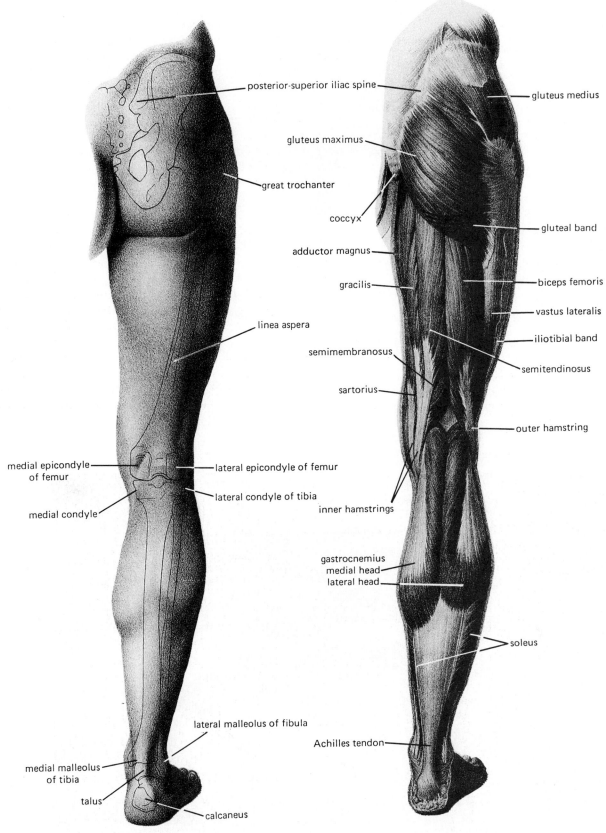

Figure 6-62. Skeletal and muscular structure of the lower limb, seen from behind. (Dr. J. Fao, *The Anatomy of the External Forms of Man* [London: Hippolyte Bailliere, 1849], plate 19. Courtesy of Countway Library, Harvard University.)

The band of muscle wedged between the peroneus and the tibialis is the *extensor digitorum longus*. Superficial for most of its length, the *extensor digitorum longus* originates with the lateral condyle of the tibia, the head of the fibula, and the ligament between the bones, or *interosseous membrane* (Figures 6-54 and 6-56).[57] Approximately midway between the knee and the ankle the extensor digitorus longus forms a tendon that passes under the transverse (annular) ligament in front of the ankle. There it divides into the individual toe tendons, except for the big toe (Figure 6-56). These fan out and reach their insertions with toes on the upper (dorsal) sides of the phalanges.[58] This radiating pattern, not unlike that on the back of the hand, becomes clear when the toes and foot are extended (raised upward). Extension of the toes and foot reveals an additional tendon, that of the *extensor hallucis longus*, the extensor muscle of the big toe (Figures 6-54 and 6-60).[59] Originating with the medial surface of the fibula and with the interosseous membrane between the fibula and the tibia, the extensor hallucis longus is covered by the extensors of the toes and by the tibialis muscle. It is superficial, however, as a tendon above and below the transverse ligament of the ankle, where it lies between tendons of the extensor digitorum longus and the tibialis. From the front of the ankle the hallucis longus tendon extends to the top (dorsal) surface of the big toe, reaching its insertion with the last phalanx of that ex-

tremity. Both the extensor digitorum longus and the extensor hallucis extend (straighten and raise) the toes and, when this action is continued, flex the foot upon the leg.[60] In addition their position on the lateral (outer) side of the leg permits them to abduct and evert the foot.

In opposition to the extensors of the toes is the *flexor digitorum longus*, a muscle that is superficial in the lower third of the leg on the medial side (Figures 6-54 and 6-60). Originating along the back surface of the tibia, the flexor digitorum longus is largely concealed by the soleus and gastrocnemius muscles, though it is partially superficial in the lower third of the leg above and behind the inner malleolus, where it fills some of the space between the Achilles tendon and the shaft of the tibia. Its tendon bends around the inner side of the calcaneus along a special groove before turning forward to pass under the sole of the foot, where it divides into four tendons that insert with the bases of the last phalanges of the four smaller toes.[61] The medial location of the flexor digitorum longus also enables this muscle to invert and adduct the foot. As is the case with the extensors of the toes, the big toe has a separate flexor muscle, the *flexor hallucis longus*, which arises from the back of the tibia and has a tendon that follows those of the other toe flexors in the groove of the calcaneus. The insertion of this tendon with the underside of the final phalanx of the big toe assists in flexing the foot (downward).

Figure 6-63. The articulated skeleton can be set in lifelike poses as a basis for figure drawing.

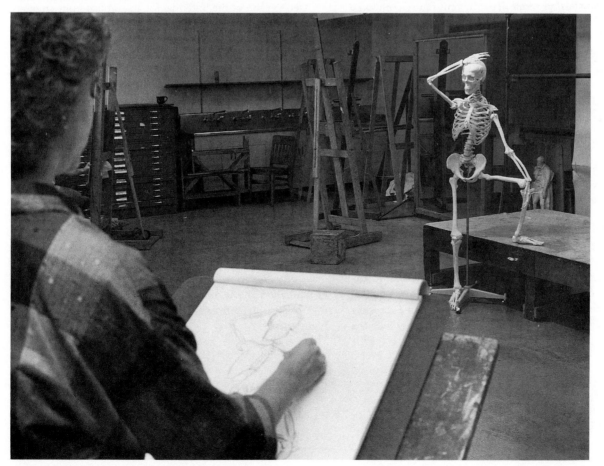

In addition to studies focusing on specific parts of anatomy it can be refreshing to test your knowledge of the muscle structure and its relation to the human form as a whole.

STUDY 47:   Drawing the Figure from the Skeleton

materials: ❑ 36 × 24″ newsprint drawing pad
  ❑ easel or straight-back chair
  ❑ Masonite or plywood panel and clamps
  ❑ sanguine and black or brown drawing crayons
reference: ❑ mounted skeleton or anatomical illustrations
time: ❑ 35 minutes

Drawing the figure based on the skeleton is another way of enhancing your understanding of the way the muscles and skeleton determine the human form. The procedure is simple: First arrange the mounted skeleton in a lifelike pose (Figure 6-63). Since the objective is to draw the figure, draw the skeleton with the figure in mind, paying special attention to those skeletal features that most affect the exterior form. Allow twenty minutes to draw it. The drawing of the skeleton, when complete, will serve as the foundation for an imaginary figure drawn over the skeleton study or beside it (Figure 6-64).

As a way of initiating the figure drawing, try drawing oval constructs over the larger skeletal features, such as the rib cage, before developing the muscle structure. This approach, described in Study 7, will result in a coherent figure composed of convex units that can be expanded or contracted according to the general build of the figure you wish to draw. After you have tested your knowledge of the muscle structure by drawing the figure from memory, refer to the anatomy plates in this section to modify or further develop the figure. If in the process you discover problem areas in the figure, these can be the subject of future anatomical studies.

SUMMARY

Upon learning about the anatomical complexities of the leg and the foot a character in a novel once became temporarily lame.[62] There is little reason to fear that a study of anatomy, properly undertaken, may similarly cripple the artist, but a sense of mental reservation is inescapable, for, as Eakins once pointed out, anatomy *as such* is of no importance to the artist.[63] Moreover, anatomical study has seldom directly influenced the direction of art, though it served as an expressive resource for artists in the Renaissance, a period in which the

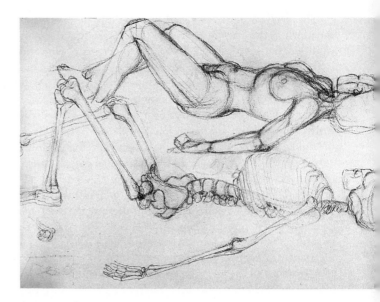

Figure 6-64. Student drawing. *Study of the Skeleton and an Imaginary Figure Based on the Skeleton.* Conté crayon on newsprint. 18 × 24″.

interests of art and science were especially close.[64] Yet, in the modern period anatomical study has been advocated by major artists of various persuasions. Paul Klee saw the study of anatomy as a means of liberation. At the age of twenty-three he wrote, "I plan . . . to learn anatomy (like a medical doctor); [and] when I know it I will be able to do everything."[65]

Klee's vision of the potential for anatomical study suggests anatomy can be studied in a way that focuses on aspects more related to problems of contemporary art by stressing structural dynamics. The body's thrusts and tensions are similar if not directly related to those found in some abstract sculpture. An affinity to body construction is apparent, for example, in the work of the contemporary American artist Kenneth Snelson, whose sculpture, like the human body, depends on tension and thrust for support (Figure 6-65).

Despite the occasional application of anatomical principles to nonfigurative art, the most direct application of anatomical study is in the figurative arts, in which the human form continues to be explored as a theme, as it has been throughout most of the history of art. The drawn figure is a poignant reminder that art is above all a human activity destined to be appreciated by fellow humans. As the British scientist Sir Julian Huxley once remarked, ". . . man alone can draw, or make unto himself a likeness. This then is the great distinction of humanity, and it follows that the most preeminently human of creatures are those who possess this distinction in the highest level."[66]

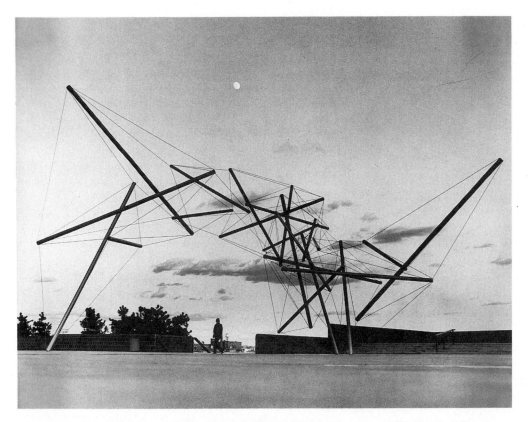

Figure 6-65. Kenneth Snelson (b. 1927), *Free Ride Home*, 1974 (photo courtesy of *The New York Times*). Though completely abstract in concept, this work depends on thrusts and tensions analogous to those of the skeletomuscular system for support. Without such tension, provided here by cables, the sculpture would collapse.

NOTES

1. The importance of this special ability is illustrated by the human heart, an organ composed largely of muscles that contract in regular beats.

2. Stephen Rogers Peck, *Atlas of Human Anatomy for the Artist* (New York: Oxford University Press, 1973), p. 89.

3. *Webster's Unabridged Dictionary* (Springfield, Mass.: Merriam, 1951).

4. In his book *Living Anatomy* (London: Faber and Faber, 1963), p. 7, R. D. Lockhart suggests that the word *relaxation* be replaced by *decontraction*, as the latter more accurately describes how muscles "relax": "When the arm is being gradually lowered," he states, "the deltoid (shoulder muscle) can still be felt firm—it is still working hard in controlling the gravitational descent of the arm, but getting longer as it pays out, like a crane lowering a weight."

5. In a relaxed standing position, however, the body requires little muscular activity, as "Ligaments may take the strain before muscles are necessary" in the hip and knee joints (R. D. Lockhart et al., *Anatomy of the Human Body* [Philadelphia: J. B. Lippincott, 1974], p. 146).

6. *Ecorché* means "skinned" in French.

7. Leonardo da Vinci, *The Treatise on Painting*, vol. 1, trans. A. Philip McMahon (Princeton, N.J.: Princeton University Press, 1956), p. 125.

8. Arthur Thomson, *A Handbook of Anatomy for Art Students* (New York: Dover, 1964), p. 171.

9. Peck, *Atlas of Human Anatomy*, p. 89.

10. *Linea alba* is Latin for "white line."

11. A fascia is a sheet or layer of tough connective tissue that covers and binds together muscle structure of the body. When fascia (instead of a tendon) forms the end of a muscle, it is called *aponeurosis*. Fascia is called intermuscular septa if it lies embedded between groupings of muscles.

12. Peck, *Atlas of Human Anatomy*, p. 89.

13. R. D. Lockhart, *Living Anatomy* (London: Faber and Faber, 1963), p. 6.

14. Arthur Thomson, whose nineteenth-century work on artistic anatomy remains a useful text, was especially sensitive to the form of the flank pads. He cautioned, "The student should be warned against the ungainly forms which are dependent on the undue accumulation of fat in the region overlying the iliac crest. This is particularly liable to occur in the female models past their prime, and imparts a grossness of form at variance with the delicacy and refinement displayed in earlier life" (Thomson, *Handbook of Anatomy*, p. 271).

15. Peck, *Atlas of Human Anatomy*, p. 49.

16. The upper origins of the latissimus dorsi are from the seventh vertebra of the rib cage on downward (Ibid., p. 102).

17. Jenö Barcsay, *Anatomy for the Artist* (London: Spring Books, 1958), p. 206.

18. Lockhart, *Living Anatomy*, p. 49.

19. Including the lowest vertebra of the rib cage, the twelfth (Henry Gray, *Anatomy* [Philadelphia: Running Press, 1974], p. 337).

20. *Infra* means "below"; hence *infraspinatus* means "below the spine" (of the scapula).

21. Peck, *Atlas of Human Anatomy*, p. 102.

22. These most useful muscle actions are listed by Gray, *Anatomy*, p. 341.

23. Connected with the base of the tongue, the hyoid bone is associated with swallowing movements. You can locate it by feeling your neck above the Adam's apple as you swallow.

24. A secondary sex characteristic, the Adam's apple becomes larger in the male about the time the voice deepens during adolescence (Thomson, *Handbook of Anatomy*, p. 365).

25. The top segment of the sternum is called the *manibrium*, after the handle of an ancient sword resembling the sternum (Gray, *Anatomy*, p. 124).

26. "Concerning the combined action of the two [sternomastoid] muscles, there is disagreement in the various textbooks: Some assert that the muscles bend forward the head and neck, whilst others state that the muscles act as extensors. The united action seems to be the bending forward of the neck on the thorax [chest] combined with the extension of the head upon the bent neck" (Thomson, *Handbook of Anatomy*, p. 373). Peck seems to agree, saying that the sternomastoids "together lift the face and tip the head backward" (Peck, *Atlas of Human Anatomy*, p. 95). Barcsay, however, asserts that the sternomastoid "flexes the head" forward, adding that the "forward flexion of the head cannot take place before the face has been lowered [so that] . . . the insertion of the muscle lies in front of the [spinal] join [with the skull]" (Barcsay, *Anatomy for the Artist*, p. 238).

27. Ibid., p. 236.

28. The platysma muscle "is a survival in man of a muscle which commonly occurs in many animals. Anyone who has watched a fly settle on a horse's neck has seen that the latter has the power of rippling or wrinkling its skin in a remarkable manner. [The] platysma belongs to the same class" (Thomson, *Handbook of Anatomy*, p. 374).

29. M. D. Vernon, *The Psychology of Perception* (Harmondsworth, Middlesex, England: Penguin, 1968), p. 51.

30. The action of the biceps on the humerus is therefore indirect.

31. The ulnar tuberosity, a bump on the front side of the ulna near the coronoid process (see Figure 6-45).

32. It is also shared with the bicep.

33. Thomson, *Handbook of Anatomy*, p. 192.

34. Gray, *Anatomy*, p. 400.

35. *Polex* is Latin for "thumb"; *pollicis*, "of the thumb."

36. Anatomical texts differ on the exact function of these muscles. Barcsay states (*Anatomy for the Artist*, p. 72) that the extensor pollicis brevis extends the distal phalanx of the thumb (even though he also states that it attaches only to the proximal or first phalanx). Peck more accurately asserts (*Atlas of Human Anatomy*, p. 112) that it "extends the first phalanx."

37. Pronation is also a weaker movement than supination. For that reason "Screws are usually made to be driven home by supination of the right forearm" (R. D. Lockhart et al., *Anatomy of the Human Body* [Philadelphia: J. B. Lippincott, 1974], p. 214).

38. The *pisiform* (pea-shaped) bone does not join with the radius, but its projection adds depth to the inner arch of the carpals, through which many tendons of the flexor muscles pass.

39. Thomson, *Handbook of Anatomy*, p. 197. According to Thomson this muscle is absent in 10 percent of the population, so do not be surprised if you cannot locate it in your wrist.

40. The term *lower limb* is used in place of the word *leg*. In common usage their meaning is identical, but in anatomical writing *leg* applies only to the part of the lower limb between the knee joint and the foot. The word *thigh* denotes the section above the knee.

41. Ibid., p. 297.

42. *Sartor* is Latin for "tailor." In times past tailors often sat cross-legged to facilitate sewing.

43. The iliopsoas, a deep muscle that attaches to the ilium, the lower vertebrae, and the femur, is sometimes included in this group, but it is omitted here because it does not act as an adductor. The muscle extends from the lower vertebrae and the inner wall of the ilium beneath the inguinal ligament to the femur, inserting with the small inner trochanter. It is largely internal, appearing superficially only in one small area between the inner angle of the sartorius and the inguinal ligament. Its function is to flex the thigh.

44. Gray warns of the danger to the adductor longus posed by horseback riding—a vivid reminder of the location of the muscle (Gray, *Anatomy*, p. 426).

45. Other fascial bands in addition to the iliotibial affect the form of the lower limb: the band of Richer, which girds the front of the thigh above the knee, causing a noticeable bulge in the vastus medialis (Figure 6-54); another that reaches under the hip muscles to form the crease below the hip (the gluteal furrow); a band lower on the limb at the knee that binds the back knee muscles in a manner similar to a garter (Figure 6-62); and the transverse ligament of the ankle, which is comparable to the annular ligament of the wrist (Figure 6-56). Not usually visible themselves, these bands of fascia help hold the muscles and tendons in place and tend to alter their appearance, especially under stress.

46. Thomson, *Handbook of Anatomy*, p. 276.

47. The gluteus medius covers a smaller, deeper muscle, the gluteus minimus, also an adductor of the thigh.

48. Ibid., p. 304. The ham is referred to as the popliteal fossa in Peck, *Atlas of Human Anatomy*, p. 132.

49. The popliteal band of fascia (see Note 48).

50. The hamstring muscles not only flex the leg but also restrict or limit the flexion of the hip joint. People with short or tight hamstring muscles are unable to touch their toes by bending at the hip. By bending the knees the distance between the insertions and the origins is shortened, facilitating the task. For an illustration of this function see Lockhart, *Living Anatomy*, p. 61.

51. The indirect action of the leg flexors on the femur recalls the indirect action of the arm biceps on the humerus (Figure 6-3).

52. *Gastrocnemius* literally means "belly of the leg" in Greek (Peck, *Atlas of Human Anatomy*, p. 131).

53. Gray, *Anatomy*, p. 437.

54. The single name for both muscles is *triceps surae* (Barcsay, *Anatomy for the Artist*, p. 151).

55. A much smaller muscle, unimportant for the artist, arises from the lower fourth of the tibia and is visible as a tendon on the lateral side of the foot (Figure 6-56). This muscle, known as the peroneus tertius, is actually part of another muscle, the extensor digitorum longus. It inserts with the upper surface of the base of the little toe's metatarsal (Gray, *Anatomy*, p. 443).

56. Ibid., p. 441.

57. The front muscles of the leg are separated from those of the back by the interosseous membrane, a thin layer of tendinous tissue that spans the gap between the inner sides of the tibia and the fibula (Ibid., p. 202).

58. The tendons insert with the second and third phalanges of the four smaller toes (Ibid., p. 435).

59. *Hallucis* is Latin for "of the big toe."

60. Ibid., p. 436.

61. Ibid., p. 439.

62. Italo Svevo, *Confessions of Zeno* (New York: Random House and Knopf, 1958), pp. 94–95.

63. John W. McCoubrey, *American Art 1700–1960* (Englewood Cliffs, N.J.: Prentice-Hall, 1965), p. 153.

64. For an interesting discussion of the relationship between scientific anatomy and the history of art see Eugenio Battisti, "Visualization and Representation of the Figure," *Encyclopaedia of the World Art*, vol. 7 (New York: McGraw-Hill, 1963), p. 666.

65. Author's translation. Tgb. *Ergänzungs manuskript*, vgl. Klee, 1960, p. 12, quoted in *Paul Klee Handzeichnungen I* (Bern: Kunstmuseum Bern, 1973), p. 109.

66. Sir Julian Huxley, July 1871, quoted in "Fifty and 100 Years Ago," *Scientific American*, vol. 225, no. 1 (July 1971), p. 10. Huxley's assessment of the humanism of drawing was made in the context of a humorous speech comparing professional disciplines with attributes of animals, part of a mock scientific search for the distinction between animals and humans. Delivered at a dinner for the Royal Academy of the Arts, the speech was in all likelihood well received.

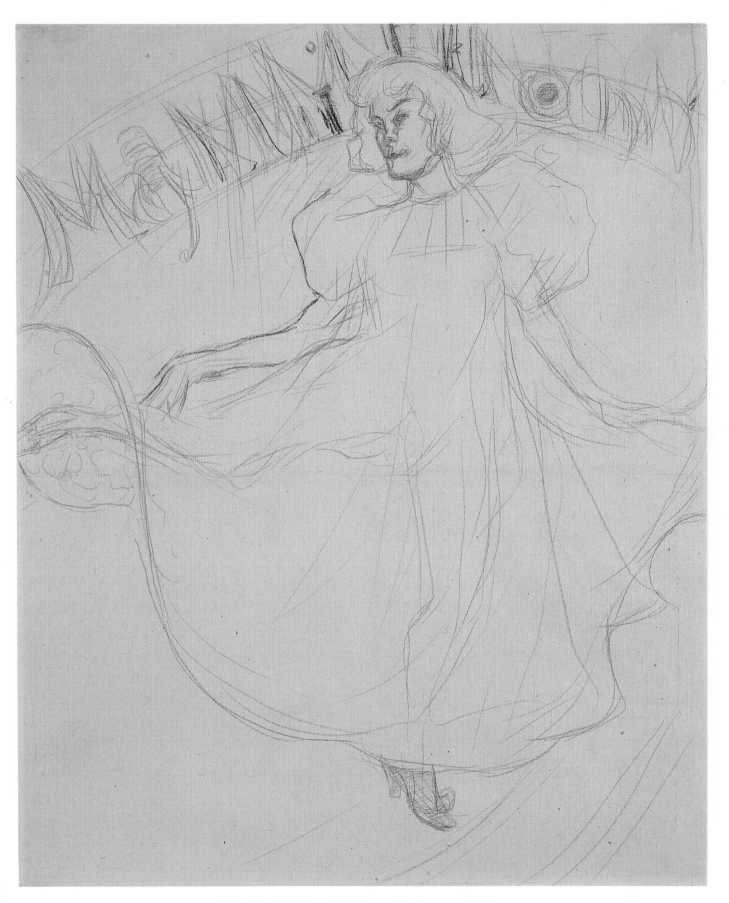

Color Plate I. Henri de Toulouse-Lautrec (1864–1901). *May Milton*, 1895. Blue and black crayon on light brown paper. 29⅛ × 23³⁄₁₆″. New Haven, Connecticut, Yale University Art Gallery. Gift of Walter Bareiss, B. S. 1940.

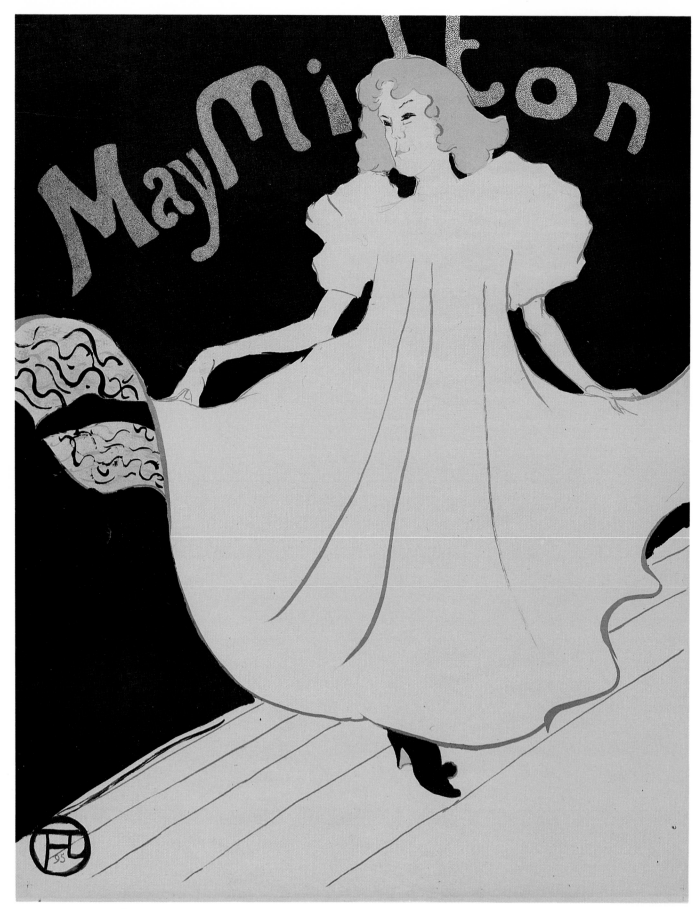

Color Plate II. Henri de Toulouse-Lautrec, *May Milton*, 1895. Colored lithographic poster. 31 × 23½".
New Haven, Connecticut, Yale University Art Gallery. Gift of Paul Mellon, B.A. 1929.

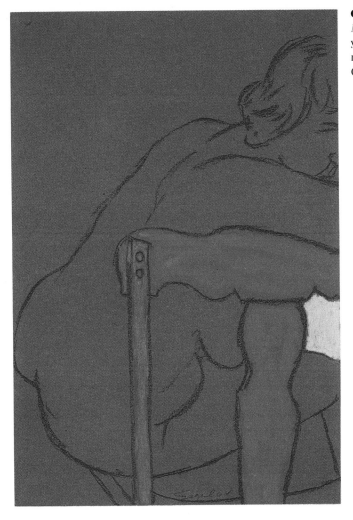

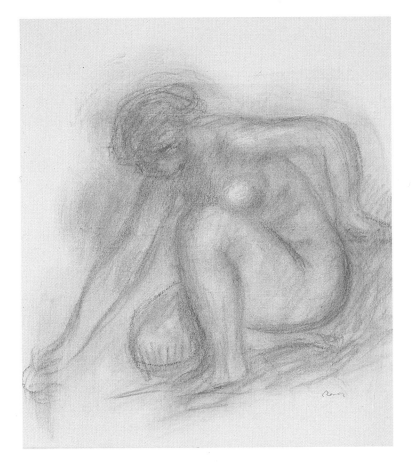

Color Plate III. George Segal (b. 1924), *Seated Nude*, 1964. Pastel (carmine red, ultramarine, and yellow). 465 × 302 mm. Oberlin, Ohio, Allen Memorial Art Museum, Oberlin College. Charles F. Olney Fund, 1964.

Color Plate IV. Pierre-Auguste Renoir (1841–1919), *Crouching Nude*, c. 1897. Red chalk on Ingres paper. 21⁹⁄₁₆ × 19¹⁄₁₆″. Ottawa, National Gallery of Canada.

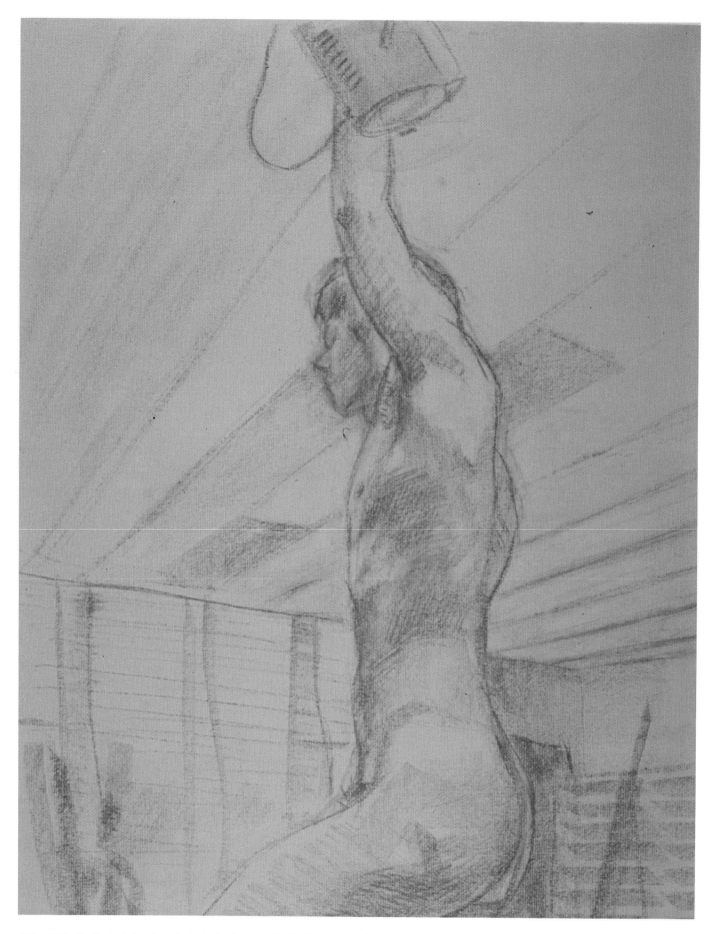

Color Plate V. Student drawing. Model in the Drawing Studio. Sanguine (red) crayon on gray-green laid paper. 25 × 19″.

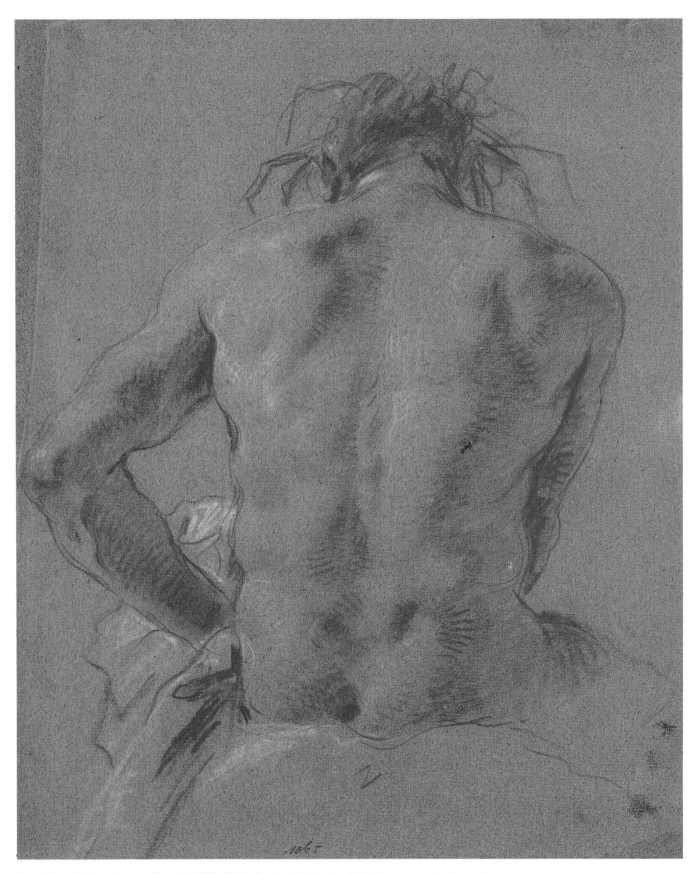

Color Plate VI: Giambattista Tiepolo (1696–1770), *Study of the Back*, c. 1745. Sanguine and white chalk on bluish paper. 344 mm. × 280 mm. Stuttgart, Kupferstichkabinett.

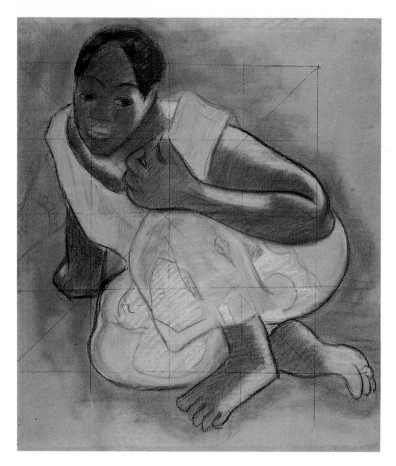

Color Pate VII. Paul Gauguin (1848–1903), *Crouching Tahitian Woman, Study for* Nafea faaipoipo (When will you marry?) (*recto*), 1892. Pastel and charcoal over preliminary drawing in graphite pencil, selectively stumped and squared in black chalk on woven paper. 21¾ × 18⅞". Courtesy of The Art Institute of Chicago. Gift of Tiffany and Margaret Blake. Combining traditional black-and-white drawing media with pastel, this is one of four surviving full-scale working drawings for the early (1891–1893) Tahitian paintings.

Color Plate VIII. Edouard Manet (1832–1883), *George Moore* (Au Café). Oil on canvas. 25¾ × 32". New York, Metropolitan Museum of Art. Gift of Mrs. Ralph J. Hines, 1955.

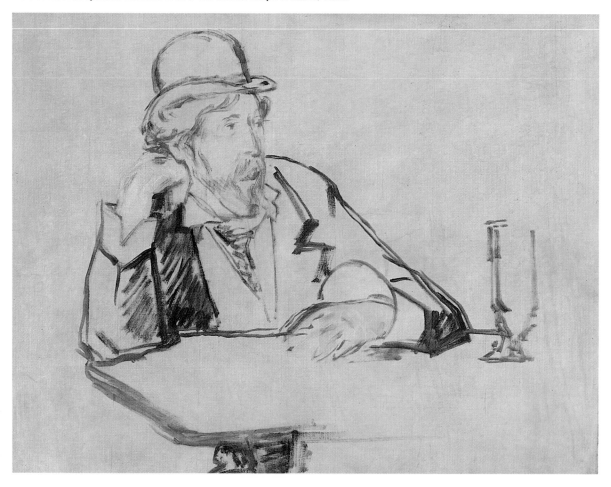

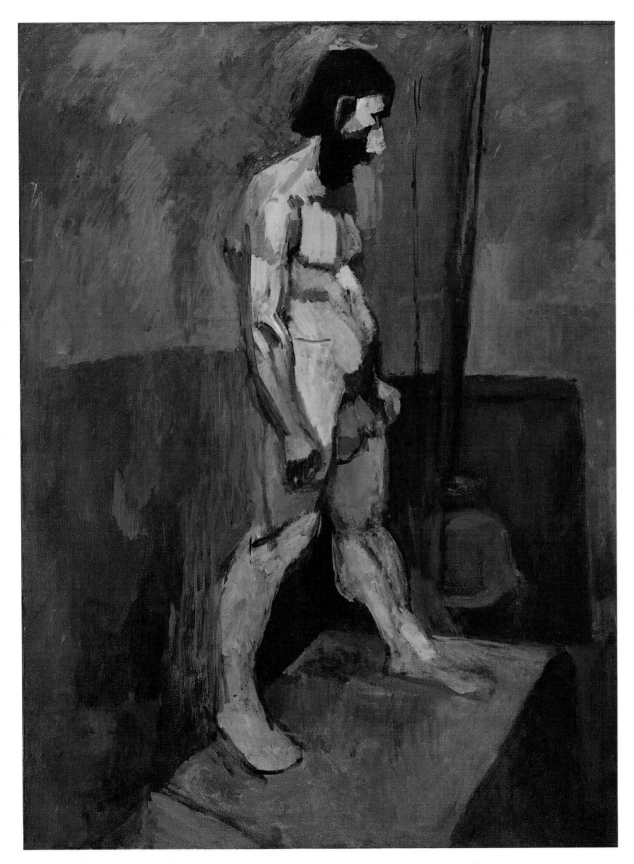

Color Plate IX. Henri Matisse, *Male Model (L'Homme Nu; "Le Serf"; Académie Bleue; Bevilacqua)*, Paris, 1900. Oil on canvas. 39⅛ × 28⅝″ (99.3 × 72.7 cm). The Museum of Modern Art, New York. Kay Sage Tanguy and Abby Aldrich Rockefeller Funds.

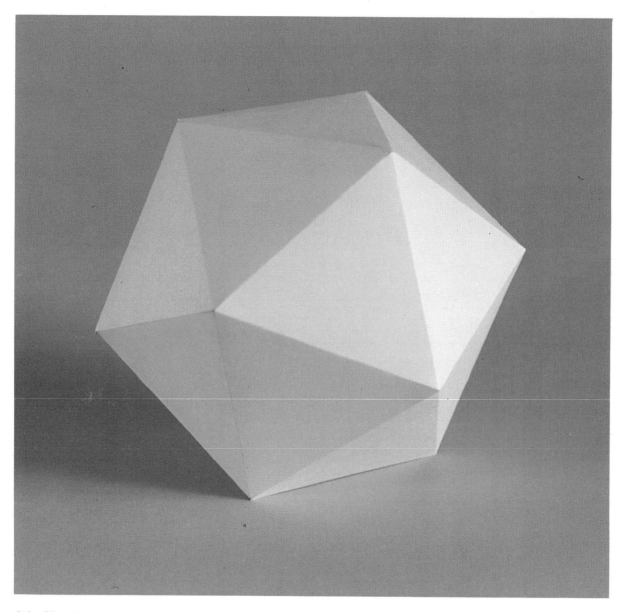

Color Plate X. *Polyhedron Model.* Natural light illuminates the right side of this white geometrical solid while an incandescent light source imparts a warm tonality to the shaded side, creating a warm-cool color contrast. The orientation of each facet of the polyhedron determines the apparent color and value of each facet in a way analogous to color modeling in drawing.

CHAPTER 7

Advanced Studies

approaches to composition, color, and modeling

The several manners I have used in my art must not be considered as an evolution, or as steps towards an unknown ideal of painting . . .

PABLO PICASSO

ALTHOUGH ART does not progress toward an ideal goal, there is an undeniable unfolding of methods and ideas that marks both the history of art and the development of the individual artist.[1] In a similar way the art of drawing also unfolds as you learn to draw the human form. The basic drawing methods introduced in Chapters 1 through 4 tend to unfold in different artistic directions. This chapter is designed to help you further explore some of these directions by focusing on technique, thematic content, and composition.

COMPOSITION

Like the gentleman who was surprised to learn he had been speaking prose all of his life,[2] you may be amused to realize that virtually all of your drawings are compositions. Even the humblest figure study, whether developed in line or modeling, has a compositional structure. Usually it consists of positive form—the figure—set off by the "empty" negative space or *ground* that fills the rest of the page. The size of the figure in proportion to the ground and its position within the ground are sources of compositional variety and expression. When the figure is contained within the page format, there

often results an effect of completeness (Figure 4-34). A proportionally large ground can produce a sense of isolation (Figure 4-46).

If the figure is cropped and seems to extend beyond the confines of the paper format, the composition can serve to dramatize interesting forms and shapes, both negative and positive, that might otherwise have gone unnoticed (Figure 6-18). To experiment with the effects of different formats try masking off a figure study with various rectangular formats using four strips of cardboard. You are likely to discover that certain proportional formats are more effective than others with your figure drawing. By framing in this way you can alter the figure-ground relationships without adding any marks to the paper. Whether it is done before or after you make the drawing, choosing an appropriate format is an important step in organizing your composition. Within the format you can observe other formal factors of composition: line and shape, repetition and variation, symmetry and balance, figure and ground as well as movement and rhythm. These terms—familiar to you already in relation to the drawing methods described in the first part of this book—will reveal their role in composition as you experiment with the studies proposed in this section. The first of these studies investigates the role of shape and local color in composition and is an extension of the line drawing method introduced in Study 9.

SHAPE AND LOCAL COLOR IN COMPOSITION

The compositions of certain works of art seem based almost exclusively on the flat shapes of things rather than on the volumetric aspects of solid form. In Utamaro's *Girl Combing Her Hair* (Figure 7-1) the positive *shapes* of black hair and patterned robe and the negative shape bounded by the hair, arms, and head are the major vehicles of expression dominating this elegant, tightly cropped composition. For Eastern artists this mode of representation was traditional, but for the European artists of the nineteenth century, trained to model form in light and shade, the use of the flat shape as a vehicle of expression was a novel and fascinating idea. Japanese prints exerted a strong influence on a number of major Western artists of the time, including Toulouse-Lautrec and Aubrey Beardsley (Color Plate II and Figure 7-3). Lautrec in particular adapted Japanese techniques in creating his poster designs, an artistic debt he acknowledged by signing his initials in the manner of a Japanese seal. Comparison of a preparatory drawing by Lautrec with the final printed poster reveals the purpose of the line drawing (Color Plates I and II). In the drawing Lautrec carefully planned the shapes of the figure and the lettering and their compositional relationships. He also recorded the form of the nude figure beneath the gown, using a freely developed angular construction of line. Although the nude figure is not visible in the poster, the preparatory study may account for the authoritative positioning of the figure elements that are visible, such as the feet and arms, as well as the subtle suggestion of body contours in the gown. Comparison of the preparatory drawing with the poster also reveals how Lautrec used contrasting color shapes to activate the composition. The basic composition is defined in the line drawing, but it is not until the addition of local color in the poster that the artist's compositional idea is realized. The deep blue color of the ground accentuates the flairing shape of the dancer's white gown and the diagonal floor line, creating a sharply contrasting figure-ground relationship, and producing a brilliant warm-cool contrast with the much smaller yellow and red color shapes of the head. The dark blue also punctuates the negative shapes between the arms and the gown on each side of the figure contributing to the uncertain balance of the dancer's gesture. These small, but lively negative shapes together with the curving lines of the figure permit an almost perfect formal integration with the rhythmically curving lettering. The broad arc of the letters of the dancer's name is echoed in the reverse curve of the hemline of the gown, adding a sense of unity to the composition.

Each color in a lithograph or woodblock print requires a separate printing. Understandably, the fewer colors, the lower

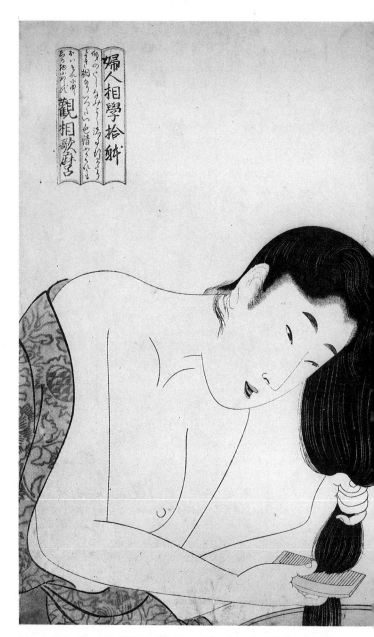

Figure 7-1. Utamaro (1753–1806), *Girl Combing Her Hair*, c. 1802. Illustration from the series *Ten Forms of Feminine Physiognomy*. Colored woodblock print. 36.3 × 24.5 cm. London, British Museum.

the printing cost. Printing restrictions of this kind do not limit the number of colors used in drawing media, of course, but if you are interested in bold color effects, you would be well advised to experiment first with a limited palette. A skillful use of a limited palette and local color can be seen in a simple figure composition by the contemporary American artist George Segal (Color Plate III). Using toned paper and pastel Segal enlivened his bold contour drawing with flat, but brilliant, local color added to the chair supporting the figure and—unexpectedly—to one negative space. Drawing with pastels like Segal, or with other color media suggested here, you may find it rewarding to try to achieve similar bold effects with local color.

**STUDY 48:   Composing with Line
                and Local Color Shapes**

materials: ❑ 1 or more sheets of colored art paper (e.g.,
                  Canson Mi-Tientes) 19 × 25″
               ❑ suggested colors: blue-gray or buff
               ❑ Masonite or plywood board and clamps
               ❑ colored pencils or other dry color medium
               ❑ suggested colors: terra cotta, sienna, light ochre
                  (or sand), white, light warm gray, light blue,
                  medium yellow, vermilion
               ❑ kneaded rubber eraser
               ❑ thin blade for sharpening pencils
               ❑ optional media: pen and ink, and for color, either
                  transparent watercolor and brush or a selection
                  of broad-tipped color markers
               ❑ white drawing paper, 11 × 14″ or a selection of
                  pastel crayons

reference: ❑ model and colored clothing or fabric
    time: ❑ 30 minutes

The main objective of this study is to explore the use of local color in drawing for compositional effects. Virtually any color medium can serve this purpose; however, colored pencils are recommended for their ease of handling. Some thought should be given to the studio setup for the model to ensure a variety of local color shapes.[3] If the model is nude, a piece of colored fabric makes a useful prop to enliven and extend the range of colors. For this study a normal diffuse lighting is preferable, in order to avoid harsh shadows.

If you wish to follow Lautrec's example, begin by making a line drawing using the visual measurement method (Study 9). Drawing with a colored pencil on tinted paper, you can produce color contrasts from the start. If your paper is blue-toned, try using a warm color, such as terra cotta; if the paper is buff, we suggest a blue pencil. This stage should be drawn lightly, as colored pencil marks do not erase completely. A lightly drawn line, however, can be lifted up by pressing a kneaded eraser against it.

The advantage of drawing on a toned paper becomes apparent when you proceed to apply the local colors, for the color of the paper itself can take on the role of a local color. You may find that, as in the George Segal drawing, the color of the paper will serve effectively as the local color of the figure (Color Plate III). Although the line drawing is a guide for laying in the local colors, there is no need to adhere to it strictly at this stage. You can modify the drawing freely as you build up the color shapes. In other words you should continue drawing while working in color.

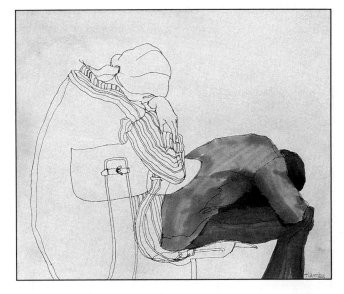

Figure 7-2. Student drawing. Two Seated Figures. India ink and color markers on drawing paper. 9½ × 13″.

In place of dry media, pen and ink can be combined effectively with color markers or watercolor for this compositional study. The India ink drawing pen is especially useful, for the ink becomes waterproof when dry, permitting color to be placed over it without smearing or blending. With these media, tinted paper is not necessary; white paper will insure the most brilliant color effects (Figure 7-2).

COLOR SHAPES IN BLACK AND WHITE

The same method of visualizing forms as color shapes can yield brilliant compositional effects in pure black and white. Aubrey Beardsley, the British graphic artist, used this approach as a way of energizing shapes in his black-and-white illustrations (Figure 7-3). By filling in outlined areas that represent dark colors with solid black he gave the remaining white areas a positive quality much like the figure-ground reversal described in Chapter 1. This is especially noticeable in the aprons and shirtfronts, which emerge as repeating abstract patterns locked in tension with the black shapes. What might have been separate black shapes are fused together to form a chainlike black construction of jackets. Since the black areas also register as positive shapes, the figure-ground reversal is incomplete, causing a formal ambivalence that is one source of the visual excitement generated by this work. The thick rectangular border serves to emphasize the relationship of the formal pattern with the surrounding pictorial space, making it clear that the expressive power of the drawing derives from the way elements of pattern were put together abstractly to form the composition.

You can see a similar approach in a self-portrait by the

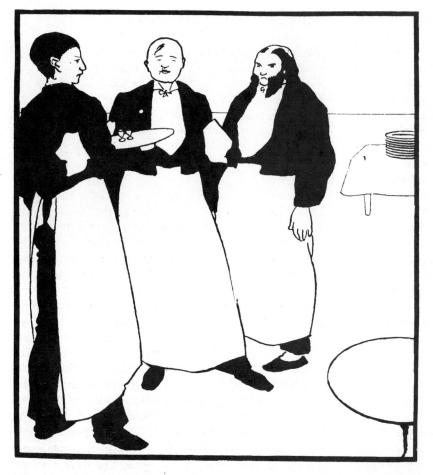

Figure 7-3. Aubrey Beardsley (1872–1898), *Garçons de Café*, 1894–1895. Illustration for *The Yellow Book*. London, Victoria and Albert Museum.

Figure 7-4. Paul Klee, *Self-Portrait*, 1909. Study for a woodcut. India ink on linen. 13 × 14.5 cm (courtesy of Felix Klee and SPADEM).

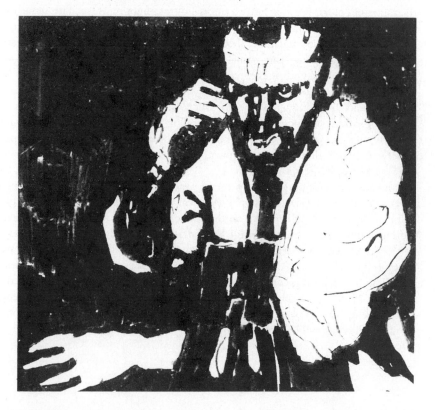

Swiss artist Paul Klee (Figure 7-4). Although a solid black tone obscures a good deal of the line in this work, the drawing is essentially a linear description of shapes. Significantly, the black tone does not serve to model effects of rounded form but rather translates color shapes into striking patterns of black and white within the framework of the line construction. Color shapes are filled in with the same directness as in a child's coloring book. What may have been different darker colors are lumped together as black; lighter variations of tone are reduced to white areas enclosed by line. The background for example fuses with the dark shape of the hair thereby stressing the asymmetrical shape of the forehead. Since the Klee self-portrait and the Beardsley drawing were conceived with printing processes in mind—the self-portrait for a woodcut and the drawing for letterpress—their similarity of approach may be partly attributable to the dictates of printing. The reduction of local color shapes to black-and-white shapes can be a productive compositional direction to pursue in drawing even when printmaking is not the objective. As a medium for this purpose you will find the modern felt pen with a broad tip useful for its capacity to fill in large flat areas (Figure 7-5).

Figure 7-5 Student drawing. Model with Patterned Blouse. Black marker on drawing paper. 12 × 9″. The interaction of pattern and shape enliven this tightly cropped sketchbook composition.

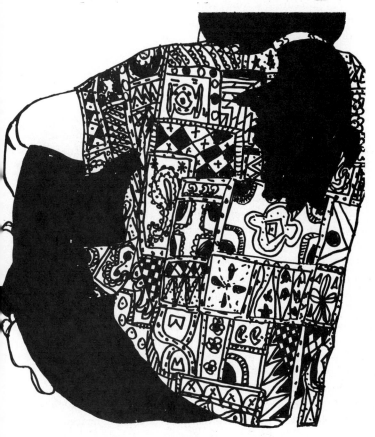

SHADOW MODELING AND COLOR

Shadow modeling makes it possible to create shapes within form, thereby adding another level of complexity to the composition, as seen in the Thiebaud drawing *Dark Background* (Figure 4-46). The artist used the shapes of cast shadows, reinforced at times with line, to create a visual counterpoint with the otherwise symmetrical composition. The formal play of shadow shapes in the figure is subtle, but its abstract character is marked in the diagonal shadow pattern cast over the platform.

When you draw the figure with color media another factor enters into the process of shadow modeling: color contrast. To some extent color contrast is present even in monochromatic drawings. In a monochromatic drawing by the French artist Renoir, for example, the artist used the sanguine crayon to model the figure in warm, reddish tones that contrast with the relatively neutral color of the paper (Color Plate IV). The pink tones of sanguine, produced by rubbing, seem to envelope the figure in a warm glow. An even more vibrant color contrast with sanguine crayon occurs when it is applied to tinted paper such as the grey-green laid paper used for a student's compositional drawing of the "Model in the Drawing Studio" (Color Plate V). Compositionally the drawing is of interest for its low view point. Drawing from a position below the model platform, the student saw the model against the perspectival lines of the ceiling and wall, elements which in the drawing activate what might have been simply empty negative space surrounding the figure. The result is an animated composition with the figure in a spatial setting.

Tinted paper was used in a slightly different way by artists in the Baroque period who augmented the color range of sanguine with white and black chalks, thereby shifting the modeling process in a decidedly chromatic direction. An heir to this tradition, the Venetian painter Giambattista Tiepolo was able to create richly coloristic effects of shadow modeling with only sanguine and white chalk on a bluish paper (Color Plate VI). Portions of the blue-gray toned paper left unmarked produce a lively warm-cool contrast with sanguine crayon. In parts of the figure that are in shadow a light tone of sanguine turns the blue of the paper into an unexpected warm gray, a source of subtle color contrast.

As Tiepolo's drawing demonstrates, a variety of hues is possible with a limited number of colored crayons. For the student a limited palette offers a convenient base on which to build a greater chromatic range. With the addition of many hues, however, drawing tends to merge with the discipline of painting, which leads beyond the scope of this book. Nevertheless, if color is your primary interest, you may wish to draw with more hues and to experiment with various color media, such as colored pencils, watercolors, and pastels. Mixed media offer another option with color. By combining color media with standard monochromatic drawing media such as charcoal and graphite, it is possible to model with color and yet retain the graphic quality associated with drawing, as demonstrated in a color drawing combining pastel with graphite pencil and black crayon by Gauguin (Color Plate VII). Even traditional painting media, such as tempera and oil, can be used for purposes of drawing with color. With these media the distinction between painting and drawing may seem arbitrary.

For Manet the painted drawing was often simply the first stage of a full-blown painting. Drawing with a flat-tipped brush and a limited warm-cool palette he deftly laid in the composition for a portrait of *George Moore* (Color Plate VIII). Is this work a drawing in color or an unfinished painting? Perhaps the question is academic, for as Cézanne once observed,

> Drawing and color are not separate at all; insofar as you paint, you draw. The more the color harmonizes, the more exact the drawing becomes. When the color achieves richness, the form attains its fullness—the contrast and connections of tone—there you have the secret of drawing and modeling.[4]

The mutually reinforcing role of color and drawing espoused by Cézanne is evident in Matisse's painting of the male model, a work which carries on the tradition of the painted *académie* of the nude (Color Plate IX). The artist departs from the earlier tradition, however, by modeling with color so that hue and intensity vary in accordance with the planes of the figure.

STUDY 49: *Shadow Modeling with Color*

materials: ❏ tinted charcoal paper or other colored art paper (e.g., Canson) with laid surface, 25 × 19″ gray-blue or gray-green, recommended
❏ colored pencils: terra cotta, sepia, ochre, white, beige (or "sand"), light and medium gray, or drawing crayons of the same hues
❏ HB graphite pencil
❏ kneaded rubber eraser

reference: ❏ model illuminated by 200-watt flood lamp (bell type with clamp)

time: ❏ 30 minutes

The method for modeling with color is essentially the same as in shadow modeling (Study 20). Color is a natural extension of shadow modeling. Shadow in nature—as well as in the studio—is seldom simply a darker tonal value. Often it is also a different color. Observed out-of-doors, shadows tend to be bluish on a clear day, because they are filled-in partially by cool light from the blue sky. In the studio it is common for the warm-cool contrast to be reversed, making the shadows seem warm, especially when the model is illuminated

both with artificial light and a stronger light from a window or skylight. The resulting warm-cool contrast is most evident when natural and artificial light sources illuminate opposite sides of a colorless (white) object (Color Plate X), but a comparable contrast can be observed with the figure. This simple contrast of color tonality can be the basis for shadow modeling with color media.

Modeling with colored pencils or crayons on a cool-tinted drawing paper can be analogous to the color modeling observed on the polyhedron in Color Plate X. The warm tones of the terra cotta pencil can serve to model the areas in shadow. The white pencil can be reserved for the planes of highest value, with the color of the paper itself functioning as an intermediary tone.

You can begin by constructing the figure lightly in line using the terra cotta colored pencil (or for easy erasing the graphite pencil) on tinted paper. As in shadow modeling, it helps to indicate the terminator lines—the shadow boundaries on the figure—though in this case they will define areas of color tones.

Color media present several options for modeling the figure. Drawing on a gray-blue (or gray-green) tinted paper you can begin by modeling the warm shadow tones of the figure with the terra cotta and warm medium gray pencils. This approach allows the paper color to function as a light cool tone in which highlights can be indicated in white. You may prefer, however, to begin by modeling the illuminated planes of the figure in light tones with white, beige, or light gray colored pencil, an approach which gives the pleasant sensation of drawing with light.

SHADOW MODELING AND SUBTLE TONAL VALUES

Shadow modeling without color was a preferred technique for drawing the nude in art academies of the nineteenth century. These carefully modeled studies, known as *académies d'après nature*, required lengthy drawing sessions and a drawing medium capable of rendering subtle nuances of tone in order to create the desired effect of light and shade.[5] Charcoal—an inexpensive medium that is both flexible and capable of rendering delicate values of tone—was most frequently used, but its very subtlety led to a smoothly polished tonal finish that sometimes robbed drawings of spontaneity, giving the term *academic* a pejorative meaning.

For the young American student Thomas Eakins—already an accomplished draftsman—the charcoal medium seemed tailor-made. His *Academic Study* is a masterful example of shadow modeling in this medium (Figure 7-6). Within the context of a well-constructed figure the artist has carefully translated his formal observations into shadow patterns apparently first indicated in line and subsequently modeled with tonal steps in accordance with an unseen single light source

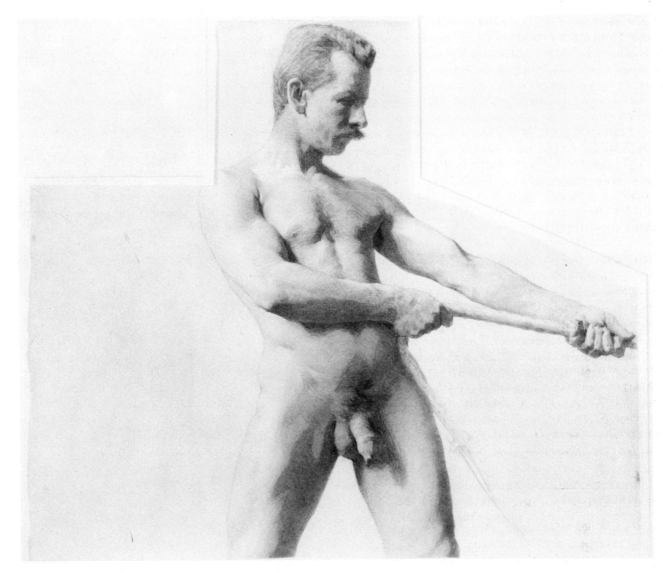

Figure 7-6. Thomas Eakins, *Academic Study*, c. 1869. Charcoal on paper. Seiden and deCuevas, Inc.

to the upper left of the subject. The tones range from pure black, used discretely within areas of dark gray, to the medium and lightest values of gray. The highlights seen in certain areas of light gray (i.e., in the region of the collarbone) result from erasures exposing the white surface of the paper.

Eakins's use of line in modeling is instructive though perhaps not immediately apparent. It is most easily seen in the larger, simpler forms, such as the thigh. Patterns of tone in the figure's right thigh reveal faint lines that mark the boundary of the shadow area. These terminator lines separate shadow patterns into several steps of tone. The sharp angularity of the shadow patterns suggests that careful angular analysis and measurement formed the basis for the remarkable accuracy of this life study, drawn while Eakins was a student in Paris. Although such structured draftsmanship is a quality sometimes identified with academic discipline, for Eakins it formed the basis of the intensely personal idiom of his mature

work.[6] Modeling with subtle tones remains a challenge for the draftsman of today.

STUDY 50:   Shadow Modeling with Subtle Tones

materials: ❑ 25 × 19″ charcoal paper with laid surface, white or toned
  ❑ Conté crayon (medium or soft) or natural vine stick charcoal
  ❑ white Conté crayon (optional)
  ❑ kneaded rubber eraser
  ❑ chamois skin or soft cloth
  ❑ blending stumps (optional)

reference: ❑ model or sculpture cast illuminated by 200-watt flood lamp (bell type with clamp)

time: ❑ 60 minutes (or three 20-minute sessions)

This exercise is essentially an extension of the method described in Study 20, and should be undertaken after you are familiar with that exercise. Visual measurement of shadow patterns is the key in both. In this study, however, no limit is placed on the number of tonal steps. Instead tonal steps are based on those you observe on the model and limited only by your own artistic judgment. Modeling with subtle tones requires a drawing session of at least one hour. One hour, however, is a long period to work continuously, and you may find it convenient—for you as well as for the model—to have a break at twenty-minute intervals.

Media Considerations

Modeling with subtle tones favors certain media. You may prefer to work with the familiar Conté crayon. Controlled effects of tone and texture are possible with Conté crayon, especially when it is held flat on the paper (Figures 4-34 and 7-7). It is wise to build up tones lightly and gradually using Conté crayon, as it resists erasures. An area drawn too lightly can be darkened easily, but it is difficult to lighten an area drawn overly dark. Rubbing the eraser over Conté crayon marks tends to produce an undesirable color change while it lightens the crayon marks. A dark area can be lightened slightly, however, by pressing the kneaded rubber eraser against the paper and lifting up. Used in this way the eraser literally picks up some of the crayon granules from the paper, leaving the paper surface intact. Because of its inflexibility Conté may require considerable practice before you can fully exploit its rich tonalities. If you wish to draw with an instrument more tolerant of errors, you may prefer charcoal.

Natural vine charcoal (carbonized vine sticks) are recommended for their softness and ease of blending—characteristics especially useful in modeling. Charcoal marks can be blended into a tone by rubbing them either with your fingers or with a paper stump—a small roll of paper made for this purpose. For blending larger areas or removing lines, a piece of fine cloth or chamois skin (a piece of soft leather) can be rubbed gently over the drawing, eradicating black lines, but leaving broad charcoal tone. If you wish, a lighter tone can be drawn into that tone by means of the kneaded eraser, which becomes in effect a negative drawing instrument.

Laid charcoal paper is well suited to the needs of sustained drawing whether in Conté crayon or charcoal. Unlike newsprint paper, a 100 percent rag charcoal paper is sufficiently tough to take repeated erasures and rubbing without feathering, a real advantage in a one-hour drawing session. Also the laid texture of charcoal paper can produce a luminous effect within dark tones, thanks to the valleys between the raised ridges of the texture. The valleys of laid paper tend to remain unmarked by the charcoal, and may appear as light marks in a shadow tone (Figures 7-7 and 7-8). If you choose to draw on a toned charcoal paper, the highest values can be

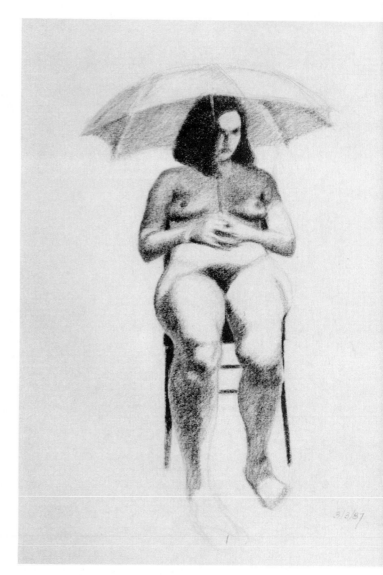

Figure 7-7. Student study in shadow modeling. Figure with Umbrella. 25 × 19″. Conté crayon on offwhite laid paper.

added with white crayon (Figure 7-9). A word of caution: Such highlights generally are most effective when applied sparingly, within areas free of charcoal. (Drawn over charcoal, white tends to turn to a cold, chalky gray.) This approach to highlights also allows the color of the paper an active role as a tonal step in the drawing—an economy of technique.

The greater flexibility of charcoal does have one disadvantage: The charcoal granules are easily rubbed off the paper. Consequently it is necessary to bind them to the surface with a light spray varnish called fixative once a drawing is completed. Fixative is also useful for the conservation of crayon and pencil drawings, even though these media tend to be less susceptible to smearing than charcoal. Unfortunately, most fixatives contain a potentially harmful solvent and therefore should be sprayed only in places with adequate ventilation or out-of-doors.

light and cast shadow on the model. In addition simple props can be employed to create cast shadows on the model. For the drawing in Figure 7-7 an umbrella was used to cast a shadow over the upper portion of the model, but instead of interpreting the shadow as a solid black shape, the student chose to model within the dark area to suggest a subtle effect of reflected light akin to relief modeling (Study 16). This shift of modeling within the shadow endows the shadow tones with a luminosity reminiscent of an effect known as chiaroscuro.

Chiaroscuro, an Italian word meaning literally *light-dark*, has much in common with shadow modeling. In a chiaroscuro drawing, form is modeled by effects of directional lighting as in shadow modeling but with special attention to modulations within areas of the lightest and darkest values. The chiaroscuro drawing seems to anticipate the eye's ability to adjust to ambient light and to see form both in shadow and in bright light. The result is a complex luminous effect that has more in common with visual experience than with the photographic image. Although chiaroscuro was pioneered by the Italian painter Caravaggio (1573–1610), it continued to be practiced in the eighteenth century. Few artists have applied the chiaroscuro method to the figure as effectively as the Venetian painter Giovanni Battista Piazzetta (1683–1754).

Close examination of a figure study by Piazzetta (Figure 7-9) reveals clues to his drawing method. As in Tiepolo's figure study (Color Plate VI) the blue tone of the paper serves as a middle tone in the figure, mediating between the shadow areas and the highest values. Within areas of the paper-tone, highlights are carefully defined in white crayon as seen on the figure's right shoulder. Light gray tones applied to the background neutralize the coolness of the blue paper and at the same time accentuate the lighter tones of the modeling within the figure.

Within the shadowed parts of the figure, such as the lower back and hips, modeling is based on light reflected from below, imparting a luminosity to the drawing even where we might expect darkness. Planes of the figure are defined by means of patches of short parallel lines (hatch marks) blended by rubbing. For deeper tones more hatch marks are added but left unblended. In addition to the texture of the hatching, the vertical lines of the laid paper run through much of the darker portion of the drawing, contributing a unifying effect in harmony with the verticality of the figure.

In true chiaroscuro fashion the tonal relationship of the figure to the background alternates throughout. The figure's right shoulder, for example, is highlighted against a darker ground, but as the eye scans downward the figural form modulates to dark against a lighter ground. It is a modulation that recurs numerous times before the eye reaches the foot. Although the structure of the figure appears solidly drawn, the exuberant effect of light streaming down on the figure predominates—so much so that light itself virtually becomes the unstated subject.

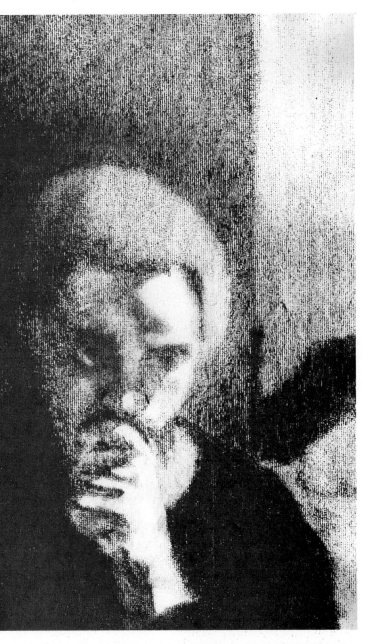

Figure 7-8. Student drawing. Self-Portrait. 25 × 19″. Conté crayon on white laid paper. Shadow modeling is here accompanied by emphatic shadow contours, as seen in the forehead, and by effects of reflected light within the shadows. The composition is unified throughout by the undisguised texture of the laid paper.

SHADOW MODELING, LIGHTING, CHIAROSCURO

Before beginning a long drawing session, the arrangement of the light source merits some consideration, especially when drawing with shadow modeling. By changing the location of the light source you can experiment with various effects of

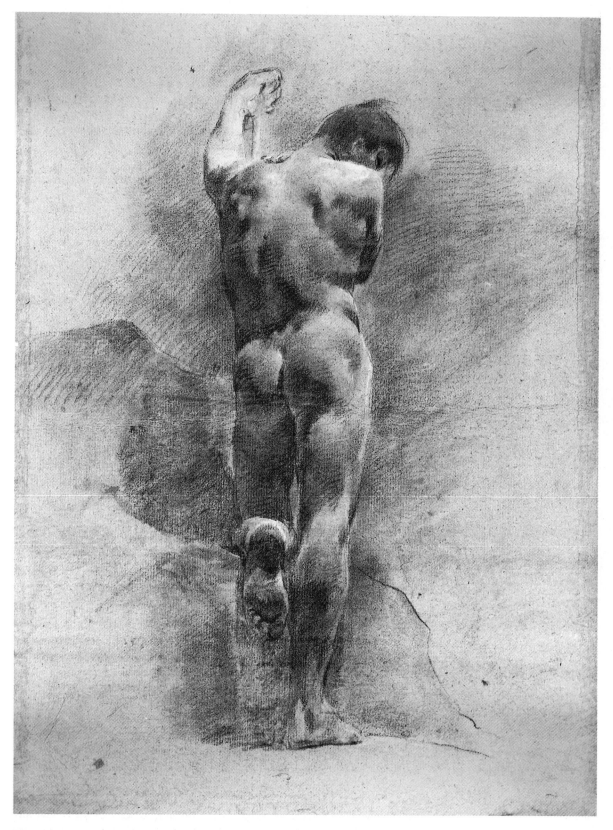

Figure 7-9. Giovanni Battista Piazzetta (1683–1754), *Nude Figure of a Young Man.* P.II. 1035. Black chalk with stump, heightened with white, on bluish-gray paper. 556 × 394 mm. University of Oxford Ashmolean Museum.

It is not by coincidence that Piazzetta's figure casts a shadow, even though the shaded studio prop—possibly a draped chair—is vague. The cast shadow is perfectly in keeping with the logic of shadow modeling, for shadow modeling lends itself to the integration of the figure with a spatial setting. Piazzetta's use of a studio prop to relate the figure to a spatial setting suggests the first of a series of four exercises we propose as strategies to expand your scope of drawing and encourage a more compositional approach to drawing the figure.

Figure 7-10. Student drawing. Model Seated on a Chair. Ballpoint pen on bond paper. 14 × 11″.

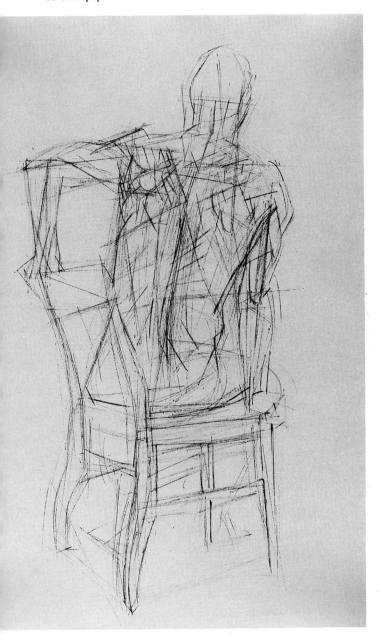

STUDY 51: **The Compositional Drawing: Four Exercises with the Figure and Spatial Setting**

materials:
❑ 35 × 24″ drawing pad or 25 × 19″ charcoal paper with laid surface, white or toned
❑ drawing crayon (medium or soft) or vine charcoal and chamois cloth
❑ white crayon (optional)
❑ kneaded rubber eraser
❑ easel or straight-back chair
❑ Masonite or plywood board and clamps
❑ alternative media: pen and ink with sketchbook, 14 × 11″ or acrylic paint, black and white
❑ gray chipboard 25 × 22″
❑ number 9 or 10 flat bristle brush
❑ aluminum muffin tin for water

reference: ❑ model and other art students in the studio
time: ❑ 20 minutes, Exercise 1
❑ 20 minutes, each figure in Exercise 2
❑ 30 minutes, Exercise 3
❑ 45 minutes, Exercise 4

The artist and the art student alike customarily draw the figure as an isolated form. The narrow focus is understandable in view of the challenging complexity of the body structure. Yet you can also consider the model in the context of the spatial setting of the studio. In the following four exercises the objective is to explore spatial relationships between the model and the studio and between the artist and the model as a basis for composition.

Exercise 1

The Model and the Immediate Spatial Setting. For your first experiments with compositional drawing, limit the scope of the drawing to the model and any supporting studio furniture, such as the platform or a chair. As a support for the weight of the body a chair is essential to the gesture of the seated figure. The relatively simple geometric structure of a chair also suggests a spatial setting for the model. In a student drawing of the seated figure (Figure 7-10) the chair structure defines the ground plane as well as the plane on which the model sits. Open spaces in the structure of the chair present simple negative shapes that offer a convenient reference for checking visual measurements of the figure as well as the chair itself.

Even the most ordinary studio furniture can be used inventively to improvise interesting spatial settings for compositional drawings of the model. The chair can be put to use in a less conventional manner, as seen in Figure 7-11, where it serves as a footrest for a model reclining on the floor. The

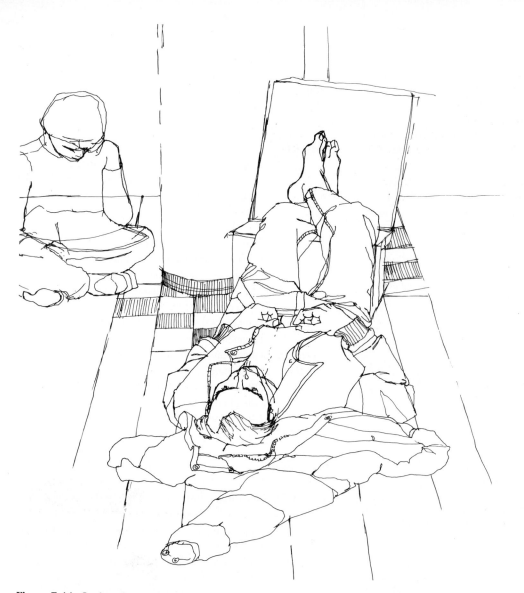

Figure 7-11. Student drawing. Model Reclining on the Floor with Legs Resting on a Chair. Pen and ink on bond paper. 14 × 11″.

relatively high viewpoint of this arrangement allows the plane of the floor to become a major element of composition, as well as a spatial setting for the foreshortened figure. When the model assumes a seated pose on the floor, the model stand can provide both physical suport for the model and a simple spatial setting for a composition with the figure (Figures 7-12 and 7-13).

A high viewpoint is also evident in a graphite drawing by Charles Cajori (Figure 3-28). In this case, however, the floor is rendered more comfortable with mattress and cushions which in the drawing function as abstract compositional shapes. A similar studio setup with cushions appears in a charcoal drawing of the resting figure by the Polish-French artist Balthus (Figure 7-14). Studio furniture is also made to play a compositional role in a study of the male model by Henri Matisse (Color Plate VII). The tilted plane of the model stand justifies the spatial position of the figure's feet and suggests that the artist painted only a short distance from the model. The slightly diagonal direction of a stovepipe counterbalances

diagonal forms of the figure. Together these compositional elements form a spatial niche for Matisse's expressive interpretation of the figure.[7]

Exercise 2

The Single Model and Multiple Figures. With one model it is possible to draw two figures in the same pose so as to construct a simple spatial composition based on repetition. When one version of the figure is clothed, the other nude, there results what amounts to a compositional theme and variation. Drawn in this way, the two figures also provide the opportunity to study the formal relationship between clothing and the body.

The focus of this problem is the spatial integration of two figures into a unified composition. Before drawing the first figure try to visualize both figures on the page. With this in mind draw the first figure leaving space for the second. In

256

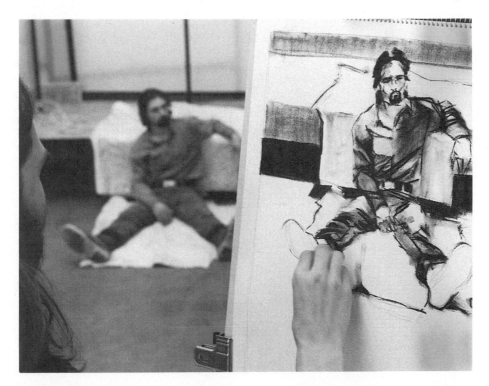

Figure 7-12. Developing a compositional drawing. The platform serves as a prop for the model, permitting a high viewpoint for the drawing student.

Figure 7-13. Student drawing. Compositional Study. Compressed charcoal crayon on newsprint paper. 25 × 19″. Interpreted as horizontal bands of black, gray, and white, the platform provides a unifying structure for the composition.

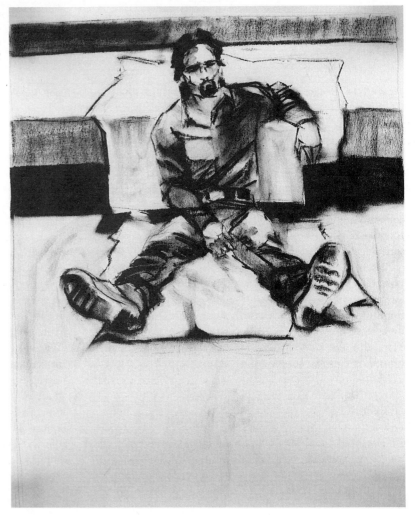

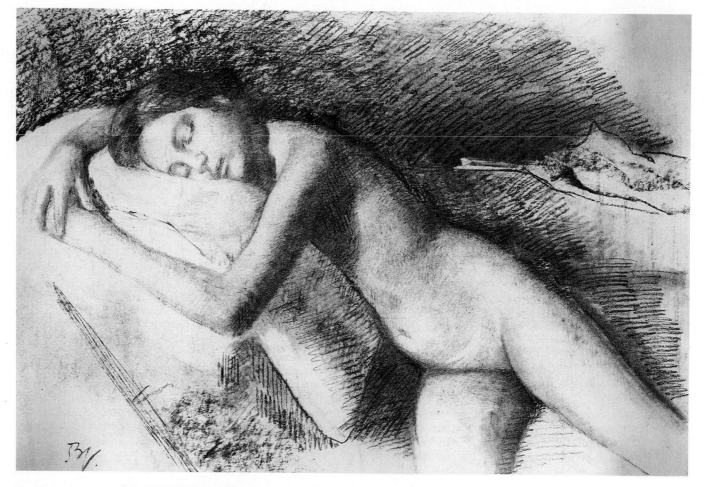

Figure 7-14. Balthus (Balthazar Klossowski de Rola) (b. 1908), *Jeune Fille Endormie.* Charcoal pencil. 65 × 94 cm. Private collection (courtesy Daniel Vareen Gallery, Geneva).

Figures 7-15 and 7-16 the two figures are placed side by side, an arrangement that facilitates repetition in the same scale. The artist has adroitly linked the figures by darkening the negative space separating the figures at the middle, thereby fusing the negative shape with the adjacent cast shadows of the arms (Figure 7-17). The compositional relationship is further solidified by the overlapping of the lower portion of each figure.

There are several variants of this exercise. In one the compositional problem assumes more complexity when the model assumes a different pose at five-minute intervals in a thirty-minute drawing session. For this study the model stand can be a reference for placing the figures in the spatial setting. Here, too, the individual figures are subordinate to the main objective: creating compositional relationships.

Exercise 3

The Model and the Reflected Image. A large plate glass mirror is a valuable tool for compositional studies with the figure. It offers an economical way to draw two figures—the model and the model's reflected image. Two mirrors can create a more complex and deliberately ambiguous spatial environment (Figures 7-18 and 7-19). The reflected image of the model is a feature in a number of drawings by Matisse. In his charcoal drawing *Reflection in the Mirror*, a central frontal figure is shown resting on one foot and leaning against a large mirror (Figure 7-20). The reflected figure, a side view, appears to counter the diagonal tilt of the leaning model while echoing her supple form in reverse. Both the model and her reflection are joined compositionally by a vertical band that frames the mirror. The vertical is repeated in various elements of the interior and recurs in the figure itself in a shadow line of the thigh.

Matisse does not hide his drawing method. The line constructs were freely redrawn in the figures as the artist refined initial visual measurements of the body. At the same time he subtly reinforced the line construction with tonal modeling, imparting a strong effect of relief, especially to the abdominal region. Tones of gray also have an important compositional role. Negative shapes are filled in with dark tone, thereby emphasizing the lighter positive forms of the model and the furniture. An exception, however, is the darkly drawn head,

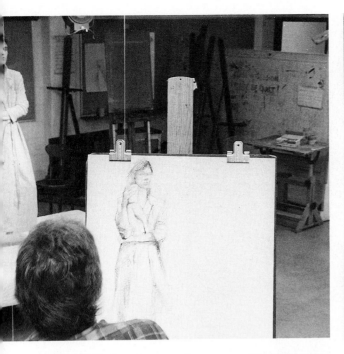 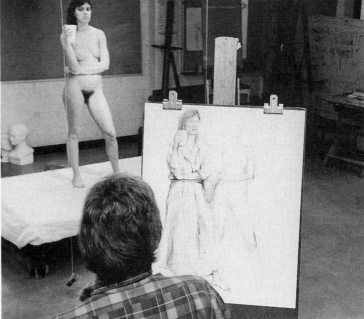

Figure 7-15. Drawing a two-figure composition, the student allows space for a second figure when drawing the first.

Figure 7-16. Integrating the second figure.

Figure 7-17. Student drawing. Two-Figure Composition. Conté crayon on bond paper. 36 × 24″. The two figures are bonded compositionally by means of skillful overlapping and by fusing negative shape with cast shadow.

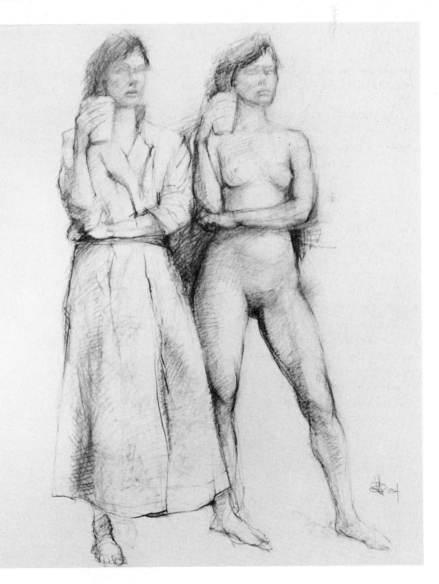

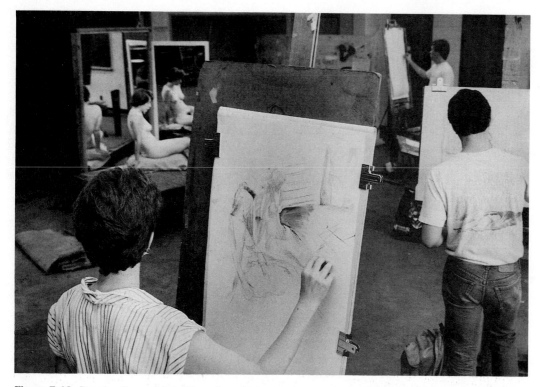

Figure 7-18. Drawing the model and the reflected image. In a first attempt at drawing the model before mirrors, the student defines lightly drawn figures with darker negative shapes of studio shelves in the background.

Figure 7-19. Student drawing. Study of the Model and Reflected Images. Compressed charcoal on bond paper. 36 × 24″. Large plate glass mirrors placed near the model stand can suggest a compositional structure as well as multiple reflections of the figure.

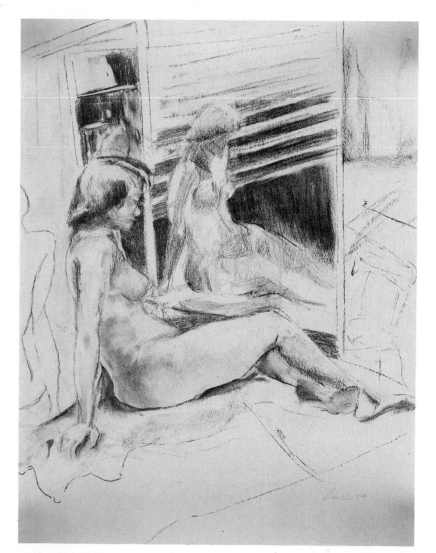

which the artist frames in white, producing an unexpected figure-ground reversal with respect to its reflection. As if to underscore the reversal the reflected head is set against a dark ground. Although the central figure alone would make a fine study in modeling, the thoughtful formal organization of the drawing make it worthy of study as composition.

Exercise 4

The Drawing Studio: The Artist and the Model. Viewed as a whole, the studio lends itself to compositional drawing. It also has the virtue of being readily available. Some thought should be given to planning a drawing that is to include the studio setting and other artists as well as the model. The point of view is an important factor. Without changing your location in the studio the visual relationship of the model to the studio changes dramatically when seen from a different height. Two student drawings—both made from locations behind the model stand—illustrate this difference of effect. A low point of view combines a foreshortened view of the model with a perspective plane of the studio ceiling in Color Plate V. A higher viewpoint, represented in Figure 7-21, allows the model stand to become a foreground plane, like a thrust stage supporting the model, who with her back to the viewer faces the artists.

Figure 7-20. Henri Matisse, *Reflection in the Mirror.* Charcoal on paper. 51 × 40 cm. New York, Metropolitan Museum of Art. Robert Lehman Collection, 1975.

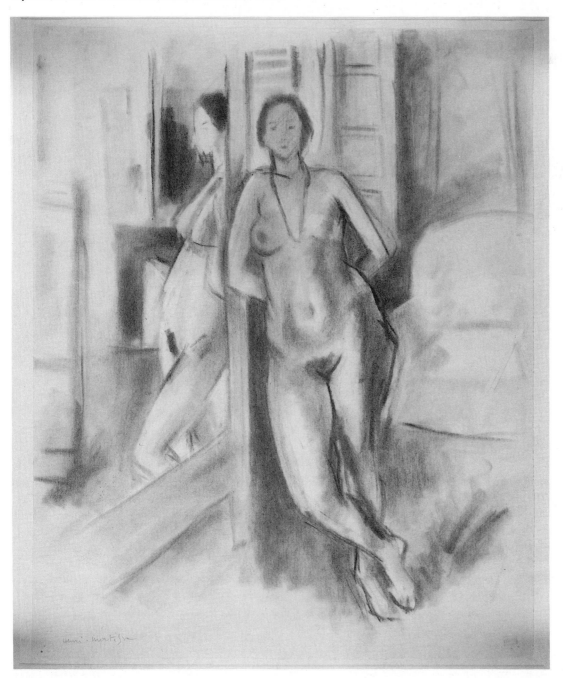

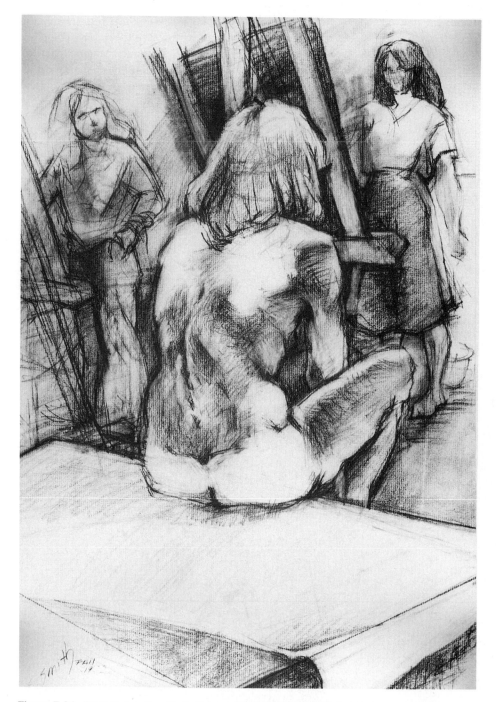

Figure 7-21. Student drawing. Studio Scene with Model. 25 × 19″. Conté crayon on white laid paper.

It is instructive to examine how the French artist Jean-Louis Forain (1852–1931) used simple geometric forms to structure his drawing *Studio Scene with Artist and Model* (Figure 7-22). A ruled line marks the vertical division of the studio walls above the reclining figure. The vertical division coincides with the projecting corner of a model stand turned isometrically toward the viewer. The rectangle of the canvas, also reinforced with ruled lines, echoes the plane of the opposite wall and frames the figure of the artist. The geometric severity of the setting is a dramatic foil for the exuberant contour drawing of the figures, heightened by washes. A similar, albeit more extreme, formal dichotomy is apparent in James Valerio's drawing of the studio (Figure 7-23). In this large pencil drawing virtually all tonal modeling is restricted to the figures. Everything else in this wide-angle view, including the centrally placed model stand, is described with the architect's ruled line, a deliberate contrast in this inventive photo-based work.

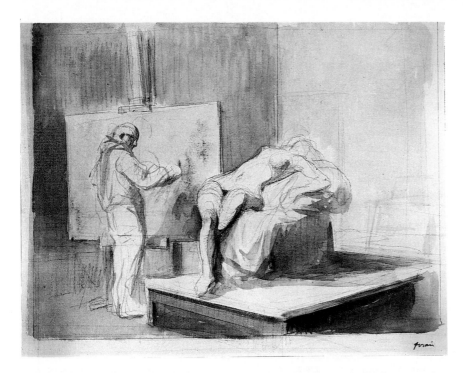

Figure 7-22. Jean-Louis Forain (1852–1931), *Studio Scene with Artist and Model.* Black chalk and wash. 12½ × 16½″ (32 × 42 cm). London, Courtauld Institute of Art.

Figure 7-23. James Valerio (b. 1938), *Studio Figures* (full-scale study), 1982. Pencil on paper. 89 × 96″. Courtesy Frumkin/Adams Gallery, New York (photo by eeva-inkeri).

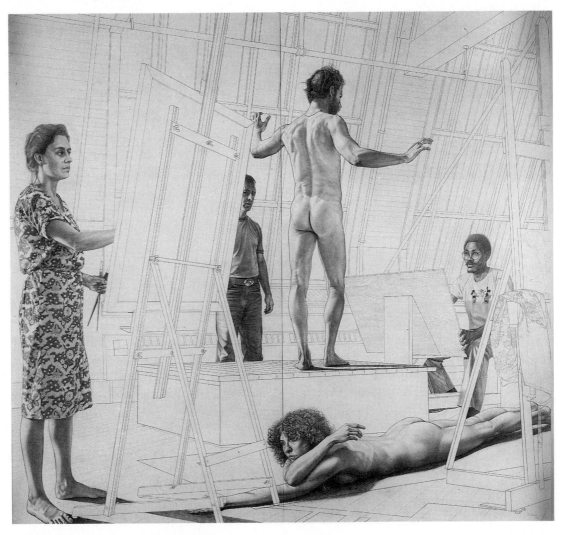

PHOTOGRAPHY AS AN AID TO THE ARTIST

For the artist to use photographs in place of direct observation has been a subject of fierce debate since the photographic process was invented in 1824. The debate involves more than one issue. The question of using photographs as an aid to the draftsman is quite different from that of using photographs in drawing instruction. For the inexperienced art student to work from photographs is, as one author observed, analogous to a language student reading a translation instead of the original text.[8] In fact, photographs have not proven to be of help in drawing instruction. Without training in life drawing, little is to be gained by trying to draw from the photograph. Yet experienced students of life drawing have little or no difficulty drawing from the photographic image; they are able to recognize the photograph for what it is: an objectified version of the optical image. Having dealt with the problem of objectifying the optical image directly as part of the drawing process, the advanced student knows what to look for in the photographic image and has the technical means to interpret it as a drawing. It is in this way that photography has been employed by artists almost since its invention.[9]

An early advocate of the photograph was the French artist Eugène Delacroix (1798–1863). He was convinced that, "if some genius were to use daguerreotype [photograph] as it should be used he could reach untold heights."[10] Delacroix himself executed a number of drawings using photographs he arranged to have taken of the nude model. Comparing the photographs with the resulting drawings is revealing, for it is clear the artist did not copy them. Instead he drew from them freely with contour hatch modeling (Figures 7-24 and 7-25). His interpretation of the photographs imparts a sense of sculptural volume only faintly discernible in the source. The fact that the artist actually saw the models holding the poses pictured in the photographs may account in part for the greater volumetric aspect of the drawing.[11] In this sense the photographs were an aid to his visual memory, and in drawing he probably used both. Above all Delacroix's photo-based drawings demonstrate his artistic independence from the tyranny of the photographic effect.

While there is nothing intrinsically wrong with emulating the photographic effect in a drawing, it is well to be aware of other approaches. Before attempting to use photographs for a more ambitious project, you may profit from Delacroix's example by sketching from photographs *you have taken.*[12]

Figure 7-24. Eugène Delacroix (1798–1863), *Studies*, 1855. Pencil. 7¼ × 8⅜″. Amherst, Massachusetts, Private collection.

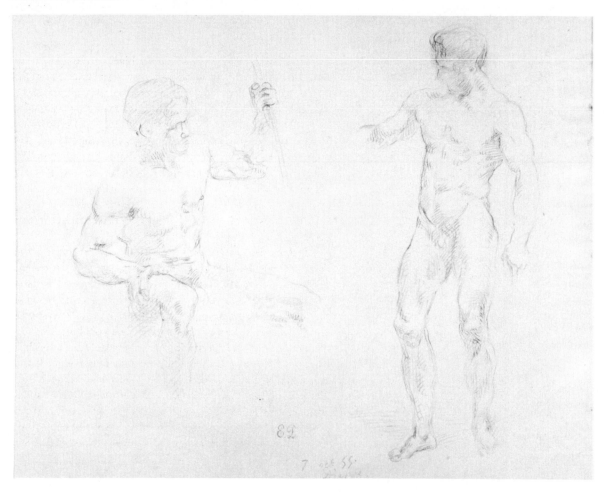

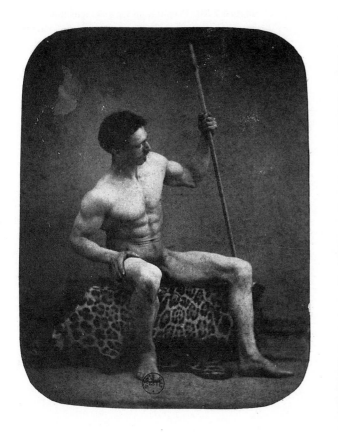

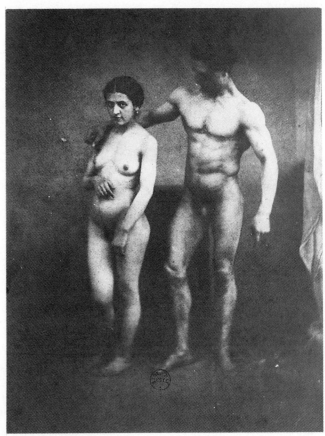

Figure 7-25. Eugène Durieu, *Nude Man and Nude Man and Woman*, c. 1854. Pair of photographs. Paris, Bibliothèque Nationale.

Rather than aiming for the tonal effects of the photograph, first make a conscious effort to translate the photographic image into the language of drawing. (One way to translate the photograph into drawing is to apply the visual measurement method described in Study 9.) The independence you may gain will be of benefit later when exploring the brilliant reflections and seamless tones peculiar to the photograph.

STUDY 52:	The Compositional Drawing and the Photograph

materials: ❏ 25 × 19″ charcoal paper with laid surface or 35 × 24″ Museumboard 2-ply, 100 percent rag
❏ graphite drawing pencils, HB, 2B, or drawing crayon
❏ kneaded rubber eraser
❏ Masonite or plywood board and clamps
❏ fixative spray
❏ white masking tape
❏ camera and film

reference: ❏ personal observation and photographs, 3 × 5″ or larger

time: ❏ two or three weeks in all

Perhaps you have wished to draw a subject you have seen but you were deterred because the setting was not convenient for drawing or sketching. With such a subject the camera can be uniquely helpful, for you can use it in place of the sketchbook to gather visual information in preparation for a composition. In this way photography can open a wider range of subjects and settings for your drawings. The camera can be especially effective for documenting readily available subjects that are off the beaten track, for example, the parking lot attendant (Figures 7-26 and 7-27), the janitor at work polishing a hallway floor (Figures 7-28 and 7-29), or the common but elusive domestic scene (Figures 7-30 and 7-31).

A major limitation of the camera—and handicap for the artist—is that the photographic image generally represents only a single point of view at an instant in time. To compensate for this limitation it is wise to take a series of photographs showing the subject you have chosen in a variety of views. Together they can provide enough visual information to make a large-scale compositional drawing. The individual photos can be mounted on a page of your drawing book and annotated, as you would preparatory sketches (Figure 7-26). Try combining elements of different photographs in small sketches to determine an optimum composition. The small sketches will also suggest the most suitable format proportion. Once chosen, the format can be scaled up and drafted on

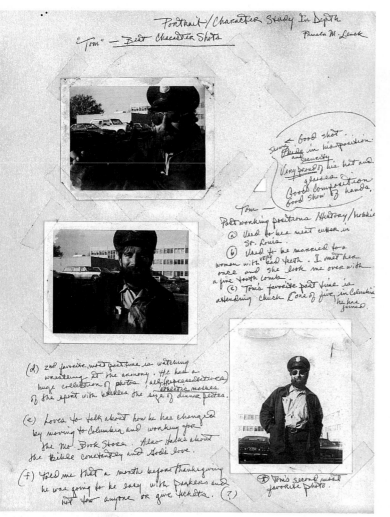

Figure 7-26. Preparation for a compositional drawing

Figure 7-27. Student drawing. The Parking Lot Attendant. Graphite pencil on Museumboard. c. 19 × 25″. Composition based on multiple photographic references.

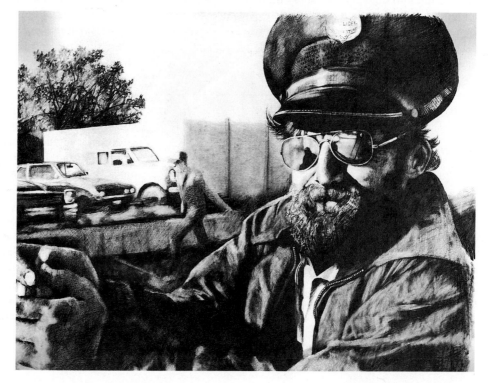

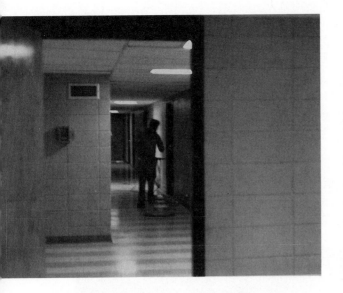

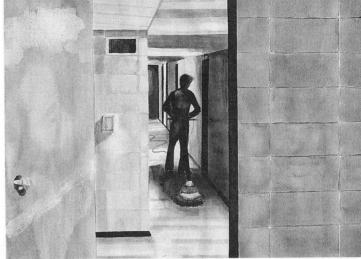

Figure 7-28. Student photograph of a hallway scene.

Figure 7-29. Student drawing. The Janitor. Monochrome wash and graphite pencil. c. 19 × 25″. Composition based on photographs.

Figure 7-30. Robert Bechtle (b. 1932), *Santa Barbara Patio*, 1981. Charcoal pencil on laid paper. 11½ × 12½″. A commonplace domestic scene is made visually memorable by a skillful balancing of formal elements in an asymmetrical composition. The densely textured foreground area is unevenly divided by the white diagonal line of a water hose leading to the figure and a linear array of bent metal garden furniture. The rounded geometry of the furniture overlaps a sharply zigzagging pattern of light and dark creating a bold series of figure-ground reversals.

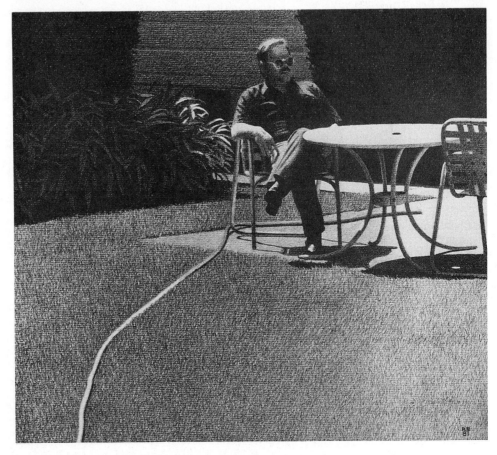

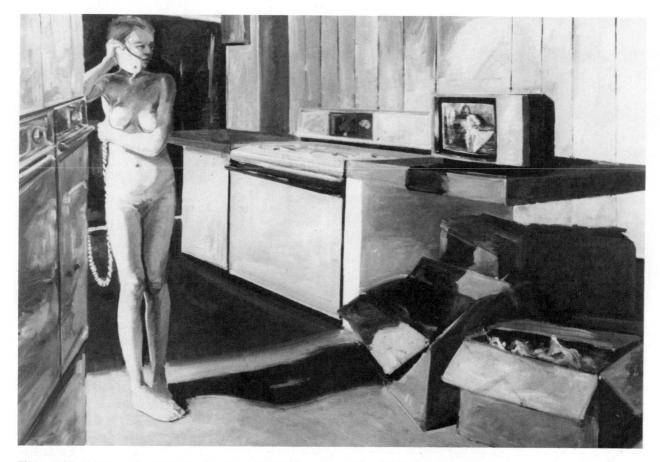

Figure 7-31. Eric Fischl (b. 1947), *The New House*, 1982. Oil on canvas. 68 × 96″. The Smorgon Family Collection of Contemporary American Art. Modern appliances provide the unexpected compositional setting for the nude figure, producing a telling contrast between the natural form of the body with the industrial geometry of machines.

the large drawing paper with pencil and straight edge (Figure 7-32).

If your compositional idea calls for a large area of the image of one photograph, it can be enlarged using the traditional grid technique. The first step is to draft a regular grid on the photograph, and a proportionally larger grid on the drawing paper. The larger grid can be drafted on the drawing paper in pencil to facilitate erasures, unless you wish to retain the grid in the finished drawing. The grid will help you position key elements of the image, but it need not limit you to a particular approach to drawing. That will remain your decision. While nothing precludes your exploring the photographic effect when drawing from photographs, you can employ any approach that best serves your purpose, just as Delacroix did.

DRAWING AS PLANNING

In the previous project photography was discussed as preparation for a drawing. Traditionally, however, drawing has been a means of planning a work to be executed in another medium (see Chapter 8). The preparatory compositional

Figure 7-32. Scaling up a format. A rectangular format here shown in solid line can be enlarged proportionally by extending a diagonal line and drafting vertical and horizontal lines from a selected point on the diagonal.

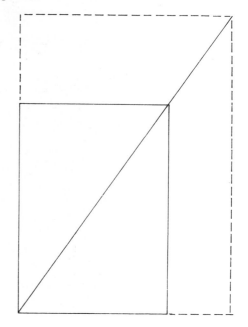

drawing remains important today, especially in projects that are large in scale, costly, and involve public spaces—as is frequently the case for sculptural monuments. The importance of the project drawing is understandable, for it is customarily submitted to the client for final approval.[13] Essentially the project drawing is a composition illustrating the completed sculpture as it would appear in a specific setting, such as a public space before a building.

STUDY 53:   **Planning a Sculpture**
                Based on a Fragment of the Human Form

materials: ❏ sketchbook, 14 × 11″
              ❏ white or tinted laid paper, 25 × 19″ or
                 Museumboard, 2-ply
              ❏ tracing paper
              ❏ drawing crayon, vine charcoal, or HB graphite
                 pencil
              ❏ colored pencils (if called for in project)
              ❏ kneaded rubber eraser
reference: ❏ previously drawn life studies
              ❏ landscape or architectural setting of your choice
time: ❏ 2 weeks in all

Requiring no experience with sculpture, this study calls on you to use your knowledge of the human form to execute a project drawing for a monument in a setting of your choice. Unlike the traditional sculptural monument that represents the whole figure, this monument is to be based on some part of the human form—either the external or skeletal form of the body. In short it is to be a fragment of the figure conceived as a monument.

You may begin by reviewing your drawings of the model, including anatomical studies in the sketchbook. Among these you are likely to discover some drawings that are practically ready-made fragments suitable as concepts for sculpture. Drawing studies of the hand for example can be the basis for a monument (7-33). Studies of anatomy (in Chapters 5 and 6) are another possibility. In addition you may find figure drawings that are suitable when cropped. With these drawings as reference material for sculpture you can turn your attention to selecting an appropriate site for the monument.

For the site you may begin by reflecting on the public spaces and buildings you know. Taking into account the functions of the buildings and spaces may help you decide which site would be best for your sculpture. For a better idea visit the site and make sketches of the setting. Experiment with a variety of viewpoints, using your rapid drawing technique to make thumbnail sketches of compositional ideas. From these you can then make larger rough sketches combining the setting with the proposed monument.

The final project drawing is intended to show your sculpture to best advantage, and several approaches are worth considering. One way might be to emphasize the sculpture by modeling it with tone, while rendering the setting in line (Figure 7-23). It can be equally effective, however, to show how well your sculpture will suit the setting, by drawing both in the same way. Regardless of the approach you choose, the overriding goal is to integrate the proposed sculpture with the setting in a composition.

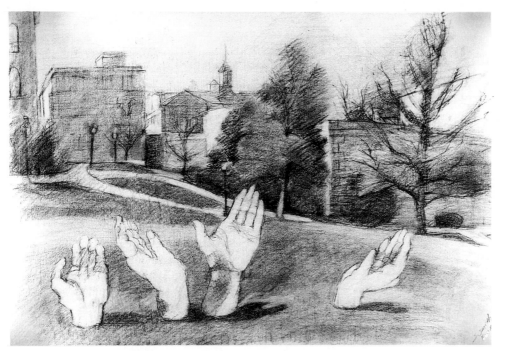

Figure 7-33. Student drawing. Proposed Sculpture and Setting, 19 × 25″. Conté crayon on white laid paper. A sheet of studies of the hand was the reference source for this large-scale sculpture project.

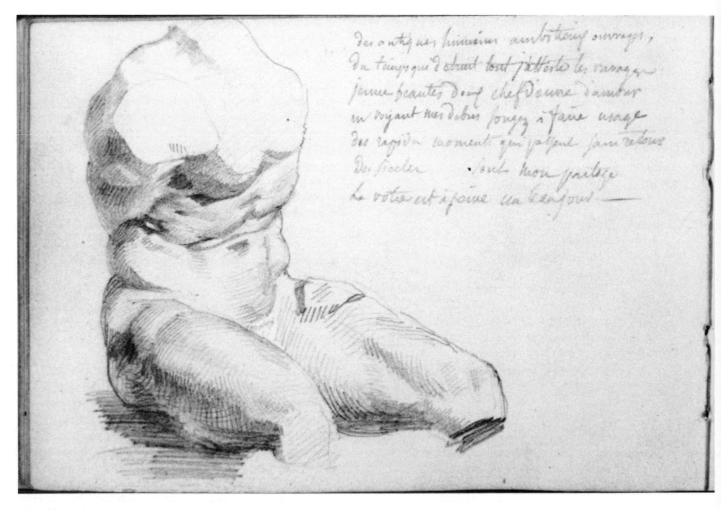

Figure 7-34. Eugène Delacroix, *The Belvedere Torso,* 1817–1821. Graphite pencil. 102 × 145 mm. Paris, the Louvre (photo courtesy of Musée Nationaux, Paris).

Composition in this instance is to be taken quite literally, for it involves putting together the proposed sculpture and the setting you have chosen. A simple way of putting them together is to execute first a drawing of the setting on a full sheet of rag paper (charcoal or Museumboard). Then prepare a separate drawing of the monument on tracing paper in the same scale as the setting. By placing the tracing paper over the drawing of the setting you will be able to discover the most suitable position for the monument. The area to be occupied by the monument can then be erased, and the monument drawn on the rag paper (Figure 7-33). Once the two drawings are combined it will be evident if any final adjustments of line or tone are needed to completely integrate the sculpture project with its setting.

If you wish to pursue further the concept of the figure fragment, you will enjoy sketching in an art museum with a collection of ancient sculpture, for ancient sculpture has survived largely in fragmentary form. Some of the finest frag-ments of ancient sculpture have stimulated the imagination and poetic sensibility of sculptors and painters alike (Figures 7-34 and 7-35).

SUMMARY

Composition, as practiced in the studio, has much in common with design. It is above all the planning of abstract relationships of shapes and structures in a drawing. The studies and exercises presented in this chapter, while emphasizing composition, are also examples of directions that can develop from your earlier studies of the basic drawing methods. Ultimately it is for you to decide the direction of your work as an artist. As you gain experience and your chosen field of drawing unfolds, your artistic compass may point in a new direction eventually. As a consequence, studies that previously held little interest may become more rewarding, and you may wish to return to them again.

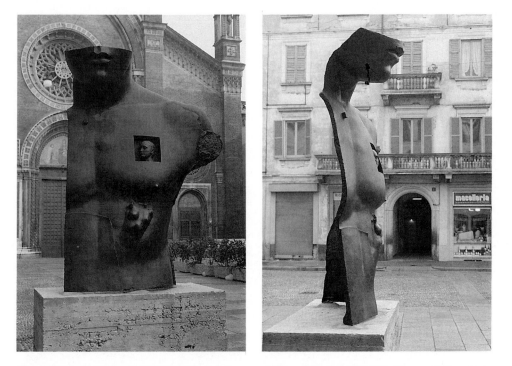

Figure 7-35. Igor Mitoraj (b. 1944), *Grande Toscano* (side and front view), 1981. Bronze. 292 cm high. Milan.

NOTES

1. Victor Hugo expressed a similar belief when he declared that, "Beauty in art is its immunity to improvement. Art as such does not by itself advance or regress. . . . Art is not capable of intrinsic progress. Retrogress as far as you please, from the palace of Versailles to the castle of Heidelberg; from the castle of Heidelberg to Notre-Dame de Paris; from there to the Alhambra; from the Alhambra to St. Sophia; from it to the Colosseum; from the Colosseum to the Acropolis, and from there to the Pyramids; you may go backward in centuries, but you will never regress in art. Art does not depend on any betterment of the future. . . ." Quoted in *Landowska on Music*, edited by Denise Restout, assisted by Robert Hawkins (New York: Stein and Day, 1964) p. 40.

2. Molière, *Le Bourgeois Gentilhomme* (1670), Act II, Scene iv.

3. Here "color" refers specifically to *local color*, the basic color of an object without the hue and value changes that often accompany shadows.

4. Emile Bernard, "Souvenir sur Paul Cézanne; une conversation avec Cézanne; la méthod de Cézanne (Paris, 1925, p. 37). Translation Joseph J. Rischel, *Masterpieces of Impressionism and Post Impressionism, the Annenberg Collection* (New York: Abrams, 1989).

5. Like life studies today the academic drawings of the nineteenth century "are not preparatory studies for one painting or another, but are generally finished works; they are above all student exercises, working drawings." Pierre Rosenberg, Foreword, James Rubin, *Eighteenth-Century French Life-Drawing* (Princeton, N.J.: Princeton University Press, 1977), p. 11.

6. It is a sad commentary on the Victorian attitudes of nineteenth-century America that Eakins found it necessary to cut his drawings of the nude into small pieces in order to hide them from customs officials when he reentered the United States. Such drawings were routinely confiscated and destroyed during inspection. The lower portion of the original drawing shown in Figure 7-6 was lost; the remainder consists of two reassembled pieces.

7. The sculptural aspect of *The Male Figure* recalls the bronze statue of *The Serf*, which Matisse executed at about the same time (1900–1903). The squared-off base of the bronze may be a reduced version of the model stand.

8. M. A. Dwight, *Introduction to the Study of Art*, 1856, as quoted by Van Deren Coke, *The Painter and the Photograph*, (Albuquerque: University of New Mexico Press, 1972), p. 11.

9. In the seventeenth and eighteenth centuries artists availed themselves of the optical image by means of the *camera obscura*, a device that focuses the image on a translucent screen, somewhat like a reflex view camera today. The *camera obscura* could not record the image, however, and was therefore of use only as an aid in the presence of the subject being observed.

10. Lorenz Eitner, *Neoclassicism and Romanticism 1750–1850 Sources and Documents*, vol. 2 (Englewood Cliffs, N.J.: Prentice-Hall, 1970), p. 118.

11. Van Deren Coke, *The Painter and the Photograph*, p. 9.

12. Photographs you have taken record what you have seen, and they have the advantage of reinforcing your visual memory, affording more latitude for interpretation. Although illustrators must often resort to using photographs of subjects they have not seen, this practice is not recommended. If you are obliged to use someone else's photographs, be sure to acknowledge your source.

13. A number of early Renaissance drawings for sculpture or painting projects have survived. Known as contract drawings, they were "often the basis of a legal contract of commission." Unlike the preparatory drawings, the contract drawing "had to be on a durable surface like paper or parchment." Francis Ames-Lewis, *Drawing in Early Renaissance Italy* (New Haven: Yale University Press, 1981), p. 7.

CHAPTER 8

Drawing as Preparation

the development
of visual concepts

*[T]he true goal to attain is to discover amongst the mass of
works produced in a given period those which contain principles
of expression capable of furnishing men with the means of
expressing and understanding themselves.*

—Pierre Francastel

Although drawing is now considered as a distinct form of visual expression embodying characteristic principles and methods, it can be misleading to study it as an isolated discipline. The historical role of drawing before the modern period was to assist in the creation of works in more permanent media. Few drawings, even in Renaissance times, were intended for public viewing: The overwhelming majority were thought of as personal artifacts, by-products of the creative process. This attitude may account for the extraordinarily free, uninhibited quality of many master drawings and for their undisguised revisions and changes, made as the visual idea developed. Like working drafts of poems, with rewritten phrases and deleted mistakes, preparatory drawings can provide insights into creative processes that are sometimes masked in a finished work of art. Moreover, a comparison of preparatory drawings with their respective finished works may offer some insight into the nature of drawing itself.[1] Such comparisons should ideally be made with original art rather than reproductions, but this is often difficult if not impossible. In some cases the original drawings, if they have survived, are now separated geographically from the finished works. In many cases, however, the preparatory drawings of masterworks are simply missing. The reasons for this situation are themselves related to the traditional use of drawing as a means of preparation.

Before paper became readily available, drawings were generally made directly on the surfaces to be painted or carved.[2] Preparatory drawings from ancient times are rare, as they were usually destroyed or obliterated in the process of making the finished work.[3] Fortunately, a few unfinished works have survived. An example of ancient Egyptian drawing preserved on an unfinished portion of a stone relief from Amarna (Figure 8-1) provides a tantalizing glimpse of figure drawing as it was practiced at the time of Akhenaten. The drawn portion of the figure consists of a linear construction, drawn in large swinging arcs deftly executed with calligraphic thick-and-thin stress. This technique is apparent in the raised forearm of the figure, in which an arc continues beyond the form of the elbow into the surrounding negative space, suggesting a free, sophisticated drawing method. The function of the Amarna drawing may be inferred by examining the way in which the artist translated its painted lines into stone relief carving. The elegant calligraphic swells and thins of the brushstrokes reappear as linear shadows in the carved lower portion of the figure, the result of the Egyptian technique of sunken-relief carving. In the carved portion of this work the ground surrounding the figure remains raised and uncarved, while the silhouette of the figure is deeply incised, capable of creating cast shadow around the edges. Within the silhouette of the figure, however, the contour lines form the basis for a delicate

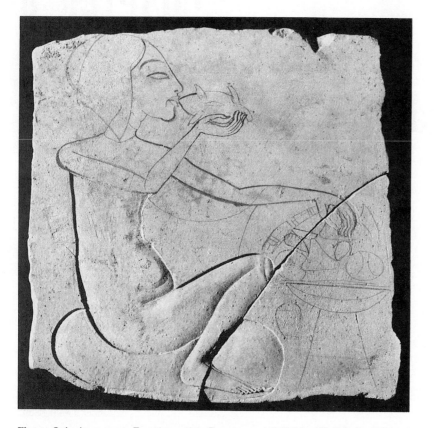

Figure 8-1. Anonymous Egyptian artist, *Drawing and Unfinished Relief of a Princess,* c. 1365 B.C. Amarna, North Palace, late Eighteenth Dynasty. Limestone with drawing lines in black pigment. 23.5 cm high. Cairo Museum.

low-relief carving, the subtle shadows of which, as in the abdominal area, suggest tonal modeling. It is not known why the sculptor left this work unfinished, nor is it known whether its unfinished aspect had any special aesthetic value to the ancient Egyptians. There is evidence, however, that certain unfinished paintings by important Greek masters were admired, sometimes more than finished works, because the preliminary drawing—still visible in the unfinished work—was appreciated (see Note 8, Chapter 3).

Like the ancient sculptor, the ancient painter usually destroyed the preparatory drawing in the course of completing the finished work of art. In medieval times the painter of panels and walls followed much the same procedure, covering the preparatory drawing as the work progressed.[4] Thanks to recent advances in conservation techniques, some preliminary drawings (*sinopie*) done by medieval and Renaissance painters as preparation for wall paintings in fresco are available to modern students (Figures 8-2 and 8-3). For the medieval and early Renaissance artist, however, such drawings were generally seen only during the creative process, a fact that must have been a serious impediment to the study of drawing. At that time, of course, drawing had no special value as an independent art form. Only when drawings became physically separate entities, divorced from the finished product, could

drawing be considered as a distinct artistic discipline. This separation was possible in medieval times—some draftsmen used parchment and vellum to preserve their drawings (Figure 1-3)—but the prohibitive cost severely restricted their use.

Not until paper became relatively inexpensive in the fifteenth century was it possible for many Western artists to work out their ideas freely on a separate surface, thereby preserving their drawings. The liberation of drawing from the final artwork tended to give artists more opportunities to experiment with different ideas before deciding on which one to execute in the more expensive materials. Paper thus gave drawing an experimental, intellectual character that it has retained to the present day.[5]

If a finished painting is seen side by side with a preparatory drawing (or drawings), as in the case of Jan Van Eyck's study and painting *Portrait of Cardinal Nicolò Albergati* (Figures 8-4 and 8-5), the drawing may sometimes seem more appealing to modern sensibilities. Compared with the drawing, the painting, though far more "finished," may appear relatively dull. Art historians believe that the drawing only was done from life. The cardinal was apparently unable to sit for the painting, for the drawing contains detailed notations on the colors to be used in the painted version. With the painting, consequently, ". . . we feel the strain of working from a draw-

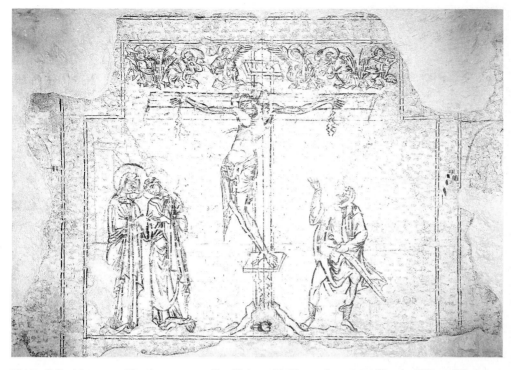

Figure 8-2. Anonymous Pistoiese master, *Crucifixion*, mid-thirteenth century. Sinopia. 315 × 452 cm. Pistoia, Church of San Domenico (photo courtesy of il Gabinetto Fotografico-Soprintendenza alle Gallerie, Firenze).

Figure 8-3. Anonymous Pistoiese master, *Crucifixion*, mid-thirteenth century. Fresco. 315 × 452 cm. Pistoia, Church of San Domenico (photo courtesy of il Gabinetto Fotografico-Soprintendenza alle Gallerie, Firenze).

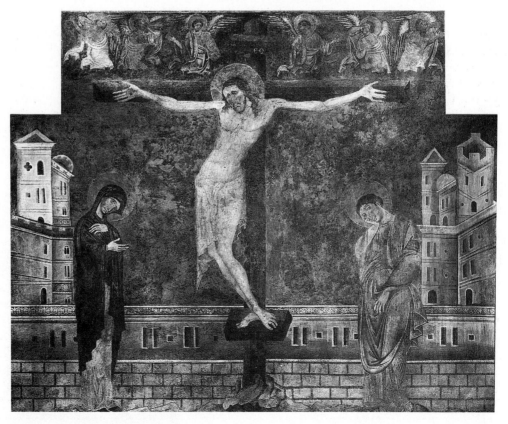

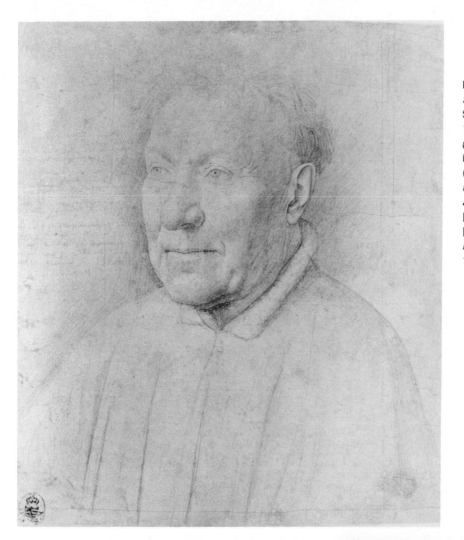

Figure 8-4. Jan Van Eyck (c. 1390–1441). *Study for* Portrait of Cardinal Nicolò Albergati. Silverpoint on grayish-white ground. 250 × 180 mm. Dresden, Staaliche Kunstsammlungen. Faintly visible on the left side of the drawing are the artist's color notes for the painting (Figure 8-5): "*Geelachitig und witte blauwachtig* [yellowish- and bluish-white]; *rotte purpurachtig* [red-purple]; *die lippen seer wittachtig* [the lips very whitish]; *die nase sanguy nachtig* [the nose suffused with blood]" (Philip Rawson, *Drawing* [London: Oxford University Press, 1969], p. 113).

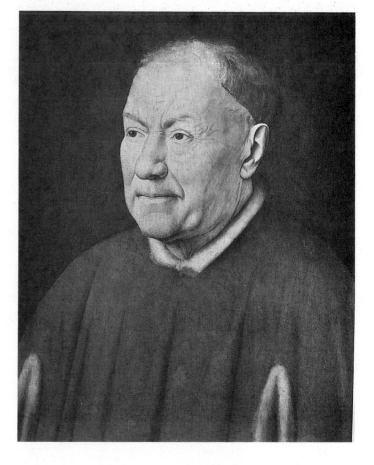

Figure 8-5. Jan Van Eyck, *Portrait of Cardinal Nicolò Albergati*. Panel painting. 13⅜ × 10¾″. Vienna, Kunsthistorisches Museum.

ing without an opportunity to refer back to the living model. . . . The result, meant to recapture a reality no longer accessible to the artist, lacks the complete integration of details to which we are accustomed in the works of Jan Van Eyck. . . ."[6] The painting, though more developed in its smaller forms, lacks the fully rounded effect of shadow modeling that is so vivid in the silverpoint drawing.

Van Eyck's use of modeling in a silverpoint drawing can be compared with that of another master, Leonardo da Vinci (Figure 8-6). Although Van Eyck's study for the *Portrait of Cardinal Nicolò Albergati* and Leonardo's *Study of the Head of a Young Girl* both utilize shadow modeling, the direction and thus the function of the hatched line are quite different. Van Eyck's hatch lines, though somewhat smoothed out, seem to follow the surfaces of the volumes observed; in Leonardo's study the orientation of the hatching is unrelated to the form of the head. The direction of the hatch marks is instead parallel to the light that appears to stream over the surface of the head from the left, modeling it in shadow patterns. The extraordinary luminosity of the drawing is due in part to a micro-ground reversal that occurs in areas where the thick sil-

verpoint lines are seen as "ground" transversed by white "lines" that are actually unmarked spaces. This purely graphic effect, a visual metaphor for light rays, enhances the volumes implied in the contour framework of the drawing and at the same time subtly shifts the focus of the drawing from the observed form to the effect of light striking the form, a shift that prophesies the future direction of European painting.

Van Eyck and Leonardo were both concerned with directional light, yet Leonardo's drawing seems less pictorial in quality. Van Eyck integrated the tones on both sides of the head with the ground, thus defining the illuminated side of the form by its contrast with the drawn tone of the ground. Likewise he carefully modeled the dark side of the head so that it merges with the values of the ground, transferring the emphasis from the linear edge to the modeled volume of the form. Leonardo, on the other hand, effectively limited his modeling to the dark side of the head, permitting contour line to define the entire illuminated side. The resulting effect is almost musical: The contour construction of the illuminated side functions as a melodic line against the tonal harmony of shadow modeling. Near the definitive contours on

Figure 8-6. Leonardo da Vinci, *Study of the Head of a Young Girl*, c. 1480. Silverpoint on a ground prepared with bister (brown pigment). 18.2 × 15.9 cm. Turin, Biblioteca Reale.

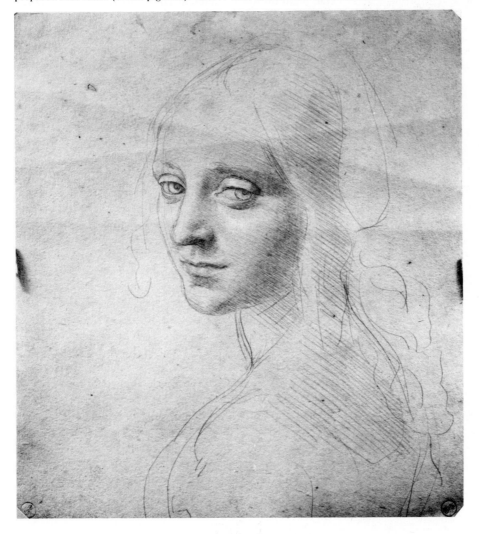

the left are two fainter, more tentative lines that were almost certainly drawn very early as Leonardo developed the general form of the head in line.

The purpose of Leonardo's study was to create a type of head suitable for the angel figure in the painting *The Virgin of the Rocks* (Figure 8-7). Kenneth Clark comments, "The drawing—one of the most beautiful . . . in the world—aims at the fullest plastic statement. The painting is sweeter, lighter, more unearthly. This is still idealization in the Gothic sense."[7] Such a critical assessment suggests that the painting is more conservative in treatment and more in accordance with the taste and standards of Leonardo's time than the drawing. Leonardo, perhaps assuming that the preparatory drawing would not be exhibited, drew with greater personal freedom of approach than he dared to apply in the commissioned work, subject as it was to the approval of a patron.[8]

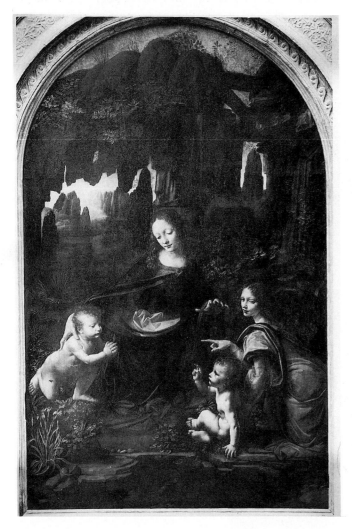

Figure 8-7. Leonardo da Vinci, *The Virgin of the Rocks*, c. 1485. Panel painting (later transferred to canvas). 75 × 43½". Paris, the Louvre.

The delicate but firm line quality seen in the Leonardo and Van Eyck drawings is characteristic of *silverpoint*, a popular drawing medium in the Renaissance. If you wish to try silverpoint, the materials, though less frequently used by modern artists, are still available in art supply stores. You need to purchase the silver wire, which produces the mark, and a stylus to hold the wire firm.[9] Silverpoint requires a specially treated surface, which can be prepared at home or purchased in the form of clay-coated papers. A thin coat of artist's gesso (either zinc or titanium white) over a smooth-surfaced paper or fiberboard panel is sufficient. In the Renaissance ground animal bones were sometimes used for this purpose.[10] The mark that silverpoint leaves on the ground may seem disappointingly faint at first, but with time it grows dark as it chemically combines with sulfur in the air to become silver sulfide, a substance that has the dark color commonly seen on unpolished silverware.[11]

Some Renaissance drawing media are the historical predecessors of modern manufactured media. Silverpoint, for example, is the ancestor of the graphite pencil, a medium that later became more popular than silver partly because it requires no special ground.[12] Similarly, the predecessors of today's drawing crayons were sticks cut from natural chalk alone without the addition of any binding material. Different minerals were mined for different colors of chalk: carbonaceous shale for black, calcite for white, and hematite for red. Natural chalk is not generally commercially available today, nor is it popular because of its inconsistent, unpredictable quality. In the nineteenth century manufacturers such as Conté in France produced crayons that in many ways surpassed natural chalk as a drawing medium. Natural chalk tends to be rather hard and is therefore not suited to large-scale drawings. Michelangelo, as Watrous points out, seems to have been aware of this limitation, for his *Studies for* The Libyan Sibyl (Figure 8-8) measures only 8⅜ by 11⅜ inches, despite the monumental size of the fresco for which it was intended (Figure 8-9).

The Michelangelo study for the Sistine ceiling is in fact not one but several drawings of the same subject on the same sheet.[13] The various drawings appear to be placed somewhat randomly: No attempt was made to organize them into a unified pictorial composition. The drawings were realized in a variety of techniques. In the combination of relief and shadow modeling used for the principal male figure as well as in the contour drawing of the torso and shoulder of the secondary figure, Michelangelo reveals his profound knowledge of anatomical form.[14] Form in this drawing is characteristically sculptural in quality. Like a statue, the figure is conceived as positive form surrounded by empty space. Notably lacking is any attempt to relate the figure tonally with the ground, as in the more pictorial study for the *Portrait of Cardinal Nicolò Albergatti* (Figure 8-4) by Van Eyck. The sculptural aspect of the Michelangelo drawing is not surprising, since the artist considered himself a sculptor rather than difference, however, may be more apparent than real: If the drawing is tilted slightly to the left, the figure appears to be inclined at the same angle as the fresco figure. A more significant change between drawing and painting is found in the gesture of the left arm: Greater foreshortening occurs in the forearm of the painted figure. The difficult foreshortened drawing of the hand, deftly realized in the studies, appears somewhat awkward in the fresco, while the drawn foot, developed in several studies, was more closely followed in the fresco.

The art of Michelangelo exercised an almost irresistible influence on younger artists of the time, particularly on Roman and Florentine painters who worked between 1520 and 1600. Prominent among those younger artists was Jacopo da Pontormo (1494–1556), a painter who was active in Florence. Like Michelangelo who inspired him, Pontormo was a brilliant draftsman who used drawing not only to visualize a compositional idea, as in his studies for the *Santa Felicità Altarpiece* (Figure 8-10 and 8-11), but also to render forms from life as a means of fleshing out an abstract concept. The subject of the altarpiece (Figure 8-12), long thought to represent the deposition from the cross, is now believed to be a scene of mourning derived from Michelangelo's celebrated *Pietà* in the

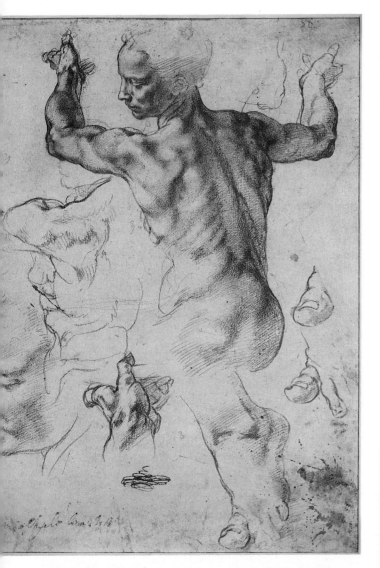

Figure 8-8. Michelangelo, *Studies for* The Libyan Sibyl [paper restored on the right side], c. 1511. Natural red chalk. 8⅜ × 11⅜″. New York, Metropolitan Museum of Art. Pulitzer Bequest.

a painter. Moreover, the fact that the finished painted figure, for which this drawing was a preparation, was intended to be set in a painted architectural framework, creating the illusion of a three-dimensional niche commonly used to hold sculpture, accounts for the sculptural appearance of the drawing.

Although both the drawing and the finished painting share sculptural qualities, a number of transformations take place between the two, the most notable of which is the change of sex. The male model in the drawing becomes a female prophetess in the painting. This change, partly explained by a difficulty in obtaining female models, was effectuated by concealing much of the figure in voluminous draperies and by generalizing or softening the undraped anatomical forms. Another change in the fresco figure as compared to the drawing is thought to lie in its greater degree of diagonal thrust. This

Figure 8-9. Michelangelo, *The Libyan Sibyl*, 1511–1512. Fresco, Rome, Sistine Chapel ceiling.

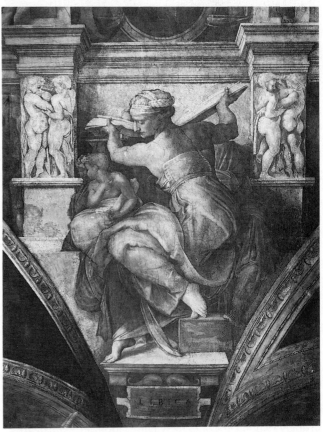

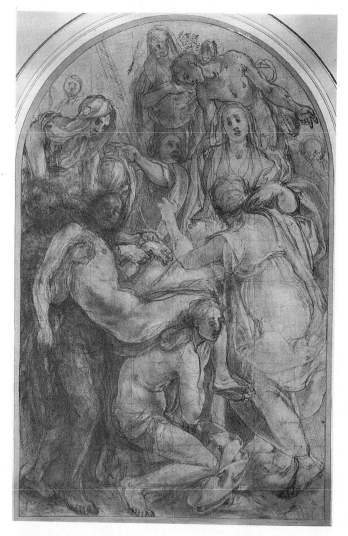

Figure 8-10. Jacopo de Pontormo, *Study for the* Santa Felicità Altarpiece, 1525–1528. Black, chalk, heightened with white and touches of bister wash, squared in red chalk. Top two figures redone in pen. 445 × 276 mm. Oxford, Christ Church.

Vatican.[15] If this analysis is correct, as seems likely, Pontormo's altarpiece and associated studies provide an interesting example of a work of sculpture by one artist inspiring a painting on a similar theme by another. Adapting a three-dimensional (i.e., sculptural) idiom to a two-dimensional work is itself a difficult problem, and Pontormo's drawings, as compared to the painting, reveal his search for a solution. The smaller life study for the altarpiece (Figure 8-11) records the artist's search for a body gesture that would be compatible with his composition as seen in the larger study. Pontormo apparently discovered in the sagging gesture of the model the large rhythmic arc formed by the back, a motif that he further developed in the painting by means of the more overtly abstract, swooping forms of drapery. The graceful arcs of the cloth, so vital to the painting's complex composition, are strongly reminiscent of drapery conventions in Roman art.[16]

The composition of Pontormo's Oxford study (Figure 8-10) generally corresponds with that of the finished painting (Figure 8-12), although a few passages, such as the supporting figure on the left, are far more developed in the latter. The fact that the large study is inscribed with a grid pattern in red chalk suggests it immediately preceded the execution of the painting, as the squaring technique was often used by Renaissance artists to simplify the task of enlarging a small drawing to fit a large surface. (In order to double the size of a drawn composition, for example, it can be copied on a grid pattern twice as large with very little distortion.) In both the drawings and the painting, linear constructs dominate. The purest con-

Figure 8-11. Jacopo da Pontormo, *Study for the* Santa Felicità Altarpiece, 1525–1528. Natural red chalk. 287 × 201 mm. Florence, Galleria degli Uffizi.

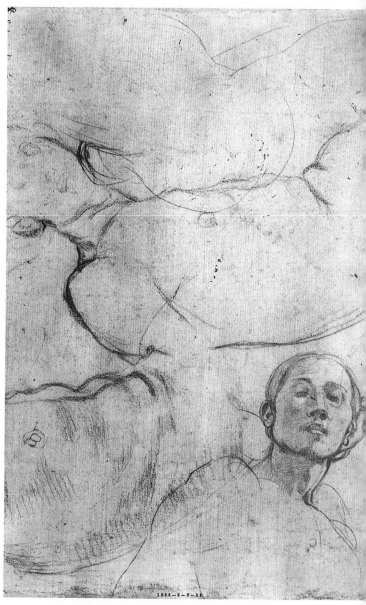

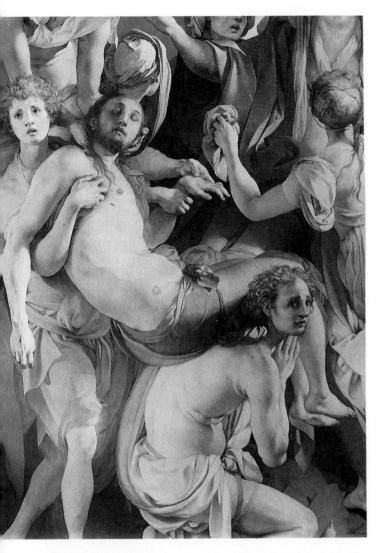

Figure 8-12. Jacopo da Pontormo, *Santa Felicità Altarpiece* (detail), 1525–1528. Panel painting. 123⅜ × 75⅝″. Florence, Santa Felicità, Capponi Chapel.

structured version of the head seen in the altarpiece— changes, however, that further remove the painting from the realism of the life drawing. The shift from realistic draftsmanship in the drawing to the more abstract structure of the painting reflects the overriding concern with stylistic refinement that is so characteristic of mannerism. Using certain features of Michelangelo's art as a creative point of departure—in particular his predilection for small-headed figures and tightly packed figural groupings in relief-like compositions—Pontormo's style moved in the direction of greater elegance and elongation of form.

The art of Peter Paul Rubens (1577–1649), the Flemish painter, exhibits a creative extension of other aspects of Michelangelo's art, such as its dynamic movement and virtuosity of draftsmanship. A study by the young Rubens of Michelangelo's *The Libyan Sibyl* (Figure 8-13), though it follows the original closely, reveals characteristics distinctive of Rubens's later work, notably a skillful use of convex-contour construc-

Figure 8-13. Peter Paul Rubens, *Study after* The Libyan Sibyl *of Michelangelo,* c. 1601. Natural red crayon. Paris, the Louvre.

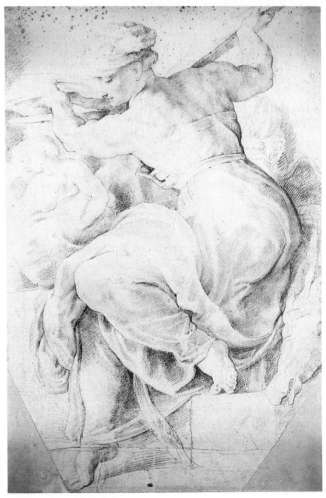

tour technique is found in the sketch of the pelvic region of the figure located in the upper portion of the Uffizi study (Figure 8-11). Below it are drawings that exhibit degrees of shadow modeling, culminating in the highly developed study of the head at the lower right. Even here, however, considerations of line override those of modeling: The drawn line remains clear even in the darkest passages. Likewise, the modeling of light and dark *chiaroscuro* never entirely obscures the essentially linear construction of the painting.

There is an appreciable difference between the drawing of the head (Figure 8-11) and the painted version. In the drawing the head lacks a consistent sense of symmetry: The base of the nose shifts too far to the right to conform to the symmetrical placement of the eyes. It is likely that Pontormo was aware of the discrepancy, for in the Oxford study (Figure 8-10) he made the changes necessary to realize the flawlessly

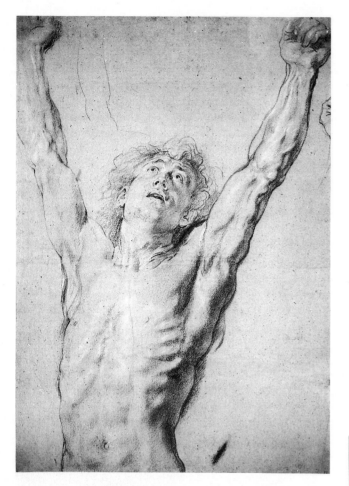

Figure 8-14. Peter Paul Rubens, *Study for the Figure of Christ,* c. 1610. Black and white chalk, touched with pale brown wash, on coarse gray paper. 528 × 370 mm. London, British Museum.

The date of both drawings coincides with the period during which the artist employed several assistants in his studio to facilitate the completion of many projects at the same time. It is believed that studies such as these were intended in part as guides for his assistants, who did much of the actual painting of *The Elevation of Christ on the Cross.*[17] The drawings may thus reflect Rubens's role as the head of a large studio, which was in effect a school for many artists. The media chosen for the two studies—natural black and white chalks—are softer than the natural red chalk used by Michelangelo for his studies for *The Libyan Sibyl.* Rubens may have preferred them for this very quality, which allows a more fluid effect comparable to that seen in his painting. The softness of the white chalk is most apparent in the British Museum drawing (Figure 8-14), in which its free application in highlighted areas enlivens the more cautiously constructed black chalk drawing.

A preference for softer, more fluid media and effects was not limited to Rubens but reflected a growing tendency that paralleled the stylistic movement in post-Renaissance art away from linearity and toward the more broadly painted effects of light and mass associated with the baroque and ro-

Figure 8-15. Peter Paul Rubens, *Study for the Figure of Christ,* 1609–1610. Black chalk with outlining in charcoal, heightened with white, on buff paper. 15¾ × 11¾″. Cambridge, Fogg Art Museum, Harvard University.

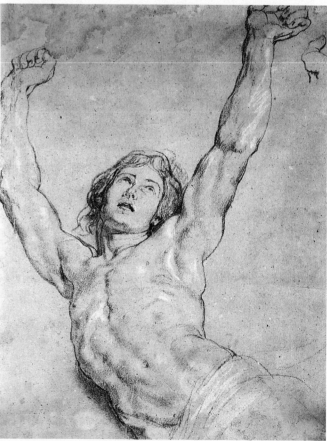

tion of form combined with angular measurement and a painterly tonal relationshp between figure and ground. Both traits can be seen in the superb *Study for the Figure of Christ on the Cross* (Figure 8-14). Like his countryman Van Eyck, Rubens established a logical though understated figure-ground relationship by applying tone outside the figure. Such a passage is noticeable on the dark side of the figure, where suggestions of very dark tone distinguish the figure from the ground and at the same time contribute to the effect of heroic scale. The British Museum study (Figure 8-14) apparently preceded a second drawing of the same subject (Figure 8-15) that is now in the Fogg Art Museum. In the latter drawing Rubens modified his idea of the Christ figure in ways that he later incorporated into the painting (Figure 8-16). The most important difference in the second drawing lies in its use of shadow modeling to suggest illumination from the right side. The second study also appears to resolve the gesture of the figure, changing it from the bolt-upright pose of the original version to the bent torso with upraised arms, a gesture that in the painting seems to be caused by the pull of gravity.

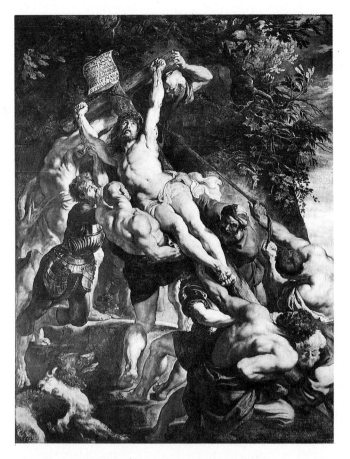

Figure 8-16. Peter Paul Rubens, *The Elevation of the Cross*, c. 1610. Wood-panel painting. 182 × 134″. Antwerp Cathedral.

cocco styles of the seventeenth and eighteenth centuries. The drawings of Goya clearly exemplify this general tendency. Significantly, one of the few Goya drawings known to be related to a painting is done in a liquid medium, sepia wash and brush (Figure 8-17). Created near the end of his long and distinguished career, the drawing *Three Men Digging* (Figure 8-17) and the painting entitled *The Forge* (Figure 8-18) reflect a singular harmony of concept and technique. In *The Forge* undisguised brushstrokes, bold use of black and white, and an unerring sense of gesture result in a graphic quality more commonly found in drawing than in painting. Likewise, the free use of brush and liquid in the drawing gives it the character of an underpainting.

Although the painting and the drawing represent different subjects—the painting is set in a blacksmith's shop, the drawing in the open fields—there is remarkably little difference in composition. Both feature gestures abound in strongly diagonal forms. Figural elements tend to be realized as color masses separated by general changes of tone. Note the lack of tonal modulation in black areas—a feature as prominent in the painting as in the drawing. If we assume the painting was done after the drawing, the most important single change was

the decision to darken the tone of the trousers of the principal figure (holding the hammer in the painting, the hoe in the drawing). This darkened tone, dictated to a certain extent by the darkened ground of the painting, binds the three figures together more tightly than in the drawing, in which the high tonal value of the principal figure visually divides the composition. The darker value of the trousers in the painting also permits a contrast with the red of the hot iron, resulting in a luminous effect that would have been more difficult if the figure's clothing had remained light in tone. By painting the principal figure's shirt white, as in the drawing, Goya focuses attention on his back, dramatizing the region essential to the powerful gesture of the blacksmith.

The precise relationship between Goya's drawing and his painting is a subject of speculation. Some authorities believe the drawing is "an independent composition on a similar theme," even though "directly related" to the painting.[18] It is not unusual for an artist to transpose compositional inventions from one work to another; thus the question is one of sequence. For purposes of discussion we have assumed that the drawing came first, but it is possible it did not. If the latter

Figure 8-17. Francisco de Goya y Lucientes (1746–1828), *Three Men Digging*, c. 1812–1823. Illustration from Album F. 51 (1472). Sepia wash. 20.6 × 14.3 cm. New York, Metropolitan Museum of Art.

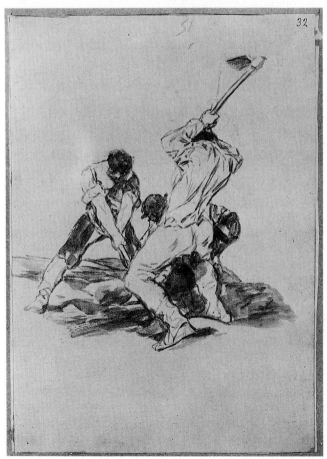

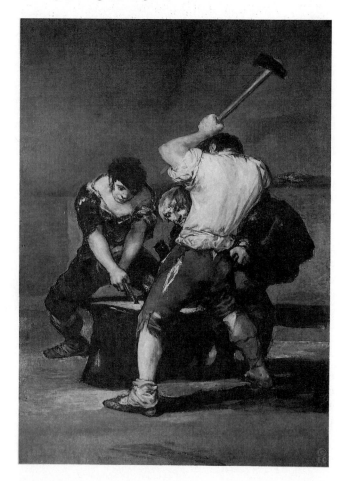

Figure 8-18. Francisco Goya, *The Forge*, c. 1812–1816. Oil painting. 181.6 × 125 cm. Copyright The Frick Collection, New York.

Japanese technique. Like many modern illustrators, Hokusai made the drawing larger than the format of the print in order to give the latter a greater sense of scale. The highly developed finish of the drawing was necessary to provide sufficient clarity to facilitate cutting the blocks; yet light wash lines such as those below the right foot of the female figure show that changes were made even at this stage. Such changes, or ghosts, in drawings and paintings are generally referred to as *pentimenti*. Other differences can be seen in the dress patterns. In order to avoid drawing repetitious patterns, Hokusai merely indicated the areas in which they were to occur and provided the woodblock cutter with a separate pattern.

The flat linearity of the Japanese print, which was destined to receive an enthusiastic acceptance by European artists in the late nineteenth century, was in some ways presaged by a French contemporary of Hokusai—Jean-Auguste-Dominique Ingres (1780–1867). In addition to his acknowledged classical inspiration (discussed in Chapter 3), ". . . the sinuous line and the absence of shadow in Ingres' best work," as Ken-

Figure 8-19. Hokusai, *Preparatory Drawing for a Wood Engraving for the Suikoden Book of 1829*. Brush and ink. 25.3 × 17 cm. London, British Museum.

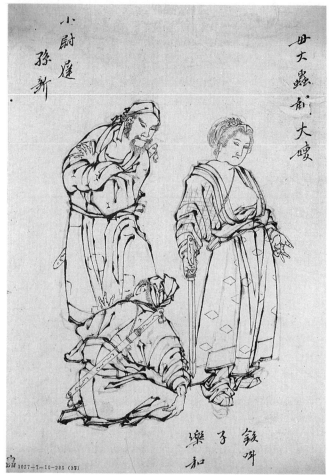

is the case, the painting then unexpectedly becomes the preparatory work for the drawing, and, given the importance of graphic work in Goya's career, he may have seen it in just that way.

The art of Goya and that of the Japanese print were destined to become a primary source of ideas and inspiration for European, particularly French, artists of the late nineteenth century. You have already witnessed one instance of the influence of the Japanese print in Lautrec's poster *May Milton* (Color Plate II). Goya was himself a contemporary of one of the most important exponents of the Japanese print—Katsushika Hokusai (1760–1849). Like Goya, Hokusai was a painter who was also known for his prints. Since it was not customary for the Japanese artist to cut his own blocks, Hokusai prepared a special drawing, like that for the *Suikoden Book* of 1829 (Figure 8-19), representing the image he wished to appear in the final print. Artisans then cut the woodblocks to realize the desired effect. A separate block was usually cut for each color. The extraordinary accuracy of the cutting can be judged by comparing the drawing (Figure 8-19) with the resulting print (Figure 8-20). Those familiar with modern photomechanical printing will recognize a similarity with the neth Clark observes, "has something oriental about it." A critic even accused Ingres of being a "Chinese painter astray in the ruins of Athens."[19] Regardless of your opinion concerning his stylistic sources, Ingres is recognized today as one of the finest draftsmen in art history.[20] Since his portraits rank among his best works, it is of special interest to consider how he utilized drawing in the course of completing a portrait commission such as that of Madame d'Haussonville (Figures 8-21, 8-22, and 8-23). A slow, methodical worker, Ingres required four years and many drawings to complete his *Portrait of Madame d'Haussonville* (Figure 8-23). Almost two dozen related drawings survive. Two such drawings (Figure 8-21 and 8-22), now in the Fogg Art Museum, suffice to give an impression of the artist's method.

Ingres's choice of the newly developed graphite pencil as his drawing instrument was in a sense a return to the metal points of an earlier era. The pencil, like silverpoint, permitted the clarity of line and delicacy of tone essential to his classical approach. In his squared study (Figure 8-21) he primarily em-

Figure 8-20. Hokusai, *Page from the Suikoden Book of 1829.* Wood engraving. 18.5 × 12.5 cm. London, British Museum.

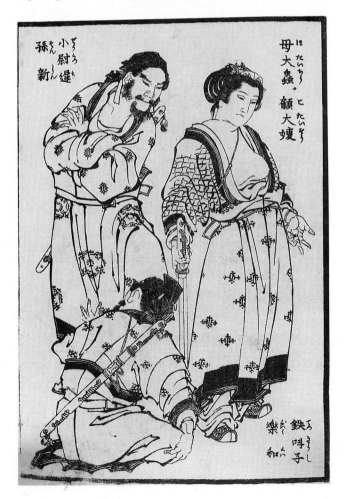

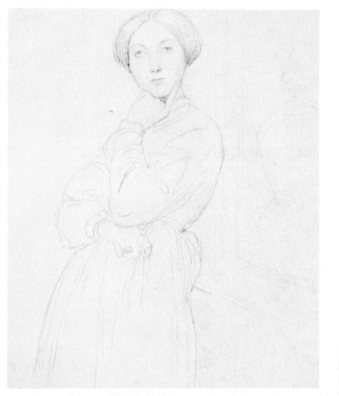

Figure 8-21. Jean-Auguste-Dominique Ingres, *Study for* Portrait of Madame d'Haussonville, c. 1842–1845. Graphite pencil on thin white woven paper, squared for transfer. 9³⁄₁₆ × 7¾". Cambridge, Fogg Art Museum, Harvard University.

ployed a linear technique except in the area of the head, where he subtly introduced tonal modeling. The restriction of modeling to the portrait figure's head, a common technical convention of his pencil portraits, was later taken up by Picasso (Figure 4-110), who admired Ingres's drawings. In another study for the portrait of Madame d'Haussonville (Figure 8-22), Ingres more boldly modeled the folds of the dress in charcoal. The subtle conflict between the linear and tonal modes in Ingres's work, a conflict often apparent in his drawings, is resolved in many of his paintings by means of a special method of modeling. In the *Portrait of Madame d'Haussonville* the sitter appears illuminated from above, near the front, an arrangement that allowed Ingres to model the form in shadow and at the same time to preserve the linear quality of the composition.[21]

The two studies focus on different though related problems associated with the finished painting. In the squared study (Figure 8-21) Ingres experimented with the compositional relationship between the sitter and the mirror. The mirror contains a reflection of almost half of the figure. He abandoned this arrangement in the painting in favor of a more classically frontal orientation, in which the mirror reflects only the head and shoulders—a solution that permitted subtle

In the pencil-and-charcoal study (Figure 8-22) Ingres develops the pose used later in the painting, a pensive attitude that appears in some female figures of classical art.[23] On the figure's right he wrote, "*plus de mouvement*" (more movement), indicating an additional contour of the figure's back. This contour, perhaps more than any other feature of the drawing, reveals Ingres's use of line to solve abstract problems of form in the painting, for the painted contour of the back exhibits a graceful continuation of the curve of the neck much like that seen in the additional contour of the drawing. Another notation on the drawing—"*grand foyer de lumière plus*" (large center of light . . .)[24]—seems to refer to a scarf, a garment discarded in the painting. The folds of the figure's dress evolve from the irregular and somewhat rumpled forms

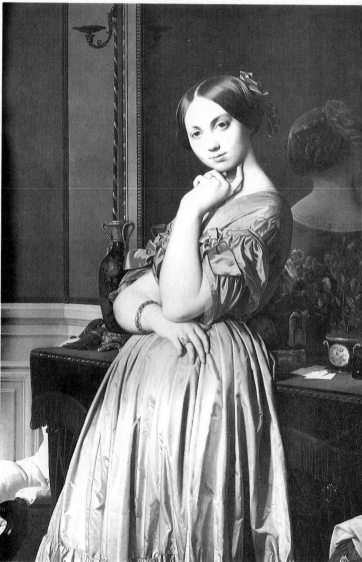

Figure 8-23. Jean-Auguste-Dominique Ingres, *Portrait of Madame d'Haussonville*, 1846. Oil on canvas. 131.8 × 92 cm. Copyright The Frick Collection, New York.

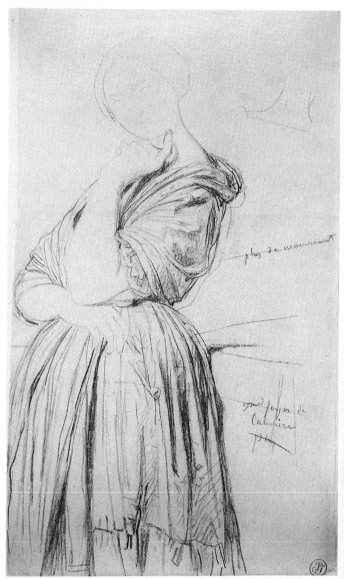

Figure 8-22. Jean-Auguste-Dominique Ingres, *Study for* Portrait of Madame d'Haussonville, c. 1842–1845. Charcoal over graphite pencil on thin white woven paper. 14⅛ × 8¹/₁₆″. Cambridge, Fogg Art Museum, Harvard University.

color gradations between the reflection and the figure that partially overlaps it.[22] In the same squared study Ingres experimented with the attitude and proportions of the figure. The head is drawn proportionally large and in a more upraised position than was finally adopted in the painting. The unstudied gesture in the drawn figure, evident in the more frontal direction of the head and in the straight-pointed finger under the chin, presents a less graceful but more realistic aspect of the sitter than Ingres chose to paint in the elegantly classical *Portrait*. This apparent shift from realism in drawing to stylization in the finished work parallels that noted earlier in connection with the angel figure in Leonardo's *The Virgin of the Rocks* (Figures 8-6 and 8-7).

suggested by the pencil pattern in the squared drawing. Acting visually as gradients of texture, the fold patterns in the skirt endow the figure with the rounded monumentality of a fluted column, a visual analogy previously expressed by a French classical painter of another era, Nicolas Poussin (1593–1665).[25]

Although the pencil-and-charcoal study (Figure 8-22) appears to be primarily a study of costume, the broader linear treatment of the exposed parts of the figure is nevertheless significant, for Ingres believed that "The simpler your lines and forms, the more beauty and strength they will possess. Whenever you divide your forms, you enfeeble them."[26] Ingres's desire to simplify the complexities of form observed in life is consistent with his interest in classical art, which often features large rhythmic, linear constructs. Underlying the simplified form of Ingres's drawing, however, is a remarkable sense of draftsmanship, which vitalizes what might otherwise seem to be merely a classical manner. The undercurrent of realism in his art became the avowed aim of some younger artists who rejected neoclassicism, which since the time of Ingres's great teacher, Jacques-Louis David, had been virtually the official style in France. Prominent among the artists of this radical persuasion was the French painter Jean-François Millet (1814–1875).

The son of a peasant, Millet's background and personal sentiment apparently attracted him to subjects very different from the elegant new aristocrats of Ingres's portraits: "Peasants," he wrote, "suit my temperament best; for I must confess, even if you think me a socialist, that the human side of art is what touches me most."[27] Millet used drawing concurrently with painting, often working and reworking a single theme over a long period of time. His drawing *The Fagot Carriers* (Figure 8-24) was preceded by an earlier painting of the same subject and followed several years later by the final painting (Figure 8-25). His choice of a soft manufactured crayon (Conté) ensured a broad quality of stroke in harmony with the brushstrokes evident on the surface of his paintings. Although the ostensible subject of the drawing and the painting is the same—peasants carrying heavy bundles of sticks— the drawing graphically realizes another theme favored by Millet, the close identity of the peasant with the field. In the drawing he modeled the figures with the same long crayon strokes used to symbolize the sticks, achieving not only a satisfying textural unity appealing to the modern sensibility but also a blurring of the distinction between the figures and the growth of the field, his way of emphasizing their poetic oneness. This strong thematic unity seems to spring directly from Millet's artistic convictions: "I try not to have things look as if chance had brought them together, but as if they had a necessary bond between them."[28] In this respect the drawing is more successful than the painting, with its clearer division of figure and background. Like Goya's *Three Men Digging* (Figure 8-17), Millet's drawing is more than a preliminary study: It stands as an independent work of art.

Figure 8-24. Jean-François Millet (1814–1875), *The Fagot Carriers*, 1852–1854. Conté crayon. 11⅜ × 18⅜". Boston, Museum of Fine Arts. Gift of Martin Brimmer.

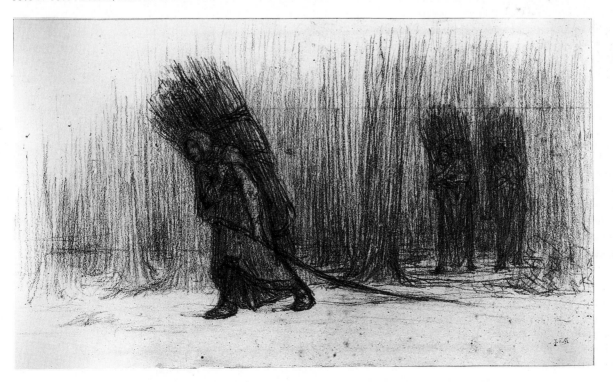

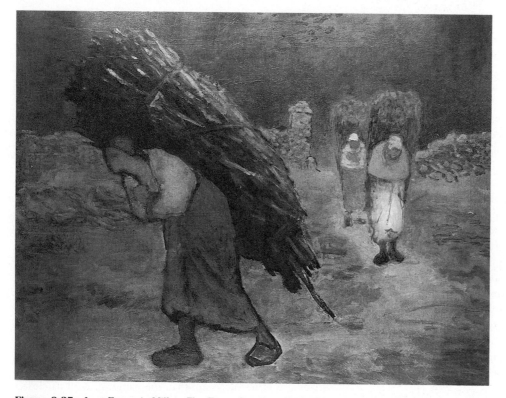

Figure 8-25. Jean-François Millet, *The Fagot Carriers*, 1875. Painting. Cardiff, National Museum of Wales.

Despite the growing tendency toward a more realistic and coloristic form of painting in the nineteenth century, as exemplified by the art of Millet, the neoclassical tradition of David and Ingres continued to prevail in many European art academies, including the provincial Art Academy of La Coruña where the youthful Picasso studied drawing in the 1890s. Although he worked in a variety of styles in his lifetime, some of his finest works recall the classical tradition in which he trained. Precociously skilled as a draftsman, Picasso grew less interested in recording the immediate perception of things (i.e., sensation)—a primary concern of many realist and impressionist artists who preceded him. He expressed instead the desire to ". . . paint things, not as I perceive them, but as I conceive them."[29] This artistic philosophy, which underlies nearly all his mature work, is the formal basis of Picasso's so-called classical Greek period (1905–1906), during which he drew and painted *The Two Brothers* (Figures 8-26 and 8-27). Reflecting the artist's involvement with conception as opposed to perception of form, both the preparatory drawing and the painting were probably done without models,[30] yet in working from memory Picasso did not simply set down a composition already fixed in his mind's eye. The pen-and-ink study (Figure 8-26), in which a similar gesture occurs, is one of a series of variations on this theme. Other preparatory sketches show a single nude figure with arms upraised. Picasso apparently decided to add a second figure of a small child to the arms of the primary figure, giving new meaning to the upraised gesture. Another study, similar to the one repro-

Figure 8-26. Pablo Picasso, *Study for* The Two Brothers, 1905. Pen and black ink. 12⅛ × 9⅜". Baltimore Museum of Art. Cone Collection.

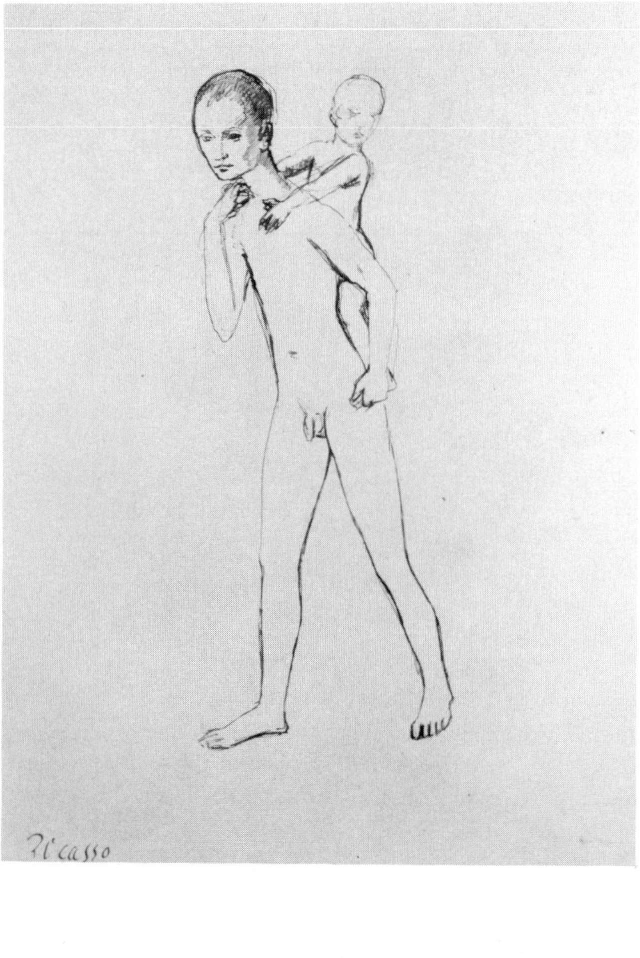

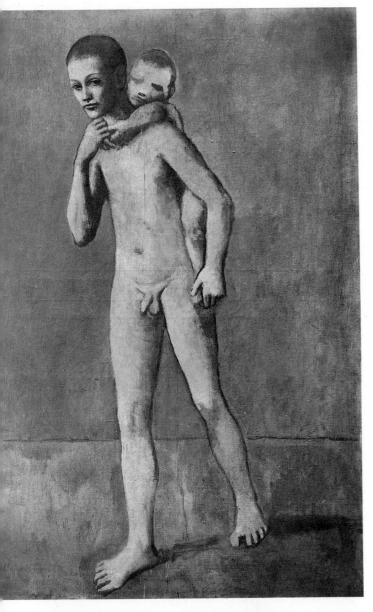

Figure 8-27. Pablo Picasso, *The Two Brothers*, 1905. Oil painting. 142 × 97 cm. Rodolphe Staechelin Foundation Collection, on loan to the Kunstmuseum, Basel.

a visual link that bonds the two figures in a compact, plastic unit; a second change is seen under the principal figure's left arm. In the drawing the line of the baby's leg, redrawn several times, appears to define and diminish the back of the principal figure, creating an ambivalent effect. In the painted version Picasso resolved this problem by carefully modeling the plane above and to the left of the baby's protruding leg, establishing the volumetric continuity of the torso form in the principal figure. Other aspects of the painting are almost directly transposed from the drawing: For example, the emphatic hatch modeling of the head, a convention noted earlier in another work by Picasso (Figure 4-110), is repeated in the painting and developed in other parts of the figure as well.

Although the positive forms in Picasso's painting appear rounded as a result of modeling, the figure as a whole is parallel with the surface of the canvas. As in a relief sculpture, few figural elements seem to project very far in space. Such an orientation of form does not disturb: It is in part responsible for the sense of calm for which classical art is noted. This very sense, however, limits classical conventions in the eyes of some artists, who strive for a more dynamic modality of expression. The forceful art of the Mexican mural painter José Clemente Orozco (1883–1949) provides an interesting contrast with Picasso's classical style.

The primal gesture of the human figure taking a step is represented in both *The Two Brothers* and Orozco's *Study of Legs* (Figure 8-28), yet the two artists saw and used the gesture

Figure 8-28. José Clemente Orozco (1883–1949), *Study of Legs*, 1938–1939. Charcoal on light gray paper. 25⅞ × 19⅝″. The Museum of Modern Art, New York. Inter-American Fund.

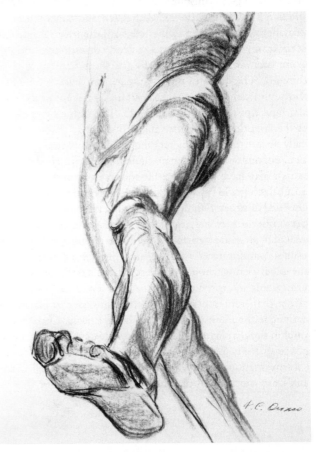

duced but showing both figures from the back, reveals that Picasso's concept of form was fully three dimensional, a quality we sense in the assertive modeling of the painting as well as in the distinctly sculptural figure-ground relationship. In addition to the preparatory drawings Picasso made at least two gouache studies of the same theme on cardboard. It seems reasonable to assume that these were also preparatory for the large oil.

The classical constructs of outline and contour noted earlier in Picasso's drawings (Figure 3-53) also prevail in *Study for* The Two Brothers (Figure 8-26), although the redrawn lines suggest a more informal approach. The same classical construction underlies the painting, which is enhanced considerably by two departures from the drawing: In the upper region of the figure the embrace and grasp of the child create

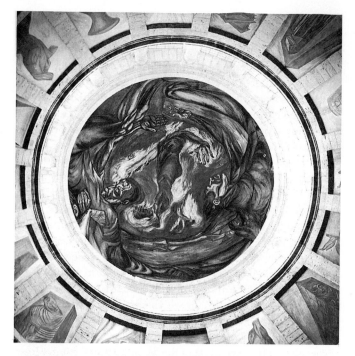

Figure 8-29. José Clemente Orozco, *El Hombre*, 1938–1939. Fresco painting in a cupola. Guadalajara, El Hospicio Cabañas.

in strikingly different ways and for different purposes. Drawing from life, Orozco apparently assumed a point of view beneath the model. Consequently, the foreshortened figure seems almost to threaten the viewer with its aggressively projecting foot and leg, an illusion that is heightened by bold contour hatching. The reason for the unusual foreshortening of the figure is apparent in the mural painting *El Hombre* (Figure 8-29), for which the drawing was a study. Painted on the curving ceiling under a dome (cupola), the fresco is normally seen from below—a direction that corresponds with the point of view represented by the foreshortened figure in the drawing. The effect of receding space conveyed by the foreshortening is further enhanced by the placement of the flaming figure painted inside the dome. The figure's feet as well as the larger circling figures are positioned so as to be physically nearer the spectator on the ground. This arrangement is also encountered in certain Renaissance frescoed domes, which may have been the artist's source of inspiration.

Orozco made use of yet another convention of European art—the allegorical figure. The flaming figure is an allegorical personification of fire, and the other three elements—earth, sea, and air—are represented by the figures that ring the dome.[31] The unusual color tonalities in the painting, such as the blue used to model the head of the sea figure, seem to justify this interpretation. Color thus takes on a symbolic rather than representational function in order to clarify and dramatize the intended allegory of the painting. Orozco's art, though highly personal, is thus a complex synthesis of artistic concepts from the past. "It is unnecessary," he once wrote, "to speak about Tradition. Certainly we have to fall in line and learn our lesson from the Masters."[32]

Yet Orozco's art is far from traditional in style. He made use of dramatic distortions of form and intensified color contrasts in a way that is reminiscent of certain twentieth-century German expressionists (e.g., Nolde and Kirchner). Orozco did not use such devices as formal ends in themselves but rather as a means of heightening the drama of the thematic content. Broadly speaking, Orozco's themes encompass the historical and political struggle of the Mexican people, whom he frequently represented in a way that is didactic in its clarity. His direct, unequivocal approach to a theme or subject is in extreme contrast to that of his Belgian contemporary René Magritte (1898–1967), who was concerned instead with the poetic ambiguities of imagery. A surrealist in the true sense of the word, Magritte based his art on a careful examination of objective reality: "If one looks at a thing with the intention of trying to discover what it means," he once wrote, "one ends up no longer seeing the thing itself, but thinking of the question that has been raised."[33] Magritte's approach transforms a real object into the surreal.[34]

We may only speculate as to the nature of the thing that Magritte utilized as the creative point of departure for his painting *Delusions of Grandeur* (Figure 8-30). A related drawing (Figure 8-31) shows a truncated figure that resembles a classical Venus without limbs and head, suggesting that such a figure may have been the object Magritte originally contemplated. The artist's transformation of the Venus figure is

Figure 8-30. René Magritte (1898–1967). *Delusions of Grandeur*, 1962. Oil on canvas. 39½ × 32″. Private collection.

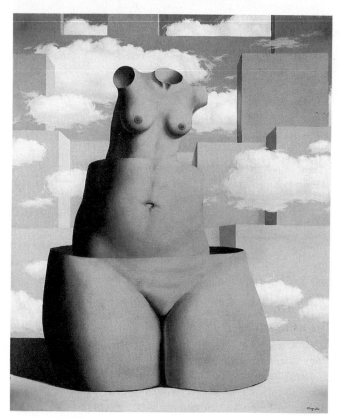

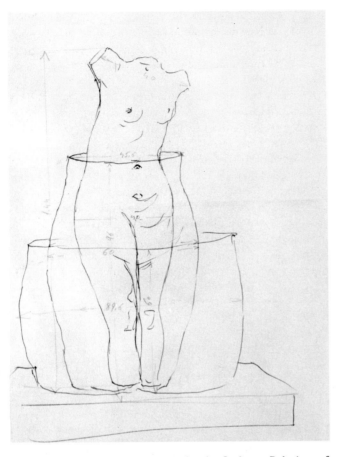

Figure 8-31. René Magritte, *Study for the Sculpture* Delusions of Grandeur, 1967. Ballpoint pen. 27½ × 21 cm. Paris, Galerie Iolas.

achieved by a device borrowed from architecture—*step construction*—which produces a systematic though unnaturalistic change of scale within the figure at discrete intervals, resulting in a towering ziggurat effect. Ironically, Magritte adopted a form of academic naturalism, disarmingly simple in technique, to realize this unnatural construction. In the painting (Figure 8-30) he developed the figure as a rounded form by means of shadow modeling and applied the same technique to the sky area, which is treated as though it consisted of solid cubes, giving the air the same sense of volume that is apparent in the figure. At the same time the hollowness suggested in the figure causes it to appear lighter in weight than the surrounding atmosphere.

The painted version of *Delusions of Grandeur* (Figure 8-30) preceded the drawings (Figures 8-31, 8-32, and 8-33) and the sculptured version (Figure 8-34) by five years: "The idea of making sculptures which would be based on a three-dimensional realization of images from Magritte's paintings was born out of a conversation with his dealer Alexandre Iolas."[35] *Delusions of Grandeur* was one of eight paintings that Magritte chose to translate into sculpture in January 1967: "He made working drawings for each one . . . deciding the scale and measurements himself, which he seemed to have no difficulty in visualizing or transposing."[36] The sculptural qual-

ity of the painting may have prompted Magritte to select it for a project in cast bronze. Magritte's drawings thus served a purpose quite unlike that of most preparatory drawings, for his were intended to assist in translating an earlier pictorial work into another artistic medium. His schematic study (Figure 8-31) shows the underlying construction of the sculpture. Dimensions are indicated to help the foundrymen assemble the work. By contrast, the two additional studies (Figures 8-32 and 8-33) present straightforward realistic views of the back and side elevations of the completed work. Freely modeled with hatch, the drawings show the telescoping section, with rounded cross sections at the top of each.

Unfortunately, Magritte died without ever seeing the sculptures completed. He did see the [full-scale] wax models, however, when he visited the foundry in June 1967, just two months before he died. At that time he made several modifications and adjustments . . . in *Delusions of Grandeur*, he altered the angles of the torso and arranged for the arms to be hollowed out.[37]

That no major changes were made indicate the effectiveness of the drawings as a means of conveying his ideas of the sculpture to the foundry.

Figure 8-32. René Magritte, *Study for the Sculpture* Delusions of Grandeur, 1967. Ballpoint pen. 27½ × 21 cm. Paris, Galerie Iolas.

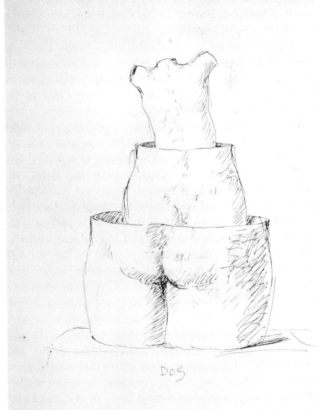

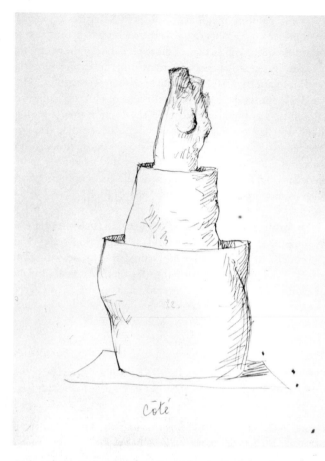

Figure 8-33. René Magritte, *Study for the Sculpture* Delusions of Grandeur, 1967. Ballpoint pen. 27½ × 21 cm. Paris, Galerie Iolas.

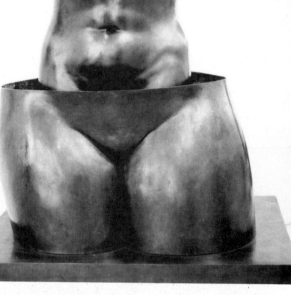

Figure 8-34. René Magritte, *Delusions of Grandeur*, 1967. Bronze sculpture. 51″ high. Paris, Galerie Iolas.

It is not easy to relate the title *Delusions of Grandeur* to either the painted or the sculptured version. This is no doubt intentional: "The titles of paintings," Magritte once wrote, "were chosen in such a way as to inspire in the spectator an appropriate mistrust of any mediocre tendency to facile self-assurance."[38] The hollow though monumental appearance of the figure set against a seemingly solid sky suggests a possible rationale of Magritte's concept. Other explanations, however, are equally plausible, though none seems conclusive. We must eventually look upon the work in the way that Magritte himself looked upon things in nature—to see the philosophical questions that underlie appearances. In *Delusions of Grandeur* Magritte raises questions that challenge our common-sense assumptions about the substance and solidity not only of the world in which we live but of the human body as well.

In some of his work Magritte exploits formal similarities in common objects for surrealistic purposes: "There is a secret affinity," he once wrote, "between certain images; it is equally valid for the objects which those images represent."[39] Such a concept was developed earlier by Arcimboldo, who substituted forms of pots and pans for similar formal constructions of the head (Figure 3-11). Magritte, however, applied the idea in such novel ways that it seems practically to have

been invented by him. The same concept has served as the source of inspiration for certain younger artists as well. It appears, for example, to underlie a sculpture by the contemporary American artist Jasper Johns (b. 1930). Entitled *The Critic Sees* (Figures 8-35 and 8-36), this work consists of a rectangular solid with a pair of glasses on one side, behind which are life casts of human mouths. The rectangular format of the sculpture brings to mind opticians' signs of the past. The use of such a visual cliché—like Magritte's use of the familiar object—is an integral part of the artist's method. The "mouth casts" set behind the glasses reveal a "secret affinity" with the form of the human eye. The ambiguity of the image, which deliberately confounds the verbal with the visual sense, raises questions in the viewer's mind. The title provides a partial answer, suggesting that the work is a comment on the role of the art critic. The artistic coherence of the comment was assured by working out the compact integration of formal elements in advance in a pencil drawing (Figure 8-35).

In making his preparatory drawing Johns did not find it necessary to resort to a new medium or method, as he did in the final sculpture, despite the avant-garde nature of his concept.[40] On the contrary, the hatch modeling and written notations recall the technique of Van Eyck over five hundred

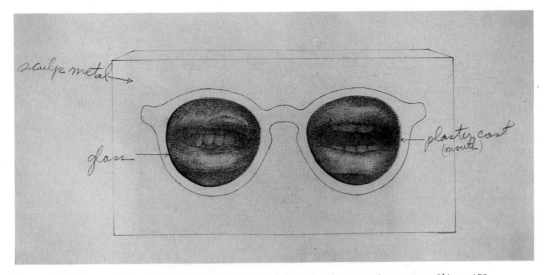

Figure 8-35. Jasper Johns, *Study for* The Critic Sees, 1961. Graphite pencil on paper. 6¼ × 12″. Collection of Mr. and Mrs. Leo Castelli.

Figure 8-36. Jasper Johns, *The Critic Sees*, 1961. Sculpmetal, plaster, and glass. 3¼ × 6¼ × 2⅛″. New York, Leo Castelli Gallery.

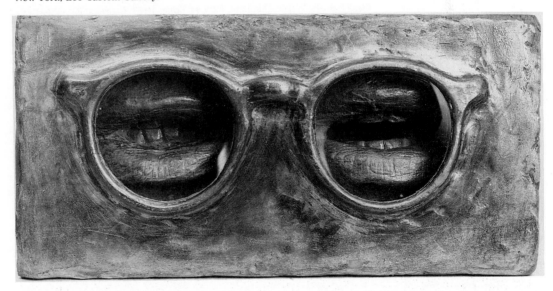

years earlier (Figure 8-4). Traditional drawing methods and materials are capable of encompassing an almost limitless range of ideas for works in other media, both old and new. This universality of application underscores the unique historical continuity that sets drawing apart from other art forms in the West. In view of the influential role that drawing continues to play in planning works of art, the advice that Cennino Cennini gave to artists six hundred years ago continues to be valid: "Do not fail, as you go on, to draw something every day, for no matter how little it is it will be well worth while, and it will do you a world of good."[41]

Today Cennini's enthusiasm for drawing is shared by many small groups of visual artists who meet on a regular basis to practice the art of drawing from the model. As a member of such a group in San Francisco, the American painter Wayne Thiebaud reports that, "For the past seven years every week at 9:00 a.m. a model and five people gather to draw and enjoy a lively gab-fest. . . . Except for our mid-point coffee break the sessions are a quiet time for working from one pose for four hours."[42] When the model arrived one day with a cast on his arm, the artists present requested that he assume a reclining pose on a table.[43] Among the drawings produced during the session are two by Thiebaud himself: a small pen-and-ink sketch (Figure 8-37) and a large drawing in charcoal (Figure 8-38). Though small in size (9⅞ × 12¾″) the sketch succeeds in resolving the basic structure of the foreshortened

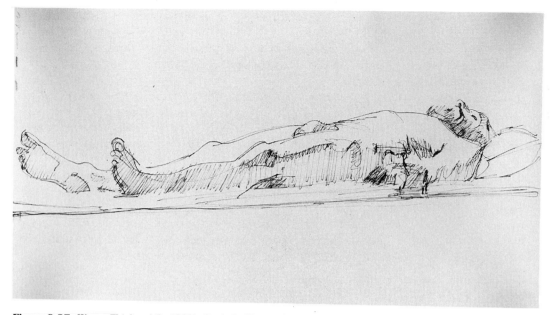

Figure 8-37. Wayne Thiebaud (b. 1920), *Study for* Man on Table, 1978. Pen and ink, brown, on brownish paper over traces of black chalk. 9⅞ × 12¾″. Private collection (photo by Pam Maddock).

Figure 8-38. Wayne Thiebaud, *Man on Table*, 1978. Charcoal on paper. 22¼ × 30″. Collection of Paul LeBaron Thiebaud (photo by Pam Maddock).

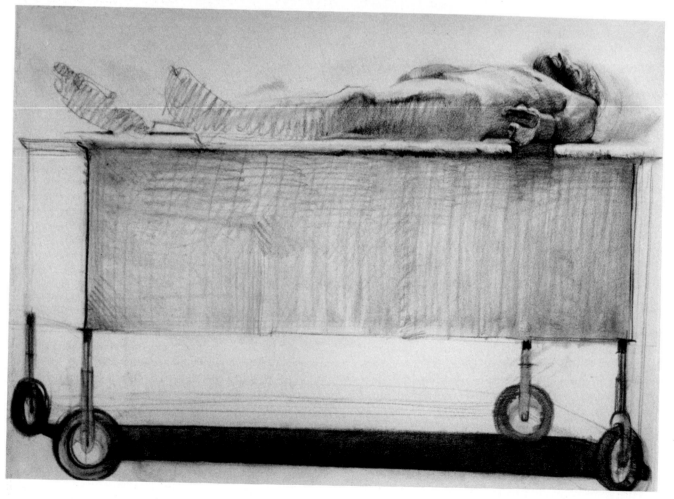

figure. The reclining pose reveals skeletal features, and several—including the bump of the great trochanter—are deftly indicated in the study by means of shadow contours.

To one who has seen only the preparatory sketch, the final drawing comes as a surprise. In a leap of creative imagination Thiebaud transformed the simple cloth-covered table on which the model actually lay into a grim hospital gurney underscored and anchored by a dark cast shadow. The lively contours of the figure are answered and supported by the severely rectilinear gurney—an effective compositional foil. The continuous white horizontal of the top is interrupted by a dark shadow cast by the arm firmly linking the figure to the gurney. Despite the clinical overtones of the scene and the prone figure reminiscent of Holbein's *Dead Christ*, there is no sense of pathos. The figure is presented simply as a fact of life . . . or death. It is, in a word, contemporary.

Beyond drawing as an autonomous art form, Thiebaud envisions a special role for figure drawing; for him it is a medium for communicating with the creative spirit of earlier artists. Through figure drawing,

> . . . it becomes possible to feel and think through the hands and minds of others. To sense origins of a Degas back, Holbein's profile lines, of the differences between the eyes drawn by Picasso and Utamaro. By studying both the history of drawing and the practice of drawing it becomes possible to reexamine the variations and novelties extended from prime origins.[44]

Viewed in this light drawing the human form becomes a means of discovering artistic roots, and by implication a way of discovering your own artistic identity.

NOTES

1. The examples selected are not all-inclusive due to limitations of space. It is hoped that the omission of significant time periods from this chapter of the book are balanced by inclusion elsewhere. My selection was motivated by didactic considerations and my intention to provide examples most useful to the student of drawing at present.

2. The invention of paper is traditionally credited to Ts'ai Lun, an officer of the Chinese imperial guard (A.D. 105), though it did not come into general use in the East until after A.D. 220. Brought to the West by the Arabs in the eighth century, paper was not generally available in Europe before 1300.

3. The rare sketches made by ancient Egyptian artists on small irregular stone slabs are an exception. The purpose of such sketches is poorly understood at present.

4. *Sinopia* is a term used to designate a preparatory drawing made directly on the plaster wall surface before beginning a fresco painting. The reddish pigment used for the wash drawing is derived from the ancient Asian town of Sinopie, from whence it was presumably exported in early times. For an interesting account of traditional sinopia and fresco techniques see Cennino Cennini's *The Book of Art*.

5. Ironically, the fragile, combustible nature of paper has contributed to the destruction of many drawings, leaving many works of art for which no preparatory drawings exist.

6. Erwin Panofsky, *Early Netherlandish Painting*, vol. 1 (Cambridge, Mass.: Harvard University Press, 1958), p. 200.

7. Kenneth Clark, *Leonardo da Vinci* (Baltimore: Penguin, 1963), p. 51.

8. Ibid. The patron in this instance was the Confraternity of the Immaculate Conception.

9. For a complete discussion of the preparation of silverpoint ground see James Watrous, *The Craft of Old-Master Drawings* (Madison: University of Wisconsin Press, 1967), pp. 3–33.

10. Ibid., p. 13.

11. One of the dubious benefits of air pollution is that it speeds up the darkening of silverpoint. You can test the quality of metal as a drawing medium by marking a painted surface with a dime or a penny (ibid., p. 22).

12. Graphite was mined in its natural form for use in art as early as 1560 in England, although it did not come into general use until the seventeenth century. In 1795 Nicolas-Jacques Conté patented a process of preparing graphite pencil rods similar to those still used today. Made from compressed graphite powder and clay, the Conté pencil rods, later known in English as leads, became very popular in the nineteenth century. Most graphite used in pencils today, however, is a synthetic product (ibid., pp. 138–144).

13. Although scholars agree that the main figure was drawn by Michelangelo, not all agree on the authorship of the smaller studies on the sheet. If the contour drawing of the shoulder and chest to the left of the principal figure and the drawing of the large profile are, as de Tolnay believes, the work of a pupil, the secondary studies represent a valuable example of the instructional use of drawing in art training. Berenson, however, concluded that the entire sheet is the work of Michelangelo. If this is so, it seems likely that the contour construction of the shoulder and chest, in which the pectoral muscle is more pronounced, was an experiment in adapting the male figure to forms more in accordance with female anatomy.

14. Amid the brilliant anatomical modeling of this drawing can be noted two pinlike indications of the tips of the shoulder clavicle bones that can be used to set the important horizontal axis of the torso. For similar markings in another drawing by Michelangelo see Figure 6-55.

15. Leo Steinberg, "Pontormo's Capponi Chapel," *The Art Bulletin*, vol. LVI, no. 3 (Sept. 1974), p. 387.

16. See the Roman frescoes of the Villa of the Mysteries, Pompeii, in Amedeo Maiuri, *Roman Painting* (Geneva: Editions Albert Skira, 1953), p. 59.

17. Julius S. Held, *Rubens Drawings*, vol. 1 (London: Phaidon Press, 1959), p. 72.

18. Pierre Gassier and Juliet Wilson, *Francisco Goya* (New York: Reynal and Company in association with William Morrow, 1971), p. 244.

19. Kenneth Clark, *The Romantic Rebellion* (New York: Harper & Row, 1973), pp. 97–98.

20. The later French artist Odilon Redon (1840–1916) objected to Ingres on the grounds of his traditionalism: "Ingres is an honest and useful disciple of the masters of another age. . . . In those false temples, with their great false gods, Ingres did not belong to his age; his mind is sterile, the sight of his work, far from increasing our moral force, lets us placidly continue on our bourgeois way of life, in no way affected or changed. His works are not true art; for the value of art lies in its power to increase our moral force or establish its heightening influence. . . ." (quoted in Robert Goldwater and Marco Treves, *Artists on Art* [New York: Pantheon, 1945], p. 359).

21. This technically subtle form of shadow modeling, also seen in portraits of Raphael, a painter Ingres greatly admired, is later encountered in paintings by the impressionist Edouard Manet (1832–1883). Such modeling creates an effect similar to that of relief modeling, as described in Chapter 5.

22. The prominence given by Ingres to the mirror and its reflection in this portrait recalls Leonardo's belief that mirrored images were among the effects impossible to create in sculpture that prove the superiority of painting as an expressive art form (*The Notebooks of Leonardo*, vol. 1 [New York: Dover, 1970], p. 329).

23. For a classical example of this pose, which Ingres may have seen, see the Greco-Roman relief carving of Medea and the Peliades in the Lateran Museum, Rome, reproduced in Rodenwaldt's *Kunst der Antike* (Berlin: Im Propläen-Verlag, 1927), p. 369.

24. In the catalog for the *Memorial Exhibition of Works of Art from the Collection of Paul J. Sachs* (Fogg Art Museum, Harvard University, 1965), p. 46, Ingres's writing is deciphered as "*grand foyer de Carmin.*" In the catalog for the *Ingres Centennial Exhibition* (Fogg Art Museum, Harvard University, 1967), p. 85, the same writing is transcribed as "*grand foyer de lumière plus*" (crossed out). The latter reading seems more accurate to this author.

25. Poussin, in a letter to his friend Chantelou in 1642, commented, "The beautiful girls whom you will have seen in Nimes will not, I am sure, have delighted your spirit any less than the beautiful columns of Maison Carrée; for the one is not more than an old copy of the other." Poussin may have been referring to the Roman author Vitruvius's account in which columns were designed according to human proportions. Kenneth Clark, *The Nude* (New York: Doubleday, Anchor, 1956), p. 45.

26. Lorenz Eitner, *Neoclassicism and Romanticism* (Englewood Cliffs, N.J.: Prentice-Hall, 1970), p. 137.

27. Kenneth Clark, *The Romantic Rebellion* (New York: Harper & Row, 1973), pp. 292–293.

28. Goldwater and Treves, *Artists on Art*, pp. 292–293.

29. As quoted in *Picasso's Private Drawings* (New York: Simon & Schuster, 1969), p. 11.

30. Pierre Daix and Georges Boudaille, *Picasso, The Blue and Rose Periods* (Greenwich, Conn.: New York Graphic Society, 1967), p. 294.

31. MacKinley Helm, *Modern Mexican Painters* (New York: Dover, 1941), p. 83.

32. Justino Fernandez, *José Clemente Orozco, Forma y Idea* (Mexico City: Liberia de Porrua Hnos. y. Cia., 1942), p. 31.

33. Magritte, as quoted by Suzi Gabelik, "A Conversation with René Magritte," *Studio International* (London), vol. 173, no. 887 (March 1967), p. 128.

34. The purposes of surrealist art were described by the French poet and critic André Breton: ". . . the strongest surrealist image is the one that pursues the highest degree of the arbitrary, the one that takes the longest to translate into practical language, whether it contains an enormous amount of apparent contradiction; whether promising to be sensational, it seems to come to a weak conclusion; whether it draws from itself a derisory formal justification; whether it is of a hallucinatory nature; whether it lends very naturally the mask of the concrete to abstraction or vice versa; whether it implies the negation of some elementary physical quality; or whether it provokes laughter" (quoted by Eddie Wolfram in *Magritte* [New York: Ballantine, 1972], p. 4). On the basis of this statement Magritte's painting and sculpture *Delusions of Grandeur* qualify as surrealist imagery on several counts.

35. Suzi Gabelik, *Magritte* (Greenwich, Conn.: New York Graphic Society, 1973), p. 181.

36. Ibid.

37. Ibid.

38. Ibid., p. 183.

39. Magritte, as quoted in Louis Scutenaire, *René Magritte* (Brussels: Librairie Selection, 1947), p. 38.

40. Sculpmetal, used to create the textured surface of this work, is the trade name for a metal solution that turns to solid metal as it dries. It can be applied to almost any surface by means of a brush or a palette knife.

41. Cennino Cennini, *The Book of the Art*, as translated in Goldwater and Treves, *Artists on Art*, p. 23.

42. Wayne Thiebaud, Introduction to catalog: *Figure Drawings, Five San Francisco Artists* (San Francisco: Charles Campbell Gallery, 1983).

43. The author is grateful to Paul LeBaron Thiebaud who graciously provided information regarding the history of the two drawings by Wayne Thiebaud.

44. Wayne Thiebaud, *Figure Drawings*.

Bibliography

THE FOLLOWING SELECTION is a basic working bibliography to assist the reader who wishes to pursue the subject further. Representing but a fraction of the works consulted in preparing this book, the list omits monographs on individual artists and references to articles in periodicals: the former, because such titles are easily found in the card catalog of any library; the latter, because they are too specific to warrant inclusion here. Since nothing is so valuable for the student of drawing as looking at original master drawings, the preponderance of works listed in the general reference category were selected to provide the next best thing—reproductions of a variety of master drawings—with the hope of stimulating both the appreciation and the production of drawings.

GENERAL REFERENCES

BEAN, JACOB, and STAMPFLE, FELICE. *Drawings from New York Collections: The Italian Renaissance.* New York: Metropolitan Museum of Art and Pierpont Morgan Library, 1965.

———. *The 17th Century in Italy (Drawings from New York Collections III).* Catalog. New York: Metropolitan Museum of Art and Pierpont Morgan Library, 1971.

BERENSON, BERNARD. *The Drawings of the Florentine Painters.* Chicago: University of Chicago, 1938.

BORDEN PUBLISHING COMPANY. *Master Draughtsman Series.* Twenty-eight inexpensive volumes reproducing drawings of individual artists from the Renaissance to the present day. Alhambra, Calif.: Borden.

BRITISH MUSEUM. *Italian Drawings in the Department of Prints and Drawings in the British Museum,* 4 vols. Vol. I: Popham, Arthur E., and Pouncey, Philip. *The 14th and 15th Centuries,* 2 vols. London: British Museum, 1950. Vol. II: Wilde, Johannes. *Michelangelo and His Studio.* London: British Museum, 1953. Vol. III: Pouncey, Philip, and Gere, John A. *Raphael and His Circle,* 2 vols. London: British Museum, 1967. Vol. IV: Popham, Arthur E. *Artists Working in Parma in the 16th Century,* 2 vols. London: British Museum, 1967.

HAVERKAMP-BEGEMANN, EGBERT. *Creative Copies, Interpretative Drawings from Michelangelo to Picasso.* New York: The Drawing Center, 1988.

HAVERKAMP-BEGEMANN, EGBERT, LAWDER, STANDISH, D. D., and TALBOT, CHARLES. *Drawings from the Clark Art Institute,* 2 vols. New Haven, Conn.: Yale University Press, 1964.

HOFMANN, WERNER. *Caricature from Leonardo to Picasso.* Translated by M. L. H. New York: Crown, 1957.

KENIN, RICHARD. *The Art of Drawing.* London: Paddington, 1974.

LAMBERT, SUSAN. *Reading Drawings.* New York: Pantheon, 1984.

LEVY, MERVYN. *The Artist and the Nude.* London: Barrie and Rockliff, 1965.

LEYMARIE, JEAN, MONNIER, GENEVIÈVE, and ROSE, BERNICE. *History of an Art, Drawing.* New York: Rizzoli, 1979.

LIBERMAN, WILLIAM S., ed. *Seurat to Matisse: Drawing in France.* New York: Museum of Modern Art, 1974.

LINDEMANN, GOTTFRIED. *Prints and Drawings: A Pictorial History.* Translated by Gerald Onn. New York: Praeger, 1970.

MARKS, CLAUDE. *From the Sketchbooks of the Great Artists.* New York: Crowell, 1972.

METROPOLITAN MUSEUM OF ART. *European Drawings,* 2 vols. New York: Metropolitan Museum of Art, 1943.

MONGAN, AGNES. *Memoral Exhibition Works of Art from the Collection of Paul J. Sachs.* Catalog. Cambridge, Mass.: Fogg Art Museum, 1965.

————. *One Hundred Master Drawings.* Cambridge, Mass.: Harvard University Press, 1949.

MONGAN, AGNES, and SACHS, PAUL J. *Drawings in the Fogg Museum of Art,* 3 vols. Cambridge, Mass.: Harvard University Press, 1946.

MOSKOWITZ, IRA, ed. *Great Drawings of All Time.* New York: Shorewood, 1962.

MUSEUM OF MODERN ART. *Modern Drawings.* Edited by Monroe Wheeler. New York: Museum of Modern Art, 1944.

POPHAM, ARTHUR E. *The Italian Drawings of the XV and XVI Centuries in the Collection of His Majesty the King at Windsor Castle.* London: Phaidon, 1949.

RAGGHIANTI, CARLO L. *Firenze 1470–1480 Disegni dal Modello.* Pisa: Instituto di Storia Dell'Arte Dell' Università di Pisa, 1975.

ROSENBERG, JAKOB. *Great Draftsmen from Pisanello to Picasso.* Cambridge, Mass.: Harvard University Press, 1959.

SACHS, PAUL J. *Modern Prints & Drawings.* New York: Knopf, 1954.

SCHOLZ, JANOS. *Italian Master Drawing. 1350–1800.* New York: Dover, 1976.

SHOREWOOD PUBLISHERS, INC. *Drawings of the Masters.* Twelve inexpensive volumes treating drawing by country and period: *French Impressionists; Italian Drawings from the 15th to the 19th Century; Flemish and Dutch Drawings from the 15th to the 18th Century; 20th Century Drawings, 1900–1940; 20th Century 1940 to Present; German Drawings from the 16th Century to the Expressionists; French Drawings from the 15th Century through Gericault; American Drawings; Spanish Drawings from the 10th to the 19th Century; Persian Drawings from the 14th through the 19th Century; From Cave to Renaissance.* New York: Shorewood, 1963. Boston: Little, Brown, 1976 (paperback edition).

TIETZE, HANS, and TIETZE-CONRAT, ERICA. *The Drawings of the Venetian Painters in the 15th and 16th Centuries.* New York: Augustin, 1944.

VAN GELDER, J. G. *Dutch Drawings and Prints.* New York: Abrams, 1959.

VAYER, LAJOS, ed. *Master Drawings from the Collection of the Budapest Museum of Fine Arts 14th–18th Centuries.* New York: Abrams, 1956.

WELCH, STUART CARY. *Indian Drawings and Painted Sketches.* Catalog. New York: Asia House Gallery, 1976.

DRAWING METHODS, MATERIALS, AND TECHNIQUES

BRO, LU. *Drawing, a Studio Guide.* New York: Norton, 1978.

CHAET, BERNARD. *The Art of Drawing.* New York: Holt, Rinehart and Winston, 1970.

DE TOLNAY, CHARLES. *History and Technique of Old Master Drawings.* New York: Bittner, 1943.

GOLDSTEIN, NATHAN. *The Art of Responsive Drawing.* Englewood Cliffs, N.J.: Prentice Hall, 1992.

HALE, ROBERT BEVERLY. *Drawing Lessons for the Great Masters.* New York: Watson-Guptill, 1964.

HOFFMAN, HOWARD S. *Vision and the Art of Drawing.* Englewood Cliffs, N.J.: Prentice Hall, 1989.

HUTTER, H. *Drawing: History and Technique.* New York: McGraw-Hill, 1968.

KAUPELIS, R. *Learning to Draw.* New York: Watson-Guptill, 1968.

KAY, REED. *The Painter's Guide to Studio Methods & Materials.* Garden City, N.Y.: Doubleday, 1972.

KLEE, PAUL. *Inward Vision: Watercolors, Drawings, and Writings.* New York: Abrams, 1959.

MAYER, RALPH W. *The Artist's Handbook of Materials & Techniques.* Rev. ed. New York: Viking, 1970.

MENDELOWITZ, DANIEL M., and DUANE A. WAKEHAM. *A Guide to Drawing.* New York: Holt, Rinehart and Winston, 1993.

NICOLAIDES, KIMON. *The Natural Way to Draw.* Boston: Houghton Mifflin, 1941.

RAWSON, PHILIP. *Drawing.* London: Oxford University Press, 1969.

WATROUS, JAMES. *The Craft of Old Master Drawings.* Madison: University of Wisconsin Press, 1950.

HISTORY AND PHILOSOPHY

AMES-LEWIS, FRANCIS. *Drawing in Early Renaissance Italy.* New Haven: Yale University Press, 1982.

BOIME, ALBERT. *The Academy and French Painting in the Nineteenth Century.* London: Phaidon, 1971.

BOREL, FRANCE. *The Seduction of Venus, Artists and Models.* New York: Rizzoli, 1990.

CLARK, KENNETH. *The Nude: A Study in Ideal Form.* Garden City, N.Y.: Doubleday, 1959.

COKE, VAN DEREN. *The Painter and the Photograph.* Albuquerque: University of New Mexico Press, 1972.

GOLDWATER, ROBERT, and TREVES, MARCO. *Artists on Art.* New York: Pantheon, 1945.

LEONARDO DA VINCI. *The Treatise on Painting.* Translated by A. Philip McMahon. Princeton, N.J.: Princeton University Press, 1956.

OZENFANT, AMEDEE. *The Foundations of Modern Art.* New York: Dover, 1952.

PANOFSKY, ERWIN. *Meaning in the Visual Arts.* New York: Doubleday, 1955.

SAGNE, JEAN. *Delacroix et la photographie.* France: Editions Herscher, 1982.

VASARI, GIORGIO. *Lives of the Artists.* Translated by E. L. Seeley. New York: Noonday Press, Farrar, Straus & Giroux, 1957.

VISUAL PERCEPTION

ARNHEIM, RUDOLF. *Art and Visual Perception.* Berkeley and Los Angeles: University of California Press, 1954.

BUSWELL, GUY THOMAS. *How People Look at Pictures: A Study of the Psychology of Perception.* Chicago: University of Chicago Press, 1935.

FRISBY, JOHN P. *Seeing.* Oxford: Oxford University Press, 1980.

GIBSON, JAMES J. *The Senses Considered as Perceptual Systems.* Boston: Houghton Mifflin, 1966.

GOMBRICH, E. H. *Art and Illusion, A Study in the Psychology of Pictorial Representation.* Princeton, N.J.: Princeton University Press, 1972.

GREGORY, R. L. *Eye and Brain: The Psychology of Seeing.* New York: McGraw-Hill, 1966.

HOCHBERG, JULIAN E. *Perception.* Englewood Cliffs, N.J.: Prentice-Hall, 1964.

MARR, DAVID. *Vision.* New York: Freeman, 1982.

Perception: Mechanisms and Models. San Francisco: Freeman, 1972.

Scientific American. New York: Scientific American, Inc. A periodical of special interest for its many articles on visual perception.

SPRINGER, SALLY P., and DEUTSCH, GEORG. *Left Brain, Right Brain.* San Francisco: Freeman, 1981.

VERNON, M. D. *A Further Study of Visual Perception.* London: Cambridge University Press, 1952.

————. *The Psychology of Perception.* Harmondsworth, Middlesex, England: Penguin, 1962.

WITTGENSTEIN, LUDWIG. *The Blue and Brown Books.* New York: Harper & Row, 1965.

WOLFE, JEREMY M. Introduction, *The Mind's Eye.* San Francisco: Freeman, 1986.

ANATOMY

BAMMES, GOTTFRIED. *Die Gestalt des Menschen.* Ravensburg: Otto Maier Verlag, 1973.

BARCSAY, JENO. *Anatomy for the Artist.* London: Spring Books, 1955.

BRIDGMAN, GEORGE B. *The Human Machine.* New York: Dover, 1972.

FAU, J. *The Anatomy of the External Forms of Man.* London: Hippolyte Bailliere, 1849.

GRAY, HENRY. *Anatomy, Descriptive and Surgical.* 1901. Reprint. Philadelphia: Running Press, 1974.

KRAMER, JACK. *Human Anatomy and Figure Drawing.* New York: Van Nostrand Reinhold, 1972.

LOCKHART, R. D. *Living Anatomy.* London: Faber and Faber, 1963.

LOCKHART, R. D. ET AL. *Anatomy of the Human Body.* Philadelphia: J. B. Lippincott, 1974.

MUYBRIDGE, EADWEARD. *The Human Figure in Motion.* New York: Dover, 1955.

PECK, STEPHEN ROGERS. *Atlas of Human Anatomy for the Artist.* New York: Oxford University Press, 1951.

SAUNDERS, J. B. DE C., and O'MALLEY, CHARLES D., trans. and annot. *The Illustrations from the Works of Andreas Vesalius of Brussels.* New York: Dover, 1973.

THOMSON, ARTHUR. *A Handbook of Anatomy for Art Students.* New York: Dover, 1964.

Procedure for Photographing Drawings

1. Arrange a pair of standard bell reflectors with 3200 floodlights spaced equidistant on each side of the picture so that each lamp is 30 inches away from the plane of the picture and 54 inches from the center line of the picture. A tape measure will help.

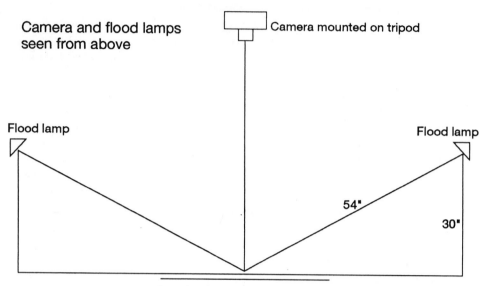

Camera and flood lamps seen from above

Camera mounted on tripod

Flood lamp

Flood lamp

54"

30"

Drawing clamped to a flat board

2. With the camera mounted on a tripod, tilt the panel and/or the camera so that the plane of the drawing parallels the plane of the back of the camera. This will prevent distortion in the photograph.

Side view of camera, tripod, drawing, and flat panel

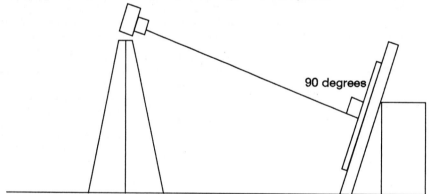

90 degrees

3. With Ektachrome EPY 135(ASA 50, tungsten) film loaded in the camera and the meter set for ASA 50, make two light readings: one with a Kodak grey card, the other directly off the picture. Use an average to obtain the basic shutter and f-stop setting for the trial roll of film. If you are shooting drawings on white paper, 1/2 second at f22/16 (halfway between f22 and f16) will be okay. Make three shots of each picture raising and lowering the f-stop setting by one-half stop and be sure to record the settings for each. When your trial roll has been processed, compare the results with the exposure settings to determine the ideal setting for your work.

Index

Boldface numbers refer to illustrations.

Abdomen, 170
Abdominal sheath, **200**, 203
Abductor pollicis muscles, 225, 231
Abel Prostrate on the Ground (Corinth), **112**
Abstract Construction (Villon), **126**
Academic Study (Eakins), **198**, 250, **251**
Academic Study of a Nude Man (Degas), **196**
Académie of the nude, 250
Académies d'après nature, 250
Acetabulum (pelvis socket), 170
Achilles tendon, 233, 239
Acromium process, 174, 205, 210
Adam's apple, 213
Adduction, 229
Adductor muscle, of legs, 229, **230**
African art, 55, 71
After Michelangelo's *Carved Relief:* "The Battle of Lapiths and Centaurs," 114, **115**, **116**
Albers, Josef, 41, **43**
Allegorical Drawing of the Plan of Saint Peter's Basilica and Square (Bernini), **53**
Allegorical Figure of a Cook (Arcimboldo), **28**
Allegory, 290
Anatomical Drawing of the Arm Musculature (Klee), **224**
Anatomical Drawing of the Musculature of the Shoulder (Klee), **207**
Anatomical Drawing of the Upper Arm Musculature (Klee), **225**
Anatomical illustrations, 147, 149–50, 173, 229

Anatomical Studies (Michelangelo), **195**
Anatomical Studies of Skulls (da Vinci), 167
Anatomical Study: Cross-Sectional Rendering of a Man's Right Leg (da Vinci), **121**
Anatomical Study of a Female Nude (Grosz), **206**
Anatomie du Gladiator Combattant (Savage), **162**, **176**, **180**, **181**, **182**
Anatomy (Gray), **153**, **154**
Anatomy of External Forms of Man, The (Fau), **149**, **153**, **156**, **157**, **200**, **204**, **209**, **218**, **219**, **222**, **223**, **226**, **228**, **230**, **232**, **234**, **236**, **237**, **238**
Anconeus muscle, 225
Angry Kaiser Wilhelm, The (Klee), **126**
Angular measurement, 35–44, **36**, **37**, **38**, **39**, 54, 55–56, 110, 137, 164, 282
Animal skeletons, study of, 185–87, **188**
Ankle, 182, 183, 185, 229, 236
bones. *See* Malleolus
Annunciation, The (Boscoli), **102**
Antagonistic muscles, 191, 224
Apelles, 26
Aphrodite and Pan Playing at Dice (Greek), **50**
Aphrodite of Melos, **117**
Aponeurosis (tendinous sheath), **200**, 207
Appendicular skeleton (limb bones), 176–80
Aquatint, 84
Arcimboldo, Guiseppe, **28**
Aristides, 26
Arms, **176**, **226**, **228**

bones. *See* Humerus; Radius; Ulna
muscles, 194, **218**, **219**–27 (*see also* individual muscles)
skeletal study, 36, 177–78
Arm Studies (Klee), **220**
Arm Studies for Adam (Dürer), **220**
Articular processes, vertebral, 154–55
Ascension of St. John the Evangelist, The (Giotto), **70**
Atlas (1st vertebra), 152, 155
Axes, body, 61–62, **159** (*see also* Medial arc; Pelvis)
Axial skeleton, **156**, **157**, 158
drawing (study 29), 155–60
Axis (2nd vertebra), 155

Back:
bones. *See* Vertebral column
muscles, 208–13, **211**
Ball-and-socket joints, 170, **176**, **181**, 192
Balthus (Balthasar Klossowski de Rola) 256, **258**
Baroque style, 249, 282
Beardsley, Aubrey, 246, 247, **248**, 249
Bechtle, Robert, **267**
Belvedere Torso, The (Delacroix), **270**
Bernini. Giovanni Lorenzo, 52, **53**, **202**
school of, **132**
Berry, William, **129**
Biceps (arm muscle), 191, 221
Biceps femoris, 231, 233

Bicipital fascia, 221
Bodygram of a Family (McCoy), **128**
Boisbaudran, Lecoq de, 34
Boscoli, Andrea, **102**
Brachialis (arm muscle), 191, **192**, 221, 226
Brachioradialis muscle, 224
Breastbone. *See* Sternum
Brush, drawing with, 30, **31**
 dry brush technique, 110
 study 7, 30–31
 study 21, 110

Cajori, Charles, **40**, 256
Calcaneus (heel bone), 180, 183, 229, 235
Calder, Alexander, **46**, 152
Calf muscles. *See* Gastrocnemius
Calligraphy, influence of, 125, **126, 127**, 273
Cambiaso, Luca, 27, 69
Caravaggio, 253
Carpaccio, Vittore, **123**
Carpal (wrist) bones, 176, 180, **181**, 182–83
Cartilage, 168, 174
Caryatid with African Sculpture (Modigliani), 73
Casts, plaster, 116
Catherine (Dürer), **2**, 136
Cennini, Cennino, 293
Cervical curve, 152
Cervical vertebrae (neck bones), 152, 153, 216
Cézanne, Paul, **40**, 41, 250
Chalks, 278, 282
Chamois skin, 252
Charcoal, 249–50, 285
Cheekbones. *See* Zygomatic bones
Chest muscles, 199, 216
Chiaroscuro, 253–55, 281
Children's drawings, 1, **2**
Chin, 213, 216, 217
Chromotypogravure, 86
Circle, in art, **5, 6**,
 study 1, 5–6
Clark, Kenneth, 278, 284–85
Classical art, 287, 289
Clavicles (collarbones), **159**, 173, 174, 176, 187, 199, 202, 205, 210, **212**
Coal Miners at Work (Moore), **136**
Coccyx (tail bone), 152, **153**, 155, 231
Collarbones. *See* Clavicles
Color, 246–49, 290
Columns, perception of, 93–95
Composition, 245–70
 with black-and-white shapes, 247
 drawing the figure in a spatial setting
  (study 51), 255–63
 with line and local color shapes
  (study 48), 247
 with photograph (study 52), 265–68
 shape and, 246–49
 symmetrical, 249
Computer Drawing (Plot) of the Proportional Volumes of a Human Subject (Herron), **54**
Contour constructs, 46–47

Contour drawing, 19–**22, 21**, 26, 46–47, 280–81, 286
 cross-section. *See* Cross-section contours
  of fabric patterns. *See* Fabric, contours of
  hatch modeling. *See* Hatch modeling, contour
 and outline, 19
 rapid, 24–27, 62
 study 4, 21–22
 study 5, 24–26
Contrapposto position, 47, 170
Convex-contour construction, 281–82
Copy After Two Figures from The Ascension of St. John the Evangelist *by Giotto* (Michelangelo), **70**
Coracobrachialis muscle, 221
Coracoid process, 174, 221
Corinth, Lovis, **112**
Coronoid process, 221, 226
Crayons, **88**, 97, 99, **100**
 colored, 249
 Conté, 250, 278
 lithographic, 89
 pastel, 247
Creation of Adam, The (della Quercia), **113**
Critic Sees, The (Johns), 292, **293**
Cross-hatching, 130–31, 137, 141
Cross-Sectional Representation of an Individual Drawn (Plotted) by Computer (Herron), **125**
Cross-section contours, 121–27
 of human form (study 25), 122–23
Crouching Nude (Renoir), **Color Plate IV**
Crouching Tahitian Woman, Study for Nafea faalpoipo (When will you marry?), **Color Plate VII**
Crucifixion (Pistoiese master), **275**
Cubism, 62, 137
Cusp joint, 221

Dance Movement, A (Rodin), **45**
Dancing Figure (Rodin), **45**
Dancing Nudes (Pollaiuolo), 47, **50**
Dark Background (Thiebaud), 105, **106**, 249
Daughter of Butades Drawing the Shadow of Her Lover (Suvée), **12**
Daumier, Honoré, 87, **89**
David, Jacques Louis, 287, 288
Dead Christ (Holbein), **295**
Degas, Edgar, 34, **60**, **187**, 194, **196, 227**, 295
Delacroix, Eugène, **264**, 268, 270
Deltoids (shoulder muscles), 193, 202–3, **205, 207, 212**, 213, 217, 221
Delusions of Grandeur (Margritte), **290**
Digastric muscle, 216
Digitations, 203, **205**
Digiti V proprius muscle, 225
Digitorum, muscles, 225
Dischinger, Rudolf, **29**
Disparate General (Goya), 142, **144**
Dix, Otto, 135, **136**
Dolls (Dischinger), **29**
Dorsal curve, 152
Dorso (Greco), **140**
Dot technique. *See* Stippling
Drama, in art, 290

Drawing and Unfinished Relief of a Princess (Egyptian), **274**
Drawing as preparation, 273–95
Dry brush drawing. *See* Brush, drawing with
Duchamp, Marcel, **17**, 65
Duchamp-Villon, Raymond, **55**, 124
Dürer, Albrecht, 1, **2, 4**, 27, 50, **51**, 55, 58, 123, **124**, 133–34, **134**, 136, **184**, 220
Durieu, Eugène, **265**
Dusty Okie (Lebrun), **29**

Eakins, Thomas, 65–68, **66**, **198**, 250, **251**
Ears, 213, **216**, 217
Ecorché (muscle cast), 193, **194**, 214
Egyptian art, 49, 62, 273, 274
Elbow, 176, 177 (*see also* Olecranon process)
Elevation of the Cross (Rubens), 282, **283**
El Hombre (Orozco), **290**
Empty space. *See* Negative space
Epicondyles (knobs), 178, 221, 224, 226
Extensor muscles, 191
 of arms, 191, 221, 224–25
 of legs, 229, 236
External oblique muscles (flank pads), 203, **205**
Extremities, 180–85
Eyeballs, 94, 168
Eyes (*see also* Visual perception):
 form, 166
 function, 94
Eye sockets (orbits), 164, 167

Fabric, contours of, 117–20, 249
 study 23, 117–19
Fagot Carriers, The (Millet), **287, 288**
Fascia, 231, 233, 235
Fat, 231, 233
Fau, J., **150, 153, 156, 157, 200, 204, 209, 218, 219, 222, 223, 226, 228, 230, 232, 235, 236, 237, 238**
Feet, 183, 185, **188**, 235, 239 (*see also* Calcaneus; Metatarsals; Talus; Tarsal bones)
 bones, 183
 compared with hands (study 38), 181–83
Female body, **148**
 protective fatty tissues of, 197
Female Model Lying on a Bed (Pearlstein), **104**
Female Nude Seen from the Back (Maillol), **81**
Femurs (thigh bones), 170, 176, 180, 228, 229, **230, 231**, 233, 235
Fibula (leg bone), 176, **177**, 179, **228**, 233, 235, 239
Figure, as construct of small units, 26–29
 -ground relationship, 7–9, 245, 247, 289
 study 6, 26–27
Figure from a Calligraphic Scroll (Pisani), **126**
Fingerpainting, 80–83
Fingers, 182
 bones. *See* Phalanges
Fischl, Eric, 268
Fixation (eye rest), 23

Flank pads. *See* External oblique muscles
Flaxman's Anatomical Studies, **172,** **173**
Flexor muscles, 221, 224, 225, 226, 233, 239
Forain, Jean-Louis, 262, **263**
Forearm, **183,** 184, 191, 224–26
Foreshortening, 39, **40,** 185, 261, 279, 290, 293–95
Forge, The (Goya), 283, **284**
Form:
    concepts of, 1–6
    perception of, 92, **128**
    and shape, 6–7
Four Anatomical Studies of the Arm Bones and Shoulder Blade, **178**
Francesca, Piero della, 123, **124,** 167
Free Ride Home (Snelson), **241**
French art, 116, 284
Fuseli, Henry, 104, **105**
Fusiform (spindle) muscle type, 191, **192**

Gan . . . L. D. (Daumier), **89**
Ganneron (Daumier), **89**
Garçons de Café (Beardsley), **248**
Gastrocnemius (calf muscle), **233,** 235, 239
Gateway, Heads, Animals, and Heraldic Eagle (Honnecourt), **3**
Gauguin, Paul, 84, 250, **Color Plate VII**
George Moore (Au Café) (Manet), **Color Plate VIII**
Géricault, Theodore, 102, **103,** 161
Gesture, drawing, 62, 181, 184, 290
Gheyn, Jacob de, II, **224**
Giacometti, Alberto, 41, **42, 167,** 169
Giotto, 3–5, **70**
Girl Combing Her Hair (Utamaro), **246**
Glenoid fossa, 221
Gluteal furrow, 231
Gluteus muscles, 231–33
Gonzalez, Julio, **165**
Goya y Lucientes, Francisco de, 79, 84, 142, **144,** 145, **283, 284,** 287
Gracilis (leg muscle), 229, **230,** 233
Great trochanter (side of hip), 179, 180, 229, 231, 295
Greco, Emilio, **140,** 141
Greek art, 47, 48–49, 54, 116, 170, 274
Groin, groove of the, 170, 203
Grosz, George, 56, **58,** 193, **206**

Hair, 167
Hamstrings, 233
Hands, **178,** 182, **183,** 184 (*see also* Carpal bones; Metacarpal bones; Phalanges)
    compared with feet, 180–83
    gestures, 181, 184
    grasping, 180, 225
    muscles, 227
Hatch marks, 129, **142,** 253
Hatch modeling, 127–33, 289, 291, 292
    (*see also* Cross-hatching)
    contour, 134–36
    and figure-ground relationship (study 28), 141–42
    and form, 133–34
    plane, 136–41, **137, 138, 139**

Head, 167, 168 (*see also* Skull)
Head (Tchelitchew), **127**
Head of a Queen from El Armana (Egyptian), **23**
Heel, 127
    bone. *See* Calcaneus
Hercules and Telephus (Roman), **73**
Hermes Waiting for a Woman (Greek), **48**
Herron, Dr. R. E., **54, 125**
Hinge joints, 176–77, **192**
Hip bones, 229 (*see also* Ilium; Os innominatum; Pelvis)
Hip joints, 233
Hokusai, Katsushika, **7, 30, 31, 32, 284, 285**
Holbein, 295
Homme Nu—Debout, Etude de Proportions (Duchamp-Villon), **55**
Homunculus, **59**
Honnecourt, Villard de, **3**
Horned Dance Mask (Baoule art), **73**
How to Hold a Brush (Hokusai), **30**
Humerus (upper arm bone), 174, 176, 177–78, **192,** 203, 205, 207, 213, 221, 225
Hyoid bone, **214,** 216
Hypothenar muscles, 227

Ideal proportions, 48, 53
Iliac crest, 203, 211, 231
Iliac furrow, 203, **205**
Iliac spines:
    anterior-inferior, 170, 180, 229
    anterior-superior, **159,** 170, 171, 229, 231
    posterior, 171
Iliofemoral ligament, 180, 229
Iliotibial band, 231
Ilium (hip bone), 170, 231
Implied line, 6
Impressionism, 288
Indian art, 62, 65, 181
Indirect action, 191
Infant body, **150**
Infrahyoid muscles, 216
Infraspinatus (back muscle), **207,** 213
Ingres, Jean Auguste Dominique, 16, 47, 71, **72,** 97, 178, **179, 233,** 285–87, **285, 286,** 288
Inguinal ligament, 170, 203
Iolas, Alexandre, 291
Ischium (pelvic bone), 170, 229, 233
Isometric tension, 192
Isotta da Rimini (Pasti), **81**
Italy, 181

Japanese prints, 246, 284
Jawbone. *See* Mandibula
Jeune Fille (Villon), 137, **139**
Jeune Fille Endormie (Balthus), **258**
Johns, Jasper, 79, **80,** 292, **293**
Joints, 184–85, 192 (*see also* Ball-and-socket joints; Cusp joint; Hinge joints)
    of the lower limb, 185

Kitaj, R. B., **203**
Klee, Paul, 16, **126,** 193, 207, **220, 224, 248,** 249
Knee, 176, 179, **180,** 185, 192, 231
Kneecap. *See* Patella
Kollwitz, Käthe, 107, **108, 109,** 110

Landseer, Henry, **172,** 173
Latissimus dorsi (back muscle), 203, 205–7, **207,** 208, 209, 213
    study 42, 205–7
Lebrun, Rico, 28, **29**
Le Corbusier, 53
Legs, 176, 178–80, 185, **188,** 203, **234** (*see also* Femurs; Fibula; Limbs, lower; Tibia)
    bones, 176, 178–80
Leonardo da Vinci, 50, 51, **52,** 58, 81, **93,** 104, 107, 109, **121,** 124, 127, **167,** 181, **184,** 193, 194, **277, 278,** 286
Levator scapulae, 213, **216**
Libyan Sibyl, The (Michelangelo), **279,** 282
Life Study of a Man's Head (Lippi), **165**
Ligaments, 192
    in the lower limb, 180
Lighting:
    directional, 107–12, 277
    effects of, 80, 81, 97, 99, 247, 282
    expressive use of, 109
    natural, 92
    and shadow modeling, 97–98, 102, 250, 253–55
    use of a flood lamp, 97–99
Limbs, 176–85
    lower, 178–80, 184–85, **236, 237, 238**
    muscles, 217–40
    upper, 176–78, 184
Line:
    and modeling, 116–20
    and shape (study 48), 247
Linea alba, 197, 199, **202**
Linea aspera, 233
Lippi, Filippino, **165,** 166
Lithographs, 79, 246
Little Girl Playing Ball (Picasso), **57**
Lopez, Francisco, **201**
López-Garcia, Antonio, **186, 208**
Lumbar curve, 152, **153**
Lumbar vertebrae (lower back bones), 153, 155, **173**

McCoy, Dan, **128**
Magritte, René, **290, 291, 292**
Maillol, Aristide, 79, **81,** 97
Male body, **148, 149, 150**
Male Model (*L'Homme Nue; "Le Serf"; Academie Bleue; Bevilacqua*) (Matisse), **Color Plate IX**
Male Nude (Kitaj), **203**
Male Nude (Lopez), **201**
Malleolus (ankle bone), 179, 183, 239
Mandibula (jawbone), 164, 168, 216, 217
Manet, Edouard, 250, **Color Plate VIII**
Man Heaving a 75-Pound Boulder (Muybridge), **195**

Man on Table (Thiebaud), **294**
Man's Head (Picasso), **59**
Marey, E. J., 65
Marey Wheel Photographs of Jesse Godley Running (Eakins), **66**
Marr, David, 44
Mary and Saint John (Netherlandish), **120**
Masseter muscle, 168
Masterworks:
    movement in (study 14), 68–69
    studying, 70–73
Mastoid processes, 213–14
Matisse, Henri, 7, **9**, 20, 26, 68, **69**, 256, 258, 261, **Color Plate IX**
May Milton (Toulouse-Lautrec), 284, **Color Plate I, Color Plate II**
Medial arc, 166
Medieval art, 169
Memory, drawing from:
    model (study 8), 32–34
    skeleton (study 40), 187–88
    skull, 169
Metacarpal bones (hand bones), 180, 182, 225
Metatarsals (foot bones), 180, 183, 235
Michelangelo Buonarroti, **68**, 69, **70**, 114, 132, **133**, 141, 176, **187**, 193, **195**, 208, **211**, **227**, 229, **231**, **235**, 278, **279**, 282
Micro-ground reversal, 277
Millet, Jean François, **287**, **288**
Mirror Polisher, The (Hokusai), **31**
Mixed media, 249–50
Modeling, 79 (*see also* Hatch modeling; Relief modeling; Shadow modeling)
    actual size, **90**
    and line, 79
Model Nizzavona, The (Toulouse-Lautrec), **101**
Modigliani, Amedeo, 55, 71, **73**
Modulor, 53
Monochromatic drawing, 249
Moore, George, 250
Moore, Henry, **136**
Mother Holding a Child and Four Studies of Her Right Hand, A (Picasso), **185**
Motion, 58–69, 191
    cinematic, 64
    double pose, 62, **63**
    and rhythm, 64–68
    rotation. *See* Rotation
    walking, **64**, 65
Muscles, 171, 192–241 (*see also* individual muscles)
    attachment to skeleton, 191, 197, 199
    components, 191, **192**
    direct action, 191, **192**
    extension, 192
    flexion, 191, **192**
    insertion, 191, 197, 205
    interaction, 203
    of lower limbs, 227–40
    relaxation, 192
    rotation, 192, 203, 213
    tension, 193
    of upper limbs, 217–27
    visibility of, 193
Muybridge, Eadweard, 65, **195**

National Aeronautics and Space Administration, 53, **54**
Neck:
    bones. *See* Cervical vertebrae
    hyoid, 213
    muscles, 199, 210, 213–17, **216**
    nape, 210
    pit of, **159**, 174, 176, 197, 199
Negative (empty) space, 7, **9**, 245, 249
Neisser, Ulric, 95
Neoclassicism, 287, 288
Netherlandish art, 119, 121
New House, The (Fischl), **268**
Nolde, Emil, **110**
Nonsequential drawing, 91, **92**
    study 19, 91
Nose, 133–34, 164, 168
Nuchal ligament, 210
Nude, drawing the, 247, 250, 256
Nude Descending a Staircase (Duchamp), 65
Nude Figure of a Young Man (Piazzetta), **254**
Nude Man and Woman (Durieu), **265**
Nude Study (Michelangelo), 132, **133**
Nude Woman (Constructed) (Dürer), **4**
Nude Woman with Staff (Constructed) (Dürer), **51**

"Objectifying" the image of the model, 42
Oblique muscles, **207**
Obturator foramen (lower pelvis), 170
Oil paints, 250, 289
Olecranon process (elbow), 177, 178, 221
Omohyoid muscles, 216
Origins of muscles, 191, 197
Orbits. *See* Eye sockets
Orozco, José Clemente, **289**, **290**
Os innominatum (pelvic bone), 170
Outline, 11–18, **12**, **14**, **20**
    and contour, 19, 44–47
    and silhouette, 11
    study 2, 13
Oval constructs, 46–47
Overlapping forms, 113
Overlay method, 160, **166**, 193, 199, **207**, 208, **210**, 213, **217**, 221, 229
Ovoid forms, 82, 166–67

Page from a Sketchbook (Picasso), **74**
Page from a Sketchbook (Pontormo), **212**
Page from a Sketchbook, Muscular Neck and Head Looking Up (Pontormo), **215**
Painted Figures of Athletes (Greek), **66**
Palmaris muscle, 226
Paper, 252, 253, 270, 274, 278
    texture, 97, 99
    toned, 247, 249, 250, 253
Pasti, Matteo d', **81**
Patella (kneecap), 179, 180, 185, 229
Patellar ligament, 229
Pearlstein, Philip, 102, **104**
Peasant Dance (Rubens), **67**, 68
Peck, Stephen, 147
Pectoralis muscles, 217
    major, 202–3, **207**
Pelvic axis, 55, 159

Pelvis, 63, **153**, 155, **159**, 160, 161, **170**–73, 180, 183, 187, 199, 228, 229, 231–33
    drawing (study 34), 171–73
Pen-and-ink drawing, 159, 208, 247
Pencils:
    colored, 247, 250 (*see also* Sanguine pencil)
    graphite, 249–50, 278, 285
Pens, felt-tip, 249
Pentimenti, 284
Peroneus muscles, 235, 239
Phalanges (toe-finger bones), 180, 182, 183
Photographs, 93, 121, 264–65
Picasso, Pablo, 40, **41**, 47, 56, **57**, **59**, **62**, 73, **74**, **96**, 97, 116, **117**, **144**, 145, **185**, 285, **288**, **289**, 295
Pisani, Geobattista, **126**
Platysma muscle, 217
Pliny, 19, 26
Plumb line, 63, **64**
Pointillism, 84
Police drawings, 133–34
Pollaiuolo, Antonio, 47, 50
Polyclitus, 50, 52
Polyhedron Model, **Color Plate X**
Pontormo, Jacopo da, **25**, **178**, **205**, **212**, **215**, 279, **280**, **281**
Portrait of Cardinal Nicolò Albergati (Van Eyck), **276**, 278
Portrait of Madame d'Haussonville (Ingres), **286**
Poseuse de Dos, La (Seurat), **86**
Poster for the German Homecrafts Exhibition (Kollwitz), **108**
Poussin, Nicolas, 113, **114**, **115**, 287
"Processes of Vision, The" (Neisser), **95**
Project drawing, 268–70
Prominens (7th vertebra), 152, 154, 210, **211**, 216
Pronation (palm down), 176, 177, **178**, 221, **222**, 225, **226**
Pronator, muscles, 224, 225, 226
Proportional System Based on a Schematic Figure, le Modulor (Le Corbusier), **53**
Proportions, 54–57
    study 10, 55–56
Pubis, 170, 197

Quadriceps muscle, 229
Quercia, Jacopo della, **113**

Radius (forearm bone), 176, **180**, 183, 221, 224, 225, 226
Raphael, 70, **71**
Realism, 288
Reclining Nude (Rembrandt), **133**–35, 141
Rectus-abdominis muscle, 203
Rectus-femoris muscle, 229, **230**
Reflected image, 258–61, **260**, 285
Reflection in the Mirror (Matisse), 258, **261**
Relief modeling, 79–97, **87**, 107, 127
    with continuous tone (study 17), 86–87
    with printing ink (study 15), 81–83
    with stippling (study 16), 83–86

Relief sculpture, 82, 87, 289
  and shadow modeling, 112–16
Rembrandt van Rijn, **33**, 70, **71**, **72**,
  133–35, 141, 142
Renaissance art, 47, 51, 53, 55, 109, 135,
  166, 169, 273, 274, 278, 280
Renoir, Pierre August, 249, **Color Plate IV**
Resist technique, 136
Retinal image, 94, **95**, **96**
Rhomboids (back muscles), 213
Rib cage, **153**, 160, **173**, 188, 203, 207,
  211, 216, 240
  and the shoulder girdle, 174–76
Ribera, Jusepe de, **168**
Robusti, Jacopo, **8**
Rodin, Auguste, 26, 34, 44–46, **45**
Rotation, 59–62, **61**
  study 10, 59–62
Rubens, Peter Paul, **67**, 68, 114, **115**, 116,
  281, **282**, **283**

Sacrospinalis (back) muscles, 153, 208, 231
Sacrum (backbone), 152, **153**, 155, 160,
  170, 174, **175**, 231
Sanguine pencil, 193, **202**, **207**, **208**, 213,
  221
Santa Barbara Patio (Bechtle), **267**
Santa Felicità Altarpiece (Pontormo), 279,
  281
Sarto, Andrea del, **216**
Sartorius muscle, 229, **230**, **231**, 233
Savage, Jean Galbert, **162**, **176**, **180**, **181**,
  182
Scalenus medius, **216**
Scapulae (shoulder blades), 160, **175**, 176,
  203, 205, 207, 210, **211**, **212**, 213,
  216, 221
Sculptor Kneeling with Model (Picasso), **144**,
  145
Sculpture, 46, 80–82, 87, 269, 270, 279,
  292 (*see also* Relief sculpture)
  line drawing as, 46
Seated Nude (Picasso), **62**
Seated Nude (Segal), **Color Plate III**
Seated Woman (Seurat), **17**
Segal, George, 246, 247, **Color Plate III**
Self-Portrait (Cézanne), 137–40, **140**
Self-Portrait (Dürer), 132–33, **133**
Self-Portrait (Fuseli), 104, **105**
Self-Portrait (Gonzalez), **165**
Self-Portrait (Klee), **248**
Self-Portrait (Nolde), **110**
Self-Portrait (Picasso), **96**, 97
Self-Portrait (Rembrandt), **72**
Self-Portrait in Profile (Duchamp), **17**
Self-Portrait IV (Albers), **43**
Self-portrait with skull (study 33), 160–66
Semimembranosus (leg muscle), 233
Semitendinosus (leg muscle), 233
Sepia wash, 283
Serratus muscles, 203, **205**, 207
Setting, spatial, 255–63
Seurat, Georges-Pierre, **17**, 84, **85**, 97, 98
Shadow, 11, 81, 274
  with a brush, 99–103, 110–11
  cast, **12**, 93, 97, 102, 104–5, 249, 255,
    295

with color, 240–50
contours, 137
and directional lighting, 107–12, 250–51
effects of, **99**
lighting and chiaroscuro, 253–55
modeling, 97–116, 137, 249–55, **253**,
  277, 285, 291
with subtle tones, 250–51
terminator lines, 111
Shape, 6–7
  and form, 6–7
  negative, 246, 258
  overlapping, 6–7
  positive, 246
Sheet of Studies for the Painting The
  Martyrdom of Saint Symphorien
  (Ingres), **233**
Shoulder, 63, 159, 174–76, 210, 212, 226,
  228
  axis, 55, 159, 160, 170
  blades. *See* Scapulae
  girdle, 153, 191
  muscles. *See* Deltoids
  and rib cage, drawing (study 35), 174–76
Silhouette, 11–18, **12**, **15**, **16**, 273
  and outline, 11
  study 3, 13–16
Silverpoint, 277, 278
Simultaneous drawing, 52
Sinopie (preliminary drawings), 274
Skeletal landmarks, **199**
Skeleton, 147–90, **188**
  drawing, from memory (study 40),
    188–90, **189**
  drawing the figure from a (study 47), 240
  introduction to (study 29), 149
  model of, 152
  mounted, **150**, 151
Sketch After Raphael's Baldassare Castiglione
  (Rembrandt), **71**
Sketchbook, artist's, 68, 70, 73–74, 269
Sketchbook Study of the Ecorché (Cézanne), **41**
Skull, 152, **153**, 160, **162**, 167–69, 216
Skull (Giacometti), **167**
Snelson, Kenneth, **241**
Soldier Holding a Lance (Géricault), **103**
Soleus muscle, 235, 239
Spinal column, 158, 176, 205 (*see also*
  Vertebral column)
  groove of, 176, 188, 197, 208
Spinous process, vertebral, 154
Splenius (neck muscle), 216
Step construction, 291
Stereometric Elaboration of Various Animals
  (Hokusai), **7**
Stereometric Man: Thirteen Cross Sections of the
  Body (Dürer), **124**
Sternohyoid muscles, **214**, 216
Sternomastoid (neck muscle), 213, **214**,
  215, **216**
Sternum (breastbone), 159, 173, 174, 176,
  187, 199, 213–14
Stippling, 83, **84**, **85**, 97
Stone Carving (Greek), **59**
Studies (Delacroix), **264**
Studies for The Libyan Sibyl (Michelangelo),
  278, **279**
Studies of a Man's Leg (Michelangelo), **231**

Studies of a Woman Adjusting Her Hair
  (Hokusai), **32**
Studies of the Bones of the Lower Limb
  (Rubens), **181**
Studies of the Head and Hands (Kollwitz),
  109
Studies of the Mouth and Nose (Ribera), **168**
Studies of the Skeletal Foot (Michelangelo),
  187
Studio Figures (Valerio), **263**
Studio Scene with Artist and Model (Forain),
  263
Studio setting, 261–62, **263**
Study (Michelangelo), **235**
Study (Picasso), **41**
Study After The Libyan Sibyl of
  Michelangelo (Rubens), **281**
Study After The Triumph of Titus (Poussin),
  114
Study for Acron (Ingres), **179**
Study for A Madonna and Child
  (Pontormo), **25**
Study for Man on Table (Thiebaud), **294**
Study for a Resurrection (Michelangelo), **68**
Study for Portrait of Cardinal Nicolò
  Albergati (Van Eyck), **276**
Study for Portrait of Madame d'Haussonville
  (Ingres), **285**
Study for St. John (Pontormo), **205**
Study for Skin I (Johns), **80**
Study for The Critic Sees (Johns), 292, **293**
Study for The Dance (Matisse), **69**
Study for the Figure of Christ (Rubens), **282**
Study for the Head of St. Elizabeth in the
  Painting Madonna with St. Elizabeth
  and the Infant St. John (Sarto), **216**
Study for The Last Judgement
  (Michelangelo), **211**
Study for the Portrait of Madame Moitessior
  (Ingres), **72**, **285**, **286**
Study for the Raft of the Medusa
  (Géricault), **161**
Study for the Santa Felicità Altarpiece
  (Pontormo), 279, **280**
Study for the Sculpture Delusions of Grandeur
  (Magritte), 290, **291**, **292**
Study for The Two Brothers (Picasso), **288**
Study for Weary (Whistler), 142, **143**
Study of a Profile (Picasso), **41**
Study of Arms (de Gheyn), **224**
Study of Arms (Michelangelo), **227**
Study of a Woman's Hands (da Vinci), **117**,
  184
Study of Legs (Orozco), **289**
Study of Proportions After Vitruvius, A (da
  Vinci), **52**
Study of the Back (Tiepolo), **Color Plate VI**
Study of the Feet and Legs (Dürer), **184**
Study of the Head of a Young Girl (da Vinci),
  277
Study of the Leg (Degas), **187**
Study of the Nude (Bernini), **202**
Study of the Nude, Backview (Degas), **227**
Study of the Proportions of the Head (della
  Francesca), **124**
Styloid process, 221
Supination (palm up), 176, 177, **178**
Supinator muscles, 224

Suprahyoid muscles, 216
Surrealism, 122, 290–92
Suvée, Joseph Benoit, **12**
Svevo, Italo, 70
Symmetry, 58, 281
    of body, 58, 159, 197
    of limbs, 217
    and proportion, 56–58
Symphysis pubis (pubis joint), 170, 171, 229

Talus (anklebone), **182**, 183
Tarsal bones (feet), 180, 183
Tchelitchew, Pavel, **127**
Teeth, 168
Tempera paints, 250
Temples (sides of forehead), 164
Temporal line, 168
Tendons, 191, **192**, 197
Tendonous fascia, 203
Tensor fasciae latae muscle, **231**
Teres-major muscle, **207**, 213
Teres-minor muscle, 213
Texture, 93, 287
    density, gradient of, 96, 97
Thenar muscles, 227
Thiebaud, Wayne, 105, **106**, 249, 293–95,
    294
Thighs, 229, 233
    bones. See Femurs
Thoracic arch (lower ribs), 174
Three-dimensional model, for drawing,
    173, 193
Three Men Digging (Goya), **283**, 287
Three-Quarter Nude, Head Partly Showing
    (Matisse), **20**
Three Studies with Drapery, Leg and Foot
    (Carpaccio), **123**
Thumb, 224, 225
Tibia (shinbone), 176, **177**, 179, 183, 185,
    229, **231**, 235
Tibialis muscle, 235, 239
Tiepolo, Giambattista, 249, 253,
    Color Plate VI
Tintoretto, il, **8**
Toes, 183, 239
    bones. See Phalanges

Tonal modeling, 83, 97, 274
Tonal values, 99, 283
Tone, 86, 89–90, 92–93, 97,107, 113–14,
    265, 277
    continuous, 86, 93
    gradation of, 93, 97, 113
    and hatching, 129
Toulouse-Lautrec, Henri de, **101**, 246, 284,
    Color Plate I, Color Plate II
Transparency of shadows, 105–7
Transverse processes, vertebral, 154
Trapezius (back muscle), 205, **207**, 210–13,
    212, 214, **215**, **216**, 217
Treatise on Painting (da Vinci), **93**
Triceps (back muscle), **207**, 221
*Triton Bearing a Draped Woman on His
    Shoulder* (Bernini, school of), **132**
Triumph of Galatea, The (Poussin), **115**
Trois Femmes Nues (Giacometti), **42**
Trunk muscles, 199–213
    back view, 208–13
    front view, 199–207
    side view, **204**
Tuberosities, 221, 229
Two Acrobats (Calder), **46**
Two Brothers, The (Picasso), 288, **289**
*Two Studies of a Begging Woman with Two
    Children* (Rembrandt), **33**
Tyndall, Robert, **129**

Ulnae (elbow knees), 176, 177, 178, **192**,
    221, 224, 225, 226
Ulnar crest, 224
Ulnar joint, **178**
Ulnar ridge, 221
Utamaro, **246**, 295

Vaillant, Wallerant, **117**
Valerio, James, 262, **263**
Value constancy, 105–7, **107**
Van Eyck, Jan, 275–77, **276**, 278, 282, 292
Vasari, Giorgio, 3
Vastus muscles, 229, **230**, 233
Venus (Matisse), 7, **9**
Vertebrae, 153

Vertebral arch, 154
Vertebral column (spine), 152–60, **153**,
    170, 174, **175**, 176
    structure of, 152–60
Viewpoint, 256, 261
Villon, Jacques (Gaston Duchamps), 124,
    126, 137, **139**
Vinci, Leonardo da. *See* Leonardo da Vinci
Virgin of the Rocks, The (da Vinci), **278**, 286
Virtual line (implied contour), 137
Visual measurement, 34–40, 151, 158, 184,
    185, 265
    angular measurement. *See* Angular
        measurement
    study 9, 35–40
Visual perception, 94, 107–8, 127
    of light, 109
Vitruvius, 49, 50, 51, 53
Volume, creating, 133

Wash modeling, 99–103
Watercolors, 99–103, 247
Watrous, Harry Wilson, 278
Watteau, Jean-Antoine, 118, **119**, 121
Whistler, James Abbott McNeill, 142, **143**
Woman and Parrot (Indian), **50**
Woman Holding a Warrior's Helmet, A
    (Achilles painter), **49**
*Woman Seated on the Ground, Seen from the
    Back* (Watteau), **119**
Woodcuts, 110, 246, 249, 284
World of the Bourgeoisie (Grosz), **58**
Wrist, 178, 224, 225–26 (see also Carpal
    bones)

Xiphoid process (lower limit of sternum),
    174

Young Artist Drawing from a Cast (Vaillant),
    117

Zygomatic (cheek) bones, 164, 168
Zygomaticus muscles, major, 168